The
Confessions

Augustinian Heritage Institute

THE WORKS OF SAINT AUGUSTINE
A Translation for the 21st Century

Part I – Books
Volume 1
The Confessions

THE WORKS OF SAINT AUGUSTINE

A Translation for the 21st Century

The Conʄessions

(Second Edition)

I/1

translation, notes and introduction by
Maria Boulding, O.S.B.

edited by
John E. Rotelle, O.S.A.

New City Press
Hyde Park, New York

Published in the United States by New City Press
202 Comforter Blvd., Hyde Park, New York 12538
©1997/2012 Augustinian Heritage Institute

Translated by Maria Boulding, O.S.B.

Library of Congress Cataloging-in-Publication Data:

Augustine, Saint, Bishop of Hippo.
  The works of Saint Augustine.
  "Augustinian Heritage Institute"
  Includes bibliographical references and indexes.
  Contents: — pt. 1., v. 1. The Confessions.
— pt. 3., v. 1. Sermons on the Old Testament, 1-19.
— pt. 3, v. 2. Sermons on the Old Testament, 20-50 — [et al.] — pt. 3,
v. 10 Sermons on various subjects, 341-400.

  1. Theology — Early church, ca. 30-600. I. Hill,
Edmund. II. Rotelle, John E. III. Augustinian
Heritage Institute. IV. Title.
BR65.A5E53 1990 270.2 89-28878
ISBN 1-56548-055-4 (series)
ISBN 1-56548-083-X (pt. 1, v. 1)
ISBN 1-56548-445-0 (pt. 1, v. 1 : pbk.)

We are indebted to Brepols Publishers, Turnholt, Belgium, for their use of the Latin critical text for *Sancti Augustini Confessionum Libri* XIII, ed. Lucas Verheijen, O.S.A., *Corpus Christianorum Latinorum* 37 (Turnholt, 1990) 1-273.

Nihil Obstat: John E. Rotelle, O.S.A., S.T.L., Censor Deputatus
Imprimatur: + Patrick Sheridan, D.D., Vicar General
Archdiocese of New York, March 25, 1996

1st printing: January 1997
15th printing (Second Edition): September 2016

Printed in the United States of America

Contents

The Confessions

Introduction

If the Bishop of Hippo looked out of his window as he picked up his pen, he saw a brilliant, colorful world, its hot details vivid in the fierce African sun. Augustine loved light, "the queen of colors" (X,34,51). He looked out at a prosperous Mediterranean country, at well-maintained roads gleaming white in the sun, at olive groves, orchards and vineyards, at municipal buildings and public baths. And everywhere was the stamp of Rome.

Augustine's "Africa" was wholly different from the vast and varied continent suggested by that name today. To the south, beyond the Aures Mountains, it was cut off from the rest of the continent by the impassable Sahara. It was equally different from any North African country of medieval or modern times. The birth of Islam was more than two hundred years in the future, and the spread of Arab culture and language nearly three centuries away. Augustine's Africa (the eastern part of Algeria and Tunisia today) was ancient Carthaginian country. Legend dated the foundation of Carthage to the ninth century B.C., and in succeeding centuries Phoenician sea-power and commerce had established trading ports along the Mediterranean coast. The Berber peasant farmers of the hinterland and the fishermen in the ports still spoke Punic, a Semitic tongue, in Augustine's day. But after a disastrous series of clashes with Rome, Carthage had been subjugated in the second century B.C., and upon the ethnic substrate Rome had imposed the rule of law, Latin culture, and the amenities of civilized life. Augustine's Africa faced north, across the tideless sea toward Italy.

Augustine picked up his pen, prayed to his God to enable him to say what he had to say, and began.

The Confessions are one long prayer, a poetic, passionate, intimate prayer. It is paradoxical, but exact, to say that he prayed for the grace to pray: "Allow me to speak in your merciful presence" (I,6,7); "Let me not weary as I confess to you those acts of mercy by which you plucked me from all my evil ways" (I,15,24); "Let me love you, Lord, and give thanks to you and confess to your name" (II,7,15); "Let me confess my disgraceful deeds to you, and in confessing praise you. Allow me this, I beg you" (IV,1,1); "Accept the sacrifice of my confessions, offered to you by the power of this tongue of mine which you have fashioned and aroused to confess to your name" (V,1,1).

He undertook this, his greatest piece of writing, in the conviction that God wanted him to make this confession: "You first willed that I should confess to you, my Lord and my God" (XI,1,1). In his heart, in his "inner ear," he heard God asking it of him; but there were practical and human promptings as well. In 397, the most probable date for *The Confessions*, or at least for his beginning to write them, Augustine was forty-three. He had been a baptized Catholic for ten years, a priest for six, and a bishop for only about two. There were probably many in the church at Hippo, and more widely in the church throughout Numidia, who were less than convinced of their good fortune in acquiring so brilliant and distinguished a man for their bishop. Cleverness was, perhaps, not highly prized. His pre-baptismal life raised questions, especially his nine years' adherence to the Manichean sect, and his polemical attitude toward the Catholic Church in earlier days. Was his conversion genuine? Finally, his elevation to the episcopate had itself been controversial, since the aged Bishop of Hippo, Valerius, had been in a hurry to snap Augustine up before any other church staked a claim, and had persuaded the Primate of Numidia to consecrate him coadjutor bishop with right of succession in canonically dubious fashion. Some kind of *apologia pro vita sua* from Augustine's pen was therefore timely, and might disarm his critics. Insofar as *The Confessions* are polemical at all (which is not very far), the Manichees are in Augustine's sights.

Beyond the critics was a wider circle of potential readers who would listen far more sympathetically. Augustine was not the only cultured and intelligent man to embrace Christianity at a mature age, after a long intellectual search. Paulinus of Nola was a kindred spirit; he and many others would be very interested in anything Augustine might have to say about his understanding of his faith and its relation to philosophy and the humanities. Many another had perhaps found in Neo-Platonism the highest and most spiritual achievement of the human mind in search of union with God, yet turned away disappointed, as Augustine had, because something was missing.

Finally there was the great company of Augustine's fellow Christians who were neither critics nor philosophers, those who would overhear his confessions and judge in charity, whose charity would itself be the medium for understanding whatever he had to say: "All whose ears are open to me by love will believe me" (X,3,3); "The charity that makes them good assures them that I am not lying" (X,3,4). These would be encouraged and praise God, for "it is cheering to good people to hear about the past evil deeds of those who are now freed from them" (ibid.).

For all these he wrote his "confessions in thirteen books" (*Revisions* II, 6,1). There was no printing, no mass-production, only laborious writing and copying by hand. It is likely that the first "readers" were groups of interested persons who gathered for reading sessions. Each of the thirteen books is an episode in the story, although the length varies.

Augustine had, therefore, both private and public inducement. He had also superb fluency and an addiction to talking about himself. Yet these facts should not blind us to what it must have cost him. It is something remarkable, even daring, for a man to write a book addressed to God which is principally about himself. For all his magnificent egoism and genius for communication, he was a highly sensitive man, and afraid of mockery. As an orator he had been professionally attuned to his audience's reaction; as a bishop he had not become indifferent to it. His desire for praise, his need to please people, were not just the weaknesses of a young man, now left behind; even as a bishop he needed to watch his motives, as he admits (X,36,59).

Clearly the first hearers were captivated, as many thousands have been over the following sixteen centuries. His own way to God had been the way of deep and searing self-knowledge, yet his confession of it could speak to others: the prefix *con-* already implies communication. Through the particular and personal experiences of his own life, time, place, and culture, Augustine searches the human heart and exposes the predicament of weak, sinful, sensual, vacillating, hopeful, graced human beings, evoking their valiant and passionate search for truth, their fascination with beauty, their disintegration when they yield to temptation and sink back to their native darkness, their longing for a happiness that will be found only in the satisfaction of the questioning mind and restless heart in God, and their unquenchable thirst for that peace and rest which may be found partially and temporarily in this life (as Augustine himself had found them for a time at Thagaste after returning from Italy to Africa as a Christian), but are finally attainable only in the vision of God, in the enjoyment of God, in the Sabbath of eternal life.

He spoke with an honesty to which Everyman and Everywoman could instinctively respond, and in powerful language. The Latin classics had been ruthlessly dinned into him in boyhood, and the phrases of Virgil, Cicero, Sallust, and Terence came readily. The verbal abilities of a promising boy had been honed and refined in the hard school of rhetoric until Augustine, always fascinated by words, was a master of vivid late Latin, with an ear for its music and a delight in its puns and paradoxes. But then had come his immersion in the scriptures, known to him in the Old Latin version which preceded the Vulgate; and by the time he came to write *The Confessions* scriptural thought and language were so thoroughly his own that nearly every page contains echoes and allusions.

So much for the setting. Now to the story Augustine had to tell.

The Two Journeys

Augustine's Africa was intensely Roman, but an intelligent lad from the provinces needed to travel. Much of the earlier part of his story is concerned with changes of place. There were geographical journeys, but also a corresponding inner journey. These two may be considered in turn.

Augustine was born at Thagaste (modern Souk Ahras in Algeria), some forty-five miles south of the coast, on 13 November 354, and went to school first at Thagaste, then at Madaura or Madaurus (modern Mdaourouch). After a year at home at Thagaste, during which his father, Patricius, saved up to send him away for higher study, Augustine became a student at Carthage. During his time there, at seventeen or so, he began to live with the loved but unnamed woman who bore him a son, Adeodatus ("God-given"), in about 372, when Augustine was perhaps eighteen. He also joined the Manichees.

In 375 he returned to Thagaste and taught there for about a year; to this period belongs the death of a friend, which afflicted him deeply, as he recounts in IV,4,7-9. He then returned to Carthage and opened a school of rhetoric there in 376. Hooliganism among his students goaded him beyond endurance, and in 383 he sailed for Rome, where the students were reputed to be better behaved, and where Manichean contacts would ensure him a welcome. Hooliganism was, however, replaced by fee-dodging, and when a professorship of rhetoric at Milan fell vacant, Augustine competed, won, and removed thither in 384. "And so I came to Milan, and to Bishop Ambrose," he says (V,13,23). This was the most momentous geographical move of his life.

After his conversion at Milan in August 386, Augustine, Monica, Adeodatus, and a company of friends left to spend the winter on a country estate at Cassiciacum, returning in the following March to Milan, where Augustine, Alypius, and Adeodatus prepared for baptism at Easter 387. Later that year they left for Ostia, to await their sailing for Africa; there Augustine and Monica together were granted the mystical experience he so famously describes in IX,10,23-25. Monica died soon after this, and with her death at the end of Book IX Augustine concludes the narrative part of his *Confessions*. He returned to Rome, and thence in 388 to Africa, where he lived a quasi-monastic life with his companions until 391. In that year he was ordained priest and founded a monastery at Hippo. In 395 he was consecrated coadjutor bishop to Valerius, whom he succeeded on the latter's death the following year.

At every stage of the journey God had led him, sometimes using even bad people like boorish students or superstitious Manichees to move him on. These journeys, so short by modern standards, but long, exhausting, and often dangerous in the fourth century, were the outer face of an inner journey, to which we must now turn.

The prodigal son, he says, "did not hire horses or carriages, nor did he board ships, nor take wing in any visible sense, nor put one foot before the other when he journeyed to that far country"; and later, on the brink of conversion, he reflects that the journey back to God "was not to be under-taken by ship or carriage or on foot ... for to travel—and more, to reach jour-ney's end—was nothing else but to want to go there" (I,18,28; VIII,8,19). In boyhood Augustine had been enthralled by the wanderings of Aeneas (I, 13, 20); his own intellectual and moral wanderings took him, like the prodigal son in whom he recognized himself, to a "far country," to "the land of unlikeness." He was running away, yet all the time the Pursuer was near, never despairing of him, calling, waiting, chiding, forcing him to face himself when Augustine tried to "put himself out of sight behind his back" (VIII, 7, 16), summoning him to confront the God within (X,27,38).

Whatever the sins, whatever the flirtations with unreality in the shape of maudlin theatrical shows or sycophancy toward the great, the spark of truth in him never entirely petered out (IV,2,2). At least in theory he acknowledged its claims: "O Truth, Truth, how the deepest marrow of my mind ached for you!" (III,6,10) At certain stages he seemed, provisionally, to find it. The nominal status of catechumen, into which he had been initiated in infancy, played little part in the search. Despite Monica's faith, Augustine seems to have received no effective Christian instruction as he grew up, though he reverenced the name of Christ and had some notion of a powerful and provident God (I,9,14).

An important moment was his reading of a now lost work by Cicero, the *Hortensius*, at the age of nineteen. Through it Augustine heard the call to philosophy in a pure form, not that of adherence to any particular school, but a dedication to the love and pursuit of wisdom wherever it might be found. The ideal he glimpsed was at odds with his disordered life at the time, but the experience was important in suggesting the possibility of breaking away from the rhetorical tradition which had thus far dominated his education, where imitation of classical models was the order of the day, into a genuine liberation of the mind to pursue wisdom beyond a set of time-bound and culturally-conditioned forms. He records, however, that he missed the name of Christ in this book (III,4,8).

Then came Manicheanism. Mani or Manes had founded a hybrid religion, or rather a theosophy, in Persia in the third century, in which elements of Christianity were mingled with Gnostic beliefs and bizarre speculation. The mixture of good and evil in the world was accounted for by the aboriginal existence of two kingdoms at war with each other: the kingdom of light, ruled by the good God, and the kingdom of darkness, ruled by Satan. These two shared a common frontier, and so limited each other, but in other respects they were infinite. The kingdom of darkness had attacked the kingdom of light, and though unable to conquer it had swallowed certain particles of the light kingdom which had offered resistance to the invaders. These light-particles were thereafter imprisoned in the universe, bound within the dominant forces of darkness or evil. Some were imprisoned in the heavenly bodies, some in trees and plants, and some in men and women. Their presence explained the tension between good and evil in human beings. The material world was evil, and the story of its creation by the good God untrue; Genesis was therefore to be rejected, along with the rest of the Old Testament. Parts of the New Testament were accepted, but the doctrine of God-made-flesh was, of course, an impossibility. Jesus was an envoy from the kingdom of light, sent to teach truth and help in the liberating work, but he had no real body, and was not truly crucified.

The inherent dualism of Manichean theory was most highly developed in the doctrine of man, who was held to be animated by two souls: a dark, evil soul which animated his body, and the light soul, really a particle of divinity, which was his true but imprisoned self. This light-soul was itself sinless, but suffered from the oppressive evil soul. Moral life consisted in the effort to liberate it, and to avoid any action which might increase the dominance of the powers of darkness over any particles of light. The corollary of this was matter-hating asceticism, including avoidance of procreation and of the plucking of fruit from trees (III,10,18). Consequent practical difficulties were solved by the division of the sect into the elect, revered for their asceticism, and the hearers, who aspired to lesser grades of sanctity and engaged in the proscribed activities, but hoped to gain merit by serving the elect.

It may surprise us that a man of Augustine's intellectual caliber could have been seduced even for a moment, let alone for nine years, by what we might consider nowadays to be a farrago of nonsense. That he was may be partly explained by the fact that Manicheanism made a serious, if bizarre, attempt to grapple with the problem of evil and its origins, a problem that preoccupied Augustine and has baffled many a brilliant mind since: if God is good and omnipotent, how can evil exist? There is horror in the notion of a universe where evil powers do their worst because the good God is helpless, yet Manichean teachings may have had a certain terrible attraction for Augustine, as a mythological projection of the fierce tensions within himself. He may also have found plenty in their hymns and ceremonies that appealed to his sense of beauty, for the Gnostics tended to specialize in these things. He was, moreover, impressed for a time by the ostensible asceticism of the elect. Though he caricatured the Manichees later, he always felt the strength of their appeal. It is likely that he never fully accepted the speculative side of their theories, and certain that he became progressively disillusioned, but drifted along for want of anything better.

Something better was, however, awaiting him at Milan. First, there was Ambrose, bishop of the city, a thoroughly cultured and intelligent man with a distinguished civic career behind him. His reputation for wisdom and eloquence attracted Augustine, who fell into the habit of listening to Ambrose's sermons, at first for their style, but imperceptibly for their content. Two aspects in particular were important. By exploring the "spiritual meaning" Ambrose made sense of various Old Testament passages which had baffled and repelled Augustine. And Ambrose was well versed in

Neo-Platonism, which informed his preaching and was integrated with his understanding of Christianity.

Augustine states that certain "books of the Platonists" were put into his hands at Milan. The Neo-Platonist philosophers whose thought and writings played the most influential part in Augustine's story were Plotinus (c. 204-270) and his disciple Porphyry (c. 232-303). Plotinus had studied for years at Alexandria under Ammonius Saccas, who was also Origen's master; but in about 244 he moved to Rome, where his subtle, penetrating thought, his genius as a teacher, and his attractive personality made him the focus of a group of disciples. In about 263 Porphyry joined him there. Many years after the master's death Porphyry wrote a *Life* of Plotinus, and systematized his teaching, somewhat artificially, into six sets of nine treatises (hence the name *Enneads*).

Plotinus drew much inspiration from a handful of Plato's treatises, notably the *Phaedo*, the *Phaedrus*, the *Symposium* and the *Timaeus*. Central to his thought was the One, or the Good, the primary, transcendent, unchanging reality. The One cannot be described, because it is beyond all definition or limitation, but it is the source of all determinate being.

From the One, said Plotinus, sprang a second hypostasis, Intellect. Some kind of rebellious self-assertion, or *tolma*, a desire for separate existence, was involved in Intellect's procession from the One, yet the One was unaffected by it. Intellect is the timeless divine mind, thinking itself, and in it are contained the Platonic "Forms" or "Ideas." Though Intellect immediately turned back toward the One in contemplation, Intellect is not pure unity, but unity in multiplicity.

A third hypostasis, which Plotinus called Soul, separated itself from Intellect by a further act of *tolma*, and thus originated time, which is a restlessness born of desire for succession in preference to simultaneous, eternal being. Discursive thought therefore became its mode of understanding; but the higher levels of soul were in immediate contact with Intellect, by which it was illumined, and through contemplation Soul could transcend itself and rise with Intellect to union with the One. The lower levels of Soul cast upon formless, primordial matter an image of the Forms contained in Intellect, thereby giving rise to the material cosmos. Soul orders the cosmos from within: Plotinus used the comparison of physical reality floating in Soul like a net in the sea, a picture which Augustine also invoked in his efforts to imagine what God could be like (VII,5,7). According to Plotinus the ordered cosmos sprang spontaneously from Soul as Soul returned to Intellect in contemplation, and similarly in human beings right action springs spontaneously and immediately from contemplation.

Human beings exist on the lowest divine level, that of Soul, but the highest part of our soul is immune to suffering and emotion, according to Plotinus; it must strive upward by purification of thought and moral behavior, and so awaken to its divine reality. The goal of philosophy must be to attain to union with the One, or the Good, by becoming what we truly are.

Plotinus was no cold theorist. Something very like love impelled him toward this sublime goal. According to Porphyry, Plotinus experienced union with the One only four times during the six years of their association in Rome, and Porphyry himself attained it only once, in old age. The love that impels the seeker must, like every other reality, have its origin in the One, and it persists in the final union where we are conformed to the One; yet the One does not love us. Nor is there any real question of sin, or any need for redemption or grace, because our origin has already endowed us with all the dynamism necessary for return to the One. Ritual activities are unnecessary, Plotinus considered, though he allowed the philosopher to engage in them if they seemed helpful.

Plotinus appears to have had little, if any, contact with orthodox Christianity, but he hated the Gnostics. Porphyry was more explicitly, and bitterly, anti-Christian; yet it was through Porphyrian spectacles that Augustine read Plotinus. He seems to have known some at least of the *Enneads*, and may have imbibed much of their substance from listening to Ambrose and in discussion with educated friends. This discovery at a critical moment in his search for truth was providential in Augustine's eyes.

Most immediately, Neo-Platonism provided him with a less inadequate, less unworthy, notion of God. His own reflections, described at length in the early part of Book VII, were leading him toward an immutable, inviolable, incorruptible reality, of necessity transcending whatever was subject to change and decay; now the Neo-Platonic books provided him with a forceful and clear-cut doctrine of such a Being, a God utterly real, purely spiritual, undivided, eternal, the One who is the source of all multiple beings. Part of Augustine's hostility toward what he had imagined to be Catholic teaching was seriously undermined by the new insight: he had hitherto been incapable of conceiving the notion of purely spiritual substance, and hence supposed that God was some huge extended body, however ethereal. This had led him to caricature as absurd Catholic belief in the creation of men and women in God's image. But now a door opened in his mind.

Similarly, he had been vividly conscious of the difference between the fleeting succession to which all creatures are subject as their existence constantly slips away from them, and the eternity which must characterize the being of God. In Book XI he pursues the mystery of time to its last, vanishing refuge in the pathetic efforts of human beings to hold onto their elusive existence and pretend to some illusory permanence; and he arrives at a "subjectivist" view of time as the tension within human consciousness. The eternal present of God's being and knowledge was perhaps already a certainty for Augustine before he encountered Neo-Platonism, but Plotinus provided him with a doctrine of processions and of the origin of time as a decline from the eternity of the One and Intellect. Neo-Platonism's final statement on the mystery of eternity was to be made more than a century later by Boethius and bequeathed to the Scholastics: eternity is "the total, simultaneous and perfect possession of endless life" (Boethius, *Consolation of Philosophy* V,6).

It is, however, simplistic to assimilate Plotinus' theory of the procession of three hypostases to Christian faith in the Trinity, and Augustine does not do so. The resemblance is more apparent than real. Plotinus' three hypostases are not only unequal; they represent a progressive decline from the primordial unity. Most significantly, Augustine emphasizes that only through Christ the Mediator, who is also the Way, is faith in the Trinity possible. Neo-Platonism had no doctrine of an incarnation of the Logos, no idea of the humility of God, no need for revelation, for redemption, or for grace to empower a response from humankind. "I read in [the Neo-Platonist books] that God, the Word, was born not of blood nor man's desire nor lust of the flesh, but of God; but that the Word was made flesh and dwelt among us, I did not read there. I certainly observed that in these writings it was often stated that the Son, being in the form of God the Father, deemed it no robbery to be equal to God ... but that he emptied himself and took on the form of a slave ... of this no mention was made in these books" (VII,9,14). He continues to spell out the contrast in the concluding paragraphs of Book VII.

What Neo-Platonism seemed immediately to offer was an invitation to self-transcendence and ecstasy, to a union of the human soul with the divine, to the flight of the alone to the Alone. This spoke to Augustine's longings as nothing else had ever done, though his attempts at mounting through created things and through his own mind to communion with the One were for the time being unsatisfactory. His initial failure, and then partial success, are related in VII,10,16 and VII,17,23. Neo-Platonism provided him with a vocabulary, and stirred in him a desire, for mystical union. Yet the One to whom Augustine aspired was not the remote, indifferent reality of Plotinus, but the God who constantly seeks, attracts, guides, heals, stoops toward us, forgives and loves us. He is the humble God of the incarnation. The Neo-Platonists had glimpsed the country Augustine sought, but could not show him the way there (VII,20,26; 21,27).

The God revealed in the Old and New Testaments is, moreover, the God who forms a people. He is the God encountered in the Church. The contrast with Neo-Platonism at this point could hardly be greater. Paradoxically, it was Neo-Platonism that helped to free Augustine's mind from the constricting misapprehensions that had held him back from the Catholic Church, but in the Church he was to find a fullness of life and an approach to God which Neo-Platonism did not offer. The flight of the alone to the Alone did not make for community. His account of the experience at Ostia, which forms a high point in his story, begins (whether consciously or not) in Neo-Platonist terms, but concludes in powerfully biblical language; and the experience, significantly, is shared with one who had no pretensions to philosophy. The "little ones," he reflected later, have a safe place in the nest of the Church, where they can grow and be nourished in the faith that gives them access to the mystery (IV,16,31).

He would certainly have found in Plotinus a robust doctrine of the goodness of the material creation as derived from the good creator. The teaching of Genesis on this point is so unambiguous that Augustine would perhaps have needed no confirmation, but it is worth noting that on embracing biblical faith he was in this respect much nearer to the positive teaching of Neo-Platonism than to Manichean dualism. The conviction that the beauty and order of the non-human world bore eloquent witness to its maker was an important element in Augustine's struggle with the problem of evil, which must be, he concluded, in some sense a negation of being.

Before his arrival in Milan, Augustine had had three major intellectual difficulties which blocked his progress toward the Christian faith. The first was a distorted notion of Catholic belief in God's creation of man in his own image, the second a revulsion from the moral crudities to be found in the Old Testament, the third his perplexity about the origin of evil. All three of these blocks were now tending to dissolve. Neo-Platonism had helped him toward a conception of spiritual substance and hence to a less inadequate idea of God. Difficulties about the Old Testament were largely resolved by the doctrine of the "spiritual sense" of some narratives, imbibed from Ambrose, together with Augustine's own reflections on development in revelation, and the differing requirements of time, place, and culture. The problem of evil still exercised his mind, but in the light of Neo-Platonic views of the universe he thought deeply about evil as a lack of being, and about the misuse of free will by rational creatures. He was almost convinced, intellectually, but not free to follow where his intelligence was leading.

Moral Struggles, Conversion

Hand in hand with this long, passionate search for truth went an equally passionate need for sexual relationships. We need to be cautious here, because popular imagination has tended to represent Augustine as extremely profligate in his youth; but for this view there is inadequate evidence. His language about his adolescent sexual behavior is lurid, but largely metaphorical, and he makes the revealing admission that he sometimes bragged to his friends about excesses he had not really committed, feeling it shameful to be thought innocent (II,3,7). This statement has the ring of truth. As a student at Carthage he began to cohabit with the woman he loved. To call her a "concubine" is too harsh, and also inaccurate. Such unions were taken for granted, and would have appeared innocent in the eyes of both. They were exclusively faithful to each other for about fourteen years, and they had a son whom Augustine dearly loved. It was a marriage in all but name. Far more questionable was Augustine's acquiescence when Monica, possibly supported by Ambrose, insisted on the dismissal of his common-law wife to clear the way for marriage to an heiress of good family, a match likely to further his career and solve his financial problems (VI,15,25). The separation was intensely painful to both parties, and Augustine does not come well out of this. His grief was dulled, though scarcely assuaged, by a temporary liaison with someone else for merely sensual gratification. This looks like a moral collapse, but it did not last long.

At this stage he discovered Saint Paul. The struggle between the good approved by the mind and the downward drag of concupiscence, evoked by Paul in Romans 7, corresponded to Augustine's own experience. He was, he tells us, like a man half asleep, who knows the force of the arguments in favor of getting up, but drowsily pleads for a few more minutes (VIII,5,12). The question that concluded Paul's description of the struggle was the crucial one for Augustine: *Who will free me from this death-doomed body, save the grace of God through Jesus Christ our Lord?* (Rom 7:24-25).

As Augustine approached the turning-point his intellectual battles were largely over, and the central issue was the apparent impossibility of continence; but Paul's influence, both now and later, was far wider and deeper than this. By immersing himself in Paul's letters Augustine discovered Christ, Christ whose absence from the Platonic books had signaled to him their insufficiency. He discovered the humility of God in the incarnation, the absolute human need for a mediator and redeemer, and the all-pervasive, healing grace of God meeting human indigence through Christ. Augustine's later doctrine of the absolute primacy of grace in our response to God was shaped by his own experience of impotence without it.

The famous conversion scene in the garden is carefully prepared for. Monica's dream, and her certainty that Augustine will eventually share her faith, are a distant prelude (III,11,19-12,21). Book VIII plays upon a series of conversions: that of the great Victorinus (who had translated into Latin the Platonic books so important to Augustine), that of the two court officials, and in the background that of Antony of Egypt. The letters of Paul are lying on an occasional table when Ponticianus arrives at the house to tell Augustine and Alypius the disturbing stories. They are again lying about in the garden when the terrible decision is made. The struggle is brilliantly described, and needs no comment—except perhaps that it is maddeningly typical of Augustine to interrupt the account with a long discussion on the nature of free will. It is relevant, certainly, to his predicament, but the reader is longing for the resolution of the contest.

After the drama of Book VIII there is a marked change of mood. Book IX is one of the most beautiful of Augustine's writings, bathed in an atmosphere of peace which seems like a preliminary realization of the eternal peace for which he has longed, from the cry of the restless heart in I,1,1 to the Sabbath rest that gently closes Book XIII. The interlude between his conversion in August 386 and the return with his friends to Milan for baptism in the following spring opens with the autumn holidays, a time of vintage, harvest, fruitfulness, and promise fulfilled.

Peace has come in some measure to Augustine, but more fully to Monica, who is now central. Her maturity, kindness, wisdom, and peace dominate Book IX, and the mystical experience shared by mother and son forms the climax of both the narrative and their relationship (IX,10, 23-25). Book IX is also a book of birth, death, and rebirth. The story of Books I-IX has led us from Augustine's birth to his sacramental death and rebirth into Christ's death and resurrection in baptism; but the book ends with Monica's death. Grief and a kind of peace fill its closing pages. And there the narrative ends.

This is highly disconcerting to most readers. When his mother died, Augustine was not yet thirty-three. The following years were packed with interest. He returned to Africa, established monastic life there, was ordained a priest, saw his close friend Alypius ordained and raised to a bishopric, was consecrated a bishop himself, preached, taught, wrote, administered the sacraments, engaged in controversy, adjudicated in disputes; and of all this he tells us virtually nothing in *The Confessions*.

There must be a cut-off point in any narrative, and so, it might be argued, the death of Monica was a fitting place to end. In that there is truth; but why, then, add four more long books?

After the Narrative

The relationship of Books X-XIII to Books I-IX has been the subject of much debate. Possibly Book X may have been added last, in response to the desire of those who had read the rest to know where Augustine stood at the time of writing. His concentration in Book X on the nature of memory, and then on his present temptations, makes this a plausible theory, but it lacks manuscript support and has not commanded general assent. Even if true, it leaves us with the question of Book XI (on time and eternity), Book XII (on conflicting interpretations of the opening verses of Genesis) and Book XIII (on the creation story in Gn 1:1-2:3).

The relevance of these long meditations to the preceding narrative is variously explained. Most persuasive are the subtle cross-references between the narrative of I-IX and the last four books. The prodigal wanders away from God, plunges into misery and frustration, and finds his way back in tears; but this is the story of all creation writ small. Augustine's personal story can be read as a particular exemplification of his thesis throughout the last books: that only in turning back to its creator can the creature, sunk in its own darkness, instability, and formless futility, find its destined happiness. If this point is validly made, the idea of conversion is a link between both (or all three) sections of *The Confessions*: Augustine's own conversion in I-IX; his continuing labor of daily conversion in X; and the "formation" of formless matter in XI-XIII. His famous words in the first chapter of Book I, *fecisti nos ad te*, come into their own.

Some scholars hold that Augustine intended to give a complete exposition of the faith, based on scripture, to which his own story would serve as an introduction, but abandoned the project. Others again see the positive doctrine of a good creator making a good world, which pervades the closing books, to be the best refutation of the Manicheanism he has negatively criticized in the earlier ones. The commentary by Professor J.J. O'Donnell draws attention to frequently recurring trinitarian patterns, and to the structural function of the threefold temptation mentioned in 1 John 2:16. The last three books together form a triadic pattern: Book XI contrasts the time-constrained, ephemeral character of creaturely being with the eternity of God the Father; Book XII evokes the plurality and fragmentation of human words as we approach the Word; Book XIII speaks of the creative and re-creative work of the Spirit.

All these observations are helpful, and all remind us that we are not reading autobiography in the modern sense. Few modern writers of autobiography or memoirs would relentlessly take us through page after exhausting page about the nature of memory, the mystery of time, or divergent views on the meaning of a single verse in Genesis. But Augustine never professed to be writing autobiography. He referred to his greatest work as "the thirteen books of my confessions" or "my confessions in thirteen books." The heart of the matter, therefore, is to find out what he means by *confessio*, or the verb *confiteri*. There are several layers of meaning.

What is Confession?

There is, first, the confession of sin, a meaning commonly understood and certainly part of Augustine's intention in this long prayer to God who had forgiven all his sins. This very forgiveness was the enabling condition for his confession of them. In addition to his sexual failings, already discussed, he confesses to vanity, concern for praise, excessive desire to excel, sycophancy toward the great, and acceptance of the compromises entailed in pleasing them. He also dwells at length on the apparently motiveless theft of pears in adolescence, scrutinizing it with a thoroughness that some readers have found bewildering. It is likely that the episode has more than its obvious significance, however; it may be presented as his personal re-enactment of the fall of our first parents described in Genesis 3, as an exposition of the essentially irrational character of sin, and as a picture of the corruptive power of friendship or camaraderie when not formed in God. Certainly, too, Augustine confesses to *curiositas*, the "lust of the eyes," indulged particularly at the theatrical shows he had enjoyed in his youth, and seen in maturity as a perversion of the desire for truth.

In proportion to Augustine's fine sense of the glory, the truth and the love to which God calls human beings was his horror of their perversion in, respectively, pride, "curiosity" and sensuality. Human beings, he believed, are poised between God above and worldly goods below (XIII, 9, 10). Their love for the one or the other is a weight which bears them toward the object of their choice.

The second level of meaning in *confessio* is confession of God's glory, the *Confitebor tibi, Domine* (*I will praise you, Lord*) of the psalms, which Augustine makes thoroughly his own. The opening words of Book I set the tone for the whole enterprise. He praises and thanks God for the great glories of creation and salvation, for the unnumbered mercies of God in his own life, for providence, for healing, for forgiveness. He praises God for what Augustine is through God's gift, after confessing what Augustine was, and still could be, of himself. He praises the mercy that stooped to his misery. The refrain is constant throughout.

Recurrently through his book Augustine begs God to enable him to make his confession. This insistent prayer for grace points us toward the third and perhaps most profound level of what Augustine understands by confession. He cannot speak, cannot find words or a voice to speak with, cannot know what to say, except because God first gives it and guarantees its veracity: "I can say nothing right to other people unless you have heard it from me first, nor can you even hear anything of the kind from me which you have not first told me" (X,2,2). He struggles to keep communication open between his own speech and the Word who is its creative source. The graced word is God's first, then Augustine's; it is most truly Augustine's in the measure that it is God's word in him. At the deepest level of creaturely being, divine creativity gives birth to human self-expression; the eternal generation of the Word is mirrored in this particular kind of creature who expresses himself by wrestling with words and meaning. None of us can know how to pray, says Saint Paul, but the Spirit prays in us (Rom 8:26); and all Augustine's labor in this book is prayer.

The graced, God-given word is therefore self-transcending, like any genuine symbol of the divine, whose function is to be transparent to the mystery beyond itself. If it is to be the means of illumination and effective communication in the world of grace it must remain open to the eternal Word of God, and allow itself to be shaped by him. Human words, however inadequate and stumbling, must remain one with the Word by self-transcendence, or they will degenerate into *loquacitas*, the chatter Augustine deplores (III,6,10). Clearly this openness is guaranteed in the case of the scriptural words, but it must be striven for also in the self-utterance on which Augustine is engaged.

It follows that the graced word is co-creative. In the closing books, and especially the last, Augustine ponders the mystery of God's creative Word which calls all creatures into being. He notes the change of formula for human creation: God who has said, *Let there be light.... Let there be a vault.... Let the earth bring forth ...* now says not "Let there be man according to his kind" but *Let us make man according to our image and likeness* (XIII,22,32), because he meant us to discern his will and respond to him. This creature comes to be in responding to God, in speaking the graced word of faith, love, and obedience back to God. The word of confession is therefore not simply a statement of what is, of the present truth of oneself, seen and admitted in the light of God's presence, with all the liberation that implies. It is more than a static recognition; it is a creative process. The human speaker is at one with God who is creating him; he becomes co-creator of himself, constituting himself in being by confession. Words, as Augustine often observed, are essentially signs; and they reach their fullest meaning as servants of self-transcendence.

In the peaceful closing chapters of Book XIII Augustine's seeing is one with God's seeing, Augustine's joy in the beauty of creation one with God's joy. And as he confesses, his voice, along with the chorus of creation, is one with God's.

Memory, Self-Knowledge, Friendship

If asked where this union between God's knowledge of him and his own self-knowledge was consummated, Augustine might have replied that it happened in his heart; or perhaps in his *memoria*, to which he devotes his long tenth book. *Memoria* includes what we mean by memory, but is much wider, and he explores it with considerable subtlety. Its contents are, first, all those traces left by sense-impressions received through past experience; these can be retrieved, associated with one another, used as imaginative building-materials, temporarily mislaid, or hopelessly lost. But then Augustine reviews other riches in his *memoria* which cannot have been deposited there by any sense-experience, such as his intuitive recognition of the principles of mathematics (X,12,19). The exploration takes him wider still, to all the realm of truth that the mind is capable of knowing, to the mind's capacity to know itself and be known by itself, and to its inner knowledge of God, against which all truth approaching from without is tested and measured. This is part of Augustine's theory of illumination. It is derived from Plato's doctrine of *anamnesis*, which held that the soul remembers eternal truths from an earlier existence before its birth in time; but Augustine discarded the reference to past experience, believing that the soul is in habitual contact with the world of intelligible truth here and now. From *memoria* wells up the universal human longing for happiness, which must be in some way known if it is longed for; and in *memoria* we know ourselves and know God.

The same Book X, where the "fields of *memoria*" are reviewed, concludes with a report by Augustine on the kinds of temptation with which he still has to grapple at the time of writing *The Confessions*. He is in no euphoric condition, and there is much less of the longed-for peace than we (or he?) might have expected. He gives a picture of conversion as a continuing, slow, and sometimes painful process, rather than a dramatic once-for-all. It must have been an immediately recognizable situation to the first readers, as it still is today.

It is a friendly picture, because Augustine was a fundamentally friendly man. Throughout *The Confessions* he never seems to be alone, even at intimate moments. When he is maneuvering to catch Ambrose alone to discuss his problems, it is "we" who have to tiptoe away disappointed; during the momentous struggle in the garden Alypius is near enough to watch and await the outcome; at the supreme moment of ecstasy at the window at Ostia he is with Monica and the experience is shared. Friendship with his mother is a major theme throughout the first nine books, and its development (which is also Monica's development toward mature holiness) is subtly suggested. But other friendships abound, and in them too there is Christward growth. In his earlier years Augustine misused his evident magnetism and gift for friendship: the pear-tree episode is a story of immature and deviant camaraderie, and he used his personal influence to lead a close (unnamed) friend astray into Manicheanism (IV,4,7). These relationships ripened into a real if still imperfect experience of life with a group of friends, delightfully described in IV,8,13; but the full flowering of his genius for friendship had to await his conversion and theirs. Initially at Cassiciacum, and again at Thagaste and Hippo after their return to Africa, Augustine and his friends found within their faith a communion of hearts and minds and life which was like a microcosm of the Church. In the last book of *The Confessions* he suggests something of his vision of the Church indwelt by the Spirit, and the glories of God's new creation in believers.

This powerfully relational side to Augustine's character prompts the question: why did he not consider life as a married Catholic after his conversion? There were probably several reasons. The pull toward community life was already strong; he and his friends had long since dreamed of an ideal common life where all things would be shared (VI,14,24), and it was precisely their (actual or possible future) wives who had been the stumbling-block; such a community life was not easily compatible with marriage. Alypius had explicitly pointed out the difficulty of combining marriage with the philosophical pursuits to which they aspired (VI,12,21). There was, further, a strong ascetical current within Christianity at the time. The story of Antony of Egypt and his radical renunciation of property and marriage was influential in the conversion of the two court officials and probably of many others. Augustine and Alypius were certainly impressed by it, as also by the other monastic stories related by Ponticianus. Paul's teaching on marriage and celibacy in 1 Cor 7 was in Augustine's mind at the time of his conversion, as he mentions at VIII,1,2, and the example of Ambrose's celibacy may have played a part. That Augustine and his friends regarded a celibate life as the only viable option for them as Christians is clear from the chagrin of Verecundus who felt himself debarred, and their reaction to him (IX,3,5-6). More particularly, Augustine's personal circumstances suggested this course. The grace of Christ offered to him at the moment of decision had appeared in the guise of a liberation from illicit sexual bonds which he had felt powerless to break; but there was no obvious prospect of honorable marriage. The woman he really loved, the mother of his son, had been "torn from his side" and was, it seems, irretrievably lost; the young girl of good family to whom he had been betrothed through Monica's efforts was still under age (which probably means only about ten or eleven years old), and since Augustine was in any case giving up his career as a teacher of rhetoric, her family was perhaps no longer interested in promoting the match.

Augustine's Understanding of the Scriptures

Augustine's struggle for truth did not end with his conversion and baptism. Wide fields opened up before him, an invitation to growth and to a stretching of mind and heart to which the later books of *The Confessions* bear witness. After the profundities of Book X he grapples in Book XI with the dizzying mystery of time as the dimension of created being. In the twelfth and thirteenth books he is searching the sacred text, and we leave him at the end still asking, seeking, and knocking at its door.

The biblical doctrine of creation came to hold rich implications for him. With his Christian mind Augustine was no more able than were the authors of Genesis before him to see the creation narrative apart from the story of salvation to which it serves as overture. The light that sprang into being on God's first day came to mean for him the light that transforms the believer in baptism, and the mature Augustine could read the story of creation only in terms of salvation experienced in the Church.

Augustine gives us scant information about the Church's sacramental life, because the discipline of secrecy was still to some extent observed, but its importance to him is beyond question. The story of Victorinus' conversion (VIII,2,3-5) emphasizes that intellectual conviction of the truth of Christianity was insufficient; initiation through baptism together with public profession of the faith and membership of the Christian community was also required. We may wonder what Augustine's own Christianity would have amounted to if he had stopped short after the garden experience in August 386, and never proceeded to baptism the following Easter.

His approach to scripture may disconcert modern readers. The allegorical method finds little favor today; it seems like a game where anything can be made to mean anything at the whim of preacher or writer. Modern scholarship is more careful of the literal sense of scripture, recognizing that authentic spiritual senses must emerge from the literal sense, not contradict or float free of it. It is only Augustine's method, however, that we may find unacceptable; his fundamental intuitions are as valid as ever. His own attitude to the scriptures evolved during the period covered by *The Confessions*, from haughty contempt for the Bible's lowly, unclassical style and distaste for unethical practices apparently sanctioned by God in the Old Testament, to puzzlement, to respect for its authority and a sense of the mystery it half revealed and half concealed, to a determination to "stand under" (or "fly under") this vault or tent that God had pitched above humankind. For him it was a coded message from God, to be pored over, prayed over, and squeezed for every drop of truth or sweetness it could distill. Through its words he communed with the Word. He prayed over it until its phrases and images, especially those of the psalms, poured out of him as the expression of his own thought and prayer, often, it would appear, when he was not consciously quoting. In the moment of personal mystical union at Ostia "we arrived at the summit of our own minds; and this too we transcended, to touch that land of never-failing plenty where you pasture Israel for ever with the food of truth" (IX,10,24). Even this experience is suggested through biblical images, and it ends with powerful longing for a perfect, eternal, uninterrupted listening to the Word, a fulfillment evoked by the gospel invitation, *Enter into the joy of your Lord*, and Paul's eschatological hope (IX,10,25). Augustine's ideal of Christian life and ministry in Book XIII is similarly shaped by Pauline teaching, for in Paul Augustine seems to have seen an icon of what he strove to be himself.

Is the Story True?

Like other Fathers of the Church, Augustine was vividly conscious of the entire mystery of salvation as embodied in a story that runs from Genesis to Revelation but still continues. He was himself caught up in it, for like the prodigal son, he had wandered far off into a land of unlikeness, but the journey home brought him to a recovery of the lost image and likeness to God with which Book XIII is concerned. It is a story still unfolding in the faithful and in the Church, and in it we are all participants.

Theology therefore cannot be an exercise in static reflection, but the struggle for truth by one who stands in the light of God's self-revelation, living as one of his people, and engaged in a history. There can be, for Augustine, no theology divorced from history. But is the converse also true; can there be history, and his own history in particular, that is not theology? In telling us his story, has he given us the plain facts, or a theological meditation? Are the first nine books history, or a symbolic presentation of Augustine's later understanding of himself in relation to God's grace, arrived at through years lived in the faith of the Church? Can we trust the story as substantially factual, or is it to be viewed as a parable, in the same light as the story of the prodigal son, with whom he often compares himself? In the latter case, his narrative would clearly have a truth of its own; should we look only for this? Must we read even the garden-scene as the symbolic construction of an artist-theologian? Even Ostia?

Undoubtedly Augustine was an artist, and there has obviously been artistic freedom in the way he presents his material. In addition to the dramatic structure of Book VIII we might instance the recurrent significance of gardens, the juxtaposition of Paul's letters and a gaming-table (VIII,6,14), the high relief given to the pear-tree episode (II,4,9), and the contrasting parallel suggested in Book IX between Monica's furtive wine-sipping and the panting of them both for the celestial fountain (IX,10,23). But every good story-teller has a right to some artistic freedom. For Augustine the story of salvation, of which his own story is a part, was essentially rooted in history. His intention to report facts is indicated by his insistence in Book X that those who are united with him in charity will believe him, together with his painstaking analysis of his situation at the time of writing. Moreover, many close friends and associates were still alive to corroborate or correct his account. The external inducements that prompted his decision to tell his story required that it have substantial factual content.

But was he, consciously or unconsciously, reinterpreting his earlier experiences in the light of a truth later apprehended? Did he, for example, really feel the lack of any doctrine of incarnation and redemption when he read the "books of the Platonists," or did he only perceive the lack later, with believer's hindsight? Could he, at that pre-conversion stage, have known what to look for?

It is simplistic to suppose that any history can be written without interpretation. Even to decide that an episode, or a sequence of events, is worth recording at all is already a value-judgment on its significance. When the historian confronts a mass of raw facts, some selection has to be made among them and some order of presentation adopted, and these decisions are necessarily interpretative. Interpretation-free history is a will-o'-the-wisp, even when the story to be told is one in which the teller has not been directly engaged.

This is the more true when the narrator is telling his own story. None of us can put the clock back; we can only speak from where we are, even if we are relating our own past. The question is sometimes put to a person after many years in some vocation—in a certain career, or a marriage, or some kind of religious life—"Would you choose in the same way again, if you had the choice now?" This is in some degree a non-question, because the person who attempts to answer it has in fact been conditioned and formed by the choice made long ago, and cannot stand objectively aloof from all the intervening experience that choice entailed.

What matters, therefore, in assessing the historical worth of Augustine's narrative is not whether he interpreted his earlier life in the light of his later Christian faith and experience, because of course he did; the significant question to ask is, how valid, how *truthful*, is his interpretation?

He came to see that all visible, existent things proclaim by their very being to anyone with ears to hear that they did not make themselves; they are God's creatures and as such bearers of his word. We see them, and hear their proclamation, insofar as our hearts are right and our love well ordered, as he makes plain in X,6,20. But the same principle holds for human experience, which is also a word of God to the believer. Human experience is an annunciation, a revelation of God, for those with ears to hear and eyes to see. Where intelligent beings are concerned, the last stage of creation is conversion to God; this idea underlies Augustine's thought on creation in Book

XIII. The *formation* of a spiritual being and its *conversion* are aspects of, or stages in, the one creative process. As angelic creatures attained their unwavering stability through perfect conversion to God and "cleaving" to him (XII,11,12-13; XII,15,19), so eventually will human creatures. Confession, in Augustine's pregnant sense, is personal engagement in the creative process. It is a willingness to stand in God's truth and become a co-creator with God in his creation of oneself. Part of this new creation in the human mind is the ability to see oneself and one's own history in God's light. To this kind of truthfulness Augustine's whole effort of confession is directed.

The Verdict of His Readers

The *Confessions* blazed a trail which others have followed, writers as varied as Abelard, Pascal, Rousseau, and Proust. It is tempting, yet patronizing and facile, to say that Augustine is "amazingly modern." Certainly his experience of God and his searching of the human heart speak to us across the centuries with so little need of transposition that the cultural gulf seems almost irrelevant. Yet we shall not hear him aright if we assume too readily (even too arrogantly) that he is like us. The words of a modern commentator make the point sharply: speaking of Augustine's doctrine of concupiscence, Professor J.J. O'Donnell writes, " ... his view of temptation excludes as illicit rich and fruitful—yet perilous—areas of human conduct. His own past, as displayed in Books 1-9, shows little that would trouble an enlightened modern for even a moment; and on the other hand *everything* to which A. converted is in some way or other alien to modern sensibilities. A. cannot be tamed and domesticated to our purposes; in fundamental ways, he is alien—to put it more gently, he is a challenge—to all of us." (*Commentary on Books 8-13*, 203-204)

In 426-427, toward the end of his life, Augustine revised many of his earlier writings and indicated how they appeared to him across the space of intervening years. Of *The Confessions*, which he had written some thirty years earlier, he wrote, "The thirteen books of my *Confessions* concern both my bad and my good actions, for which they praise our just and good God. In so doing they arouse the human mind and affections toward him. As far as I am concerned, they had this effect upon me in my writing of them, and still do when I read them now. What others think about them is for them to say; but I know that they have given pleasure in the past, and still do give pleasure, to many of my brethren." (*Revisions* II,6,1) For all our blind spots and selective responses, we, like readers over sixteen centuries, may find ourselves in agreement with this judgment.

Note on this Translation

The Latin text principally used is that of Lucas Verheijen, O.S.A., in *Corpus Christianorum, Series Latina,* Volume XXVII (Turnhoult, 1990), with an occasional departure where the text established by Professor J.J. O'Donnell clarifies matters, particularly with regard to punctuation.

The earliest manuscripts recognized only a division into thirteen books. Separate chapters within these were marked in printed editions from the late fifteenth century; and paragraphs were numbered within the chapters by the Maurist edition of 1679. In the present translation all three sets of numbers are shown; thus X,31,43 means Book X, Chapter 31, numbered paragraph 43.

The title to each book, and the subheads within the text, have been added by the translator, and to these subheads the list of contents corresponds.

The magisterial work of Professor J.J. O'Donnell, Augustine, *Confessions,* Volume I, *Introduction and Text;* Volume II, *Commentary on Books 1-7;* Volume III, *Commentary on Books 8-13* (Oxford, 1992), will transform the task of translation for generations to come. The debt of the present translator to this work will be evident on every page.

Chronological Outline of Augustine's Life for the Period Covered by The Confessions

A.D.

354 13 November, Augustine born at Thagaste in Numidia Proconsularis, to Patricius and Monica. He had at least one brother, Navigius, and two sisters whose names are not recorded.

365-369 Schooling at Madaura or Madauros (modern Mdaurouch).

369-370 A year of idleness at home while his father saves up to enable him to continue his studies.

370 Conversion of Patricius.

371-374 Augustine as a student at Carthage. He lives with an unnamed woman. In 372 Patricius dies. Augustine's son Adeodatus born. Augustine reads the *Hortensius*.

375 Returns from Carthage to Thagaste to teach rhetoric. Friend dies.

376-383 Teaches at Carthage. Writes *De Pulchro et Apto* (*The Beautiful and the Harmonious*), now lost.

383 To Rome.

384 To Milan as professor of rhetoric. Meets Ambrose.

385 Monica arrives in Milan.

386 February, persecution by Justina. June, finding of bodies of Saints Gervasius and Protasius. Augustine reads "Platonic books." Talks with Simplicianus. Is visited by Ponticianus. August, conversion in garden. September, goes to Cassiciacum.

387 March, returns to Milan. On Easter night, 24 April, is baptized with Alypius and Adeodatus. Autumn, vision at Ostia. Death of Monica.

* * * *

34

After this Augustine, his friends, and his son remained in Rome until August 388, when they returned to Thagaste. There they lived a quasi-monastic life. Augustine studied and wrote. In 389 or 390 Adeodatus died. In 391 while visiting Hippo on a Sunday morning Augustine was singled out by Bishop Valerius and persuaded by the congregation to accept ordination to the priesthood. In 395-396 he was coadjutor bishop to Valerius, whom he succeeded as bishop of Hippo in 396. In 397 Ambrose died, and was succeeded by Simplicianus, though Augustine apparently did not know of this when he wrote, or at least began, *The Confessions* in 397.

Revisions II, 6 (32)

Thirteen Books of The Confessions

1. The thirteen books of my *Confessions* concern both my bad and my good actions, for which they praise our just and good God. In so doing they arouse the human mind and affections toward him. As far as I am concerned, they had this effect upon me in my writing of them, and still do when I read them now. What others think about them is for them to say; but I know that they have given pleasure in the past, and still do give pleasure, to many of my brethern. The first ten books were written about myself; the last three about holy scripture, from the words *In the Beginning God created heaven and earth*[1] as far as the Sabbath rest.[2]

2. In the fourth book, after I confessed the misery of my soul on the death of a friend, saying that in some way our soul had been made one from two, I say: "And perhaps I was so afraid of death because I did not want the whole of him to die, whom I had loved so dearly."[3] This seems to me, as it were, a trifling pronouncement rather than a serious confession, although this absurdity may be moderated to some extent by the word "perhaps" which I added.

And what I said in the thirteenth book: "The barrier" was made "between the spiritual waters on high and the lower waters,"[4] was said without sufficient deliberation. The subject, however, is exceedingly obscure.

This work begins as follows: *Magnus es, domine.*

---

1. Gn 1, 1.
2. See Gn 2, 2.
3. See *Confessions* IV,6,11.
4. Ibid. XIII,32,47.

The Confessions

Book I

Infancy and Boyhood

Opening prayer and meditation

1, 1. Great are you, O Lord, and exceedingly worthy of praise;[1] your power is immense, and your wisdom beyond reckoning.[2] And so we humans, who are a due part of your creation, long to praise you—we who carry our mortality about with us,[3] carry the evidence of our sin and with it the proof that you thwart the proud.[4] Yet these humans, due part of your creation as they are, still do long to praise you. You stir us so that praising you may bring us joy, because you have made us and drawn us to yourself, and our heart is unquiet until it rests in you.

Grant me to know and understand, Lord, which comes first: to call upon you or to praise you? To know you or to call upon you? Must we know you before we can call upon you? Anyone who invokes what is still unknown may be making a mistake. Or should you be invoked first, so that we may then come to know you? But how can people call upon someone in whom they do not yet believe? And how can they believe without a preacher?[5] But scripture tells us that those who seek the Lord will praise him,[6] for as they seek they find him,[7] and on finding him they will praise him. Let me seek you, then, Lord, even while I am calling upon you, and call upon you even as I believe in you; for to us you have indeed been preached. My faith calls upon you, Lord, this faith which is your gift to me, which you have breathed into me through the humanity of your Son and the ministry of your preacher.

---

1. See Pss 47:2(48:1); 95(96):4; 144(145):3.
2. See Ps 146(147):5.
3. See 2 Cor 4:10.
4. See 1 Pt 5:5.
5. See Rom 10:14.
6. See Ps 21:27(22:26).
7. See Mt 7:7-8; Lk 11:10.

2, 2. How shall I call upon my God, my God and my Lord, when by the very act of calling upon him I would be calling him into myself?[8] Is there any place within me into which my God might come? How should the God who made heaven and earth[9] come into me? Is there any room in me for you, Lord, my God? Even heaven and earth, which you have made and in which you have made me—can even they contain you? Since nothing that exists would exist without you, does it follow that whatever exists does in some way contain you? But if this is so, how can I, who am one of these existing things, ask you to come into me, when I would not exist at all unless you were already in me? Not yet am I in hell, after all, but even if I were, you would be there too; for if I descend to the underworld, you are there.[10] No, my God, I would not exist, I would not be at all, were you not in me. Or should I say, rather, that I should not exist if I were not in you, from whom are all things, through whom are all things, in whom are all things?[11] Yes, Lord, that is the truth, that is indeed the truth. To what place can I invite you, then, since I am in you? Or where could you come from, in order to come into me? To what place outside heaven and earth could I travel, so that my God could come to me there, the God who said, *I fill heaven and earth?*[12]

3, 3. So then, if you fill heaven and earth, does that mean that heaven and earth contain you? Or, since clearly they cannot hold you, is there something of you left over when you have filled them? Once heaven and earth are full, where would that remaining part of you overflow? Or perhaps you have no need to be contained by anything, but rather contain everything yourself, because whatever you fill you contain, even as you fill it? The vessels which are full of you do not lend you stability, because even if they break you will not be spilt. And when you pour yourself out over us,[13] you do not lie there spilt but raise us up; you are not scattered, but gather us together.[14] Yet all those things which you fill, you fill with the whole of yourself. Should we suppose, then, that because all things are incapable of

---

8. The point is more forceful in Latin: *invocare*, "to call upon," is literally "to call into."
9. See Gn 1:1.
10. See Ps 138(139):8.
11. See Rom 11:36; 1 Cor 8:6.
12. Jer 23:24.
13. See Jl 2:28-29; Acts 2:17-18.
14. The immediate background here is probably the yearning of dispersed Israel for ingathering at the end-time, as expressed in many psalms; but there may also be echoes of the

containing the whole of you, they hold only a part of you, and all of them the same part? Or does each thing hold a different part, greater things larger parts, and lesser things smaller parts? Does it even make sense to speak of larger or smaller parts of you? Are you not everywhere in your whole being, while there is nothing whatever that can hold you entirely?

4, 4. What are you, then, my God? What are you, I ask, but the Lord God? For who else is lord except the Lord, or who is god if not our God?[15] You are most high, excellent, most powerful, omnipotent, supremely merciful and supremely just, most hidden yet intimately present, infinitely beautiful and infinitely strong, steadfast yet elusive, unchanging yourself though you control the change in all things, never new, never old, renewing all things[16] yet wearing down the proud though they know it not;[17] ever active, ever at rest, gathering while knowing no need, supporting and filling and guarding, creating and nurturing and perfecting, seeking although you lack nothing. You love without frenzy, you are jealous yet secure, you regret without sadness,[18] you grow angry yet remain tranquil, you alter your works but never your plan; you take back what you find although you never lost it; you are never in need yet you rejoice in your gains, never avaricious yet you demand profits.[19] You allow us to pay you more than you demand, and so you become our debtor, yet which of us possesses anything that does not already belong to you? You owe us nothing, yet you pay your debts; you write off our debts to you, yet you lose nothing thereby.

After saying all that, what have we said, my God, my life, my holy sweetness? What does anyone who speaks of you really say? Yet woe betide those who fail to speak, while the chatterboxes go on saying nothing.[20]

5, 5. Who will grant me to find peace in you? Who will grant me this grace, that you would come into my heart and inebriate it, enabling me to

---

Neo-Platonic doctrine of the return of the many to the One, and possibly of Manichean beliefs concerning the dispersal of the divine being into fragments.

15. See Ps 17:32 (18:31).
16. See Wis 7:27.
17. See Jb 9:5.
18. See Gn 6:6-7.
19. See Mt 25:27.
20. Possibly an allusion to the Manichees, whose verbosity Augustine mentions in V,7,12.

forget the evils that beset me[21] and embrace you, my only good? What are you to me? Have mercy on me, so that I may tell. What indeed am I to you, that you should command me to love you, and grow angry with me if I do not, and threaten me with enormous woes? Is not the failure to love you woe enough in itself? Alas for me! Through your own merciful dealings with me, O Lord my God, tell me what you are to me. Say to my soul, *I am your salvation.*[22] Say it so that I can hear it. My heart is listening, Lord; open the ears of my heart and say to my soul, *I am your salvation.* Let me run toward this voice and seize hold of you. Do not hide your face from me:[23] let me die so that I may see it, for not to see it would be death to me indeed.[24]

6. The house of my soul is too small for you to enter: make it more spacious by your coming. It lies in ruins: rebuild it. Some things are to be found there which will offend your gaze; I confess this to be so and know it well. But who will clean my house? To whom but yourself can I cry, *Cleanse me of my hidden sins, O Lord, and for those incurred through others pardon your servant?*[25] I believe, and so I will speak.[26] You know everything, Lord.[27] Have I not laid my own transgressions bare before you to my own condemnation, my God, and have you not forgiven the wickedness of my heart?[28] I do not argue my case against you,[29] for you are truth itself; nor do I wish to deceive myself, lest my iniquity be caught in its own lies.[30] No, I do not argue the case with you, because *if you, Lord, keep the score of our iniquities, then who, Lord, can bear it?*[31]

---

21. See Jer 44:9.
22. Ps 34(35):3.
23. See Dt 32:20.
24. See Ex 33:23.
25. Ps 18(19):13.
26. See Ps 115(116):10; 2 Cor 4:13.
27. See Jn 21:17.
28. See Ps 31(32):5.
29. See Jb 9:2-3.
30. See Ps 26(27):12.
31. Ps 129(130):3.

Infancy

6, 7. Yet allow me to speak, though I am but dust and ashes,[32] allow me to speak in your merciful presence, for it is to your mercy that I address myself, not to some man who would mock me. Perhaps you too are laughing at me,[33] but still you will turn mercifully toward me;[34] for what is it that I am trying to say, Lord, except that I do not know whence I came into this life that is but a dying, or rather, this dying state that leads to life? I do not know where I came from.[35] But this I know, that I was welcomed by the tender care your mercy provided for me, for so I have been told by the parents who gave me life according to the flesh, those parents through whose begetting and bearing you formed me within time, although I do not remember it myself. The comforts of human milk were waiting for me, but my mother and my nurses did not fill their own breasts; rather you gave me an infant's nourishment through them in accordance with your plan, from the riches deeply hidden in creation. You restrained me from craving more than you provided, and inspired in those who nurtured me the will to give me what you were giving them, for their love for me was patterned on your law,[36] and so they wanted to pass on to me the overflowing gift they received from you. It was a bounty for them, and a bounty for me from them; or, rather, not from them but only through them, for in truth all good things are from you, O God. Everything I need for health and salvation flows from my God. This I learned later as you cried the truth aloud to me through all you give me, both within and without. At that time I knew only how to suck and be deliciously comforted, and how to cry when anything hurt my body, but no more.

8. After this I began to smile, at first only in my sleep and then when I was awake.[37] So I have been told, and I believe it on the strength of what we see other babies doing, for I do not remember doing it myself. Little by little I began to notice where I was, and I would try to make my wishes

32. See Gn 18:27; Jb 42:6.
33. See Pss 2:4; 36(37):13; Wis 4:18. Augustine is markedly sensitive to the mockery. Elsewhere he speaks of his own mocking attitude in earlier days (for example, III,10,18; IV,4,8), and regards the mocking spirit that delights in the discomfiture of others as typical of gratuitous evil-doing; see III,8,16.
34. See Jer 12:15.
35. All his life Augustine remained agnostic about the origin of the human soul.
36. Human love derived from and conformable to divine love, a very Augustinian idea.
37. Possibly an allusion to Virgil, *Eclogues* IV,60. It was common in ancient wisdom to think of man as the only animal that could laugh: *animal cachinnabile*.

known to those who might satisfy them; but I was frustrated in this, because my desires were inside me, while other people were outside and could by no effort of understanding enter my mind. So I tossed about and screamed, sending signals meant to indicate what I wanted, those few signs that were the best I could manage, though they did not really express my desires. Often I did not get my way, either because people did not understand or because what I demanded might have harmed me, and then I would throw a tantrum because my elders were not subject to me, nor free people willing to be my slaves; so I would take revenge on them by bursting into tears.[38] I have learned that babies behave like this from those I have been able to watch, and they without knowing it have taught me more surely what I was like myself than did my nurses who knew me well.

9. My infancy has been so long dead now, whereas I am alive. But you, O Lord, are ever living and in you nothing dies, for you exist before the dawn of the ages, before anything that can be called "before"; you are God and Lord of everything that you have created. In you stand firm the causes of all unstable things; in you the unchangeable origins of all changeable things abide; in you live the eternal ideas of all irrational and transient creatures. Tell me, I beg you, tell your miserable suppliant, O merciful God, whether my infancy was itself the sequel to some earlier age, now dead and gone. Was there nothing before it, except the life I lived in my mother's womb? Some information about that has been given me, and I have myself seen pregnant women. But then, my God, my sweetness, what came before that? Was I somewhere else? Was I even someone? I have nobody to tell me: neither father nor mother could enlighten me, nor the experience of others, nor any memory of my own. Are you laughing at me for asking you these questions,[39] and are you perhaps commanding me to praise you and confess to you simply about what I do know?

10. Confess to you I will, Lord of heaven and earth,[40] and praise you for my earliest days and my infancy, which I do not remember. You allow a person to infer by observing others what his own beginnings were like; we can learn much about ourselves even from the reports of womenfolk. Already I had existence and life, and as my unspeaking stage drew to a

---

38. Throughout these paragraphs Augustine is continually conscious of the literal meaning of *in-fans*, one who is unable to speak.
39. See Pss 2:4; 36(37):13; Wis 4:18.
40. See Mt 11:25.

close I began to look for signs whereby I might communicate my ideas to others. Where could a living creature like this have come from, if not from you, Lord? Are any of us skillful enough to fashion ourselves? Could there be some channel hollowed out from some other source through which existence and life might flow to us, apart from yourself, Lord, who create us? Could we derive existence and life from anywhere other than you, in whom to be and to live are not two different realities, since supreme being and supreme life are one and the same? You are supreme and you do not change,[41] and in you there is no "today" that passes. Yet in you our "today" does pass, inasmuch as all things exist in you, and would have no means even of passing away if you did not contain them. Because your years do not fail,[42] your years are one "Today." How many of our days and our ancestors' days have come and gone in this "Today" of yours, have received from it their manner of being and have existed after their fashion, and how many others will likewise receive theirs, and exist in their own way? Yet you are the selfsame: all our tomorrows and beyond, all our yesterdays and further back, you will make in your Today, you have made in your Today.

What does it matter to me, if someone does not understand this? Let such a person rejoice even to ask the question, "What does this mean?" Yes, let him rejoice in that, and choose to find by not finding rather than by finding fail to find you.

7, 11. O God, hear me. Alas for the sins of humankind! A human it is who here bewails them, and you treat him mercifully because you made him, though the sin that is in him is not of your making. Who is there to remind me of the sin of my infancy (for sin there was: no one is free from sin in your sight, not even an infant whose span of earthly life is but a single day);[43] who can remind me of it? Some little mite who is a tiny child now, in whom I might observe conduct I do not remember in myself? What then was my sin at that age? Was it perhaps that I cried so greedily for those breasts? Certainly if I behaved like that now, greedy not for breasts, of course, but for food suitable to my age, I should provoke derision and be very properly rebuked. My behavior then was equally deserving of rebuke, but since I would not have been able to understand anyone who

41. See Mal 3:6.
42. See Ps 101:28(102:27); Heb 1:12.
43. See Jb 14:4-5.

scolded me, neither custom nor common sense allowed any rebuke to be given. After all, we eradicate these habits and throw them off as we grow up. Yes, but I have never seen any sensible person throw away good things when clearing out, so can we suppose that even in an infant such actions were good—the actions of a child who begs tearfully for objects that would harm him if given, gets into a tantrum when free persons, older persons and his parents, will not comply with his whims, and tries to hurt many people who know better by hitting out at them as hard as his strength allows, simply because they will not immediately fall in with his wishes or obey his commands, commands which would damage him if they were carried out?

The only innocent feature in babies is the weakness of their frames; the minds of infants are far from innocent. I have watched and experienced for myself the jealousy of a small child: he could not even speak, yet he glared with livid fury at his fellow-nursling. Everyone has seen this. Mothers and nurses claim to have some means of their own to charm away such behavior.[44] Is this to be regarded as innocence, this refusal to tolerate a rival for a richly abundant fountain of milk, at a time when the other child stands in greatest need of it and depends for its very life on this food alone? Behavior of this kind is cheerfully condoned, however, not because it is trivial or of small account, but because everyone knows that it will fade away as the baby grows up. This is clear from the fact that those same actions are by no means calmly tolerated if detected in anyone of more mature years.

12. Your will is that I should praise you, O Lord my God, who gave life and a body to that infant; you will me to praise you who equipped him with faculties, built up his limbs, and adorned him with a distinctive shape, as we can see. You implanted in him all the urges proper to a living creature to ensure his coherence and safety; and now you command me to praise you for those gifts, and to confess to you and sing to your name, O Most High,[45] because you are God, almighty and good, and would be so even if you had wrought no other works than these, since none but yourself, the only God, can bring them into existence. From you derives all manner of

---

44. Possibly a reference to some pagan custom, or perhaps only to the device of distracting the child's attention.
45. See Ps 91:2(92:1).

being, O God most beautiful, who endow all things with their beautiful form and by your governance direct them in their due order.[46]

But it irks me, Lord, to link that phase of my existence with my present life, the life I live now in this world; I do not remember passing through it, I have to rely on the reports of others concerning it, and I can only infer from my observation of other infants that I went through it too, though certainly this inference is well founded. As far as the dark blank in my memory is concerned, that period of infancy is on a par with the time I spent in my mother's womb. And if I was even conceived in iniquity, and with sin my mother nourished me in her womb,[47] where, I beg of you, my God, where was I, your servant, ever innocent? Where, Lord, and when?

So I will leave that period aside. What does it matter to me now, since it has vanished without trace from my memory?

Learning to speak

8, 13. Did I make my way from that infant stage into boyhood? Or should I rather say that boyhood caught up with me and took over from infancy? Yet infancy did not depart, so what happened to it? It did not stay with me, for I was no longer an infant who lacked the faculty of speech,[48] but a boy who could talk. I remember this, and later I turned my attention to the way in which I had learned to speak. It was not that older people taught me by offering me words by way of formal instruction, as was the case soon afterward with reading. No, I taught myself, using the mind you gave me, O my God, because I was unable to express the thoughts of my heart by cries and inarticulate sounds and gestures in such a way as to gain what I wanted or make my entire meaning clear to everyone as I wished; so I grasped at words with my memory;[49] when people called an object by some name, and while saying the word pointed to that thing, I watched and

---

46. *A quo est omnis modus, formosissime, qui formas omnia et lege tua ordinas omnia,* an invocation of the Trinity. Triadic patterns occur frequently in Augustine, though the vocabulary varies. The allusion is sometimes directly to the persons of the Trinity, at other times to aspects of the created world, especially human nature, which reflect the triune Creator. Here *modus* suggests the initial creation of as yet unformed matter; *forma* the principle of differentiation which gives to each thing its distinctive identity; *ordo* the animating, dynamic force of interrelatedness and love.

47. See Ps 50:7(51:5).

48. The rare form *farer* links this verb with the literal meaning of *infans*.

49. *Prensabam memoria*: variant readings for *prensabam* include *pensabam* ("I weighed in my memory"), and *praesonabam* ("I practiced the sounds in my mind beforehand"). But textual criticism favors the rare *prensabam*, and this accords with the "grasping" character of

remembered that they used that sound when they wanted to indicate that thing. Their intention was clear, for they used bodily gestures, those natural words which are common to all races, such as facial expressions or glances of the eyes or movements of other parts of the body, or a tone of voice that suggested some particular attitude to things they sought and wished to hold on to, or rejected and shunned altogether.

In this way I gradually built up a collection of words, observing them as they were used in their proper places in different sentences and hearing them frequently. I came to understand which things they signified, and by schooling my own mouth to utter them I declared my wishes by using the same signs. Thus I learned to express my needs to the people among whom I lived, and they made their wishes known to me; and I waded deeper into the stormy world of human life, although I was still subject to the authority of my parents and the guidance of my elders.

Augustine goes to school

9, 14. Ah, God, my God, what wretchedness I suffered[50] in that world, and how I was trifled with! The program for right living presented to me as a boy was that I must obey my mentors, so that I might get on in this world and excel in the skills of the tongue, skills which lead to high repute and deceitful riches. To this end I was sent to school to learn my letters, though I, poor wretch, could see no point in them. All the same, I would be beaten whenever I was lazy about learning. This punishment was taken for granted by grown-up people and many a pupil had undergone it before we did, laying down those rough roadways along which we were now being driven, as we bore our part in the heavy labor and pain allotted to the sons of Adam.[51]

We did, however, meet at school some people who prayed to you, Lord, and we learned from them, imagining you as best we could in the guise of some great personage who, while not evident to our senses, was yet able to hear and help us. So it came about that even then in boyhood I began to

---

Augustine's conduct at this stage. As he clutched greedily at food and other objects, so he now grabs at words.
50. See Terence, *Adelphoe* 867.
51. See Gn 3:16; Sir 40:1.

pray to you, my aid and refuge.[52] By calling upon you I untied the knots of my tongue and begged you, in my little-boy way but with no little earnestness, not to let me be beaten at school. You did not hear my prayer, lest by hearing it you might have consigned me to a fool's fate; so my stripes were laughed at by my elders and even my parents, who would not have wished anything bad to happen to me. But bad it was, and very dreadful for me.

15. Is it possible, Lord, that there exists anyone so courageous, so united to you by intense love, that he could make light of rack, hooks and similar torments, from which other people the world over pray to you to be delivered? Is there any such person who could rise above them through devout union with you, rather than out of mere cloddish insensibility that counterfeits courage? But if this person loved others who are terrified of such tortures, could he still make light of them, as did our parents, who laughed at the torments we boys suffered? We were just as terrified of punishment as other people of torture, and our prayers to you were no whit less heartfelt as we begged that we might escape.

All the same, we were blameworthy, because we were less assiduous in reading, writing and concentrating on our studies than was expected of us. It was not that we lacked intelligence or ability, Lord, for you had endowed us with these in a measure appropriate to our age; it was simply that we loved to play, and we were punished by adults who nonetheless did the same themselves. But whereas the frivolous pursuits of grown-up people are called "business," children are punished for behaving in the same fashion, and no one is sorry for either the children or the adults; so are we to assume that any sound judge of the matter would think it right for me to be beaten because I played ball as a boy, and was hindered by my game from more rapid progress in studies which would only equip me to play an uglier game later?[53] Moreover, was the master who flogged me any better himself? If he had been worsted by a fellow-scholar in some pedantic dispute, would he not have been racked by even more bitter jealousy than I was when my opponent in a game of ball got the better of me?

10, 16. O Lord God, you are the disposer and creator of everything in nature, but of our sins the disposer only; and I did sin at that time, Lord my

52. See Pss 93(94):22; 17:3(18:2).
53. *Deformius luderem*: see note on I,7,12. "Deformed" persons or activities are those which fail to reflect the "form" or beauty instilled into them by the second person of the Trinity. Compare Augustine's lament in X,27,38.

God, by disobeying the instructions of my parents and teachers, for I was later able to make good use of the lessons my relatives wanted me to learn, whatever may have been their intention in so directing me. I sinned because I disobeyed them not in order to choose something more worthwhile, but simply because I loved games. I hankered to win myself glory in our contests, and to have my ears tickled by tall stories which only made them itch more hotly;[54] and all the while that same curiosity more and more inflamed my eyes with lust for the public shows which are the games of grown-ups.[55] The people who provide these entertainments enjoy such celebrity and public esteem that nearly all of them hope their children will follow their example; and yet they are quite prepared to see those children beaten for watching similar shows to the detriment of their study, study which, as their parents hope, will bring them to a position in which they in turn will provide the shows!

Look with mercy on these follies, Lord, and set us free who already call upon you. Set free those also who do not yet call upon you, so that they may invoke you and you may give them freedom.

His baptism is deferred

11, 17. While still a boy I had heard about the eternal life promised to us through the humility of our Lord and God, who stooped even to our pride; and I was regularly signed with the cross and given his salt even from the womb of my mother, who firmly trusted in you.[56] You saw, Lord, how one day in my boyhood I was suddenly seized by stomach pains and, as my fever mounted, came near to death. You saw, my God, because even then you were guarding me, with what distress and what faith I earnestly

---

54. See 1 Tm 4:3-4.
55. The triad of vices to which Augustine here confesses seems to correspond to the *sin of the world* in 1 Jn 2:16. He will develop the thought more fully in X,30,41, but the pattern is already here in his boyhood faults: *amore ludendi* is an early manifestation of *the lust of the flesh, superbas victorias* of *the pride of life*, and *curiositate* of *the lust of the eyes*.
56. That is, he was initiated into the catechumenate. Although this sentence indicates an awareness of the elements of Christian belief (incarnation and promise of eternal life), it appears that his initiation was not followed by any systematic Christian instruction. The imperfect tenses *signabar ... condiebar* probably suggest a rite performed not only on admission to the catechumenate but at regular intervals.

begged to be baptized into your Christ, who is my God and my Lord;[57] you saw how I pleaded with my loving kindly mother and with the mother of us all, your Church. She who had given me life according to the flesh was very anxious, because in her pure heart, through her faith in you and with a love still more tender, she was bringing my eternal salvation to birth. She would have hastened to ensure that I was initiated into the saving sacraments and washed clean by confessing you, Lord Jesus, for the forgiveness of my sins, had I not rapidly recovered.

My cleansing was therefore deferred on the pretext that if I lived I would inevitably soil myself again, for it was held that the guilt of sinful defilment incurred after the laver of baptism[58] was graver and more perilous. I was already a believer, as were my mother and all the household, with the sole exception of my father. He, however, did not overrule the influence my mother's piety exercised over me, by making any attempt to stop me believing in Christ, in whom he did not at that time believe himself. My mother did all she could to see that you, my God, should be more truly my father than he was, and in this endeavor you helped her to win the argument against a husband to whom she, though a better person, was ordinarily subject, for in taking this course she was in fact subjecting herself to you, who so commanded her.

18. My God, I beg you to tell me—for I would very much like to know, if it is your will—to what purpose my baptism was postponed, and whether it was for my good that the restraints against sinning were in some degree slackened for me; it is true, is it not, that they were slackened? Why is it that we still hear nowadays people saying on all sides of another person, "Let him be, let him do as he likes, he is not baptized yet"? Where bodily health is at stake we do not say, "Let him be, let him go on injuring himself, he is not cured yet." How much better it would have been if I had been healed at once, and if everything had been done by my own efforts and those of my family to ensure that the good health my soul had received should be kept safe in the care of you who had given it. Yes, how much better it would have been! But many towering waves of temptation seemed to be looming in the period beyond boyhood. My mother already

---

57. See Jn 20:28.
58. *Lavacrum*: see Ti 3:5; Sg 6:5. The word became common among Christian writers as a synonym for baptism. The practice of deferring baptism until the recipient was on his deathbed was not unusual; in later life as a bishop Augustine opposed it. See his remarks in the following paragraph.

anticipated them and thought it better to risk in them the clay from which I would later be molded than the new-formed man himself.[59]

12, 19. Yet even during that time of my boyhood, when it was supposed that I was safer than I would be in adolescence, I was not fond of study, and hated being driven to it. Driven I was, though, and that did me good, though my own attitude was far from good, because I learned only under compulsion, and no one is doing right who acts unwillingly, even if what he does is good in itself. The people who forced me on were not acting well either, but good accrued to me all the same from you, my God. They did not foresee to what use I would put the lessons they made me learn: they thought only of sating man's insatiable appetite for a poverty tricked out as wealth and a fame that is but infamy. But you, who have even kept count of our hairs,[60] turned to my profit the misguided views of those who stood over me and made me learn, just as you also turned to my profit my own perverse unwillingness to learn by using it to punish me, for I certainly deserved punishment, being a great sinner for such a tiny boy. In this way you turned to my good the actions of those who were doing no good, and gave me my just deserts by means of my sin itself. Matters are so arranged at your command that every disordered soul is its own punishment.

Latin and Greek studies

13, 20. Even to this day I have been unable to make up my mind why I hated the Greek that was dinned into me in early boyhood.[61] Latin studies, on the contrary, I loved, not the elementary kind under my first teachers, but the lessons taught by masters of literature;[62] for the early lessons in reading, writing and arithmetic had been no less burdensome and boring to me than all the elements of Greek. What other reason could there be for this than the sinful, inane pride in my life, flesh as I was, a passing breath

---

59. The thought emerges from Gn 1:2 and 1:26-27. "Clay" represents unformed matter. *Effigies* is used by Augustine elsewhere of Christ, that is, God in human form. Baptism stamps this form of Christ upon us.
60. See Mt 10:30.
61. The real extent of Augustine's knowledge of Greek is controverted. It seems that he may have had a rudimentary working knowledge of the language throughout most of his life, and have improved it at a date later than the writing of *The Confessions*. He rubbed shoulders with Greek-speaking clergy, and Bishop Valerius, under whom Augustine was a presbyter, was certainly familiar with Greek.
62. "Grammarians," but the term had a wider connotation than our modern word, more like "teachers in secondary schools."

that comes not again?[63] Those early lessons in literacy were unquestionably more profitable because more dependable; by means of them I was gradually being given a power which became mine and still remains with me: the power to read any piece of writing I come across and to write anything I have a mind to myself. Far more useful, then, were those studies than others in which I was forced to memorize the wanderings of some fellow called Aeneas, while forgetting my own waywardness, and to weep over Dido, who killed herself for love, when all the while in my intense misery I put up with myself with never a tear, as I died away from you, O God, who are my life.

21. What indeed is more pitiful than a piteous person who has no pity for himself? I could weep over the death Dido brought upon herself out of love for Aeneas, yet I shed no tears over the death I brought upon myself by not loving you. O God, you are the light of my heart, bread for the inward mouth of my soul,[64] the virtue wedded to my mind and the innermost recesses of my thought; yet I did not love you, and breaking my troth I strayed away from you.[65] Even in this troth-breaking the approval of people all around me rang in my ears: "Fine! Well done."[66] To pander to this world is to fornicate against you, but so loudly do they shout "Well done!" that one feels ashamed to fall short of their expectations. For these things I did not weep, yet I wept for Dido, "slain as she sought her last end by the sword,"[67] while I myself was abandoning you to seek the last dregs of your creation; dust I was, and unto dust returning.[68] If forbidden to read those tales, I was saddened at being prevented from reading what would sadden me. How insane it is to regard these studies as more civilized and rewarding than the elementary lessons in which I learned to read and write!

22. But now let my God cry more loudly in my soul, so that your truth may tell me, "No, that is not the case; it is not true. The primary teaching is better in every respect." I am undoubtedly more ready today to forget the

---

63. See Ps 77(78):39.
64. "Light" and "bread" are both images used by Christ of himself in the gospel of John.
65. See Ps 72(73):27. The background to this metaphor is the bridal relationship established by God with Israel in the covenant and consummated in Christ's marriage to the Church. Hence serious sin, and especially resort to false gods, was called "fornication" or "adultery" in the prophetic tradition, and Augustine's use of the psalmist's words in the present context need not refer to sexual sin.
66. See Pss 34(35):21; 39:16(40):15; 69:4(70):3.
67. See Virgil, *Aeneid* VI, 6 456-457.
68. See Gn 3:19.

wanderings of Aeneas and so forth than how to write or read. Curtains may well hang at the entrance to schools of literature, but they serve less to signal the prestige of elite instruction than to conceal error.[69] Let not those buyers and sellers of literary studies shout me down, my God, as I confess to you according to my soul's need, and acquiesce as you chide me for those evil ways of mine and bring me to love your good ways; let them not shout me down, for I fear them no longer. If I put to them the question whether the poet spoke truly when he affirmed that Aeneas once came to Carthage, the uneducated will say they do not know, while the more scholarly will admit that it is untrue. If, on the other hand, I ask how to spell the name "Aeneas," everyone who has studied the subject will give me a correct answer in accordance with the settled convention which people have made among themselves in fixing those signs. If I then go further and ask which would be a graver handicap in this life, to forget how to read and write, or to forget those poetic fantasies, can one doubt what answer would be given by anyone in his right mind?

Sin I did, then, in boyhood, by preferring those frivolous tales to much more useful attainments, or rather by loving the one and loathing the other. Already the jingle, "One and one make two, two and two make four," was hateful to me, whereas a wooden horse full of armed men, Troy afire, and the shade of Creusa[70]—these were a spectacle on which I delighted to gaze, and as empty as they were entertaining.

14, 23. Why was it, then, that I hated studying Greek literature, which had similar songs to sing? Homer was just as skilled at weaving stories, and he too was empty in a thoroughly entertaining way, yet as a boy I found him distasteful. I expect Virgil is equally distasteful to Greek boys, when they are forced to study him as I was Homer. It was so difficult; and the difficulty of thoroughly mastering a foreign language seemed to sprinkle bitterness over those fabulous narratives for all their Greek sweetness, because I knew none of the words, and the threat of savage, terrifying punishments was used to make me learn them. Time was, in my infancy, when I had known no Latin words either, but those I had learned

---

69. These schools were sometimes open-sided buildings, divided from the street only by columns, between which curtains were hung. Augustine refers to them in Sermon 51,4,5: "The higher the honor in which a master is held, the more curtains hang at his doorway. They are there to ensure privacy, but lifted to admit anyone who will do him honor." He may be sarcastically alluding to curtains which screened shrines, creating an atmosphere of mystery.
70. See Virgil, *Aeneid* II,772.

by paying attention, without any fear or pain at all, amid the cuddles of my nurses, and teasing, and playful, happy laughter. So I learned then without the painful pressure of people pestering me, because my own heart prompted me to bring forth its ideas, as it never could have done had I not learned words. Only I learned in infancy not from teachers but from speakers, into whose ears I in my turn was able to give utterance to what I had conceived in my mind. It is evident that the free play of curiosity is a more powerful spur to learning these things than is fear-ridden coercion; yet in accordance with your laws, O God, coercion checks the free play of curiosity. By your laws it constrains us, from the beatings meted out by our teachers to the ordeals of the martyrs, for in accord with those laws it prescribes for us bitter draughts of salutary discipline to recall us from the venomous pleasure which led us away from you.

15, 24. Hear my prayer, Lord.[71] Let not my soul faint under your discipline, nor let me weary as I confess before you those acts of mercy[72] by which you plucked me from all my evil ways.[73] I long for you to grow sweeter to me than all those allurements I was pursuing. You have enabled me to love you with all my strength and with passionate yearning grasp your hand, so that you may rescue me from every temptation until my life's end.[74] See, Lord, you are my king and my God;[75] let every useful thing I learned as a boy be devoted now to your service; let whatever I speak, write, read or count serve you, for even as I was learning such vanities you were schooling me, and you have forgiven the sins of self-indulgence I committed in those frivolous studies. Through them I acquired a great many useful words, though admittedly the same words can be learned just as well from texts which are by no means frivolous, and would make a safer path for children to tread.

16, 25. Woe, woe to you, you flood of human custom! Who can keep his footing against you? Will you never run dry? How long will you toss the children of Eve into a vast, terrifying sea, which even those afloat on the saving wood can scarcely cross?[76] Did you not give me a story to read in which Jupiter is both the Thunderer and an adulterer? He could not

---

71. See Ps 60:2(61:1).
72. See Ps 106(107), passim.
73. See 2 Kgs 17:13.
74. See 1 Cor 1:8.
75. See Pss 5:3(2);43:5(44:4).
76. Combined imagery: (1) the tree of life, the cross; (2) Noah's ark, referred to in Wis 14:7 as "the wood whereby righteousness was established."

possibly be both; yet so he was represented, to the end that his real adultery might seem to establish itself as deserving of imitation because a faked thunder-clap acted as go-between. Who among our hooded masters of oratory[77] give sober consideration to the cry of one who was of the same clay as themselves, "Homer invented these stories and attributed human actions to the gods, but I wish he had rather provided us with examples of divine behavior"?[78] It would be truer to say that Homer did indeed make up these tales, and thereby seemed to invest the disgraceful deeds of human beings with an aura of divinity, so that depraved actions should be reckoned depraved no longer, since anyone who behaved so could pretend to be imitating not abandoned humans but the gods above.

26. O hellish river, human children clutching their fees are still pitched into you to learn about these exploits, and general interest is aroused when education is publicly touted in the forum, in view of the law which decrees that a state salary be paid to teachers over and above the pupils' fees. You clash your rocks and set up a great din: "This is the place to acquire literacy; here you will develop the eloquence essential to persuasion and argument." Really? Could we not have learned those useful words elsewhere, words like "shower," "golden," "lap," "trick," "heavenly temples," if Terence had not presented to us a young scoundrel who took Jupiter as a model for his own fornication? This young man looks at a mural painting which shows how Jupiter tricked a woman by sending a golden shower into Danae's lap.[79] Watch the dissolute youth making use of heavenly instruction to work up his lust! "What a god!" he exclaims, "a god who makes the temples of heaven ring with his thunder!" Well, a poor little fellow like me can't do that, but I have imitated him in the other thing, and what fun it was![80]

It is simply not true that such words are more conveniently learned from obscene stories of this type, though it is all too true that under the influence of the words obscene deeds are the more boldly committed. I am blaming

---

77. The *paenula* or hood was originally a hooded cloak worn in the rain. Tacitus mentions orators who wore it even when pleading before a judge, implying that this was a scruffy but common practice (*Dialogus de oratoribus* 39). It is unclear whether the *paenula* had become a recognized sign of masters of oratory by Augustine's time.
78. Cicero, *Tusculan Disputations* I,26.65.
79. *Eunuchus* 584-591.
80. See ibid. 585, 589-590. The four standard Latin authors read by schoolboys in Augustine's day were Virgil, Cicero, Terence, and Sallust.

not the words, which are finely-wrought, precious vessels,[81] but the wine of error mixed for us in them by teachers who are drunk themselves. If we as boys refused to drink it we were caned, and no appeal to a sober judge was open to us. Wretch that I was, I learned these things eagerly and took pleasure in them; and so I was accounted a boy of high promise. But in your presence, my God, I can remember it now and be at peace.

17, 27. Allow me to say something, my God, about the intelligence which was your gift to me,[82] and the crazy employments in which I frittered it away. An exercise was set for me which was fraught with worrying implications, for I hoped to win praise and honor if I succeeded, but if not, I ran the risk of being caned. I was required to produce a speech made by Juno expressing her anger and grief at being unable to repulse the Trojan king from Italy,[83] but in words which I had never heard Juno use. We were obliged to follow the errant footsteps[84] of poetic fantasies and to express in prose what the poet had said in verse. That boy was adjudged the best speaker who most convincingly suggested emotions of anger and grief and clothed them in apt words, as befitted the dignity of the person represented. What did it profit me, O God, my true life,[85] that my speech was acclaimed above those of my many peers and fellow-students? Was it not all smoke and wind? Was there no other material on which I could have exercised my intelligence and my tongue? Yes, there was: your praise, O Lord; your praise in the words of the scriptures would have supported the drooping vine of my soul, and then it would not have yielded a crop of worthless fruit for the birds to carry off. Sacrifice can be offered to those birds of prey, the rebel angels, in more ways than one.

18, 28. Small wonder, then, that I was swept off helplessly after profitless things and borne away from you, my God. The models proposed to me for imitation were people who would have been caught out and covered with confusion if they had related any of their doings—deeds not wrong in themselves—in a barbaric accent or with grammatical blunders, whereas to relate licentious deeds in correct and well-turned phrases, in ample and elegant style, would have won them praise and honor. You see this, Lord,

---

81. See Prv 20:15.
82. Augustine opened Book I with a prayer asking God to enable him to speak; he introduces its concluding section similarly.
83. See Virgil, *Aeneid* I,38.
84. As in I,13,20.22, Augustine plays on the double meaning of *erro*, to wander (geographically) or to go astray.
85. See Jn 11:25; 14:6.

but you are very patient and look on silently; you are exceedingly merciful and worthy of our trust.[86] Will you always remain silent?[87] From this vast, deep sea you are even now drawing out to safety[88] a soul that seeks you and thirsts to enjoy you,[89] one whose heart pleads with you, *I have sought your face, O Lord, your face will I seek,*[90] for at that time I was far away from your countenance in darkness of spirit. Not with our feet or by traversing great distances do we journey away from you or find our way back. That younger son of yours in the gospel[91] did not hire horses or carriages, nor did he board ships, nor take wing in any visible sense nor put one foot before the other when he journeyed to that far country where he could squander at will the wealth you, his gentle father, had given him at his departure. Gentle you were then, but gentler still with him when he returned in his need. No, to be estranged in a spirit of lust, and lost in its darkness, that is what it means to be far away from your face.[92]

29. Look upon all this, O Lord God and, as you look, patiently consider how carefully human beings observe those orthographic conventions and syllabic quantities which they have received from earlier orators, while neglecting the eternal rules directed to unending salvation which they have received from you. A speaker who wishes to maintain and teach those long-standing conventions will give greater offense to his fellow-men by pronouncing the word "human" without sounding the "h," in defiance of grammatical discipline, than if he, human as he is, flouts your commands by hating a fellow-human. Does he suppose that another human being who is his enemy can do him more harm than does the very hatred with which he regards that other person, or that anyone can do more serious damage to another by hostile behavior than he does to his own soul by harboring hostile intent? Knowledge of letters lies less deep in us than the law written in our conscience[93] which forbids us to do to another what we would not have done to ourselves.[94]

---

86. See Pss 102(103):8; 85(86):15.
87. See Is 42:14.
88. See Ps 85(86):13.
89. See Pss 41:3(42:2); 62:2(63:1).
90. Ps 26(27):8.
91. See Lk 15:32.
92. In these last lines Augustine combines imagery from the parable of the prodigal son (Lk 15:11-32) with a remembered passage from Plotinus (*Enneads* I,6.8.16-27).
93. See Rom 2:15.
94. See Tb 4:16; Mt 7:12; Lk 6:31.

How hidden you are, dwelling on high[95] in your silence, great and only God, who by your unfaltering law spread the punishment of blindness over unlawful human lusts! A man in persistent search of fame pleads before a merely human judge, with a crowd of other humans standing round, and accuses his adversary with savage hatred. He takes the utmost care that no slip of the tongue betrays him into saying, "Them fellows ... , " while caring not a whit that by his rage he is about to remove a fellow-human from human society.

Childish sins

19, 30. Such were the moral standards of the world at whose threshold I lay, a wretched boy; this was the arena in which I was to struggle. It made me more wary of committing some barbarism in speech than of being jealous of others who did not commit it when I did. I tell you this, my God, and confess to you those efforts for which I was praised; for at that time I believed that living a good life consisted in winning the favor of those who commended me. I failed to recognize the whirlpool of disgraceful conduct into which I had been flung, out of your sight.[96] What could have been fouler in your eyes at that time than myself? I was earning the disapproval even of those same people by the countless lies with which I deceived the slave who took me to school, my teachers and my parents, and all because of my love for play and the absurd anxiety with which I craved to gawk at worthless shows and imitate what I watched.

I stole from my parents' larder too, and their table, either out of gluttony or to get something with which I could bribe other boys to let me join in their games, for they exacted a price even though they enjoyed our play as much as I did. In those games I would often seek to dominate by fraudulent means, because I was myself dominated by a vain urge to excel.[97] And what was it that I was so unwilling to excuse, what did I so fiercely condemn if I detected it in others, but the very cheating I practiced myself? If I was caught out and accused of cheating I was more apt to lose my temper than to admit it. Is this boyhood innocence? No, Lord, it is not; hear

---

95. See Is 33:5.
96. See Ps 30:23(31:22).
97. Another instance of the threefold temptation: curiosity about seeing, gluttony, vanity. See note on I,10,16.

me, dear God, it is not. These same sins grow worse as we grow older: first it is offenses against pedagogues and teachers, or cheating over nuts and balls and sparrows; then later it is crimes against prefects and kings, and fraud in gold and estates and slaves, just as a schoolboy's canings are succeeded by heavier punishments. It was only the small stature of a child that you mentioned with approval as a symbol of humility, O Lord our king, when you declared that *of such is the kingdom of heaven.*[98]

Thanksgiving

20, 31. In spite of all this, O Lord our God, I give thanks to you, the most perfect, most good creator and ruler of the universe, and I would still thank you even if you had not willed me to live beyond boyhood. Even then I existed, I lived and I experienced;[99] I took good care to keep myself whole and sound and so preserve the trace in me of your profoundly mysterious unity, from which I came. By means of my inner sense[100] I coordinated my sensible impressions, and in my little thoughts about little things I delighted in truth. I was unwilling to be deceived, I had a lively memory, I was being trained in the use of words, I was comforted by friendship, and I shrank from pain, groveling and ignorance.

> In a living creature such as this
> everything is wonderful and worthy of praise,
> but all these things are gifts from my God.
> I did not endow myself with them,
> but they are good, and together they make me what I am.
> He who made me is good, and he is my good too;
> rejoicing, I thank him for all those good gifts
> which made me what I was, even as a boy.
> In this lay my sin,
> that not in him was I seeking pleasures, distinctions and truth,

---

98. Mt 19:14.
99. See note at I,7,12 above on trinitarian allusions. That the present triad, *eram ... vivebam ... sentiebam* is an intentional reference to the Trinity is evident from the next phrase Augustine uses of himself, *vestigium secretissimae unitatis.* He is made in the image of God, Three in One.
100. The "common sense" of Aristotelian and Stoic philosohy which correlates impressions received through the external senses. The "outer man" is for Augustine an image of the "inner man" who can know both God and the self.

but in myself and the rest of his creatures,
and so I fell headlong into pains, confusions and errors.
But I give thanks to you, my sweetness, my honor, my confidence;
to you, my God, I give thanks for your gifts.
Do you preserve them for me.
So will you preserve me too,
and what you have given me will grow and reach perfection,
and I will be with you; because this too is your gift to me
— that I exist.

Book II

Adolescence

Sexual awakening

1, 1. Now I want to call to mind the foul deeds I committed, those sins of the flesh that corrupted my soul,[1] not in order to love them, but to love you, my God. Out of love for loving you I do this, recalling my most wicked ways and thinking over the past with bitterness so that you may grow ever sweeter to me; for you are a sweetness that deceives not, a sweetness blissful and serene.[2] I will try now to give a coherent account of my disintegrated self, for when I turned away from you, the one God, and pursued a multitude of things, I went to pieces. There was a time in adolescence when I was afire to take my fill of hell. I boldly thrust out rank, luxuriant growth in various furtive love affairs; my beauty wasted away and I rotted in your sight, intent on pleasing myself and winning favor in the eyes of men.

2, 2. What was it that delighted me? Only loving and being loved. But there was no proper restraint, as in the union of mind with mind, where a bright boundary regulates friendship. From the mud of my fleshly desires[3] and my erupting puberty belched out murky clouds that obscured and darkened my heart until I could not distinguish the calm light of love from the fog of lust. The two swirled about together and dragged me, young and weak as I was, over the cliffs of my desires, and engulfed me in a whirlpool of sins. Your anger had grown hot at my doings, yet I did not know. I was deafened by that clanking chain of my mortal state which was the punish-

---

1. The image of God in man is "corrupted" by sin; Book II recounts this process in Augustine's adolescence. It is refashioned by God's saving work, as he confesses at XIII,34,49.
2. The sweet Spirit of love is contrasted with the bitterness of his recollected sins, as Augustine embarks on the history of his disordered loves. In the following sentence the contrast between unity and multiplicity is reminiscent of Porphyry.
3. See 1 Jn 2:16.

ment for my soul's pride, and I was wandering away from you, yet you let me go my way. I was flung hither and thither, I poured myself out, frothed and floundered in the tumultuous sea of my fornications; and you were silent.[4] O my joy, how long I took to find you! At that time you kept silence as I continued to wander far from you and sowed more and more sterile seeds to my own grief, abased by my pride and wearied by my restlessness.

3. Who was there to alleviate my distress? No one took thought to arrange a marriage for me, so that my pursuit of fleeting beauties through most ignoble experiences might be diverted into useful channels. Some bounds might have been set to my pleasures if only the stormy surge of my adolescence had flung me up onto the shore of matrimony. Or again, if I had been unable to find tranquillity in that way, content to use my sexuality to procreate children as your law enjoins,[5] O Lord (since you propagate the stock of our mortal race by this means, powerfully using your gentle hand to control the thorns which have no place in your paradise,[6] for your almighty power is never far from us, even when we are far from you), if, as I say, I could not have found peace in marriage, this at all events is certain, that I ought to have listened more attentively to the voice from your clouds[7] which proclaimed, *Those who marry will have trials in their married life; and I would wish to spare you;*[8] and again, *It is a good thing for a man not to touch a woman;*[9] and, *An unmarried man is preoccupied with the affairs of God, and with pleasing God; but a married man is preoccupied with the affairs of the world, and with pleasing his wife.*[10] Yes, I could have listened more attentively to those words, and made myself a eunuch for the kingdom of heaven.[11] In that way I might have waited more contentedly for your embrace.

---

4. See Is 42:14.
5. See Gn 1:28.
6. See Gn 3:18.
7. Augustine frequently uses clouds as a symbol of the preachers of God's word, who produce the thunder of his threats and the rain that gives life. In the present text the reference is to the scriptural words themselves.
8. 1 Cor 7:28.
9. 1 Cor 7:1.
10. 1 Cor 7:32-33.
11. See Mt 19:12.

4. But I was far too impetuous, poor wretch, so I went with the flood-tide of my nature and abandoned you. I swept across all your laws,[12] but I did not escape your chastisements, for what mortal can do that? You were ever present to me, mercifully angry, sprinkling very bitter disappointments over all my unlawful pleasures so that I might seek a pleasure free from all disappointment. If only I could have done that, I would have found nothing but yourself, Lord, nothing but you yourself who use pain to make your will known to us,[13] and strike only to heal,[14] and even kill us lest we die away from you. Where was I, and how far was I exiled from the joys of your house[15] in that sixteenth year of my bodily age, when the frenzy of lust imposed its rule on me, and I wholeheartedly yielded to it? A lust it was licensed by disgraceful human custom, but illicit before your laws. Yet none of my family made any attempt to avert my ruin by arranging a marriage for me; their only concern was that I should learn to excel in rhetoric and persuasive speech.

A year at home

3, 5. In that same year, my sixteenth, my studies were interrupted and I was brought back from Madaura, a nearby city where I had been lodging for instruction in literature and rhetoric. The reason for this was that my father was saving up to send me further afield, to Carthage, though it was his shameless ambition that suggested the plan, not his wealth, for he was no more than a fairly obscure town councillor at Thagaste. But to whom am I telling this story? Not to you, my God; rather in your presence I am relating these events to my own kin, the human race, however few of them may chance upon these writings of mine. And why? So that whoever reads them may reflect with me on the depths from which we must cry to you.[16]

---

12. See Lv 10:11.
13. See Ps 93(94):20. The original meaning of the psalm is different, but the obscurity of the Latin translation led Augustine to take it in the sense that God uses suffering to teach his people.
14. See Hos 6:2.
15. See Lk 15:13.
16. See Ps 129(130):1.

What finds a readier hearing with you than a heart that confesses to you, a life lived from faith?[17]

At the time I speak of anyone would have heaped praise upon my father, a man prepared to go beyond his means in spending as much money as was needed to send his son away to study, even in a distant city. No such efforts were made on behalf of the children of many other citizens who were far richer; yet all the while this same father of mine was unconcerned about how I would grow up for you, and cared little that I should be chaste, provided I was intellectually cultivated. It would be truer to say that I was left fallow[18] of your cultivation, O God, who are the only true and good owner of your field, my heart.[19]

6. Owing to the state of family finances in this sixteenth year of my life there was an interval of leisure for me, during which, being free from all schooling, I began to spend time in my parents' company. The thorn-bushes of my lust shot up higher than my head, and no hand was there to root them out. Least of all my father's; for when at the baths one day he saw me with unquiet adolescence as my only covering[20] and noted my ripening sexuality, he began at once to look forward eagerly to grandchildren, and gleefully announced his discovery to my mother. His glee sprang from that intoxication which has blotted you, our creator, out of this world's memory and led it to love the creature instead,[21] as it drinks the unseen wine of its perverse inclination and is dragged down to the depths. In my mother's soul, however, you had already begun to build your temple and prepare for your holy indwelling,[22] whereas my father was still a catechumen, and a recent one at that. She therefore started up in devout fear and trembling, for she was afraid for me even though I was not yet a Christian. She saw the twisted paths I followed, those paths trodden by people who turn their backs to you, not their faces.[23]

---

17. See Hb 2:4; Rom 1:17; Gal 3:11; Heb 10:38.
18. A pun on *disertus* (skilled, dexterous) and *desertus* (abandoned, left fallow).
19. See Mt 13:24-30.
20. *Inquieta indutum adulescentia*: the adjective "restless" or "unquiet" is understandable enough in reference to this stage, but is also significant in view of the antithesis of restlessness and repose which pervades *The Confessions*; see I,1,1. It is also possible that the "disquieting" revelations of nakedness echo Gn 3:7. Patricius' delight may suggest that Augustine was their eldest child.
21. See Rom 1:25.
22. See 1 Cor 3:16-17.
23. See Jer 2:27.

Adolescent lust

7. Alas for me! Do I dare to say that you were silent, my God, when I was straying from you? Were you really silent to me at that time? Whose, then, were the words spoken to me by my mother, your faithful follower? Were they not your words, the song you were constantly singing into my ears? None of it sank down to my heart, though, to induce me to act on it. She urged me to keep clear of fornication, and especially not to commit adultery with any man's wife. I remember in my inmost heart the intense earnestness with which she cautioned me against this; but these warnings seemed to me mere woman's talk, which I would have blushed to heed. In truth they came from you, but I failed to realize that, and assumed that you were silent and she alone was talking. By using her you were not silent to me at all; and when I scorned her I was scorning you—I, her son, the son of your handmaid, I your servant![24] But I was quite reckless; I rushed on headlong in such blindness that when I heard other youths of my own age bragging about their immoralities I was ashamed to be less depraved than they. The more disgraceful their deeds, the more credit they claimed; and so I too became as lustful for the plaudits as for the lechery itself. What is more to be reviled than vile debauchery? Afraid of being reviled I grew viler,[25] and when I had no indecent acts to admit that could put me on a level with these abandoned youths, I pretended to obscenities I had not committed, lest I might be thought less courageous for being more innocent, and be accounted cheaper for being more chaste.

8. With companions like these I roamed the streets of Babylon[26] and wallowed in its filth as though basking amid cinnamon and precious ointments. My invisible enemy trampled on me[27] and seduced me in order to fix me still faster in the center of that city, for I was easy enough to seduce. My natural mother had by this time fled from the center of Babylon,[28] though she still lingered in its suburbs. She warned me to live chastely, but did not extend her care to restraining within the bounds of conjugal love (if it could not be cut right back to the quick) this behavior of mine, of which

24. See Ps 115(116):16.
25. This and the preceding sentence contain assonances which the translation attempts to suggest: *libebat ... libidine; vituperatione ... vitium; vituperarer ... vitiosior.*
26. Babylon is for Augustine the biblical type of the earthly city; he will develop the theme later in *The City of God.*
27. See Ps 55:2(56:1).
28. See Jer 51:6.

she had heard from her husband, even though she judged it to be corrupt already and likely to be dangerous in the future. Her reluctance to arrange a marriage for me arose from the fear that if I were encumbered with a wife my hope could be dashed—not hope in you for the world to come, to which she held herself, but my hope of academic success. Both my parents were very keen on my making progress in study: my father, because he thought next to nothing about you and only vain things about me; and my mother, because she regarded the customary course of studies as no hindrance, and even a considerable help, toward my gaining you eventually. So, at least, do I interpret their respective attitudes, as I remember them now as best I can.

The restraints placed upon my amusements were also slackened more than strict discipline would have approved, with the result that I strayed into various disreputable amours. Throughout these experiences a dark fog cut me off from your bright truth, my God, and my sin grew sleek on my excesses.[29]

He robs a pear tree

4, 9. Beyond question, theft is punished by your law, O Lord,[30] and by the law written in human hearts,[31] which not even sin itself can erase; for does any thief tolerate being robbed by another thief, even if he is rich and the other is driven by want? I was under no compulsion of need, unless a lack of moral sense can count as need, and a loathing for justice, and a greedy, full-fed love of sin. Yet I wanted to steal, and steal I did. I already had plenty of what I stole, and of much better quality too, and I had no desire to enjoy it when I resolved to steal it. I simply wanted to enjoy the theft for its own sake, and the sin.

Close to our vineyard there was a pear tree laden with fruit. This fruit was not enticing, either in appearance or in flavor. We nasty lads went there to shake down the fruit and carry it off at dead of night, after prolonging our games out of doors until that late hour according to our abominable custom. We took enormous quantities, not to feast on ourselves but perhaps to throw to the pigs; we did eat a few, but that was

---

29. See Ps 72(73):7.
30. See Ex 20:15; Dt 5:19.
31. See Rom 2:14-15.

not our motive: we derived pleasure from the deed simply because it was forbidden.[32]

Look upon my heart, O God, look upon this heart of mine, on which you took pity in its abysmal depths. Enable my heart to tell you now what it was seeking in this action which made me bad for no reason, in which there was no motive for my malice except malice. The malice was loathsome, and I loved it. I was in love with my own ruin, in love with decay: not with the thing for which I was falling into decay but with decay itself, for I was depraved in soul, and I leapt down from your strong support into destruction, hungering not for some advantage to be gained by the foul deed, but for the foulness of it.

Question of motives

5, 10. The beautiful form of material things attracts our eyes, so we are drawn to gold, silver and the like. We are powerfully influenced by the feel of things agreeable[33] to the touch; and each of our other senses finds some quality that appeals to it individually in the variety of material objects. There is the same appeal in worldly rank, and the possibility it offers of commanding and dominating other people: this too holds its attraction, and often provides an opportunity for settling old scores. We may seek all these things, O Lord, but in seeking them we must not deviate from your law. The life we live here is open to temptation by reason of a certain measure and harmony between its own splendor and all these beautiful things of low degree. Again, the friendship which draws human beings together in a tender bond is sweet to us because out of many minds it forges

---

32. Augustine's heavy emphasis on this episode has sometimes puzzled readers, who have seen in it no more than a teenager's prank. He depicts it as sin, rebellion against God's law, with no mitigating motive other than lust for the wrongness itself. In view of his habitual preoccupation with the opening chapters of Genesis it is not difficult to see the pear tree episode as a parallel to the fall in Gn 3, which was followed by the awakening of disordered sexual concupiscence in Adam and Eve: here we have a symbolic "fall" in Augustine's life, though his sexual concupiscence is already disordered. The mention of throwing the fruit to pigs evokes the plight of the prodigal son, who is never far from Augustine's mind in these pages (see Lk 15:15-16).

33. *Congruentia*, a suitability, fittingness, correspondence, is central to Augustine's idea of beauty.

a unity.[34] Sin gains entrance through these and similar good things when we turn to them with immoderate desire, since they are the lowest kind of goods and we thereby turn away from the better and higher: from you yourself, O Lord our God, and your truth and your law. These lowest goods hold delights for us indeed, but no such delights as does my God, who made all things; for in him the just man finds delight, and for upright souls[35] he himself is joy.

11. So then, when people look for the reason why some criminal act has been committed, their account is usually reckoned credible only when it is evident that there may have been greed on the malefactor's part to gain possession of goods belonging to someone else—those goods we have called "lowest"—or fear of losing his own; for these good things truly are beautiful and lovely in their own way, even though base and mean in comparison with the higher goods that bring us true happiness. Suppose someone has committed homicide. Why did he do it? Perhaps he was in love with the victim's wife, or coveted his estate, or wanted to steal from him in order to support himself, or feared to be robbed of the like himself by the other man, or had been injured and burned for revenge. Is it likely that he would kill another person without any motive, simply because he enjoyed killing? Who could believe that? Admittedly it is reported of a certain frenzied and outrageously cruel man that "he preferred being evil and cruel with no provocation,"[36] but a motive for his crimes was nonetheless declared: he wished to ensure, the historian tells us, that "neither hand nor mind should atrophy from inaction."[37] We might further ask, "And what else did he intend?" He meant to use crime for the training of his young conspirators, in order eventually to gain control of the city and win honors, power and riches: thus he would be free from fear of the law and from the difficulties in his circumstances arising from "shortage of money and his guilty record."[38] Even Catiline, then, did not love his criminal acts for their own sake, but only the advantages he had in view when committing them.

---

34. The first hint of the only possible good that, Augustine will eventually admit, played a part in his motives for the theft.
35. See Ps 63:11(64:10).
36. Sallust, *Catilina* 16,3. Augustine will name Catiline at the end of the paragraph.
37. Ibid. 5,5.
38. Ibid. 5,7.

6, 12. How does this apply to me, poor wretch? What did I love in you, O my theft, what did I love in you, the nocturnal crime of my sixteenth year? There was nothing beautiful about you, for you were nothing but a theft. Are you really anything at all, for me to be speaking to you like this?

O good God, creator of all things[39] and more beautiful than all of them, those pears we stole did have a certain beauty because they were your creation—yours, O God, who are the highest good and the true good for me. Those pears were beautiful, but they were not what my miserable soul loved. I had plenty of better ones, and I plucked them only for the sake of stealing, for once picked I threw them away. I feasted on the sin, nothing else, and that I relished and enjoyed. Even if some morsel of the pears did enter my mouth, it was only the criminal act that lent it savor. So now, Lord my God, when I ask what it was that gave me pleasure in that theft, I find nothing of fair, seductive form at all. I do not mean simply that it lacked the beauty to be found in justice and prudence, or the beauty of the human mind and intelligence, or that of our senses and bodily life, or the beauty inherent in the stars, so lovely in their appointed places, or in the earth and the sea full of young life born there to replace the things that die. No, I mean more: my theft lacked even the sham, shadowy beauty with which even vice allures us.[40]

13. For in vice there lurks a counterfeit beauty: pride, for instance —even pride apes sublimity, whereas you are the only God, most high above all things. As for ambition, what does it crave but honors and glory, while you are worthy of honor beyond all others, and eternally glorious? The ferocity of powerful men aims to inspire fear; but who is to be feared except the one God? Can anything be snatched from his power or withdrawn from it—when or where or whither or by whom? Flirtatiousness aims to arouse love by its charming wiles, but nothing can hold more charm than your charity, nor could anything be loved to greater profit than your truth, which outshines all else in its luminous beauty. Curiosity poses as pursuit of knowledge, whereas you know everything to a supreme degree. Even ignorance or stupidity masquerades as simplicity and innocence, but nothing that exists is simpler than yourself; and what

---

39. See 2 Mc 1:24; Ambrose, *Hymn* 1,2.
40. Augustine has here traced four grades of goodness or beauty in descending order: moral (justice and prudence), intellectual (mind and intelligence), sensuous, and organic; he closes the sequence with a sham beauty that fades almost to nothing.

could be more innocent than you, who leave the wicked to be hounded by their own sins? Sloth pretends to aspire to rest, but what sure rest is there save the Lord? Lush living likes to be taken for contented abundance, but you are the full and inexhaustible store of a sweetness that never grows stale. Extravagance is a bogus generosity, but you are the infinitely wealthy giver of all good things. Avarice strives to amass possessions, but you own everything. Envy is contentious over rank accorded to another, but what ranks higher than you? Anger seeks revenge, but who ever exacts revenge with greater justice than yourself? Timidity dreads any unforeseen or sudden threat to the things it loves, and takes precautions for their safety; but is anything sudden or unforeseen to you? Who can separate what you love from you?[41] Where is ultimate security to be found, except with you? Sadness pines at the loss of the good things with which greed took its pleasure, because it wants to be like you, from whom nothing can be taken away.[42]

14. A soul that turns away from you therefore lapses into fornication[43] when it seeks apart from you what it can never find in pure and limpid form except by returning to you. All those who wander far away and set themselves up against you are imitating you, but in a perverse way;[44] yet by this very mimicry they proclaim that you are the creator of the whole of nature, and that in consequence there is no place whatever where we can hide from your presence.

With regard to my theft, then: what did I love in it, and in what sense did I imitate my Lord, even if only with vicious perversity? Did the pleasure I sought lie in breaking the law at least in that sneaky way, since I was unable to do so with any show of strength? Was I, in truth a prisoner, trying to simulate a crippled sort of freedom, attempting a shady parody of omnipotence by getting away with something forbidden? How like that servant of yours who fled from his Lord and hid in the shadows![45] What rottenness, what a misshapen life! Rather a hideous pit of death! To do

---

41. See Rom 8:35.
42. All through this paragraph Augustine is demonstrating that each vice is a dishonest imitation of some attribute of God, and a pretension to possess apart from God something that he alone can give, since he alone possesses it authentically and in fullness.
43. See Ps 72(73):27.
44. The tempter's promise to Adam and Eve is in the background: *You shall be like gods* (Gn 3:5).
45. Adam (Gn 3:8-10), with whom Augustine identifies.

what was wrong simply because it was wrong—could I have found pleasure in that?

7, 15. How can I repay the Lord[46] for my ability to recall these things without fear? Let me love you, Lord, and give thanks to you and confess to your name, because you have forgiven my grave sins and wicked deeds.[47] By your sheer grace and mercy you melted my sins away like ice.[48] To your grace also do I ascribe whatever sins I did not commit, for what would I not have been capable of, I who could be enamored even of a wanton crime? I acknowledge that you have forgiven me everything, both the sins I willfully committed by following my own will, and those I avoided through your guidance.

Is there anyone who can take stock of his own weakness and still dare to credit his chastity and innocence to his own efforts? And could such a person think to love you less, on the pretext that he has had smaller need of your mercy, that mercy with which you forgive the sins of those who turn back to you? If there is anyone whom you have called, who by responding to your summons has avoided those sins which he finds me remembering and confessing in my own life as he reads this, let him not mock me; for I have been healed by the same doctor who has granted him the grace not to fall ill, or at least to fall ill less seriously. Let such a person therefore love you just as much, or even more, on seeing that the same physician who rescued me from sinful diseases of such gravity has kept him immune.

8, 16. What fruit did I ever reap from those things which I now blush to remember,[49] and especially from that theft in which I found nothing to love save the theft itself, wretch that I was? It was nothing, and by the very act of committing it I became more wretched still. And yet, as I recall my state of mind at the time, I would not have done it alone; I most certainly would not have done it alone. It follows, then, that I also loved the camaraderie with my fellow-thieves. So it is not true to say that I loved nothing other than the theft? Ah, but it is true, because that gang-mentality too was a nothing. What was it in fact? Who can teach me, except the One who illu-

---

46. See Ps 115(116):12.
47. Professor O'Donnell's comment cannot be bettered here: "Memory without fear is the fruit of forgiveness; love, thanksgiving, and confession are repayment to God for the forgiveness that has preceded all confession" (vol. 2, p. 140).
48. See Sir 3:17.
49. See Rom 6:21.

mines my heart[50] and distinguishes between its shadows? Why has this question come into my mind now, to be examined and discussed and considered? If the object of my love had been the pears I stole, and I simply wanted to enjoy them, I could have done it alone; similarly, if the act of committing the sin had sufficed by itself to yield me the pleasure I sought, I would not have further inflamed my itching desire by the stimulation of conspiracy. But since my pleasure did not lie in the pears, it must have been in the crime as committed in the company of others who shared in the sin.

9, 17. What kind of attitude was that? An extremely dishonorable one, certainly; alas for me, that I entertained it! Yet what exactly was it? Who understands his faults?[51] The theft gave us a thrill, and we laughed to think we were outwitting people who had no idea what we were doing, and would angrily stop us if they knew. Why could I not have derived the same pleasure from doing it alone? Perhaps because it is not easy to enjoy a joke by oneself? Not easy, to be sure, but it does sometimes happen that people who are entirely alone, with no one else present, are overcome by laughter, if something very funny presents itself to their senses or their thoughts. Possibly ... but I would not have done that deed alone; in no way would I have done it alone. In your presence I declare it, my God, this is my soul's vivid remembrance. On my own I would not have perpetrated that theft in which I felt no desire for what I stole, but only for the act of stealing; to do it alone would have aroused no desire whatever in me, nor would I have done it.

What an exceedingly unfriendly form of friendship that was![52] It was a seduction of the mind hard to understand, which instilled into me a craving to do harm for sport and fun. I was greedy for another person's loss without any desire on my part to gain anything or to settle a score. Let the others only say, "Come on, let's go and do it!" and I am ashamed to hold back from the shameless act.

---

50. See Sir 2:10.
51. See Ps 18:13(19:12).
52. Augustine held a very high view of friendship, but here it is corrupt and corrupting friendship, a theme of Book II.

The prodigal's wanderings begin

10, 18. Who can unravel this most snarled, knotty tangle? It is disgusting, and I do not want to look at it or see it. O justice and innocence, fair and lovely, it is on you that I want to gaze with eyes that see purely and find satiety in never being sated. With you is rest and tranquil life. Whoever enters into you enters the joy of his Lord;[53] there he will fear nothing and find his own supreme good in God who is supreme goodness. I slid away from you and wandered away, my God; far from your steadfastness I strayed in adolescence, and I became to myself a land of famine.[54]

---

53. See Mt 25:21.
54. See Lk 15:14. In this last sentence Augustine sums up his adolescent re-enactment of the prodigal's story.

Book III

Student Years at Carthage

1, 1. So I arrived at Carthage, where the din of scandalous love-affairs raged cauldron-like around me.[1] I was not yet in love, but I was enamored with the idea of love, and so deep within me was my need that I hated myself for the sluggishness of my desires. In love with loving, I was casting about for something to love; the security of a way of life free from pitfalls seemed abhorrent to me, because I was inwardly starved of that food which is yourself, O my God. Yet this inner famine created no pangs of hunger in me. I had no desire for the food that does not perish, not because I had my fill of it, but because the more empty I was, the more I turned from it in revulsion. My soul's health was consequently poor. It was covered with sores and flung itself out of doors,[2] longing to soothe its misery by rubbing against sensible things; yet these were soulless, and so could not be truly loved. Loving and being loved were sweet to me, the more so if I could also enjoy a lover's body; so I polluted the stream of friendship with my filthy desires and clouded its purity with hellish lusts; yet all the while, befouled and disgraced though I was, my boundless vanity made me long to appear elegant and sophisticated. I blundered headlong into the love which I hoped would hold me captive, but in your goodness, O my God, my mercy,[3] you sprinkled bitter gall over my sweet pursuits. I was loved, and I secretly entered into an enjoyable liaison, but I was also trammeling myself with fetters of distress, laying myself open to

---

1. The city was very prosperous when Augustine arrived there in his seventeenth year, and had for more than a century rivaled Alexandria in its claim to be the second city of the empire. Christianity had taken root there early, but paganism was still strong.
2. The reference may be to Job (Jb 2:7-8), but Lazarus is probably in mind too (Lk 16:20).
3. See Ps 58:18(59:17).

the iron rods and burning scourges of jealousy and suspicion, of fear, anger and quarrels.[4]

2, 2. I was held spellbound by theatrical shows full of images that mirrored my own wretched plight and further fueled the fire within me.[5] Why is it that one likes being moved to grief at the sight of sad or tragic events on stage, when one would be unwilling to suffer the same things oneself? In the capacity of spectator one welcomes sad feelings; in fact, the sadness itself is the pleasure. What incredible stupidity! The more a person is buffeted by such passions in his own life, the more he is moved by watching similar scenes on stage, although his state of mind is usually called misery when he is undergoing them himself and mercy[6] when he shows compassion for others so afflicted. But how real is the mercy evoked by fictional dramas? The listener is not moved to offer help, but merely invited to feel sorrow; and the more intensely he feels it the more highly he rates the actor in the play. If these tragic human stories—whether referring to events long past or fictional—are played in such a way that they fail to move the spectator to sadness, he walks out in disgust, criticizing the performance; but if he feels sad, he stays on, keenly attentive, and enjoys a good cry.

3. So it is possible to enjoy sad feelings; yet there can be no doubt that everyone aspires to be happy. Can this be the reason: that no one wants to be miserable, but we do like to think ourselves merciful, and mercy must entail some sorrow? Can it be for this reason alone that sorrowful feelings are welcomed? To be sure, this power of sympathy derives from the stream of friendship. But where does it flow to, whither is it bound? Why does it debouch into a torrent of boiling pitch, into seething passions of monstrous lust, so that it loses itself in them, is diverted and thrown off course, and deviates by its own choice from its heavenly serenity? Is mercy, then, to be rejected? By no means; it is sometimes right to entertain compassionate feelings. But beware of impurity, my soul: under the

---

4. See Gal 5:20.
5. The *spectacula* on offer included plays (Augustine's particular addiction), gladiatorial contests (Alypius' weakness; see VI,8,13) and the circus races.
6. Misery ... mercy: *miseria* ... *misericordia*. Augustine likes to play on these correlative words. In *The Catholic Way of Life* 27,53 he says that *misericordia* is so called because it makes *miserum* the heart (*cor*) of someone who feels compassion for another's misfortune.

guardianship of my God, the God of our fathers who is to be praised and most highly exalted for ever,[7] beware of impurity.

Even today I am not devoid of merciful sensibility, but at that time it was different; I rejoiced with lovers on the stage who took sinful pleasure in one another, even though their adventures were only imaginary and part of a dramatic presentation, and when they lost each other I grieved with them, ostensibly merciful; yet in both instances I found pleasure in my emotions. Today I feel greater pity for someone who takes delight in a sinful deed than for someone else who seems to suffer grievously at the loss of pernicious pleasure and the passing of a bliss that was in fact nothing but misery. This is unquestionably a truer mercy, but the sadness it entails holds no attraction for me. A person who sorrows for someone who is miserable earns approval for the charity he shows, but if he is genuinely merciful he would far rather there were nothing to sorrow about. If such a thing as spiteful benevolence existed (which is impossible, of course, but supposing it did), a genuinely and sincerely merciful person would wish others to be miserable so that he could show them mercy!

We must conclude that, while some sorrow is commendable, no sorrow is to be valued for its own sake. You, Lord God, lover of souls, show mercy far more purely than we can, and in a way free from all taint, because no sorrow can wound you. Which of us is sufficient for this?

4. At that time I was truly miserable, for I loved feeling sad and sought out whatever could cause me sadness. When the theme of a play dealt with other people's tragedies—false and theatrical tragedies—it would please and attract me more powerfully the more it moved me to tears. I was an unhappy beast[8] astray from your flock and resentful of your shepherding, so what wonder was it that I became infected with foul mange? My love for tragic scenes sprang from no inclination to be more deeply wounded by them, for I had no desire to undergo myself the woes I liked to watch. It was simply that when I listened to such doleful tales being told they enabled me superficially to scrape away at my itching self, with the result that these raking nails raised an inflamed swelling, and drew stinking discharge from a festering wound. Was that life I led any life at all, O my God?

---

7. See Dn 3:52.
8. *Infelix pecus*: the words echo Virgil, *Eclogues* III,3, *infelix O semper, oves, pecus!* as well as the lost sheep of the gospel, Mt 18:22; Lk 15:4-7; see 1 Pt 2:25. Augustine may also have had in mind the last verse of Ps 118 (119), *I have gone astray like a sheep: seek your servant,* on which Ambrose commented very beautifully: see Ambrose, Sermon 22 on Psalm 118,3,27-30.

3, 5. Far above me your faithful mercy was hovering. How great were the sins on which I spent all my strength, as I followed my impious curiosity! It led me to abandon you and plunge into treacherous abysses, into depths of unbelief and a delusive allegiance to demons, to whom I was offering my evil deeds in sacrifice.[9] And in all these sins your scourges beat upon me. Even within the walls of your church, during the celebration of your sacred mysteries, I once made bold to indulge in carnal desire and conduct that could yield only a harvest of death;[10] and for this you struck me with severe punishments, though none that matched my guilt. O my God, you were immensely merciful to me,[11] and were my refuge from the terrible dangers amid which I wandered, head held high. I withdrew further and further from you, loving my own ways and not yours, relishing the freedom of a runaway slave.

The "wreckers"

6. The prestigious course of studies I was following looked as its goal to the law-courts, in which I was destined to excel and where I would earn a reputation all the higher in the measure that my performance was the more unscrupulous. So blind can people be that they glory even in their blindness! Already I was the ablest student in the school of rhetoric. At this I was elated and vain and swollen with pride; but as you know, O Lord, I was a good deal quieter than the "wreckers" and kept well clear of their destructive activities. I was ashamed of the sense of shame that held me back from being like these "wreckers,"[12] whose perverse and diabolical nickname is almost a badge of good education; I associated with them and sometimes enjoyed friendly contacts, but always recoiled from their acts of violence. They would chase sensitive freshmen relentlessly, taunting and hounding them on no provocation, simply for their own malicious amusement. Nothing is more like demonic activity than this behavior. What apter name could be found for such people than "wreckers"? They are first wrecked and twisted themselves; then the spirits who secretly seduce and deceive them laugh to see them deceiving and laughing at other people.

---

9. See Dt 32:17; 1 Cor 10:20.
10. See Rom 7:5.
11. *O tu praegrandis misericordia mea*: this phrase, and the similar but less strong *Deus meus, misericordia mea* in III,1,1, bracket by an invocation of God's true mercy Augustine's reflections on pseudo-mercy in the preceding paragraphs.
12. *Eversores*, literally those who upset, overthrow, sack a city.

The quest for wisdom: Cicero's Hortensius

4, 7. Still young and immature, I began in the company of these people to study treatises on eloquence. This was a discipline in which I longed to excel, though my motive was the damnably proud desire to gratify my human vanity. In the customary course of study I had discovered a book by an author called Cicero, whose language is almost universally admired, though not its inner spring. This book of his is called the *Hortensius*[13] and contains an exhortation to philosophy. The book changed my way of feeling and the character of my prayers to you, O Lord, for under its influence my petitions and desires altered. All my hollow hopes suddenly seemed worthless, and with unbelievable intensity my heart burned with longing for the immortality that wisdom seemed to promise. I began to rise up, in order to return to you.[14] My interest in the book was not aroused by its usefulness in the honing of my verbal skills (which was supposed to be the object of the studies I was now pursuing, in my nineteenth year, at my mother's expense, since my father had died two years earlier); no, it was not merely as an instrument for sharpening my tongue that I used that book, for it had won me over not by its style but by what it had to say.

8. How ardently I longed, O my God, how ardently I longed to fly to you away from earthly things! I did not understand then how you were dealing with me. Wisdom resides with you,[15] but love for wisdom is called by the Greek name "philosophy," and this love it was that the book kindled in me. There are people who lead others astray under the pretense of philosophy, coloring and masking their errors under that great, fair, honorable name. Nearly all who did so in Cicero's own day are mentioned and shown up in his book; and there too one can almost find an exposition of the salutary warning given by your Spirit through your good, devout servant: *Take care that no one deceives you with philosophy and empty, misleading ideas derived from man-made traditions, centered on the elemental spirits of this world and not on Christ; for in him all the fullness of the Godhead dwells in bodily wise.*[16] At the time these words of the apostle were still unknown to me; but you know, O light of my heart, that there was one thing and one only that brought me joy in the exhortation to wisdom: that

---

13. This book is lost, but known in fragments, mainly through the quotations elsewhere in Augustine's works. He continued to allude to and quote from it for more than fifty years.
14. The prodigal again; see Lk 15:18-20.
15. See Jb 12:13.16.
16. Col 2:8-9.

by its call I was aroused and kindled and set on fire to love and seek and capture and hold fast and strongly cling not to this or that school, but to wisdom itself, whatever it might be. Only one consideration checked me in my ardent enthusiasm: that the name of Christ did not occur there. Through your mercy, Lord, my tender little heart had drunk in that name, the name of my Savior and your Son, with my mother's milk, and in my deepest heart I still held on to it. No writing from which that name was missing, even if learned, of literary elegance and truthful, could ever captivate me completely.[17]

Distaste for scripture

5, 9. Accordingly I turned my attention to the holy scriptures to find out what they were like. What I see in them today is something not accessible to the scrutiny of the proud nor exposed to the gaze of the immature, something lowly as one enters but lofty as one advances further, something veiled in mystery. At that time, though, I was in no state to enter, nor prepared to bow my head and accommodate myself to its ways. My approach then was quite different from the one I am suggesting now: when I studied the Bible and compared it with Cicero's dignified prose, it seemed to me unworthy.[18] My swollen pride recoiled from its style and my intelligence failed to penetrate to its inner meaning. Scripture is a reality that grows along with little children, but I disdained to be a little child[19] and in my high and mighty arrogance regarded myself as grown up.

He joins the Manichees

6, 10. In reaction to this disappointment I fell among a set of proud madmen, exceedingly carnal and talkative people in whose mouths were diabolical snares[20] and a sticky mess compounded by mixing the syllables of your name, and the names of the Lord Jesus Christ and the Holy Spirit,

---

17. The Manichean writings, which he will shortly encounter, had the advantage over Cicero in this respect.
18. Augustine was reading the second-century Old Latin translation. Jerome was similarly put off; see his Letter 22,30.
19. See Mt 7:27.
20. See 1 Tm 3:7; 2 Tm 2:26.

who is our Paraclete and Consoler.[21] These names were never far from their mouths, but amounted to no more than sound and the clacking of tongues, for their hearts were empty of the truth. They would say, "Truth, truth!" and had plenty to tell me on the subject, but truth had no place in them. They told me lies not only about you, who are truly the Truth, but also about the elements of this world that is your creation. I ought to have gone beyond them and beyond what even truthful philosophers have taught out of love for you, my Father, who are the highest good and the loveliness in all lovely things.

O Truth, Truth, how the deepest and innermost marrow of my mind ached for you, even then while they prattled your name to me unremittingly and in so many ways, though only in words and in their huge, copious tomes! I was hungering for you, but their teachings were like plates on which they served me not you but the sun and moon, which are your beautiful works, to be sure, but still your works, not yourself, and not even your primary works at that; for your spiritual creations are nobler than material creatures, nobler even than these brilliant heavenly bodies. I was hungering and thirsting for you, not for your creations, not even for your spiritual creations, but for yourself, O Truth, *in whom there is no variation, no play of changing shadow;*[22] and all they set before me were dishes of glittering myths. It would have been more profitable to love the sun in the sky, which at least our eyes perceive truly, than those chimeras offered to a mind that had been led astray through its eyes.[23] Yet I ate those offerings, believing that I was feeding on you; I ate them without appetite, for there was no taste in my mouth of you as you are, since those insubstantial shams were not you. I derived no nourishment from them, but was left

---

21. He is referring to the Manichees. Their system was immensely powerful for minds preoccupied with the perennial tension between good and evil in every person. The Manichees grappled with the problem through the medium of myths concerning the origins of the cosmos. The system was radically dualistic: evil in the material world was explained by relegating God to its fringes and denying his omnipotence. There was a ruler of the realm of light (very different from the God of orthodox Christianity), and a cosmic "Christ" whose "power" dwelt in the sun and his "wisdom" in the moon. The historic Christ was not truly human. Mani himself, the founder of the sect, was identified with the Paraclete. Followers of the sect were divided into the "elect" and a lower grade of "hearers." Augustine himself seems never to have gone beyond the hearer stage.
22. Jas 1:17. The quotation is the more apt for the background it evokes in James' letter, where God is referred as the "Father of lights" in a completely un-Manichean sense.
23. In Manichean belief the sun and the moon served as vehicles for conveying elements of light, purified and released from this world, back to the realm of light. Sun and moon were therefore important, and in some sense divine.

the more drained. The food we dream we are eating in our sleep is very like the food we eat when awake, but it does not nourish the dreamers, because they are asleep. Those mythical objects, however, did not even come near to resembling you as you are when you speak to me today, because they were nothing but figments of the imagination invested with bodily form, counterfeit bodies. The material objects we see with our eyes of flesh, in the sky or on earth, are more real than they; what we see in company with the beasts and birds is far more dependable than images of the same things conjured up in our imagination. Yet even if we do but see these things in our mind's eye, still they are more real than other objects of which we might form some notion from them—greater, supposedly infinite beings which have no reality whatever. On such inanities was I being fed, and unfed I remained.

But you, O my love, for whom I faint with longing that I may be strong, you are not those material objects we can see, in heaven though they are, nor are you the beings we do not see there, for you have created them and do not even count them as your highest works. How much more distant are you, then, from mere figments of my imagination, fantasy-bodies that have no reality at all! More real are the memory-pictures we form of objects which at least do exist, and more real again than these are the physical beings themselves; yet none of these are you. Better and more certain than the bodies of material creatures is the soul that gives life to their bodies, yet you are not the soul either. You are the life of souls, the life of all lives, the life who are yourself living and unchanging, the life of my own soul.

11. Where were you at that time? How far from me? I was certainly roving far away from you, and debarred even from the pods I was feeding to pigs.[24] The fables of schoolmasters and poets are far better than the snares then being set for me; yes, verses, songs and tales of Medea in flight are undeniably more wholesome than myths about the five elements being metamorphosed to defeat the five caverns of darkness.[25] These latter have no truth in them at all and are lethal to anyone who believes them, whereas I can turn verse and song into a means of earning real food. When I sang of

---

24. See Lk 15:16.
25. According to the Manichees the realm of darkness comprised five caverns: of darkness, smoke, evil, wind, evil fire and evil water. Against them the cosmic man waged war, armed with the good elements of light, air, wind, fire, and water.

Medea in her flying chariot I was not vouching for any of it as fact, nor, when I listened to someone else singing of it, did I believe the story; but I did believe the Manichean lies. All the worse for me! By these stages I was led deeper into hell,[26] laboring and chafing under the scarcity of truth, because I was seeking you, my God, not through that power of the mind by which you have chosen to rank me above the beasts, but only through carnal inclination. To you do I confess this, for you showed mercy to me before ever I could confess it. You were more intimately present to me than my innermost being, and higher than the highest peak of my spirit.

But I stumbled upon that bold woman devoid of prudence in Solomon's allegory; she was sitting outside on her stool and inviting me: *Come and enjoy eating bread in secret, and drink sweet, stolen water.*[27] She seduced me because she found me living outside, in my carnal eyes, and ruminating within myself only on what I had devoured through them.

7, 12. The trouble was that I knew nothing else; I did not recognize the other, true reality. I was being subtly maneuvered into accepting the views of those stupid deceivers by the questions they constantly asked me about the origin of evil, and whether God was confined to a material form with hair and nails, and whether people who practiced polygamy, killed human beings and offered animal sacrifices could be considered righteous.[28] Being ignorant of these matters I was very disturbed by the questions, and supposed that I was approaching the truth when I was in fact moving away from it. I did not know that evil is nothing but the diminishment of good to the point where nothing at all is left. How could I see that, I whose power of sight was restricted to seeing material shapes with my eyes and imaginary forms with my mind?

---

26. See Prv 9:18.
27. Prv 9:17. Folly, this temptress in Prv 9:13-17, is the antithesis of wisdom, who is personified in the preceding verses as a woman inviting passers-by to her banquet.
28. Augustine is not concerned to give a full or fair account of the Manichean system, but he mentions here three problems that puzzled him, and which the Manichees at least raised, even if their answers were less than satisfactory. In Books V-VII he discusses the solutions (in reverse order). The first question (origin of evil), though clearly not new, was forced upon Jews and Christians in acute form by their belief in a good and omnipotent God, the second and third (spirituality of God and moral crudities in the Old Testament) by the anthropomorphisms and progressive character of biblical revelation. At this stage Augustine lacked the understanding to find adequate answers. Three times in this paragraph and the beginning of the next he says, "I did not know."

Nor did I know that God is spirit,[29] not a being with limbs stretching far and wide, and having a certain size. The notion of size implies that a body is smaller in a single part than in the whole of itself; so that, if it is infinite, it would somehow be smaller in a spatially defined section than spread out through infinity—rather than present everywhere in its entirety, as a spirit is and as God is. Moreover I had no inkling of what there could be in us which would give grounds for saying that we are made in the image of God, as scripture rightly says we are.[30]

13. I did not know either that true inward righteousness takes as its criterion not custom but the most righteous law of almighty God, by which the morality of countries and times was formed as appropriate to those countries and times, while God's law itself has remained unchanged everywhere and always, not one thing in one place and something different elsewhere. By this norm Abraham, Isaac, Jacob, Moses, David and all those of whom God spoke approvingly were indeed righteous; they are accounted guilty only by persons of limited experience who judge *by some human day of reckoning*[31] and measure the conduct of the human race at large by the standard that befits their own. They are like someone who knows nothing about armor, or which piece belongs where, and tries to cover his head with the greaves and his feet with the helmet, and then grumbles because they do not fit properly. Or again, they are like a man who on a certain day which is appointed a public holiday from noon onward is indignant because he is not allowed to set out his goods for sale in the afternoon, although this was allowed in the morning; or like a person who in one and the same house sees something being handled by one servant which another one, who serves drinks, is not allowed to touch, or something being done behind the stables which is not properly done at table, and gets angry about this, complaining because, while there is one house and one staff of servants, the same actions are not permitted to everybody in all places.[32] Equally foolish are people who grow indignant on hearing that some practice was allowed to righteous people in earlier ages which is forbidden to the righteous in our own day, and that God laid down one rule for the former and a different one for the latter, as the differ-

29. See Jn 4:24.
30. See Gn 1:27.
31. 1 Cor 4:3.
32. Three similes from Roman life: the army, the forum, and the household. Augustine will pick them up twice more before the end of the paragraph.

ence between the two periods of time demands; whereas in fact both sets of people have been subject to the same norm of righteousness. This attitude is just as stupid as being upset because, with regard to a single man or a single day or a single house, one perceives different pieces of armor to be designed for different limbs, and an activity to be lawful until a certain hour but not afterward, and something to be permitted or even ordered in a corner but forbidden and punished elsewhere. Does this mean that justice is fickle and changeable?[33] No, but the epochs over which she rules do not all unfold in the same way, precisely because times change. Human beings live on earth for a brief span only, and they lack the discernment to bring the conditions of earlier ages, of which they have no experience, into the same frame of reference with those they know well; but they can easily perceive in one body or one day or one house what is appropriate for each limb, each period of time and all persons and places. Thus while they may be scandalized by the one, they readily submit to the other.[34]

14. All this was beyond my comprehension at the time and I made no allowance for it; although these truths leapt to the eye, I failed to see them. Yet I was quite accustomed to compose songs in which I was not free to place the metrical foot anywhere I fancied: different meters demanded different placing of the stress, and sometimes even within one line the feet were not uniform throughout. In spite of this, the art of poetry itself, in accordance with which I sang, was not different in different places, but worked always on the same principles. I lacked the insight to understand that justice, of which good and holy people are the servants, contains in itself, in a far more excellent and sublime way, the principles of all it prescribes, and is unvaryingly self-consistent, yet does not impose all its demands at once, but adjusts and allots to different periods the provisions most apt for them. In my blindness I censured the holy patriarchs, who not only made use of the opportunities available to them in the way ordained and inspired by God, but also prefigured what was to come, as God revealed it through them.

---

33. Augustine is quoting Virgil, *Aeneid* IV,569, where the epithets are applied to woman by Mercury, who is instructing Aeneas to terminate his affair with Dido, who scarcely merits them.

34. It is part of Augustine's greatness that he tentatively applies to some problems of the Old Testament principles of interpretation based on historical development, which would be elaborated centuries later.

8, 15. Can we suppose that it is ever or anywhere unjust to love God with one's whole heart, whole soul and whole mind, and to love one's neighbor as oneself?[35] By the same token, vices contrary to nature are everywhere and always to be detested and punished. Such were the sins of the Sodomites. If all nations behaved as the Sodomites did, they too would be held guilty under the divine law, which did not make men to have that kind of relationship with each other. The very fellowship which ought to hold between ourselves and God is violated when our nature is defiled by perverted lust, since our nature is his creation.

Transgressions against human codes are a different matter: they vary in accordance with variable customs; but they are to be avoided all the same, lest an agreement made by citizens or compatriots among themselves, and rendered stable by custom and law, be violated at the whim of any citizen or foreigner; for a part which fails to harmonize with the whole is a source of mischief. If, on the other hand, God commands something which conflicts with the customs or rules of any human society, then it is to be done, even if it has never been done there before; if it has fallen into abeyance, it must be restored, or if not established previously, it must be established now. After all, a king has the right to command that something be done in the state over which he reigns, even if neither he nor any of his predecessors has ever ordered it before. To obey him in such an instance does not undermine that community; indeed, to disobey him would harm it, for a general contract to obey its rulers holds good in human society. How much more, then, are we bound unhesitatingly to serve God, the Ruler over all creation, in any matter where he commands us! As in the hierarchy of human society a more powerful official is placed above one of lesser rank and is to be obeyed, so God stands above all.

16. It is the same with crimes against the person. They may spring from a desire to hurt another person, whether by insulting language or by injury, and in either case may be prompted by a spirit of revenge, as when someone attacks his enemy. Or the motive may be to secure something belonging to another, as when a robber attacks a traveler, or to forestall some evil, when one attacks a person of whom one is afraid. Again, crime may be motivated by envy, as when a person in wretched circumstances envies one more fortunate, or one who is successful in an enterprise jealously injures another because he fears the other will catch up with him, or

---

35. See Mt 22:37.39; Mk 12:30.33; Lk 10:27.

is chagrined because that person already has. Or it may simply be pleasure in the misfortunes of others that tempts people to crime: this is the pleasure felt by those who watch gladiators, and anyone who laughs and mocks at other people.

These are the chief kinds of sin, which sprout from a craving for domination, or for watching shows, or for sensory pleasure,[36] or from any two of these, or all three together. The consequence is an evil life in opposition to that other "three plus seven," the ten-stringed harp, your decalogue, O God most high and most sweet.[37]

But how can our vices touch you, who are incorruptible? What crimes can be committed against you, who are immune from harm? You avenge them nonetheless by causing the sin to rebound on the sinner, for even when people sin against you, they are maliciously damaging their own souls. Iniquity plays itself false[38] when it corrupts and perverts its own nature, to which you gave life and order, or when it makes intemperate use of lawful things, or again when it burns with desire for other things not permitted, lusting to enjoy them in a way contrary to nature. Or again, the guilt of sinners may lie in rebelling against you in word or intention, thereby kicking against the goad,[39] or in casting off the restraints of human society and defiantly enjoying private alliances and feuds, as dictated by their own likes and dislikes. This is what happens when anyone abandons you, the fountain of life,[40] the One, the true creator and ruler of the universe, and in self-sufficient arrogance chooses to love a part of it only, a bogus "one."[41]

Yet through loving humility we find our way back to you. You purify our evil dispositions; you are merciful toward the sins of those who confess to you; you hear the groans of captives[42] and set us free from the bonds we have forged for ourselves, provided only we no longer defy you in the arrogance of a spurious freedom, greedy to have more and thereby

---

36. The three classic temptations once more.
37. The first three of the ten commandments relate to God, the remaining seven to relationships with one's neighbors; hence for Augustine 3+7 makes up the ten-stringed harp of Ps 32(33):2, on which we praise God.
38. See Ps 26(27):12.
39. See Acts 9:5; 26:14.
40. See Jer 2:13.
41. According to the Neo-Platonists the destiny of human beings is to love and cleave to the One; sin consists in turning away from the One and becoming engrossed in the life of the senses, and thus setting up a false center, or false "One."
42. See Ps 101:21(102:20).

incurring the loss of everything, loving some advantage of our own better than yourself, who are the good of all.

9, 17. Particularly deserving of mention among vices, crimes and the many other kinds of iniquity are the sins of those who are making some progress, sins which in the eyes of people qualified to judge are at the same time blameworthy when measured by ideal standards yet praiseworthy inasmuch as they offer hope for the future, as green shoots promise the crop. There are also certain deeds which look like vices or crimes against others, yet are not really sins, for they offend neither you, our Lord and God, nor the human community. So, for instance, someone may accumulate goods for use in ordinary life or to meet some particular need, yet it is by no means sure that any avarice was involved; or again, people are punished by someone in authority zealous for their correction, but there it is not clear whether vindictiveness played any part. It happens, therefore, that many things are done which to human judgment would seem to merit condemnation, yet are expressly commended by you, while many actions approved by human reckoning are by you explicitly condemned, because often there is a discrepancy between the appearance of an action and the intention of the agent; and the circumstances of the time, which may be obscure, make a difference too.

When you suddenly command some unusual, unexpected course of action, then even if it is something you have hitherto forbidden, even if for the time being you conceal the reason for your behest, and even if it contravenes the accepted norms of a human society, can we doubt that it is right to obey, seeing that a human society is just precisely insofar as it serves you? Blessed are they who know that you have commanded them. Everything that is done by your servants is done either to make plain what needs to be revealed at present, or to foreshadow the future.

10, 18. I knew nothing of all this, and so I derided your holy servants and prophets. Even as I laughed at them I deserved to be laughed at by you, for gradually, little by little, I was being lured into such absurdities as the belief that a fig wept when plucked, and its mother tree too wept milky tears. Then, I was told, if one of the saints ate the fig (plucked, of course, not by any fault on his part but by someone else's[43]), it would be absorbed by his digestive system and then when he belched or groaned in prayer he

---

43. That is, by one of the hearers, content with a lower grade of sanctity, and privileged to provide food for the elect.

would spew out angels, or even particles of God. These particles of God most high, of the true God, would have remained trapped in the fruit unless liberated by the teeth and belly[44] of one of the holy elect! I believed, poor wretch, that it was accordingly a higher duty to show mercy to the fruits of the earth than to human beings, for whom they came into existence; for if some hungry person who was not a Manichee asked for one, it was believed that to give it to him entailed passing a death-sentence on that morsel.

Monica, grieved, is consoled by a vision

11, 19. You stretched out your hand from on high and pulled my soul[45] out of these murky depths because my mother, who was faithful to you, was weeping for me more bitterly than ever mothers wept for the bodily death of their children. In her faith and in the spiritual discernment she possessed by your gift she regarded me as dead; and you heard her, O Lord, you heard her and did not scorn those tears of hers which gushed forth and watered the ground beneath her eyes wherever she prayed. Yes, you did indeed hear her, for how else can I account for the dream by which you so comforted her that she agreed to live with me and share my table, under the same roof? She had initially been reluctant to do so, repelled by my blasphemous errors, which were loathsome to her. But she dreamt that she was standing on some kind of wooden ruler,[46] and saw a young man of radiant aspect coming toward her; he cheerfully laughed at her, whereas she was sorrowful, overwhelmed with grief. He asked her the reason for her gloom and daily tears, though as usual his question was intended to teach her, not to elicit information for himself.[47] She replied that she was mourning my ruin. He then instructed and admonished her to take good heed and see that where she stood, there also stood I. This was to reassure her. She took heed, and saw me standing close beside her on the same rule.

---

44. *Dente ac ventre*, a contemptuous assonance.
45. See Ps 143(144):7.
46. *In quadam regula linea.* The most obvious translation would evisage a wooden ruler of inordinate size, and this may be right. Alternatively it has been suggested that the *regula* was a leveling device used in building aqueducts, raised a few feet off the ground. in either case there is probably a conscious reference to the *regula fidei*, the faith professed at baptism.
47. This may suggest that the young man was Christ, who was in the habit of asking leading questions.

How else could this have happened, if not because your ears were open to the plea of her heart, O good and all-powerful God, who care for each of us as though each were the only one, and for all alike with the same tenderness you show to each?

20. Another telling point was that when she had related the vision to me, and I had launched into an attempt to persuade her that she must not give up hope of some day becoming what I was, she promptly replied, without the slightest hesitation, "No: I was not told, 'Where he is, you will be too,' but, 'Where you are, he will be.' " I confess to you, Lord, that, as my memory serves me—and I have often spoken of this episode—I was more deeply disturbed by this answer that came from you through my sharp-eyed mother than by the dream itself. She was not worried by the false interpretation that had come to me so pat, but saw immediately what needed to be seen, as I had not done until she spoke. The dream foretold, so long in advance, the joy in store for this devout woman many years later, and so gave her comfort in her present anxiety. Nearly nine years were to follow during which I floundered in the mud of the deep[48] and the darkness of deception, often struggling to extricate myself but crashing heavily back again. Yet throughout those years my mother, a chaste, God-fearing, sensible widow of the kind so dear to you, though more eager in her hope was no less assiduous in her weeping and entreaty, never at any time ceasing her plangent prayers to you about me. Her pleas found their way into your presence, but you left me still wrapped around by the fog, and enveloped in it.

"A son of tears"

12, 21. Meanwhile you gave another answer, as I recall. (I am, of course, omitting many things, being in a hurry to get to those which more powerfully impel me to praise you; and in any case there are many that I do not remember.) You gave this second answer through a priest of yours, a certain bishop who had been nurtured in the Church and well versed in your scriptures. The woman asked him if he would be so kind as to talk to me, to rebut my errors, disabuse me of my harmful persuasions and teach me good ones; for he was used to doing this, whenever he happened to find anyone apt to profit by it. He refused, however, and very wisely, as I subsequently understood. He replied that I was as yet unteachable; I was puffed up with the

---

48. See Ps 68:3(69:2).

novelty of my heresy and had been tormenting plenty of unskilled persons with finicky little questions, as she told him. "Leave him alone," he advised. "Simply pray for him to the Lord. He will find out for himself through his reading how wrong these beliefs are, and how profoundly irreverent." At the same interview he told her how he had himself been handed over to the Manichees as a little boy by his mother, who had also been led astray; he had not only read nearly all their books but had even written some himself,[49] and without anyone having to argue or persuade him it had become clear to him that the sect was something he should flee from. So he had fled.

These assurances did not satisfy her. She pleaded all the more insistently and with free-flowing tears that he would consent to see me and discuss matters with me. A little vexed, he answered, "Go away now; but hold on to this: it is inconceivable that he should perish, a son of tears like yours." In her conversations with me later she often recalled that she had taken these words to be an oracle from heaven.[50]

---

49. Or, perhaps, merely copied Manichean works. The story of this unnamed bishop, like that of Victorinus later, mirrors Augustine's own.

50. This "voice from heaven" that solemnly closes Book III is paralleled by that at the end of the garden scene in Book VIII.

Book IV

Augustine the Manichee

Augustine sells rhetorical skills

1, 1. Throughout those nine years, from my nineteenth to my twenty-eighth year, I and others like me were seduced and seducers, deceived ourselves and deceivers of others amid a welter of desires: publicly through the arts reputed "liberal," and secretly under the false name of religion.[1] In the one we were arrogant, in the other superstitious, and in both futile; under the auspices of the former we pursued trumpery popular acclaim, theatrical plaudits, song-competitions and the contest for ephemeral wreaths, we watched trashy shows and indulged our intemperate lusts; through the latter we sought to be purged of these defilements by providing food for the so-called "elect" or "saints," in the hope that they would turn the food into angels and gods for us in the workshops of their bellies to be the agents of our liberation. These ends I pursued, these things I did, in the company of friends who through me and with me were alike deceived.

Let the haughty laugh at me, let them laugh who have never yet been flat on their faces, felled for their own good by you, my God; but let me confess my disgraceful deeds to you, and in confessing praise you. Allow me this, I beg you, and grant me to trace today the twisting arguments that led me astray at that past time, shouting my joy to you as I offer you this sacrifice.[2] Without you, what am I to myself but a guide to my own downfall? Or, when things go well with me, what am I but a child suckled on

---

1. Secretly because the sect had been proscribed by both Church and state during most of the fourth century, though the law was not rigorously enforced. But the distinction may be simply between public and private life.
2. See Ps 26(27):6.

your milk and fed on you, the food that perishes not?[3] What kind of human being is anyone who is human and nothing more? Let the strong and mighty laugh at us, then, but let us weak and needy folk confess to you.

2, 2. During these years I was teaching the art of rhetoric, selling talkative skills apt to sway others because greed swayed me. Yet I preferred to have good pupils, or such as passed for good, as you know, O Lord; and without any trickery on my part I taught them the tricks of the trade, never such as would secure the condemnation of the innocent, though sometimes such as were calculated to get the guilty acquitted. And you saw from afar, O God, how I was losing my foothold on slippery ground, but how amid the smoke a spark of integrity still guttered in me; for though I taught students who loved worthless things and sought falsehood,[4] in which pursuits I bore them company, I did try to teach them honestly.

He begins to cohabit with an unnamed girl

At this time too I lived with a girl not bound to me in lawful wedlock but sought out by the roving eye of reckless desire; all the same she was the only girl I had, and I was sexually faithful to her. This experience taught me at first hand what a difference there is between a marriage contracted for the purpose of founding a family, and a relationship of love charged with carnal desire in which children may be born even against the parents' wishes—though once they are born one cannot help loving them.[5]

3. Another thing I remember is that once when I had decided to enter a dramatic poetry contest some sorcerer fellow sent word to me to ask what I was prepared to pay him to ensure that I would win. I replied that I detested and loathed those obscene rites, and would not countenance the killing of a fly to bring me victory, even if the crown to be won were of gold that would last for ever. This fellow was prepared to offer living creatures in sacrifice, and I suspected that he intended by these rites to enlist demonic support for my cause. But it was not out of reverence for your purity that I

---

3. See Jn 6:27.
4. See Ps 4:3.
5. From IX,6,14 it appears that Augustine's son, Adeodatus, must have been born about 371/2, when Augustine was still a student; so Augustine's relationship with his partner had begun before the time he is directly discussing now. The chronology of these nine years is not precise. Possidius (*Life* 1,2) tells us that a period of teaching "grammar" at Thagaste had preceded Augustine's teaching of rhetoric at Carthage.

rejected this evil thing, O God of my heart, for I had not yet learned to love you; all I had learned was to think about brilliant material objects. Is not a soul that sighs for such make-believe gods wantonly forsaking you, trusting in illusions and feeding the winds?[6] Yet while refusing to have sacrifice offered to demons on my behalf I was all the while offering myself in sacrifice to them through my superstition; for what does "feeding the winds" mean but feeding demons, providing pleasure and amusement for them by our errors?

He investigates astrology

3, 4. I made no move whatever to break off my habit of consulting those charlatans whom people call "mathematicians,"[7] for I took the view that no sacrifice was being offered by them, nor any prayer addressed to spirits in the practice of divination. Nonetheless true Christian piety is consistent with its own principles in rejecting and condemning astrology. It is good to confess to you, O Lord, and to say, *Have mercy on me; heal my soul, for I have sinned against you;*[8] it is good to beware of abusing your forgiveness by regarding it as a license to sin, and good to remember our Lord's warning, *See now, you are healed: sin no more, lest some worse fate befall you.*[9] When people say, "The sky is responsible for your sin, so you cannot avoid it," or "Venus did this, or Saturn, or Mars," they invalidate our whole salvation. They are suggesting that human beings are guiltless—humans who are flesh and blood and putrid pride!—and that the fault lies with the creator and controller of sky and stars. And who is this? You, our God, sweetness and the fount of justice, who will repay each of us as our actions deserve, and do not disdain a broken and humbled heart.[10]

5. At this time there was a certain man of deep insight, very skilled and highly reputed in the art of medicine, who as proconsul had set his hand on my unsound head, but only to crown me with the wreath won in the contest. No healer's hand did he lay upon me, for you, Lord, were the only

---

6. See Ps 72(73):27; Prv 10:4; Hos 12:1.
7. Astrologers: from an earlier application to scholars who made mathematical calculations about astronomy the currency of the term was now debased, to denote those who superstitiously sought the causes of human actions in the stars. Astrologers and those who consulted them were declared liable to the death penalty under Valentinian I.
8. Ps 40:5(41:4); for the preceding words see Ps 91:2(92:1).
9. Jn 5:14.
10. See Mt 16:27; Rom 2:6; Ps 50:19(51:17).

healer of my sickness, you who thwart the proud but give grace to the humble.[11] Were you deserting me, or giving up the task of curing my soul? No; even through that old man you were at work. It happened like this. I had become quite well known to him, and listened regularly and attentively to his speeches, for although unpolished in style they were pleasant to the ear and weighty for the vigorous ideas they expressed. Through conversation with me he learned that I was deeply interested in the writings of those who professed to cast birth horoscopes. In kindly and fatherly fashion he advised me to throw them away, and not to waste on such rubbish the care and effort better spent on more useful enterprises. He told me that as a young man he had learned astrology with such zeal that he had wanted to make it his career and earn his living by it. If he had the intelligence to understand Hippocrates, he pointed out, he was certainly capable of mastering those books. Later, however, he abandoned them and took up medicine, for no other reason than that he had discovered them to be entirely misleading, and as an honorable man he did not want to make his living by deceiving others. "But you," he said, "you can support yourself and maintain your social position by the profession of rhetoric, so you are pursuing this fraudulent study as a hobby, not from any economic necessity. All the more reason, then, for you to believe me when I inform you about this subject in which I was so well versed myself that I meant to make my living by it alone."

I asked him how, in that case, it came about that astrologers could often make predictions which proved true. He gave the best answer available, saying that this was due to chance, a force prevalent throughout nature. Think how frequently it happens, he said, that a person looks for guidance in the pages of some poet who was singing of an unrelated matter and had something quite different in mind, yet a line stands out which is wonderfully apposite to the question in hand; [12] well, then, surely we should not wonder if, in response to some prompting from above, an utterance issues from a human mind unaware of what is happening in it, and this utterance

---

11. See Jas 4:6; 1 Pt 5:5. The physician was probably Vindicianus, named in VII,6,8. He had been physician to the emperor Valentinian, and was rewarded with a proconsulship.
12. The *sortes vergilianae*, a practice of opening a book at random, especially one of Virgil, and taking the first passage that springs to the eye as an oracle. The proconsul argues that if this haphazard method can sometimes yield remarkable results, the subtlety of a human mind can surely do more.

corresponds to the circumstances and actions of the client. This would be chance, not skill.[13]

6. By the answer he gave me, or which you gave me through him, you made provision for my needs and sketched in my memory an outline of the truth I was later to search out for myself. Yet at the time neither he nor my very dear friend, Nebridius, a fine and extremely sensible young man[14] who ridiculed the whole business of divination, was able to persuade me to throw those books away, because the authority of the writers weighed with me too heavily, and because I had as yet found no certain teaching which could convince me beyond doubt that any truthful statements delivered by diviners were due to chance and coincidence, rather than to genuine skill on the part of stargazers.

Death of a friend at Thagaste

4, 7. At this same period, when I first began to teach in the town where I was born,[15] I had a friend who shared my interests and was exceedingly dear to me. He was the same age as myself and, like me, now in the flower of young manhood. As a boy he had grown up with me; we had gone to school together and played together. He was not then such a friend to me as he was to become later, though even at the later time of which I speak our union fell short of true friendship, because friendship is genuine only when you bind fast together people who cleave to you through the charity poured abroad in our hearts by the Holy Spirit who is given to us.[16] I did love him very tenderly, though, and similarity of outlook lent warmth to our relationship; for I had lured him from the true faith, which he had held in a thoroughly immature way and without conviction, to the superstitious and baneful fables which my mother deplored in me. Already this man was intellectually astray along with me, and my soul could not bear to be without him. Ah, but you were pursuing close behind us, O God of

---

13. Perhaps Vindicianus suspected the possibility of unconscious thought-reading. But Augustine's own view is different: see VII,6,10.

14. Some manuscripts offer *castus*, chaste, instead of *cautus*, prudent, sensible, circumspect. Nebridius was to follow Augustine to Milan and remain a close friend until his premature death.

15. The year of teaching at Thagaste, 375/376, when Augustine was twenty-one years of age, antedates the spell of teaching at Carthage of which he has spoken in the two preceding chapters.

16. See Rom 5:5.

vengeance[17] who are the fount of all mercy and turn us back to yourself in wondrous ways. You took him from this life after barely a year's friendship, a friendship sweeter to me than any sweetness I had known in all my life.

8. Who can of himself alone extol your deeds, even those you have wrought in him alone? O my God, what was it that you then did for me? How unfathomable the abyss of your judgments![18] As my friend struggled with fever he lay for a long time unconscious and sweating at death's door; and as hope for his recovery dwindled he was baptized without his knowledge. I cared little for this, since I took it for granted that his mind was more likely to retain what he had received from me, irrespective of any rite performed on his unconscious body. How wrong I was; for he rallied and grew stronger, and immediately, or as soon as I possibly could (which is to say at the first moment that he was fit for it, for I did not leave him, so closely were we dependent on each other), I attempted to chaff him, expecting him to join me in making fun of the baptism he had undergone while entirely absent in mind and unaware of what was happening. But he had already learned that he had received it, and he recoiled from me with a shudder as though I had been his enemy, and with amazing, new-found independence warned me that if I wished to be his friend I had better stop saying such things to him. I stood aghast and troubled, but deferred telling him of my feelings in order to let him get better first, thinking that once he was in normal health again I would be able to do what I liked with him. But he was snatched away from my mad designs, to be kept safe with you for my consolation: a few days later the fever seized him anew and he died. And I was not there.

9. Black grief closed over my heart[19] and wherever I looked I saw only death. My native land was a torment to me and my father's house unbelievable misery. Everything I had shared with my friend turned into hideous anguish without him. My eyes sought him everywhere, but he was missing; I hated all things because they held him not, and could no more say to me, "Look, here he comes!" as they had been wont to do in his lifetime when he had been away. I had become a great enigma to myself, and I questioned my soul, demanding why it was sorrowful and why it so disqui-

---

17. See Ps 93(94):1.
18. See Rom 11:33.
19. See Lam 5:17.

eted me, but it had no answer. If I bade it, "Trust in God,"[20] it rightly disobeyed me, for the man it had held so dear and lost was more real and more lovable than the fantasy in which it was bidden to trust. Weeping alone brought me solace, and took my friend's place as the only comfort of my soul.

5, 10. All this is over now, Lord, and my hurt has been assuaged with time. Let me listen now to you who are truth; bring the ear of my heart close to your mouth, that you may tell me why weeping is a relief to the wretched. Can it be that although you are everywhere present you have flung our wretchedness far away from you, abiding unmoved in yourself[21] while we are tossed to and fro amid human trials? Surely not, for if we could not weep into your very ears, no shred of hope would be left to us. How comes it, then, that such sweet fruit is plucked from life's bitterness, the sweetness of groans, tears, sighs and laments? Does the comfort lie in this, that we hope you will hear? This is certainly true of our prayers, for they presuppose a desire to reach you. But is it true of sorrow for what we have lost, and of the grief that overwhelmed me then? No, for I neither hoped that he would come back to life nor made my tears a plea that he should; I simply mourned and wept, for I was beset with misery and bereft of my joy.[22] Or is it that bitter tears match the weariness we feel over what we once enjoyed, but find attractive no more?

6, 11. But why am I talking thus? This is no time for asking questions, but for confessing to you. I was miserable, and miserable too is everyone whose mind is chained by friendship with mortal things, and is torn apart by their loss, and then becomes aware of the misery that it was in even before it lost them. This was my condition at the time; I wept very bitterly and found repose in the bitterness. Miserable as I was, I held even this miserable life dearer than my friend; for although I might wish to change it, I would have been even less willing to lose it than I was to lose him. I do not even know if I would have been willing to lose it for him, after the manner of Orestes and Pylades, who wanted to die for one another or, failing that, to die together, because for either to live without the other would have been worse than death—or so the story goes, though it may not

---

20. For echoes in all these lines, see Pss 41:6.12(42:5.11); 42(43):5.
21. See Wis 7:27.
22. See *Miser ... eram et amiseram*, an Augustinian assonance.

be true.[23] Some kind of emotion opposed to this had sprung up in me, so that although my weariness with living was intense, so too was my fear of dying. I believe that the more I loved him, the more I hated death, which had taken him from me; I hated it as a hideous enemy, and feared it, and pictured it as ready to devour all human beings, since it had been able to make away with him. Yes, this was my state of mind: I remember it.

Look upon my heart, O my God, look deep within it. See, O my hope, who cleanse me from the uncleanness of such affections, who draw my eyes to yourself and pull my feet free from the snare,[24] see that this is indeed what I remember. I was amazed that other mortals went on living when he was dead whom I had loved as though he would never die, and still more amazed that I could go on living myself when he was dead—I, who had been like another self to him. It was well said that a friend is half one's own soul.[25] I felt that my soul and his had been but one soul in two bodies,[26] and I shrank from life with loathing because I could not bear to be only half alive; and perhaps I was so afraid of death because I did not want the whole of him to die, whom I had loved so dearly.[27]

7, 12. Woe to the madness which thinks to cherish human beings as though more than human! How foolish the human heart that anguishes without restraint over human ills, as I did then! Feverishly I thrashed about, sighed, wept and was troubled, and there was no repose for me, nor any counsel. Within me I was carrying a tattered, bleeding soul that did not want me to carry it, yet I could find no place to lay it down. Not in pleasant countryside did it find rest, nor in shows and songs, nor in sweet-scented gardens, nor in elaborate feasts, nor in the pleasures of couch or bed, nor even in books and incantations.[28] All things loured at me, even daylight itself, and everything that was not what he was seemed to me offensive and hateful, except for mourning and tears, in which alone I found some slight relief. Whenever my soul was drawn away from this, it burdened me with a

---

23. Mentioned in Cicero, *On Friendship* 7,24, where it is attributed to Pacuvius.
24. See Ps 24(25):15.
25. Horace, *Carmen* I,3,5-8.
26. The idea comes from Ovid, *Tristia* IV,4,72 and is applied to Orestes and Pylades. A similar definition of a friend is ascribed to Aristotle by Diogenes Laertius, VI,1,20.
27. In his *Revisions* II,6,2, written in 426/427, thirty years later than *The Confessions*, Augustine distanced himself from the rhetorical vehemence of his statement, considering it unsuited to the gravity of the confessional mode, and perhaps excessively influenced by sentimental classical models. But the tones may well represent his mood at twenty-one years of age.
28. He enumerates the objects of the five senses in formal order: sight, hearing, smell, taste, touch. All his earlier temptations have let him down; the last resort is to theurgy.

great load of misery. I should have lifted it up to you, Lord,[29] to be healed, but I was neither willing nor able to do so, especially because when I thought about you you did not seem to be anything solid or firm. For what I thought of was not you at all; an empty fantasy and my own error were my god. If I tried to lodge my soul in that, hoping that it might rest there, it would slip through that insubstantial thing and fall back again on me, who had remained to myself an unhappy place[30] where I could not live, but from which I could not escape. Whither could my heart flee to escape itself? Where could I go and leave myself behind? Was there any place of refuge where I would not be followed by my own self? Yet flee I did from my native land, for my eyes were less inclined to look for him where they had not been wont to see him before. So I left Thagaste and came to Carthage.

Consolation in other friends at Carthage

8, 13. Time does not stand still, nor are the rolling seasons useless to us, for they work wonders in our minds. They came and went from day to day, and by their coming and going implanted in me other hopes and other memories. Little by little they set me up again and turned me toward things that had earlier delighted me, and before these my sorrow began to give ground. Yet its place was taken, not indeed by fresh sorrows, but by the seeds of fresh sorrows; for how had that sorrow been able so easily to pierce my inmost being, if not because I had poured out my soul into the sand by loving a man doomed to death as though he were never to die? What restored and re-created me above all was the consolation of other friends, in whose company I loved what I was loving as a substitute for you. This was a gross fable and a long-sustained lie, and as our minds itched to listen they were corrupted by its adulterous excitation,[31] but the fable did not die for me when any of my friends died.

There were other joys to be found in their company which still more powerfully captivated my mind—the charms of talking and laughing together and kindly giving way to each other's wishes, reading elegantly written books together, sharing jokes and delighting to honor one another,

---

29. See Ps 24(25):1.
30. See II,10,18, "I became to myself a land of famine."
31. See 2 Tm 4:3-4. The "gross fable" is the Manichean system.

disagreeing occasionally but without rancor, as a person might disagree with himself, and lending piquancy by that rare disagreement to our much more frequent accord. We would teach and learn from each other, sadly missing any who were absent and blithely welcoming them when they returned. Such signs of friendship sprang from the hearts of friends who loved and knew their love returned, signs to be read in smiles, words, glances and a thousand gracious gestures. So were sparks kindled and our minds were fused inseparably, out of many becoming one.

9, 14. This is what we esteem in our friends, and so highly do we esteem it that our conscience feels guilt if we fail to love someone who responds to us with love, or do not return the love of one who offers love to us, and this without seeking any bodily gratification from the other save signs of his goodwill. From this springs our grief if someone dies, from this come the darkness of sorrow and the heart drenched with tears because sweetness has turned to bitterness, so that as the dying lose their life, life becomes no better than death for those who live on. Blessed is he who loves you, and loves his friend in you and his enemy for your sake.[32] He alone loses no one dear to him, to whom all are dear in the One who is never lost. And who is this but our God, the God who made heaven and earth and fills them, because it was by filling them that he made them?[33] No one loses you unless he tries to get rid of you, and if he does try to do that, where can he go, whither does he flee,[34] but from you in your tranquillity to you in your anger? Does he not encounter your law everywhere, in his own punishment? Your law is truth, as you yourself are truth.[35]

Transience of created things

10, 15. Turn us toward yourself, O God of Hosts, show us your face and we shall be saved;[36] for wheresoever a human soul turns, it can but cling to what brings sorrow unless it turns to you, cling though it may to beautiful things outside you and outside itself. Yet were these beautiful things not from you, none of them would be at all. They arise and sink; in their rising they begin to exist and grow toward their perfection, but once perfect they

32. See Mt 5:44; Lk 6:27.
33. I, 2,2.
34. See Ps 138(139):7.
35. See Ps 118(119):142; Jn 14:6.
36. See Ps 79:8(80:7).

grow old and perish; or, if not all reach old age, yet certainly all perish. So then, even as they arise and stretch out toward existence, the more quickly they grow and strive to be, the more swiftly they are hastening toward extinction. This is the law of their nature. You have endowed them so richly because they belong to a society of things that do not all exist at once, but in their passing away and succession together form a whole, of which the several creatures are parts. So is it with our speaking[37] as it proceeds by audible signs: it will not be a whole utterance unless one word dies away after making its syllables heard, and gives place to another.

Let my soul use these things to praise you,
O God, creator of them all,
but let it not be glued fast to them by sensual love,
for they are going whither they were always destined to go,
toward extinction;
and they rend my soul with death-dealing desires,
for it too longs to be, and loves to rest in what it loves.
But in them it finds no place to rest,
because they do not stand firm;
they are transient, and who can follow them with the senses of the body?
Or who can seize them, even near at hand?
Tardy is carnal perception, because it is carnal;
such is the law of its nature.
Sufficient it is for another purpose, for which it was made,
but insufficient to catch the fleeting things
that rush past from their appointed beginning
to their appointed end.
In your Word, through whom they are created,
they hear your command,
"From here begin, and thus far you shall go."

11, 16. Be not vain, my soul, and take care that the ear of your heart be not deafened by the din of your vanity.[38] You too must listen to the selfsame Word who calls you back, and there find a place of imperturbable quiet, where love is

---

37. *Sermo noster:* probably human language in general, but possibly his confession to God in this work. The transience of the sounds that make an intelligible whole was a favorite image with Augustine. In the present context he means that human sounds and words are as fleeting as all beautiful things; only the Word of God abides, as he goes on to say.
38. Compare the famous passage, X,27,38, where he confesses that God has penetrated his deafness.

never forsaken unless it chooses to forsake. See, those things go their way that others may succeed them, and that a whole may exist comprised of all its parts, though a lowly whole indeed. "But I," says the Word of God, "shall I depart to any place?" Fix your dwelling there,[39] my soul, lay up there for safe-keeping whatever you have thence received, if only because you are weary of deceits. Entrust to Truth whatever of truth is in you, and you will lose nothing; your rotten flesh will flower anew,[40] all your diseases will be healed,[41] all your labile elements will be restored and bound fast to you; they will not drag you with them in their own collapse, but will stand firm with you and abide, binding you to the ever-stable, abiding God.[42]

17. Why follow your flesh, perverted soul? Rather let it follow you, once you are converted. Whatever you experience through it is partial, and you do not know the whole, of which these experiences are but a part, although they give you pleasure. Were your carnal perception able to grasp the whole, were it not, for your punishment, confined to its due part of the whole, you would long for whatever exists only in the present to pass away, so that you might find greater joy in the totality. When with this same carnal perception you listen to human speech, you do not want to halt the succession of syllables: you want them to fly on their way and make room for others, so that you may hear the whole. So is it always with the constituent elements of a simple object, constituents which do not all exist simultaneously: in their entirety they give us greater pleasure, provided we can perceive them all together, than they do separately. But better still, better by far, is he who made all things. He is our God, who does not pass away, for there is nothing else to supplant him.

12, 18. If sensuous beauty delights you, praise God for the beauty of corporeal things, and channel the love you feel for them onto their Maker, lest the things that please you lead you to displease him. If kinship with other souls appeals to you, let them be loved in God, because they too are changeable and gain stability only when fixed in him; otherwise they would go their way and be lost. Let them be loved in him, and carry off to God as many of them as possible with you, and say to them:[43]

---

39. See Jn 14:23.
40. See Ps 27(28):7, which Augustine refers to the resurrection in his *Exposition of Psalm* 27,7.
41. See Mt 4:23; Ps 102(103):3.
42. See Ps 101:13(102:12); Heb 1:11; 1 Pt 1:23.
43. This central section of Book IV began with a prayer to God (10,15) and continues with Augustine's apostrophe to his own soul (11,16-12,19), but within this latter section he addresses other souls (12,18-19).

Let us love him, for he made these things and he is not far off,[44] for he did not make them and then go away: they are from him but also in him. You know where he is, because you know where truth tastes sweet. He is most intimately present to the human heart, but the heart has strayed from him. Return to your heart, then, you wrongdoers, and hold fast to him who made you. Stand with him and you will stand firm, rest in him and you will find peace. Where are you going, along your rough paths? Tell me, where are you going? The good which you love derives from him, and insofar as it is referred to him it is truly good and sweet, but anything that comes from him will justly turn bitter if it is unjustly loved by people who forsake him. Why persist in walking difficult and toilsome paths?[45] There is no repose where you are seeking it. Search as you like, it is not where you are looking. You are seeking a happy life in the realm of death, and it will not be found there. How could life be happy, where there is no life at all?

19. He who is our very life came down[46] and took our death upon himself. He slew our death by his abundant life and summoned us in a voice of thunder[47] to return to him in his hidden place, that place from which he set out to come to us when first he entered the Virgin's womb. There a human creature, mortal flesh, was wedded to him that it might not remain mortal for ever; and from there he came forth like a bridegroom from his nuptial chamber, leaping with joy like a giant to run his course.[48] Impatient of delay he ran, shouting by his words, his deeds, his death and his life, his descent to hell and his ascension to heaven,[49] shouting his demand that we return to him. Then he withdrew from our sight,[50] so that we might return to our own hearts and find him there. He withdrew, yet look, here he is. It was not his will to remain with us, yet he has not abandoned us either; for he has gone back to that place which he never left, because the world was made through him,

---

44. See Ps 99(100):3; Acts 17:27.
45. See Wis 5:7.
46. See Jn 6:33.
47. See I, 16, 25: Christ has now stolen Jove's thunder.
48. See Ps 18:6-7 (19:5). Patristic tradition interpreted this psalm as an allegory of the incarnation, by which divinity and humanity were married in the person of Christ. The idea was celebrated in a famous hymn (6,17-20) by Ambrose, which Augustine doubtless knew.
49. See Eph 4:8-9.
50. See Lk 24:51; Acts 1:9.

and though he was in this world he had made[51] he came into it to save sinners.[52] To him my soul confesses, and he heals this soul that has sinned against him.[53] O mortals, how long will you be heavy-hearted?[54] Life has come down to you, and are you reluctant to ascend and live? But what room is there for you to ascend, you with your high-flown ways and lofty talk?[55] Come down, that you may ascend, ascend even to God, for you have fallen in your attempts to ascend in defiance of God.

This is what you must tell them, to move them to tears in this valley of weeping,[56] and by this means carry them off with you to God, because if you burn with the fire of charity as you speak, you will be saying these things to them by his Spirit.

What is beauty? He writes a book

13, 20. Being ignorant of all this at the time, and in love with beautiful things below me, I was plunging into the depths. To my friends I would say, "Do we love anything save what is beautiful? And what is beautiful, then? Indeed, what is beauty? What is it that entices and attracts us in the things we love? Surely if beauty and loveliness of form were not present in them, they could not possibly appeal to us." I applied my mind to these questions and it struck me that in material objects there was both a quality inherent in the whole—beauty—and a different quality that was seemly in something that was harmoniously adapted to something else, as a part of the body to the whole, or a sandal to the foot, and other similar things. This realization welled up in my mind from my innermost heart, and I wrote some books entitled *The Beautiful and the Harmonious*, two or three books, I think—you know, O God, but it escapes me, for I no longer have them; they have somehow been lost.[57]

14, 21. What was it, O Lord my God, that prompted me to dedicate those books to an orator in Rome, Hierius? I did not know him personally, but I had come to esteem him for his splendid reputation for learning; I had also heard

---

51. See Jn 1:10-11.
52. See 1 Tm 1:15. The general shape of a baptismal profession of faith is discernible in this paragraph.
53. See Ps 40:5(41:4).
54. See Ps 4:3(2).
55. See Ps 72(73):9.
56. See Ps 83:7(84:6).
57. At the nadir of his fall, Augustine thought of himself as a lover of beauty. Much later, from a perspective given him by the life of grace, he deplored his tardiness in loving it: see X,27,38.

him quoted, and liked what I had heard. But what I liked still better was the fact that he found favor with others, people who extolled him highly and marveled that a Syrian, previously formed in Greek eloquence, had reached such eminence as a Latin orator and was at the same time so exceedingly learned in philosophical matters. When a man is praised, then, it is possible to love him, even in his absence: does this mean that love is transmitted from the mouth of the person who praises him to the heart of the listener? Certainly not; but one lover can be set on fire by another. We can truly love a person who is the subject of eulogy as long as we believe that the one who proclaims his merits is not doing so with intent to deceive: that is, that the person spoken of is being praised by one who loves him sincerely.

22. At that time I admired people simply because they were judged praise-worthy by others, not on the strength of any judgment of yours, O my God, by which no one is deceived. All the same, why was the esteem in which I held Hierius not like that evoked, say, by some noble charioteer, or a gladiator made widely famous by popular enthusiasm, but something far different, more serious, and akin to the commendation I hoped to win myself? I had no wish to be celebrated and loved in the way actors are, even though I myself celebrated and loved them; I would have preferred obscurity to notoriety like theirs, and would rather have been hated than loved in that manner. How can these contrasted and warring loves be carried in a single soul and balanced against each other? How can I love in another what I loathe and ward off from myself, and this when both of us are human? A good horse can be admired by someone who would not want to be a horse himself, even if he could; but the case is different with an actor, for he shares our own nature. Do I then love in another man what I would hate to be myself, when I too am a man? A human being is an immense abyss, but you, Lord, keep count even of his hairs,[58] and not one of them is lost in you; yet even his hairs are easier to number than the affections and movements of his heart.

23. This orator, however, was the sort of man I loved in the sense of wanting to be like him. I was driven off course by my pride and tossed about by every wind,[59] for your guidance of me was very unobtrusive. How do I know, how can I confess to you with such certainty, that I had come to love him more for the love he aroused in those who sang his praises than for the achievements by which he won them? I know it because if, instead of praising him, those same people had recounted his

---

58. See Mt 10:30.
59. See Eph 4:14.

deeds with disparagement and contempt, I would not have warmed to him or felt any interest; and yet neither the facts nor the man himself would have been different; the difference would have lain only in the attitude of those who related them. To such weakness is a soul reduced when it is not yet anchored in the solid ground of truth. It is tossed and turned, whirled and spun, by every breath of opinion from the mouths of those who think they know, its light is obscured by clouds and it cannot see the truth. But look! Truth is straight ahead of us.

Accordingly I set great store by bringing my oratory and my research to this man's notice. If he approved them I would glow with satisfaction, but if he did not, a heart vain and empty for lack of your solid strength would be wounded. But I continued to enjoy turning over in my mind the question of the beautiful and the harmonious about which I had written to him; I considered it with a contemplative eye and admired it, although no one shared my appreciation.

15, 24. I did not yet see that the whole vast question hinged on your artistry,[60] almighty God, who alone work wonders.[61] My mind scanned material forms, and I defined and distinguished what was beautiful in itself from what was harmonious because fittingly adapted to something else, supporting my distinction with material examples. I turned to the nature of the soul, but here I was balked by the false opinion which I held concerning spiritual entities, and unable to discern the truth. Truth was thrusting itself upon me, staring me in the face, but I averted my trembling thought from incorporeal reality and looked instead toward shapes and colors and distended mass, and, since in the soul I could not see these, concluded that I was not able to see the soul. I loved the peace that accompanied virtue, and hated the discord inseparable from a vicious way of life, and I observed that in the former unity was to be found, but in the latter fragmentation. Hence it appeared to me that unity, in which the rational mind subsisted, was itself the essence of truth and of the supreme good, whereas I believed that in disintegration some indefinable substance of irrational life was to be found, which was the essence of supreme evil. I thought this to be not only a substantial reality but also life in the fullest

---

60. *In arte tua*, probably a reference to the second person of the Trinity in the mind of the mature Augustine who wrote *The Confessions*. From this later perspective his lost work, *The Beautiful and the Harmonious*, which he discusses here, could be seen as an early attempt to trace the manifestations of the second and third persons in creation.

61. See Pss 71(72):18; 135(136):4.

sense—life not derived from you, my God, from whom are all things.[62] This was my opinion, wretch that I was.[63] I called the unity "Monad," conceiving it as a sexless soul; but the other I called "Dyad," to include the anger that issues in crimes and the self-indulgent cravings that lead to vice. But I did not understand what I was talking about. I did not know, never having learned, that evil is no substance at all, and that our mind is not the supreme, immutable good.[64]

25. When the impetuous power of the soul is viciously inclined, and it swaggers in mutinous, insolent pride, violent crimes are the outcome; when that appetite of the soul which thirsts for carnal pleasures is not moderated, vices are the result; so too, if the rational mind itself is vicious, errors and wrong-headed opinions corrupt our life. Such was the condition of my mind at this time. I did not realize that it needed to be open to the radiance of another light in order to become a partaker in the truth, for it is not itself the essence of truth. Rather it is you, Lord, who will light my lamp: O God, you will illuminate my darkness[65] and from your fullness we have all received.[66] For you are *the true light, which illumines every human person who comes into this world,*[67] and in you *there is no variation, no play of changing shadow.*[68]

26. Instead I was striving to reach you by my own efforts, and you thrust me away to taste death, because you *thwart the proud.*[69] What could be prouder than my outlandish delusion, whereby I laid claim to be by nature what you are? I was subject to change, as was obvious to me from the fact that I was clearly seeking to be wise in order to change for the better, yet I was prepared even to think you changeable rather than admit that I was not what you are. Therefore I was thrust away, and you thwarted my puffed-up obstinacy. I conjured up material forms in my imagination, and I who was flesh disparaged the flesh, for I was *a roving spirit that had not yet*

---

62. See Rom 11:36; 1 Cor 8:6.
63. Augustine's first, fumbling attempt to make a philosophical ascent from creatures to God comes to grief because he cannot grasp the notion of purely immaterial reality: the nature of the soul eludes him, so he cannot go further. Much later he will know that God is unity; here he imagines that unity must be God.
64. The terms "Monad" and "Dyad" derived from Pythagoras but were well known in fifth-century Africa. Augustine apparently tried to reformulate the mythological doctrines of his Manicheanism in terms more acceptable to his own intelligence and that of his hearers.
65. See Ps 17:29(18:28).
66. See Jn 1:16.
67. Jn 1:9.
68. Jas 1:17.
69. Jas 4:6; 1 Pt 5:5.

returned to you.[70] I persisted in walking after things that had no existence either in you or in me or in any creature, ideas not created for me by your truth but invented in material shape by my own vanity. To your little ones,[71] faithful Christians and my fellow-citizens,[72] from whom I was unwittingly exiled, I babbled away in my petulant fashion, asking, "If God made the soul, why does it fall into error?" But I did not like to hear in reply, "On your showing, we might ask why God falls into error." I was readier to assert that your immutable substance had been forced into error[73] than to confess that my own mutable substance had gone astray by its own will, and that its error was its punishment.

27. I was about twenty-six or twenty-seven when I wrote those volumes.[74] The materialistic images on which I was speculating set up a din in the ears of my heart, ears which were straining to catch your inner melody, O gentle Truth. I was thinking about the beautiful and the harmonious, and longing to stand and hear you, that my joy might be perfect at the sound of the Bridegroom's voice,[75] but I could not, because I was carried off outside myself by the clamor of my errors, and I fell low, dragged down by the weight of my pride. No joy and gladness from you reached my ears, nor did my bones exult, for they had not yet been humbled.[76]

He reads Aristotle's Categories

16, 28. When I was about twenty a certain writing of Aristotle had been put into my hands, entitled *The Ten Categories*. What a proud mouthful it was when my rhetoric master at Carthage, and others reputedly learned, rattled off the list of them! At the very name of the book I would hang on his words agape, as though expecting some important divine revelation. Yet I read them in private and understood them, though I wonder now what profit that was to me.[77] When I compared notes with other students, who admitted that they had scarcely understood the *Categories* from the

---

70. Ps 77(78):39; See Prv 2:19.
71. See Mt 11:25.
72. That is, proleptically so, according to the usual interpretation, those who will be his companions in the city of God; but some think he means his fellow-citizens at Thagaste.
73. The Manichean Light-Deity was not omnipotent.
74. If precise, this indication would place the work between November 380 and November 382, toward the end of his nine years as a Manichee.
75. See Jn 3:29.
76. See Ps 50:10(51:8).
77. See Eccl 2:15.

most expert masters—masters who not only gave oral instruction but even drew plenty of diagrams in the dust—I found that they were unable to tell me anything that I had not already grasped from my private reading. The categories seemed clear enough to me as they spoke of substances (a man, for example) and of accidents inhering in them, such as his appearance (what he is like), his stature (how many feet high), his relationship (whose brother), where he is, when he was born, his posture (standing or sitting), whether he is wearing sandals or is armed, whether he is doing anything or whether anything is being done to him; or spoke of any of the innumerable attributes to be found in any of these nine catgories, a few of which I have mentioned by way of example, or in the main genus of substance.

29. What profit had it been to me? Supposing that these ten predicates covered everything that exists, I mistakenly attempted to understand even you, my God, in terms of them, you who are wonderfully simple and changeless, imagining that you were the subject of your greatness and beauty, and that those attributes inhered in you as in their subject, as they might in a material thing. I did not realize that you are yourself identical with your greatness and beauty, whereas a material thing is not great and beautiful simply because it is that thing, because even if it were smaller or less beautiful it would still be the material thing it is. No, the reading had been no profit to me—a hindrance, rather. My conclusions about you were falsehood, not truth, the figments of my misery, not the firmament of your happiness. As you had commanded, so did it befall me: the earth brought forth thorns and thistles for me, and I garnered my bread by much labor.[78]

30. Furthermore, what profit was it to me that I, rascally slave of selfish ambitions that I was, read and understood by myself as many books as I could get concerning the so-called liberal arts? I enjoyed these, not recognizing the source of whatever elements of truth and certainty they contained. I had turned my back to the light and my face to the things it illuminated, and so no light played upon my own face, or on the eyes that perceived them.[79] Whatever I understood of the arts of grammar and rhet-

---

78. See Gn 3:18-19.

79. This striking metaphor recalls Plotinus, *Enneads* V,5,7,16-19. See also *their faces*, II,3,6. In Jer 2:27 the phrase occurs in the context of a denunciation of pagan practices and, by implication, sacrifice to false gods; and here too Augustine says he was not offering to God the sacrifice of his intellect.

oric, of dialectic, geometry, music and arithmetic,[80] without much difficulty or tuition from anyone, I understood because my swift intelligence and keen wits were your gift; you know it, O Lord my God. Yet from this gift I offered you no sacrifice. It therefore worked not to my advantage but rather to my harm, because I took care that this excellent part of my substance[81] should be under my own control, and I did not guard my strength by approaching you,[82] but left you and set out for a distant land to squander it there on the quest for meretricious gratifications. What profit was this good gift to me when I failed to use it well? It only made me less able to appreciate how very difficult these liberal arts were for even the most zealous and clever to understand. I found this out only when I tried to expound them to my pupils, among whom only the brightest could follow my explanation without dragging.

31. But what profit was that to me, since I supposed that you, my God, you who are truth, were an immense, luminous body, and that I was a particle of it? What outrageous perversity! But that is what I was like, and I am not ashamed to confess to you your own deeds of mercy toward me and to invoke you, my God, since I was not ashamed then to profess to my human hearers my own blasphemous views and to bay doglike against you. What profit to me then was the ingenuity that nimbly picked its way amid those teachings, and the plethora of intricate books I had unraveled without human tuition to support me, if I was crippled and led astray by sacrilegious depravity where the teachings of true godliness were concerned? On the other hand, what disadvantage was it to your little ones that they were much more slow-minded than I? They did not forsake you, but stayed safely in the nest of your Church[83] to grow their plumage and strengthen the wings of their charity on the wholesome nourishment of the faith.[84]

---

80. An incomplete list of the traditional seven.
81. *Tam bonum substantiae meae*: more idiomatically "of my character," "of my make-up"; but the Vulgate version of Lk 15:12-13 uses *substantia* for the father's fortune, shared with, and dissipated by, his prodigal son. This latter is certainly referred to in the following lines.
82. See Ps 58:10(59:9). Augustine's comment on this verse in *Exposition of Psalm* 58,1,18 clarifies the present passage: "I will guard my strength by approaching you, because if I leave you, I fall; but if I draw near, I grow stronger.... There is a land of unchangeable truth, and if the soul moves away from it, it is darkened; but when it approaches, it is illumined. I will guard my strength, then, by approaching you; I will not leave you or trust in myself."
83. See Ps 83:4(84:3).
84. See Jb 39:26.

O Lord our God,
grant us to trust in your overshadowing wings:
protect us beneath them and bear us up.[85]
You will carry us as little children,
and even to our grey-headed age you will carry us still.[86]
When you are our strong security, that is strength indeed,
but when our security is in ourselves, that is but weakness.
Our good abides ever in your keeping,
but in diverting our steps from you we have grown perverse.
Let us turn back to you at last, Lord, that we be not overturned.
Unspoilt, our good abides with you,
for you are yourself our good.
We need not fear to find no home again
because we have fallen away from it;
while we are absent our home falls not to ruins,
for our home is your eternity.

---

85. The imagery seems to originate in the great wings of the cherubs overspreading the mercy-seat (see Ex 25:17-21), but is widely used in the psalms: see Pss 16(17):8; 35:8(36:7); 56:2(57:1); 60:5(61:4); 62:8(63:7); 90:(91):4; see also Mt 23:37.
86. See Ex 19:4; Dt 32:11; Is 46:4.

Book V

Faustus at Carthage,
Augustine to Rome and Milan

1, 1. Accept the sacrifice of my confessions, offered to you by the power of this tongue of mine which you have fashioned and aroused to confess to your name;[1] bring healing to all my bones[2] and let them exclaim, *Lord, who is like you?*[3] A person who confesses to you is not informing you about what goes on within him, for a closed heart does not shut you out, nor is your hand pushed away by human obduracy; you melt it when you choose, whether by showing mercy or by enforcing your claim, and from your fiery heat no one can hide.[4]

But allow my soul to give you glory that it may love you the more, and let it confess to you your own merciful dealings,[5] that it may give you glory. Your whole creation never wearies of praising you, never falls silent; never a breath from the mouth[6] of one who turns to you but gives you glory, never is praise lacking from the universe of living creatures and corporeal beings as they laud you through the mouths of those who contemplate them. Supported by these things you have made let the human soul rise above its weariness and pass through these creatures to

---

1. See Prv 18:21. In *The City of God*, X,5-6, Augustine expressed his most mature thought on the nature of sacrifice: "A visible sacrifice is the sacrament, or sacred sign, of the sacrifice which is unseen.... True sacrifice is any work which is done so that we may cleave to God in holy fellowship.... When the soul offers itself to God in such a way that, inflamed by his love, it lets go worldly concupiscence and subjects itself to God as to the unchangeable pattern of its being, and hence becomes pleasing to him as sharing in his beauty, then the soul itself becomes a sacrifice."
2. See Ps 6:3(2).
3. Ps 34(35):10.
4. See Ps 18:7(19:6).
5. See Ps 106(107):8, and recurrently.
6. See Ps 150:7(6).

you, who have made them so wonderfully. There it will find refreshment, there is its true strength.

2, 2. Wicked, restless folk may go their way and flee from you as they will. You see them, for your eyes pierce their darkness, and how lovely is the whole of which they are part, lovely though they are foul![7] And how have they harmed you? Have they in any point brought your rule into disrepute, that rule which is just and perfect from highest heaven to the lowest of creatures? Where have they fled, in fleeing from your face? Is there any place where you cannot find them?[8] They have fled all the same, to avoid seeing you who see them, and so in their blindness they have stumbled over you—for you abandon nothing you have made; yes, stumbled over you, these unjust folk, and justly hurt themselves; for they distanced themselves from your gentleness only to trip over your probity and fall upon the rough edges of your anger.[9] Clearly they do not know that you are everywhere, for you are not confined to any place, and you alone are present to those who run far away from you.

Let them turn back, and seek you,
for you do not forsake your creation
as they have forsaken their creator.
Let them only turn back,
see! there you are in their hearts,
in the hearts of all those who confess to you,
who fling themselves into your arms and weep against your breast
after their difficult journey,
while you so easily will wipe away their tears.[10]
At this they weep the more,
yet even their laments are matter for joy,
because you, Lord, are not some human being of flesh and blood,
but the Lord who made them,
and now make them anew and comfort them.

And what of myself: where was I as I sought you? You were straight ahead of me, but I had roamed away from myself and could not find even myself, let alone you!

---

7. In the sense that black can be used in a painting to enhance the beauty of the whole: Augustine suggests this idea in *The City of God*, XI,23, as Plotinus also had done in *Enneads* III,2,11,10.
8. See Ps 138(139):7-8.
9. Echoes of Rom 11:7-11.
10. See Is 25:8; Rv 7:17; 21:4.

Augustine hopes to question Faustus

3, 3. Now, in my God's presence, I will describe my twenty-ninth year.[11] A certain Manichean bishop, Faustus by name,[12] had lately arrived in Carthage. He was a lethal trap set by the devil. Many people were ensnared by the persuasive sweetness of his eloquence, and I too was ready to admire it, but I was beginning to distinguish it from the truth I hungered to learn. What interested me was not the dainty verbal dish on which he served his offerings, this Faustus of such high renown, but how much knowledge he could provide for me to eat; for I had been told earlier how extremely well informed he was in all branches of reputable scholarship, and how particularly learned in the liberal arts.

Now, I had read widely in the works of philosophers, committed a good deal to memory and still retained it, and I began to compare certain elements from my reading with the long-winded myths of the Manichees. The philosphers' conclusions seemed to me more probable, since these men had been clever enough to make calculations about the world, even though they were quite unsuccessful in discovering its Lord.[13] For great are you, Lord, and you look kindly on what is humble, but the lofty-minded you regard from afar.[14] Only to those whose hearts are crushed do you draw close.[15] You will not let yourself be found by the proud, nor even by those who in their inquisitive skill count stars or grains of sand, or measure the expanses of heaven, or trace the paths of planets.

Valid observations of the natural world by "philosophers"

4. With their intellect and the intelligence you have given them they investigate these things, and so they have discovered much, and predicted eclipses of the sun's light, or the moon's, many years in advance, indicating precisely the day, the hour, and the extent of the eclipse. And their calculations have been accurate. It has therefore been possible for them to make forecasts and draw up rules from their research. On the basis of these rules, which are still studied today, it can be predicted in which year, in

---

11. That is, 13 November 382 to 13 November 383.
12. That is, "The Lucky One."
13. See Wis 13:8-9; Rom 1:18-25, which underlie the following paragraphs.
14. See Ps 137(138):6.
15. See Ps 33:19(34:18).

which month, on which day of the month and at what hour an eclipse will occur, and what proportion of its light the sun or moon will lose. And, as forecast, it happens. People think this wonderful: those who are ignorant of such matters are dumbfounded, while the experts strut and make merry. In their impious pride they draw away from you and lose your light, because these scholars who foresee a future eclipse of the sun long beforehand fail to see their own in the present, for want of inquiring in a religious spirit from whom they have received the very intelligence which enables them to inquire into these phenomena. If they discover that you have made them, they do not give themselves to you so that you may preserve what you have made, nor do they slay in your honor those selves of their own making, nor immolate their high-flown pride as though it were a sacrifice of birds, nor make into an offering of fish that curiosity whereby they walk the secret pathways of the deep, nor sacrifice their self-indulgent habits like beasts of the field,[16] so that you, O God, who are a devouring fire,[17] may consume their dead ambitions and re-create the seekers for eternal life.

5. They do not know him who is the Way,[18] your Word through whom you made[19] those very things they are reckoning, together with themselves who do the reckoning, and the senses with which they perceive the things they reckon, and the mind with which they reckon; yet your wisdom is beyond reckoning.[20] Your only-begotten Son has become our wisdom, our righteousness and our sanctification,[21] yet he was reckoned as one of us and paid tribute to Caesar. They do not know him as the Way whereby they can climb down from their lofty selves to him, and thus by him ascend to him. Of this Way they know nothing; they think themselves exalted to the stars and brilliant. But they have crashed down to earth[22] and their foolish hearts are darkened.[23] Many true statements do they make about creation, but they do not find the Truth who is artificer of creation because they do not seek him with reverence. Or, if they do find him and recognize God, they do not honor him as God or give him thanks; their reasoning grows

---

16. See 1 Jn 2:16.
17. See Dt 4:24; Heb 12:29.
18. See Jn 14:6.
19. See Jn 1:3.
20. See Ps 146(147):5.
21. See 1 Cor 1:30.
22. See Is 14:12-13.
23. See Rom 1:21-25, here and in the following lines.

unsound as they claim to be wise and arrogate to themselves what is yours. This in turn leads them into an extreme of blind perversity, where they will even ascribe to you what is theirs, blaming you, who are Truth, for their own lies, and changing the glory of the incorruptible God into the likeness of corruptible humans, or birds or four-footed beasts or crawling things. They distort truth into a lie, and they worship and serve the creature instead of the creator.

6. For all that, I kept in mind many true conclusions which they had drawn from creation itself, and I saw that these could be verified by calculation, by observing the succession of the seasons and by the visible evidence of the stars. I then compared them with the assertions of Mani, who had written voluminously (and incoherently) on these subjects. What I read there was confirmed neither by any rational account of solstices and equinoxes and eclipses, nor by anything else of this kind that I had learned from books of secular philosophy. I was simply bidden to believe, and what I was required to believe did not correspond to the rational explanations I had worked out and discovered by my own observations; in fact there was a wide discrepancy.

4, 7. Lord God of truth, it surely cannot be that simply knowing these things renders a person pleasing to you? Unhappy is anyone who knows it all but does not know you, whereas one who knows you is blessed, even if ignorant of all these. Nor is anyone who knows both you and them more blessed for knowing them, but blessed on your account alone, provided that such a person recognizes you as you are, and glorifies you and gives you thanks, and does not drift off into unsound reasoning. Someone who knows enough to become the owner of a tree, and gives thanks to you for the benefits it brings him, is in a better state, even if ignorant of its height in feet and the extent of its spread, than another who measures and counts all its branches but neither owns it nor knows its creator nor loves him.[24] Similarly a person who lives by faith owns the whole world's wealth, for though he may have nothing he possesses all things if he but clings to you,[25] the master of them all: he may have scanty acquaintance with the wheeling paths of the Great Bear, yet it would be foolish to doubt that he is better off than a man who measures the sky and numbers the stars and

---

24. The verbs "measures," "counts" and "loves" prepare for the allusion to Wis 11:21 below.
25. See 2 Cor 6:10.

weighs the elements, yet leaves you out of his reckoning, you who have disposed all things according to measure and number and weight.[26]

Manichean assertions about natural phenomena are astray

5, 8. Who ever thought of asking some fellow called Mani to write on these subjects? People could perfectly well have learned true piety without any such expertise. Your advice to us is, *Reverence for God, that is true wisdom.*[27] Obviously Mani might have been thoroughly conversant with scientific truths, even if a stranger to piety. In fact, however, he was ignorant of them, but still had the effrontery to teach them, and from this it emerges that he knew nothing about piety either; for to profess these theories about the world is a mark of vanity, whereas piety is proved by confession to you. It was providential that this man talked so much about scientific subjects, and got it wrong, because this gave people who had truly studied them the chance to convict him of error; and then by implication his insight into other, more recondite matters could be clearly assessed. Mani was content with no modest evaluation: he tried to persuade his followers that the Holy Spirit, who comforts your faithful people and enriches them with his gifts, was with full authority present in him personally. It followed, therefore, that when he was caught out in untrue statements about the sky and the stars, or the changes in sun or moon, his presumption was plainly revealed as sacrilegious, because although these matters are not directly relevant to religious doctrine, he was not simply discoursing on things of which he was ignorant, but even, in his insane, pretentious vanity, passing off his erroneous opinions as those of a divine person—himself, no less.

9. When I hear one or other of my fellow-Christians expressing a mistaken opinion arising from his ignorance in these fields, I regard with tolerance the person who entertains the notion. As long as he does not believe anything unseemly about you, O Lord, creator of all things, I do not see that it does him any harm if he chances to be ignorant of the position or characteristics of a material creature. It does harm him, however, if he thinks his view forms an essential part of our doctrine and belief, and

---

26. See Wis 11:21, which text was significant for Augustine's idea of the structure of created being. The image of the Trinity is imprinted on creation.
27. Jb 28:28.

presumes to go on obstinately making assertions about what he does not know. Yet when this kind of weakness occurs while faith is in its cradle, our mother, charity, bears with it, looking forward to the day when newly-created humanity will grow to the stature of perfect manhood, and no longer be tossed about by every gust of teaching.[28]

The case was quite different with a man who set himself up as a teacher and writer, and as the leader and principal guide of those to whom he propounded his views, and this so persuasively that his disciples thought they were following no ordinary man but your Holy Spirit. If ever such a man were proved to have spoken untruly, could anyone doubt that he must have been grossly deranged, and that his ideas were abhorrent, and to be rejected outright?

I, however, had not yet clearly determined whether variations in the length of day and night, eclipses of the moon and the sun, and similar phenomena of which I had read in other books could be explained equally well by his account of them. If by chance they could, it would still be possible for me to keep open the question of whether his version or theirs more plausibly represented things as they really were, and thus to prefer his authority as a guide to my faith, on the grounds of his alleged holiness.

Augustine is disappointed in Faustus

6, 10. All through that period of about nine years, during which I was spiritually adrift as a hearer among the Manichees, I had been awaiting the arrival of this Faustus with an expectancy that had been at full stretch too long. Whenever I had been in contact with others of the sect, and their replies to the questions I raised on these topics failed to satisfy me, they would put me off with promises about him. Once he had arrived, they assured me, and I had an opportunity to discuss things with him, these points, together with any more serious problems I might raise, would quite easily be sorted out and resolved. When he came, then, he did indeed impress me as a man of pleasant and smooth speech, who chattered on the usual themes much more beguilingly than the rest. A man adept at serving finer wines, then; but what was that to me in my thirst? My ears were sated with such offerings already. The content did not seem better to me for being better presented, nor true because skillfully expressed, nor the man

---

28. See Eph 4:24; 4:13-14.

wise of soul because he had a handsome face and a graceful turn of speech. Those who had held out promises to me were not good judges; to them he seemed wise and prudent merely because they enjoyed the way he talked. But I realized that there were people of a different stamp who doubted even the possibility of truth, and were unwilling to trust anything conveyed in elegant and fluent style.

For some time, though, you had been teaching me in wondrous, hidden ways, my God (and I believe what you have taught me because it is true; there is no other teacher of truth except you, though teachers aplenty have made a name for themselves in many a place); so I had already learned under your tuition that nothing should be regarded as true because it is eloquently stated, nor false because the words sound clumsy. On the other hand, it is not true for being expressed in uncouth language either, nor false because couched in splendid words. I had come to understand that just as wholesome and rubbishy food may both be served equally well in sophisticated dishes or in others of rustic quality, so too can wisdom and foolishness be proffered in language elegant or plain.

11. After waiting so long and so eagerly for this man, I was certainly delighted with his lively and spirited style in debate, and by his apt choice of words to clothe his thought, words that came to him readily. Yes, I was delighted, and along with others I praised and extolled him; indeed, I was in the forefront of those who did so. But I was annoyed that amid the crowd who went to hear him I was unable to catch his attention or share my anxious questionings with him in intimate conversation and the give and take of discussion. If ever I did succeed in gaining a hearing with him in the company of intimate friends and at a time which was not unsuitable for an exchange of ideas, and I put to him some of the problems that preoccupied me, then, before even coming to anything deeper, what I found was a man ill-educated in the liberal arts, apart from grammar, and even in that schooled only to an average level. He had read a few of Cicero's speeches and one or two books by Seneca, and some volumes fairly well written in Latin for his own sect, and because in addition to this he was accustomed to preach daily, he had acquired a fair command of language, which was rendered the more glib and seductive by his skillful management of what ability he had and a certain natural charm.[29]

---

29. In about 397/399, just after writing *The Confessions*, Augustine wrote his main refutation of Manicheanism in the form of a polemic against Faustus' version of it, the *Answer to Faustus, a Manichean.*

Is my recollection not accurate, Lord God, judge of my conscience? My heart and my memory of these things lie open before you,[30] who were leading me by your hidden, secret providence, and were already bringing my shameful errors round in front of my face,[31] that I might see and hate them.

7, 12. Once it had become sufficiently clear to me that he was poorly informed about the very disciplines in which I had believed him to excel, I began to give up hope that he could elucidate and clear up for me the problems with which I was concerned. To be sure, he could have been ignorant about these and still have had a grasp of religious truth, but only on condition of not being a Manichee. Their books are full of interminable myths concerning sky, stars, sun and moon, and it had been my earnest wish that by comparing these with the numerical calculations I had read elsewhere he would demonstrate to me that the phenomena in question could be more plausibly explained by the account given in Mani's books, or at least that an equally valid explanation could be found there; but now I no longer deemed him capable of explaining these things to me with any precision.

I must say, however, that when I raised these points for consideration and discussion he refused courteously enough, reluctant to risk taking on that burden; for he knew that he did not know about these matters, and was not ashamed to admit it. He was not one of the talkative kind, of whom I had suffered many, who tried to teach me but said nothing. His heart was, if not right with you,[32] yet not without discretion. He was not altogether unaware of his own lack of awareness and was unwilling to enter rashly into argument that might leave him cornered, with no way out and no easy means of retracting. This attitude endeared him to me all the more, for the restraint of a mind that admits its limitations is more beautiful than the beautiful things about which I desired to learn. I found him consistent in this approach to all the more difficult and subtle questions.

13. The keen attention I had directed toward Mani's writings was therefore rebuffed, for I felt more hopeless than ever in respect of their other teachers now that this man, for all his reputation,[33] had turned out to be so incompetent in many of the subjects that mattered to me. I began to spend

---

30. See Num 10:9.
31. See Ps 49(50):21, and IV,16,30.
32. See Ps 77(78):37; Acts 8:21.
33. *Ille nominatus*: either "this man of renown" or, possibly, with a punning allusion to the name Faustus, "this man with the lucky name."

much time in his company on account of his ardent enthusiasm for the literature that I, as a master of rhetoric, was teaching to the young men of Carthage, and thereafter I fell into the habit of reading with him any works which he had heard of and wished to study, or which were, in my judgment, suited to his ability. Apart from this, all the plans I had formed for advancement in the sect lapsed into oblivion now that I had come to know this man: not that I severed my connection with it entirely, but since I had found nothing better than this sect into which I had more or less blundered, I resolved to be content with it for the time being, unless some preferable option presented itself.

Thus it came about that this Faustus, who was a death-trap for many, unwittingly and without intending it began to spring the trap in which I was caught, for thanks to your hidden providence, O my God, your hands did not let go of my soul. Through my mother's tears the sacrifice of her heart's blood was being offered to you day after day, night after night, for my welfare; and you dealt with me in wondrous ways. You, my God, you it was who dealt so with me; for *our steps are directed by the Lord, and our way is of his choosing.*[34] What other provision is there for our salvation, but your hand that remakes what you have made?

Indiscipline among his students prompts move to Rome

8, 14. You dealt with me in such a way that I was persuaded to move to Rome, to teach there instead what I had been teaching at Carthage. I must not omit to confess to you the reasons why I was so persuaded, because in them your deep, secret providence was at work, and your ever-present mercy, and these are to be pondered and proclaimed. I did not want to go to Rome because my friends promised me that there I would command higher fees and enjoy greater prestige—though these arguments were not without force for me; the principal and almost the sole reason was that I heard that young men there study more quietly and are controlled by a more systematic regime of strict discipline to prevent them from rushing pell-mell and at random into the school of a teacher with whom they are not enrolled; in fact they are not admitted at all except by his permission. At Carthage things are very different: the unbridled licentiousness of the

---

34. Ps 36(37):23.

students is disgusting. Looking almost like madmen they burst in reck-lessly and disrupt the discipline each master has established to ensure that his pupils make progress. With boorishness that defies belief they commit many acts of violence which would attract legal penalties if custom did not seem to plead in their defense; yet this in itself proves that the perpetrators are the more to be pitied, inasmuch as they do with apparent legality what will never be permitted by your eternal law, and think they are acting so with impunity, whereas the very blindness that dictates their behavior is itself their punishment, and they suffer far worse damage themselves than they inflict on others.

Accordingly while teaching these youths I was being forced to endure those very forms of misconduct I had been chary of adopting myself in my student days; and I decided to depart for a place where, by all accounts, such things did not happen.

But in truth it was you, *my hope and my inheritance in the country of the living,*[35] who for my soul's salvation prompted me to change my country, and to this end you provided both the goads at Carthage that dislodged me from there and the allurements at Rome that attracted me; and this you did through the lovers of a life that is no more than death, who on the one hand behaved insanely and on the other held out to me vain promises. To bring my steps back to the straight path you secretly made use of both their perversity and mine; for those who disturbed my tranquillity were blinded by disgusting frenzy, while those who invited me elsewhere were wise only in the things of this earthly country,[36] while I, for my part, loathed real misery in the one place and craved spurious happiness in the other.

Monica's opposition; Augustine departs by stealth

15. You knew all along, O God, the real reason why I left to seek a different country, but you did not reveal it either to me or to my mother, who bitterly bewailed my departure and followed me to the seashore. She held on to me with all her strength, attempting either to take me back home with her or to come with me, but I deceived her, pretending that I did not

---

35. Ps 141:6 (142:5).
36. See Phil 3:18-19, a description which seems to fit the Manichees, who were *enemies of Christ's cross* (believing the crucifixion to be a phantasm), and *made a god of their bellies* in the sense derided by Augustine at III,10,18; IV,1,1. Augustine's Manichean connections probably helped him to establish himself in Rome.

want to take leave of a friend until a favorable wind should arise and enable him to set sail. I lied to my mother, my incomparable mother! But I went free, because in your mercy you forgave me. Full of detestable filth as I was, you kept me safe from the waters of the sea to bring me to the water of your grace; once I was washed in that, the rivers of tears that flowed from my mother's eyes would be dried up, those tears with which day by day she bedewed the ground wherever she prayed to you for me.

At the time, however, she refused to go home, and it was only with difficulty that I persuaded her to spend the night in a place very near our ship, a memorial chapel to Blessed Cyprian.[37] That same night I left by stealth; she did not, but remained behind praying and weeping. And what was she begging of you, my God, with such abundant tears? Surely, that you would not allow me to sail away. But in your deep wisdom you acted in her truest interests: you listened to the real nub of her longing and took no heed of what she was asking at this particular moment, for you meant to make me into what she was asking for all the time. So the wind blew for us and filled our sails, and the shore dropped away from our sight as she stood there at morning light mad with grief,[38] filling your ears with complaints and groans.

You took no heed, for you were snatching me away, using my lusts to put an end to them and chastising her too-carnal desire with the scourge of sorrow. Like all mothers, though far more than most, she loved to have me with her, and she did not know how much joy you were to create for her through my absence. She did not know, and so she wept and wailed, and these cries of pain revealed what there was left of Eve in her, as in anguish she sought the son whom in anguish she had brought to birth.[39] Yet when she had finished blaming my deception and cruelty, she resumed her entreaties for me, and returned to her accustomed haunts, while I went to Rome.[40]

---

37. Cyprian, bishop of Carthage, champion of the unity of the Church, had been martyred under Valerian in 258. Augustine was to be much influenced by his writings and his memory, and would later preach at Cyprian's shrines.
38. The parallel with Dido, left on the shore by Aeneas, is surely conscious and deliberate, though the outcome in the two cases was very different.
39. See Gn 3:16.
40. Probably in 383.

Illness in Rome; Manichean contacts

9, 16. For me too a scourge was waiting there, in the guise of a bodily illness that brought me to death's door loaded with all the sins I had committed against you, against myself and against other people, evil deeds many and grievous over and above the original sin that binds all of us who die in Adam.[41] For no single one of them had you pardoned me in Christ: he had not broken down the barrier of enmity[42] I had piled up against you by my sins, for how could the crucifixion of a phantom do that for me? And that was all I thought he was. The more illusory for me was his death in the flesh, the more real was the death of my soul. But in truth his bodily death was real; it was my unbelieving soul that was living on illusion. My fever worsened. I was on my way to perdition; for where should I have gone, if I had departed at this time? Inevitably to the fire and torments[43] my deeds deserved, according to your just ordinance.

Meanwhile my mother, who knew nothing of this, persevered in praying for me; she was far away, but you are present everywhere, so you heard her in that land where she was, and took pity on me where I was. I recovered my bodily health, though I remained sick in my sacrilegious heart. Even in that dire peril I had no desire for your baptism; better had been my state in boyhood when I begged for it from my loving mother, as I have recalled and confessed already. But I had meanwhile grown up into my disgraceful condition, and like one demented had fallen into the habit of mocking your healing prescriptions, though it was you who now had saved me from dying in that state and so incurring a twofold death.[44] If a blow like that had struck my mother's heart, she would never have recovered. I can find no words to express how intensely she loved me: with far more anxious solicitude did she give birth to me in the spirit than ever she had in the flesh.

17. I cannot see, therefore, how she could possibly have been healed if so terrible a death had overtaken me, and transfixed her too in the tenderest depths of her loving heart. Where would her passionate prayers have gone, those prayers so frequently, so ceaselessly offered?[45] Nowhere, surely, if

---

41. See 1 Cor 15:22.
42. See Eph 2:14-16.
43. See Mt 25:41.
44. See Rv 20:6,14; 21:8, the "second death."
45. See 1 Thes 5:17.

not into your keeping; and would you, O God of all mercy,[46] spurn the broken, humbled heart[47] of a chaste and temperate widow who was untiring in her acts of charity,[48] attentive to the needs of your saints and faithful in serving them? Never a day would pass but she was careful to make her offering at your altar. Twice a day, at morning and evening, she was unfailingly present in your church, not for gossip or old wives' tales but so that she might hearken to your words, as you to her prayers. Could you, then, whose grace had made her what she was, disdain those tears and rebuff her plea for your aid, when what she tearfully begged from you was not gold or silver, not some insecure, ephemeral advantage, but the salvation of her son? No, Lord, that would have been unthinkable; rather you were present, you heard her, and you acted: it was done as you had predestined that it should be. Could you have deceived her in those visions and assurances you had given her, those I have already recorded and others not mentioned, to which she held fast in her faithful heart and which she regularly in prayer presented for your attention, as pledges bearing your own signature?[49] Perish the thought! Though you forgive us all our debts, you deign by your promises to make yourself our debtor, for your merciful love abides for ever.[50]

10, 18. This is why you restored me from my sickness; you saved your handmaid's son,[51] and gave me back my bodily health for the time being, preserving me so that you might endow me with better and more dependable health[52] later.

At this time I joined the company of the so-called Saints in Rome, who were deceived themselves and deceivers of others; for I was mixing not only with their Hearers, one of whom was the man in whose house I had been ill and had recovered, but also with those whom they call the Elect. It still seemed to me that it is not we who sin, but some other nature within us that is responsible. My pride was gratified at being exculpated by this theory: when I had done something wrong it was pleasant to avoid having to confess that I had done it, a confession that would have given you a

---

46. See 2 Cor 1:3.
47. See Ps 50:19(51:17).
48. The description recalls 1 Tm 5:10.
49. See Col 2:14.
50. See Ps 117(118):1.
51. See Pss 85(86):16; 115:7(116:16).
52. *Salutem*: used for either "health" or "salvation."

chance to heal this soul of mine that had sinned against you.[53] On the contrary, I liked to excuse myself and lay the blame on some other force that was with me but was not myself. But in truth it was all myself. My impious ideas had set up a division, pitting me against myself,[54] and my sin was the more incurable for my conviction that I was not a sinner.

It was a detestable wrong, almighty God, to prefer the lie that you were suffering defeat in me for my destruction[55] to the truth that I was being mastered by you for my salvation. You had not yet set a guard over my mouth or a chaste gate at my lips to keep my heart from straying into evil talk, and from making excuses for itself in its sins as it consorted with evil-doers;[56] and so I continued to associate with their Elect. By now I had given up hope of making any progress in that false doctrine, so I held onto the teachings half-heartedly and without giving them much thought, simply because I had resolved to make do with them in default of anything better.

Appeal of Academic skepticism

19. In fact, though, a suspicion had arisen in my mind that another class of philosophers, known as Academics, were more likely to be right. These men had recommended universal doubt, announcing that no part of the truth could be understood by the human mind.[57] Adopting the commonly held view of them I too believed that they had seen clearly in this matter, though I did not yet understand their real intention. I did not neglect to restrain my host from what I considered his excessive credulity with regard to the fabulous statements of which Manichean books are full, yet I was more comfortable in friendly association with Manichees than with others not of that heresy. No longer did I defend it with my original vehemence, yet familiar acquaintance with these people, of whom Rome harbors a fair number, made me lazy about seeking anything else. This was especially the case because I had despaired of the possibility that

---

53. See Ps 40:5(41:4).
54. See Mt 12:26.
55. Manichees believed that man's "good soul" was a particle of the divine; therefore when a person sinned, God was suffering defeat.
56. See Ps 140(141):3-4.
57. The Skeptics of the New Academy. Augustine was to write a treatise against them in about 386.

anything true could be discovered in your Church, O Lord of heaven and earth,[58] creator of all things, both seen and unseen.[59] The Manichees had turned me away from the Church, and I thought it contemptible to believe that you bore the appearance of human flesh and were confined to our bodily shape and our members.[60] When I wanted to think about my God I did not know how to think otherwise than in terms of bodily size, for whatever did not answer to this description seemed to me to be nothing at all. This misapprehension was the chief and almost sole cause of the error I could not avoid.

20. Consistently with this I believed that there was a similar substance of evil as well, a dark, deformed mass; this was either gross, and called earth, or ethereal and rarefied like an airy body, which the Manichees picture as a malevolent mind creeping about through the earth. Some kind of reverence on my part forced me to believe that a good God could not have created any evil nature, so I mentally constructed two masses opposed to each other: both were infinite, but the evil one I conceived rather more narrowly, the good on a larger scale. From this tainted premise other sacrilegious ideas followed. When my mind attempted to speed back once more to the Catholic faith I was repelled, because the Catholic faith is not what I thought it was. Further, it seemed to me more reverent, O God, God to whom your own merciful dealings with me confess,[61] to believe that you were at any rate infinite on all other sides, even though I was forced to admit that you were finite on that one side where the mass of evil opposed you, than to hold that you were limited on every side by the form of a human body. Since in my ignorance I thought that evil was not only a substance, but even a bodily substance (for I did not know how to envisage a mind except as an ethereal body spread out through space), it seemed to me better to believe that you had not created any evil than to believe that what I thought of as the nature of evil could have proceeded from you.

I even thought that our Savior himself, your only-begotten Son, had been detached from the mass of your huge, brilliant substance for our salvation; so fixed was I in this worthless notion that I believed nothing

---

58. See Mt 11:25, a significant echo: Augustine was not yet among the "little ones."
59. See Col 1:16, and the Nicene Creed.
60. The statement in Gn 1:26-27 that human beings are made in God's image provoked Manichean ridicule and deeply puzzled Augustine until he came to grasp the notion of spiritual substance.
61. See Ps 106(107):8 and recurrently.

else of him but what I could picture in terms of it. In conseqence I held that a nature of this kind could not have been born of the Virgin Mary without becoming intermingled with flesh; yet a nature such as I pictured it could not be so intermingled without being defiled. I was therefore afraid to believe in One who was born in the flesh, lest I should be forced to believe him defiled by the flesh.[62] Your spiritually-minded faithful will gently and lovingly laugh at me if they read these confessions of mine; all the same, that is what I was like.

11, 21. Moreover, I did not consider that your scriptures could be defended on those points where the Manichees had censured them; but there certainly were times when I longed to discuss these one by one with somebody who had studied those books thoroughly, to find out his view of them. While still at Carthage I had been influenced in a preliminary way by the lectures of a certain Elpidius[63] who disputed with the Manichees face to face, for he drew arguments from the scriptures which could not easily be gainsaid. The Manichees' reply seemed feeble to me, and they were understandably disinclined to bring it out openly, preferring to give it to us in private. They alleged that the New Testament writings had been falsified by some unknown persons bent on interpolating the Christian faith with elements of the Jewish law; but they produced no incorrupt exemplars themselves.

But most of all it was those massive substances that weighed me down as I thought in terms of bodies; it was as though they pinned me fast and choked me as under their weight I gasped for the pure and unpolluted air of your truth, but found myself unable to breathe it.

Augustine teaches in Rome

12, 22. I now set myself to work hard at teaching rhetoric in Rome, the task for which I had come. My first move was to gather students together at my house, and I began to make a name for myself among them, and more widely through them. But what did I then discover, but that abuses prevailed in Rome which I had not been obliged to contend with in Africa?

---

62. *In carne natum ... ex carne inquinatum,* an Augustinian assonance.
63. One of the few people from the time prior to his conversion whom Augustine mentions by name, possibly because the name itself ("Hopeful") was significant for him. This Book V has many references to despair and incipient hope.

It was obviously true that acts of vandalism by young hooligans did not occur there, but, I was told, "A crowd of these young men conspires together, and in order to avoid paying their fees to their teacher they suddenly leave him for another. They betray their good faith, and because they hold wealth so dear they account justice cheap." My heart was filled with hatred for these youths, but it fell short of *perfect hatred,* [64] for I probably hated what I might suffer at their hands more than the crimes they might commit against anyone else. Still, people of this type are depraved and break faith with you [65] by setting their hearts on the fleeting baubles of this passing life and the filthy lucre that sullies the hand that grasps it. [66] They embrace an elusive world while despising you who abide for ever, you who call them back again and forgive the wanton human soul that returns to you. Today I hate such people for being depraved and twisted, but I will love them insofar as they may be corrected, and may come to prefer the education to the money, and prefer even to the education you yourself, O God, who are truth and overflowing wealth of goodness that deceives not, and pure, inviolate peace. But at that time, when harm from these bad students threatened me, my desire to avoid it for my own sake was stronger than any desire that they should become good for yours.

He wins a teaching post in Milan

13, 23. A message had been sent from Milan to Rome, addressed to the prefect of the city, asking for a master of rhetoric. A pass had also been issued, authorizing the person chosen to use the official post-horses. Against the background of unsatisfactory student behavior I therefore canvassed [67] support among citizens drunk on Manichean nonsense, in the hope that after prescribing a subject for a trial discourse the prefect Symmachus would recommend and dispatch me. [68] My real reason for

---

64. Ps 138(139):22. Augustine explains this in his *Exposition of Psalm* 138.28: "To hate with perfect hatred means that we neither hate sinners on account of their sins, nor love the sins for the sake of the sinners."
65. See Ps 72(73):27.
66. See Ti 1:7; 1 Pt 5:2.
67. *Ambivi*, the verb from which is derived *ambitio*, a motivating force for Augustine.
68. Symmachus was himself a celebrated orator, and is likely to have been consulted in this capacity rather than as prefect. He had been proconsul in Africa in Augustine's student days (373); his recommendation of Augustine now was probably in the autumn of 384.

going was to get away from the Manichees, though this was not apparent
either to them or to me at the time.

He arrives in Milan and meets Ambrose

So I came to Milan and to Bishop Ambrose,[69] who was known throughout the world as one of the best of men. He was a devout worshiper of you,
Lord, and at that time his energetic preaching provided your people with
choicest wheat and the joy of oil and the sober intoxication of wine.[70]
Unknowingly I was led by you to him, so that through him I might be led,
knowingly, to you.

This man of God welcomed me with fatherly kindness and showed the
charitable concern for my pilgrimage that befitted a bishop. I began to feel
affection for him, not at first as a teacher of truth, for that I had given up
hope of finding in your Church, but simply as a man who was kind to me.
With professional interest I listened to him conducting disputes before the
people, but my intention was not the right one: I was assessing his
eloquence to see whether it matched its reputation. I wished to ascertain
whether the readiness of speech with which rumor credited him was really
there, or something more, or less. I hung keenly upon his words, but cared
little for their content, and indeed despised it, as I stood there delighting in
the sweetness of his discourse. Though more learned than that of Faustus it
was less light-hearted and beguiling; but such criticism concerns the style
only, for with regard to the content there was no comparison. While
Faustus would wander off into Manichean whimsy, this man was teaching
about salvation in a thoroughly salutary way. But salvation is far from
sinners,[71] and a sinner I was at that time. Yet little by little, without
knowing it, I was drawing near.

14, 24. I was taking no trouble to learn from what Ambrose was saying,
but interested only in listening to how he said it, for that futile concern had

---

69. Milan was the residence of the Western Emperor from Diocletian's time until it was captured
by Attila. Ambrose, the son of a prefect of Gaul, had been nominated bishop of Milan by
popular acclamation while still a catechumen. He had been bishop there since 374 and was
now in his prime.
70. Though the subject of the verb is Ambrose's preaching, the language is unmistakably
sacramental. For wheat see Pss 80:17(81:16); 147:14; for the connection wheat-oil-wine see
Pss 4:8(7); 103(104):15. The phrase *sobria ebrietas* occurs in a well-known hymn composed
by Ambrose (1,7,25-26); see Eph 5:18.
71. See Ps 118(119):155.

remained with me, despairing as I did that any way to you could be open to humankind. Nonetheless as his words, which I enjoyed, penetrated my mind, the substance, which I overlooked, seeped in with them, for I could not separate the two. As I opened my heart to appreciate how skillfully he spoke, the recognition that he was speaking the truth crept in at the same time, though only by slow degrees. At first the case he was making began to seem defensible to me, and I realized that the Catholic faith, in support of which I had believed nothing could be advanced against Manichean opponents, was in fact intellectually respectable. This realization was particularly keen when once, and again, and indeed frequently, I heard some difficult passage of the Old Testament explained figuratively; such passages had been death to me because I was taking them literally.[72] As I listened to many such scriptural texts being interpreted in a spiritual sense I confronted my own attitude, or at least that despair which had led me to believe that no resistance whatever could be offered to people who loathed and derided the law and the prophets.[73] However, I did not yet consider the Catholic way the one to follow simply because it too could have its learned proponents, men who were capable of refuting objections with ample argument and good sense; nor did I yet consider the Manicheanism I professed was to be condemned because I had observed that the party of the defense could make out an equally good case. The Catholic Church appeared to me unconquered, but not so clearly as to appear the conqueror.

25. I then expended much mental effort on trying to discover if I could in any way convict the Manichees of falsehood by some definite proofs. If only I had been capable of envisaging a spiritual substance, all their elaborate constructions would have fallen to pieces at once and been thrown out of my mind; but this I could not do. All the same, as I gave more and more thought to the matter and made comparisons, I judged that many philosophers had held far more probable views on this physical world and on whatever in nature comes within reach of our senses. Accordingly I adopted what is popularly thought to be the Academic position, doubting everything and wavering: I decided that I ought to leave the Manichees, since at this period of uncertainty it was not right for me to continue as a member of a sect to which I judged some philosophers superior; but I flatly

---

72. See 2 Cor 3:6.
73. That is, the Old Testament. See Mt 5:17; 7:12; Lk 16:6.

refused to entrust the cure of my soul's sickness[74] to philosophers who were strangers to the saving name of Christ. I resolved therefore to live as a catechumen in the Catholic Church, which was what my parents had wished for me, until some kind of certainty dawned by which I might direct my steps aright.

---

74. See Mt 9:35; Lk 9:1.

Book VI

Milan, 385:
Progress, Friends, Perplexities

1, 1. O you who have been my hope since my youth[1] where were you when I sought you? How was it that you had gone so far away?[2] Had you not created me and marked me out *from the four-footed beasts, and made me wiser than the birds in the sky?*[3] Yet I was walking a dark and slippery path, searching for you outside myself[4] and failing to find the God of my own heart.[5] I had sunk to the depth of the sea,[6] I lost all faith and despaired of ever finding the truth.

Monica comes to Milan

Steadfast in her fidelity, my mother had by this time rejoined me, for so completely did she trust in you that she had not feared to follow me over land and sea.[7] Indeed, amid the perils of the voyage it was she who kept up the spirits of the sailors, though in the ordinary way it is to them that inexperienced and frightened travelers look for reassurance. She, however, had dared to promise them that they would come safely to port, because you had yourself made this promise to her in a dream. She found me, by contrast, beset by mortal danger as I despaired of discovering the truth. When I told her that I was no longer a Manichee, though not a Catholic Christian either, she was overjoyed, but not as though this news had taken

---

1. See Ps 70(71):5.
2. See Ps 9:22(10:1).
3. Jb 35:11 (Old Latin).
4. This sounds Neo-Platonic, but the more significant comparison is with X,27,38.
5. See Ps 72(73):26.
6. See Ps 67:23(68:22); there may also be an allusion to Jonah.
7. See Virgil, *Aeneid* IX,492. Monica's voyage would probably have been in the spring of 385, when sailing became possible after the winter storms.

134

her by surprise. She was already confident with regard to my wretched condition to this extent, that while she constantly wept over me in your sight as over a dead man, it was over one who though dead could still be raised to life again; she offered me to you upon the bier of her meditation, begging you to say to this widow's son, *Young man, arise, I tell you,*[8] that he might live again and begin to speak, so that you could restore him to his mother.[9] Accordingly, when she learned that what she tearfully begged of you every day had been partially granted, inasmuch as I had now been delivered from falsehood, even if I had not yet found the truth, there was no wild excitement or agitation in her heartfelt joy. So certain was she that you, who had promised her everything, would grant what was still lacking, that she told me very tranquilly and with full confidence that in Christ she believed she would see me a faithful Catholic before she departed from this life.

So much she said to me; but to you, the fount of all mercy, she redoubled her prayers and tears, imploring you to make haste to my help[10] and enlighten my darkness.[11] She hurried all the more eagerly to church and hung upon Ambrose's preaching, in which she found a spring of water leaping up to eternal life.[12] She revered that man as an angel of God,[13] for she realized that it was thanks to him that I had meanwhile been brought to my present point of wavering; and she foresaw with certainty that I would have to pass through a still more dangerous condition—a crisis, as the physicians call it—on my way from sickness to health.

2, 2. In Africa she had been accustomed to make offerings of pottage, bread and wine at the tombs of the martyrs. When she attempted to do the same here, she was prevented by the doorkeeper; but as soon as she learned that it was the bishop who had forbidden the practice she complied in so devoted and obedient a spirit that I marveled at the attitude she had so readily adopted: criticizing her own custom rather than sitting in judgment

---

8. Lk 7:14.
9. The translation offered here assumes the punctuation *sed neque catholicum christianum, non quasi inopinatum aliquid audierit exilivit laeticia, cum iam secura....* Some editors of the Latin text place a comma after *non*, which would oblige us to understand that Monica was not overjoyed, because she had expected the news.
10. See Ps 69:2(70:1).
11. See Ps 17:29(18:28).
12. See Jn 4:14.
13. See Gal 4:14. *Diligebat:* she revered or esteemed him, a verb with fewer carnal overtones than *amo*. Augustine makes the same distinction in V,13,23 between Ambrose's attitude to himself and his to Ambrose.

on his prohibition.[14] And no wonder, for her mind was not enslaved to any habit of wine-bibbing, nor did addiction to wine incite her to hatred of the truth, as is the case with many men and women who are as disgusted by any commendation of sobriety as are drunkards when offered watered-down wine. With my mother it was otherwise: she would bring her basket containing the festive fare which it fell to her to taste first and then distribute; but she would then set out no more than one small cup, mixed to suit her abstemious palate, and from that she would only sip for courtesy's sake. If it happened that there were many shrines of the dead to be honored in this manner she would carry round this same single cup and set it forth in each place. She thus served to her fellow-worshipers extremely sparing allowances of wine which was not only heavily diluted but by this time no more than lukewarm. What she sought to promote at these gatherings was piety, not intemperance.

Once she had ascertained, however, that Ambrose, illustrious preacher and exemplar of piety as he was, had forbidden the celebration of these rites even by those who conducted them with restraint, lest any opportunity might be given to drunkards to indulge in excess, and also because the custom resembled the cult of ancestors and so was close kin to the superstitious practices of the pagans,[15] she most willingly gave it up. She had now seen the wisdom of bringing to the martyrs' shrines not a basket full of the fruits of the earth, but a heart full of more purified offerings, her prayers. In consequence she was now able to give alms to the needy, and it was also possible for the sacrament of the Lord's Body to be celebrated at these shrines—and fittingly, since it was in imitation of his passion that the martyrs offered themselves in sacrifice and were crowned.

All the same, O Lord my God—and in your presence I speak truly from my heart on this matter—it seems to me unlikely that my mother would have yielded easily over the abolition of this custom had it been forbidden by anyone other than Ambrose, whom she highly revered. It was above all for the part he played in my salvation that she esteemed him; and he for his part held her in like esteem for her deeply religious way of life. Her spiritual fervor[16]

---

14. Later, in Africa, Augustine made efforts to stamp out similar grave-cults there too. In addition to their pagan associations, they lent themselves to drunkenness and licentious revelry, but they died hard, since they also contained a core of genuine piety.

15. The Roman pagan festival, *Parentalia*, celebrated 18-21 February, was marked by offerings to the shades of the ancestors.

16. See Rom 12:11.

prompted her to assiduous good works[17] and brought her constantly to church; and accordingly when Ambrose saw me he would often burst out in praise of her, telling me how lucky I was to have such a mother. Little did he know what a son she had: I was full of doubts about all these things and scarcely believed it possible to find the way of life.[18]

Bishop Ambrose

3, 3. Not yet had I begun to pour forth my groans to you in prayer, begging you to help me; rather was my mind intent on searching and restlessly eager for argument. Now I regarded Ambrose as a fortunate man as far as worldly standing went, since he enjoyed the respect of powerful people; it was only his celibacy which seemed to me a burdensome undertaking. I had not begun to guess, still less experience in my own case, what hope he bore within him, or what a struggle he waged against the temptations to which his eminent position exposed him, or the encouragement he received in times of difficulty, or what exquisite delights he savored in his secret mouth, the mouth of his heart, as he chewed the bread of your word.

Nor was he aware of my spiritual turmoil or the perilous pit before my feet.[19] There were questions I wanted to put to him, but I was unable to do so as fully as I wished, because the crowds of people who came to him on business impeded me, allowing me little opportunity either to talk or to listen to him. He was habitually available to serve them in their needs, and in the very scant time that he was not with them he would be refreshing either his body with necessary food or his mind with reading. When he read his eyes would travel across the pages and his mind would explore the sense, but his voice and tongue were silent.[20] We would sometimes be present, for he did not forbid anyone access, nor was it customary for anyone to be announced; and

---

17. See 1 Tm 5:10; 6:18.
18. For the "way of life" see Ps 15(16):11; Prv 6:23; 10:17; 15:10. All these passages from Proverbs associate the way of life with acceptance of discipline.
19. See Mt 15:14.
20. This famous passage has sometimes been taken to imply that Ambrose invented silent reading. It was undoubtedly known earlier. See Cicero, *Tusculan Disputations* V,40,116 on the advantage the deaf may derive from reading poetry. Augustine himself silently peruses scripture at VIII,12,29. But reading aloud or in a muttered undertone was the more common practice and long continued so. Saint Benedict's *Rule* (48,5) reminds monks who read while lying on their beds to do so without disturbing their neighbors. Until at least the end of the Middle Ages the reading of scripture was understood as an activity involving the whole person, physical as well as mental and spiritual; gastronomic metaphors of mastication such as chewing the cud were commonly used for it, as is the case a few lines above.

on these occasions we watched him reading silently. It was never otherwise, and so we too would sit for a long time in silence, for who would have the heart to interrupt a man so engrossed? Then we would steal away, guessing that in the brief time he had seized for the refreshment of his mind he was resting from the din of other people's affairs and reluctant to be called away to other business. We thought too that he might be apprehensive that if he read aloud, and any closely attentive listener were doubtful on any point, or the author he was reading used any obscure expressions, he would have to stop and explain various difficult problems that might arise, and after spending time on this be unable to read as much of the book as he wished. Another and perhaps more cogent reason for his habit of reading silently was his need to conserve his voice, which was very prone to hoarseness. But whatever his reason, that man undoubtedly had a good one. [21]

4. This meant, however, that no opportunity at all was given me to find out what I longed to know from your holy oracle, Ambrose's heart. At most, I could only put a point to him briefly, whereas my inner turmoil was at such a feverish pitch that I needed to find him completely at leisure if I were to pour it all out, and I never did so find him. Nonetheless I listened to him *straightforwardly expounding the word of truth*[22] to the people every Sunday, and as I listened I became more and more convinced that it was possible to unravel all those cunning knots of calumny in which the sacred books had been entangled by tricksters who had deceived me and others. I came to realize that your spiritual children, whom you had brought to a new birth by grace from their mother, the Catholic Church, did not in fact understand the truth of your creating human beings in your image[23] in so crude a way that they believed you to be determined by the form of a human body. Although I had not even a faint or shadowy notion[24] of what a spiritual substance could be like, I was filled with joy, albeit a shamefaced joy, at the discovery that what I had barked against for so many years was not the Catholic faith but the figments of carnal imagination. I had been all

---

21. The contrast is clear between Ambrose and the glib and available Faustus in Book V. Augustine had approached Faustus hoping for wisdom and found only a ready tongue; he initially approached Ambrose (in public) to enjoy his eloquence, only to find himself attracted willy-nilly by its content. Ambrose's apportioning of his time was similar to what Augustine would aim at himself as a bishop; see XI,2,2. Augustine was also very conscious that one who expounds the scriptures to others must do a great deal of silent listening himself.

22. 2 Tm 2:15.

23. See Gn 1:26-27; 9:6; Sir 17:1.

24. See 1 Cor 13:12.

the more foolhardy and impious in my readiness to rant and denounce where I ought to have inquired and sought to learn.[25]

O God, most high, most deep, and yet nearer than all else, most hidden yet intimately present, you are not framed of greater and lesser limbs; you are everywhere, whole and entire in every place, but confined to none. In no sense is our bodily form to be attributed to you, yet you have made us in your own image, and lo! here we are, from head to foot set in our place!

Augustine finds some enlightenment

4, 5. Since I did not know how your image could exist in us I would, given the chance, have knocked at the door[26] and proposed my question about how the doctrine was to be believed, instead of opposing it with insults as though it had been believed in the absurd way I had assumed. The anxiety which gnawed at my inner self to determine what I could hold onto as certain was the more intense in proportion to my shame at remembering how long I had been deluded and beguiled by assurances that falsehoods were certain, and had in my headstrong, childish error babbled about such very dubious things as though they were proven. Later on it became clear to me that these tenets were false; but at the time I was at least certain of this, that while they were uncertain I had for a while held them to be certain, and had been arguing blindly in the objections I raised against your Catholic Church. I had not yet come to accept her teachings as true, but at least I now knew that she did not teach the doctrines to which I had gravely objected.

Thus it was that I was put to shame and forced to turn about.[27] I rejoiced to find that your one and only Church, the body of your only Son,[28] that Church within which I had been signed with Christ's name in my infancy, did not entertain infantile nonsense or include in her sound teaching any belief that would seem to confine you, the creator of all things, in any place however vast and spacious, in any place that would hem you in on every side after the manner of human bodies.

---

25. Reading *discere*. Some manuscripts have *dicere*, "I ought to have spoken in an inquiring spirit."
26. See Mt 7:7.
27. See Ps 6:11, the psalmist's plea against his enemies. Augustine reverses the order of the verbs, and with it the sense.
28. See Col 1:18.24.

6. Another thing that brought me joy was that the ancient writings of the law and the prophets were now being offered to me under quite a different aspect from that under which they had seemed to me absurd when I believed that your holy people held such crude opinions; for the fact was that they did not. I delighted to hear Ambrose often asserting in his sermons to the people, as a principle on which he must insist emphatically, *The letter is death-dealing, but the spirit gives life.*[29] This he would tell them as he drew aside the veil of mystery[30] and opened to them the spiritual meaning of passages which, taken literally, would seem to mislead. He said nothing which offended me, even though I still did not know whether what he said was true. In my heart I was hanging back from any assent, dreading a headlong fall, and nearly died by hanging instead. I longed to become as certain of those things I could not see as I was that seven and three make ten. I was not so demented as to think that even this simple truth was beyond comprehension; but I wanted to have the same grasp of other things, both material entities not immediately present to my senses and spiritual realities of which I did not know how to think in any but a materialistic way. The possibility of healing was, ironically, within my reach if only I had been willing to believe, because then I could with a more purified mind have focused my gaze on your truth, which abides for ever[31] and is deficient in nothing. But just as someone who has suffered under a bad physician may often be afraid to entrust himself to a good one, so it was in my soul's case. It could be healed only by believing, yet it shirked the cure for fear of believing what was false. It struggled in your hands,[32] though it is you who have prepared the healing remedies of faith and spread them over the ills of the world, enduing them with marvelous potency.

5, 7. Against this background, however, I now began to prefer Catholic doctrine. True, some of its propositions were not demonstrated rationally, either because there might be no one present to whom they could be demonstrated or because they were not demonstrable at all; but I came to see that in commanding that certain things must be believed without demonstration the Church was a good deal more moderate and very much less deceitful than those parties who rashly promised knowledge and

---

29. 2 Cor 3:6.
30. See 2 Cor 3:14-16.
31. See Ps 116(117):2.
32. See Dn 4:32(35).

derided credulity, but then went on to demand belief in a whole host of fabulous and absurd myths which certainly could not be demonstrated.

So it was, Lord, that you began little by little to work on my heart with your most gentle and merciful hand, and dispose it to reflect how innumerable were the things I believed and held to be true, though I had neither seen them nor been present when they happened. How many truths there were of this kind, such as events of world history, or facts about places and cities I had never seen; how many were the statements I believed on the testimony of friends, or physicians, or various other people; and, indeed, unless we did believe them we should be unable to do anything in this life. With what unshakable certainty, moreover, did I hold fast to the belief that I had been born of my particular parents, yet I could not have known this without believing what I had heard.

So you persuaded me that the truly blameworthy people were not those who believed in your scriptures, the scriptures which you had established with such authority throughout almost all nations,[33] but those who refused to believe in them; and it was to these people that I should beware of listening if by chance any of them might challenge me by asking, "How do you know that those books were provided for the human race by the Spirit of the one, real and most truthful God?" It was precisely this fact that most commended itself to belief, because not one of the slanderous disputes to be found in the works of philosophers who disagreed among themselves, in any of the vast number of books I had read, had ever been able to wrench away from me the belief that you exist, whatever may be your nature (and of this I was ignorant) and that the course of human affairs concerns you.[34]

8. This conviction was sometimes strong in me, sometimes feeble; but I always believed in your existence and your care for us, even though I did not know what to think about your essential nature, or conceive what way

---

33. The scriptures were not some esoteric documents reserved for initiates, but publicly available; the Christian Church was a visible, historical community whose message concerned historical facts. These claims were constantly and proudly made, and they carried weight with Augustine even before he came to accept the message. His approach to Christian faith was by way of an initial acceptance of the authority of scripture as authentically from God, as an incarnation of the Word in the sacred text, before he was ready to assent to its specific teachings.

34. Most philosophers, including the Stoics and the Neo-Platonists, in fact agreed on the fundamental truths of the existence of God and his governance of the world; see Cicero, *On the Nature of the Gods* II,1,3.

could lead me, or lead me back, to you.[35] It was because *we were weak*[36] and unable to find the truth by pure reason that we needed the authority of the sacred scriptures; and so I began to see that you would not have endowed them with such authority among all nations unless you had willed human beings to believe in you and seek you through them.

Having already heard many parts of the sacred books explained in a reasonable and acceptable way, I came to regard those passages which had previously struck me as absurd, and therefore repelled me, as holy and profound mysteries.[37] The authority of the sacred writings seemed to me all the more deserving of reverence and divine faith in that scripture was easily accessible to every reader, while yet guarding a mysterious dignity in its deeper sense. In plain words and very humble modes of speech it offered itself to everyone, yet stretched the understanding of those who were *not shallow-minded*.[38] It welcomed all comers to its hospitable embrace, yet through narrow openings[39] attracted a few to you—a few, perhaps, but far more than it would have done had it not spoken with such noble authority and drawn the crowds to its embrace by its holy humility.

All the while, Lord, as I pondered these things you stood by me; I sighed and you heard me; I was tossed to and fro and you steered me aright. I wandered down the wide road of the world, but you did not desert me.

Hollowness of his secular ambitions; the drunken beggar

6, 9. I was hankering after honors, wealth and marriage, but you were laughing at me.[40] Very bitter were the frustrations I endured in chasing my desires, but all the greater was your kindness in being less and less prepared to let anything other than yourself grow sweet to me. Look at my heart, Lord, you who have willed me to remember this and confess to you. You freed my soul from the close-clinging, sticky morass of death; let it

---

35. *Via*, the Way, Christ. Compare "the Truth," just below.
36. Rom 5:6.
37. *Ad sacramentorum altitudinem referebam*. The word *sacramentum* (originally a military oath) acquired rich content in the Christian Fathers. In Augustine it covers both the mysterious meanings hidden in the sacred text, and the grace-giving rites of the Church, both being sacred signs. The Christian bishop has the duty of dispensing both.
38. Sir 19:4.
39. See Mt 19:24, the eye of the needle, and Mt 7:13, the narrow gate. Contrast the "wide road" at the end of this chapter.
40. See Pss 2:4; 36(37):13.

now cling to you.[41] How wretched it was! You probed its wound to the raw, to persuade it to leave all else behind[42] and be converted to you[43] who are above all things,[44] without whom nothing whatever would exist—be converted to you and find healing.[45]

I recall how miserable I was, and how one day you brought me to a realization of my miserable state. I was preparing to deliver a eulogy upon the emperor in which I would tell plenty of lies with the object of winning favor with the well-informed by my lying; so my heart was panting with anxiety and seething with feverish, corruptive thoughts. As I passed through a certain district in Milan I noticed a poor beggar, drunk, as I believe, and making merry. I groaned and pointed out to the friends who were with me how many hardships our idiotic enterprises entailed. Goaded by greed, I was dragging my load of unhappiness along, and feeling it all the heavier for being dragged. Yet while all our efforts were directed solely to the attainment of unclouded joy, it appeared that this beggar had already beaten us to the goal, a goal which we would perhaps never reach ourselves. With the help of the few paltry coins he had collected by begging, this man was enjoying the temporal happiness for which I strove by so bitter, devious and roundabout a contrivance. His joy was no true joy, to be sure, but what I was seeking in my ambition was a joy far more unreal; and he was undeniably happy while I was full of foreboding; he was carefree, I apprehensive. If anyone had questioned me as to whether I would rather be exhilarated or afraid, I would of course have replied, "Exhilarated"; but if the questioner had pressed me further, asking whether I preferred to be like the beggar, or to be as I was then, I would have chosen to be myself, laden with anxieties and fears. Surely that would have been no right choice, but a perverse one? I could not have preferred my condition to his on the grounds that I was better educated, because that fact was not for me a source of joy but only the means by which I sought to curry favor with human beings: I was not aiming to teach

41. See Pss 62:9(63:8); 72(73):28.
42. See Lk 5:11.28, on the call of the apostles.
43. See Pss 21:28(22:27); 50:15(51:13).
44. See Rom 9:5.
45. See Is 6:10; Mt 13:15.

them but only to win their favor; and this was why you broke my bones[46] with the rod of your discipline.[47]

10. I have no patience with anyone who would say to my soul, "But it makes a difference what a person is happy about; that beggar was enjoying his intoxication, you longed to bask in glory." What kind of glory was that, Lord? No glory that was to be found in you;[48] for just as his was no true joy, so mine was no true glory, and it turned my head more fatally. He would sleep off his intoxication that same night, whereas I had slept with mine and risen up again, and would sleep and rise with it again ... how many days! I know that it does indeed make a difference what one is joyful about, and the joy of faithful hope is incomparably distant from that empty enjoyment; but even as things were then there was a vast distance between us: he was the happier, not only inasmuch as he was flooded with merriment while I was torn with cares, but also because he had earned his wine by wishing good-day to passers-by, while I was seeking a swollen reputation by lying.

I spoke fully to my friends on these lines, and often in similar circumstances took stock of my reactions. It grieved me that I should be like this, and I took it badly, and this in itself increased my grief. If some good fortune did smile upon me, I felt it not worthwhile to seize it, because almost before I had hold of it, away it would fly.

Alypius

7, 11. Those of us who lived as friends together sighed deeply over these experiences, and I discussed them most especially and intimately with Alypius and Nebridius.[49] Alypius and I had been born in the same town, where his parents were leading citizens. He was younger than I, and had been among my students when I began to teach in our town.[50] He studied under me again at Carthage and held me in high esteem, because I seemed to him good and learned, while I for my part was fond of him on account of

---

46. See Ps 52:6(53:5).
47. See Ps 22(23):4.
48. See 1 Cor 1:31.
49. For Nebridius see IV,3,6 and Augustine's Letter 98,8. Alypius was with Augustine at the famous conversion scene, VIII,12,28-30, was converted with him, was with him at Cassiciacum and later became bishop of Thagaste.
50. That is, in 375/376, the year Augustine's other great friend died.

his great nobility of character, which was unmistakable even before he reached mature years. However, the whirlpool of Carthaginian immoral amusements sucked him in; it was aboil with frivolous shows, and he was ensnared in the madness of the circuses. At the time when he was being wretchedly tossed about in it, I as a professor of rhetoric had opened a school and was teaching publicly, but he did not attend my courses on account of a quarrel which had arisen between me and his father. I had discovered that he loved the circuses with a passion likely to be his undoing, and I was extremely anxious because he seemed to me bent on wasting his excellent promise, if indeed he had not already done so. I had, however, no opportunity to restrain him by any kind of pressure, either out of goodwill as a friend or by right as his teacher, for I presumed that his attitude to me was the same as his father's, though in fact he was not like that. Accordingly he disregarded his father's wishes and took to greeting me when we met; he also began to frequent my lecture hall, where he would listen awhile, then go away.

12. I did not tackle him about his reckless addiction to worthless shows, or attempt to save him from ruining his fine intelligence on them, because it slipped my memory; but you, Lord, guide the courses of all your creatures, and you had not forgotten this man who one day would be set over your children as dispenser of your mysteries. You brought about his correction through my agency, but without my knowledge, so that it might be clearly recognized as your work. One day when I was sitting in my usual place with my students around me he came, greeted me, sat down and applied his mind to the subject we were studying. I chanced to have a text in my hands, and while I was expounding it an apt comparison with the circuses occurred to me, which would drive home the point I was making more humorously and tellingly through caustic mockery of people enslaved by that craze. You know, our God, that I did not think at the time about curing Alypius of this bane. Yet he took my illustration to himself, believing that I had used it solely on his account; and what another person might have regarded as a reason for being angry with me this honest young man regarded rather as a reason for being angry with himself and loving me more ardently. Long ago you had told us, weaving the advice into your scriptures: *Offer correction to a wise man, and he will love you for it.*[51] Yet I had not corrected him myself. You make use of all of us, witting or unwit-

---

51. Prv 9:8 (Old Latin).

ting, for just purposes known to you, and you made my heart and tongue into burning coals with which to cauterize a promising mind that was wasting away, and heal it.[52]

If anyone is insensitive to your merciful dealings, let such a person silently withhold your praise, but from the marrow of my being those same dealings cry out in confession to you;[53] for after hearing my words he wrenched himself away from that pit in which he had been willfully sinking, and finding incredible pleasure in his blindness. With a strong resolve of temperance he shook his mind free, and all the filth of the circuses dropped away from him. Never again did he go there. Then he overcame his father's opposition to his taking me for his teacher; his father gave in and gave him leave.

Once he had begun to study with me again, he became entangled in the same superstition as I, for he loved the display of continence put up by the Manichees, believing it to be real and authentic. In fact it was insane and seductive. It captivated precious souls[54] who were still too ignorant to penetrate the depth of virtue and liable to be deceived by the superficial appearance of a virtue that was but feigned and faked.

8, 13. He had been drawn toward a worldly course by his parents' siren song, and he was unwilling to abandon it, so he had gone to Rome ahead of me to study law, and there he was assailed by an entirely unexpected craving for gladiatorial entertainments. This came about in a way no one could have foreseen. He shunned such displays and loathed them; but some of his friends and fellow-students, returning from their midday meal, happened to find the stadium open to them and, as is the way with close friends, drew him in by force, despite his vehement protests and struggles. It was one of the days for cruel and murderous sport, and he kept telling them, "You may drag my body into that place and fix me there, but can you direct my mind and my eyes to the show? I will be there, and yet be absent, and so get the better both of you and of the performance." They heard what he said but took him along with them all the same, wishing perhaps to know if he could make good his claim. When they arrived and settled themselves in what seats they could find, the whole place was

---

52. See Ps 139:11(140:10). In his *Exposition of Psalm* 139,14 (compare ibid. 119,5) Augustine explains that burning is necessary to clear the ground, so that grace may build.
53. See Ps 106(107):8 and recurrently.
54. See Prv 6:26.

heaving with thoroughly brutal pleasure. He kept the gateways of his eyes closed, forbidding his mind to go out that way to such evils. If only he could have stopped his ears too! At a certain tense moment in the fight a huge roar from the entire crowd beat upon him. He was overwhelmed by curiosity, and on the excuse that he would be prepared to condemn and rise above whatever was happening even if he saw it, he opened his eyes, and suffered a more grievous wound in his soul than the gladiator he wished to see had received in the body. He fell more dreadfully than the other man whose fall had evoked the shouting; for by entering his ears and persuading his eyes to open the noise effected a breach through which his mind—a mind rash rather than strong, and all the weaker for presuming to trust in itself rather than in you, as it should have done[55]—was struck and brought down. As he saw the blood he gulped the brutality along with it; he did not turn away but fixed his gaze there and drank in the frenzy, not aware of what he was doing, reveling in the wicked contest and intoxicated on sanguinary pleasure. No longer was he the man who had joined the crowd; he was now one of the crowd he had joined, and a genuine companion of those who had led him there. What more need be said? He watched, he shouted, he grew hot with excitement, he carried away with him a madness that lured him back again not only in the company of those by whom he had initially been dragged along but even before them, dragging others.

Nonetheless you rescued him from his plight with your mighty and most merciful hand, and taught him to rely not on himself but on you;[56] but this was long afterward.

9, 14. The foregoing episode was stored up in his memory and contributed to his future healing, as also did another. Once when he was still a student and attending my classes at Carthage, he was in the market-place at midday, thinking over the passage he had to declaim, as is customary in scholastic training. You allowed him to be arrested by the temple-guards as a thief; and I think, our God, that you did so for no other reason than to ensure that this youth, who was destined to be such a great man, should learn even at this early stage that in judicial hearings one person ought not to be condemned too easily through the rash gullibility of another.

---

55. See Jdt 6:15.
56. See Prv 3:5; Is 57:13.

This is what happened. He was walking up and down alone in front of the lawcourt with his tablets and pen when a certain young student (the real thief) secretly brought an axe and, without Alypius being aware of it, gained access to the leaden gratings over the part of the market assigned to the silversmiths, and began to hack away the lead. The silversmiths below heard the sound of the axe, and softly discussed what to do; then they sent men to arrest anyone they might find. Hearing their voices the thief fled, leaving the axe behind because he was afraid of being caught with it in his possession. But Alypius, who had not seen him go in, observed him come out and take to his heels, and, wishing to know the reason, went into the place, picked up the axe, and stood there holding it, considering the matter in some surprise. The men who had been sent came and found him, alone and holding the very tool which had alerted them by its noise. They seized him and dragged him off, boasting to a crowd of bystanders in the market-place that they had caught the thief red-handed. Then they led him away to stand trial.

15. But his lesson had gone far enough. You promptly came to the defense of his innocence, O Lord, you who were the sole witness of it.[57] As he was being led off either to imprisonment or to corporal punishment there chanced to meet them a certain architect who had prime responsibility for public buildings. The guards were glad that he in particular should have met them, because they were often suspected by him of having themselves stolen any items which were missing from the market-place, and now they thought that he would at last realize who had committed these thefts. However, this man had frequently seen Alypius at the house of a certain senator whom he used often to visit to pay his respects. He recognized him at once, took him by the hand and drew him aside from the throng, inquiring the reason for this calamity. When he heard what had happened, and heard all the bystanders making a commotion and uttering angry threats, he ordered Alypius to come away with him.

They arrived at the home of the youth who had committed the crime. At the gate was a youngster naive enough to blurt out the whole truth without worrying about the consequences for his master; and he was the slave who had been in attendance on his master in the market-place. Alypius remem-

---

57. See Wis 1:6; Jer 29:23.

bered this and told the architect, who showed the axe to the child and asked him whose it was. "Ours," he promptly replied, and on being questioned further revealed the rest of the story.

The case thus shifted to that household, and the crowds who had already begun to jeer at Alypius were balked, while the man who would one day be the dispenser of your word and the judge of many a case in your Church departed more experienced and better informed.

10, 16. I had caught up with him in Rome, and since a very strong bond of friendship kept him close to me, he set out for Milan in my company; for he did not want to leave me, and he also hoped to make some use of the legal expertise he had acquired, though this was in response to his parents' wishes rather than his own. Three times already he had acted as assessor, and aroused the amazement of others by his integrity, though for his part he found it still more amazing that they could value gold above honor.

His character was put to the test not only by the lure of covetousness but also by the sting of intimidation. In Rome he served as Assessor to the Chancellor of the Italian Treasury. Now there was at this time a certain very powerful senator who had placed many people under an obligation by his favors, and dominated others by instilling terror. He sought to gain permission for some course of action not permitted by the law, as his influence usually enabled him to do; but Alypius withstood him. A bribe was offered; Alypius laughed heartily. Threats were made, but he spurned them. Everyone marveled at the rare soul which neither sought to make a friend nor feared to make an enemy of this great man, who was widely famed for the innumerable means at his disposal either to do others a good turn or to harm them. The judge to whom Alypius stood as counsel had himself no wish to grant the petition but dared not openly refuse; he therefore threw the responsibility for the decision onto Alypius, alleging that he was prevented by his counsel from granting the request, though the truth was that if he had done so Alypius would have left the court.

Almost the only source of temptation for him lay in literary studies, for he had the opportunity to have books copied for his own use at palace prices; but after considering the claims of justice he changed his mind for the better, judging that equity, which forbade him so to act, had more to recommend it than the privilege of office, which enabled him to. This was a trifling matter, but anyone who is trustworthy in a small thing is trustworthy in a great one too, and that saying uttered by your Truth can never be without force: *If you have not proved trustworthy over dishonest money, who will give you what is real? And if you have not been trustworthy over what belongs to another, who will give you any of your own?*[58]

This is what he was like, this man so closely united with me, the friend who concurred with me as we debated the right way to live.

Nebridius

17. Nebridius too shared our aspirations and was tossed to and fro along with us, for he was an ardent fellow-seeker of the happy life and an exceedingly keen researcher into the most difficult questions. He had left behind his home territory near Carthage, left Carthage itself where he had spent most of his time, left his father's fine estate,[59] his home and his mother (who did not attempt to follow him), and come to Milan for no other purpose than to live with me and share in our fiercely burning zeal for truth and wisdom. So then there were three gaping mouths, three individuals in need, gasping out their hunger to one another and looking to you to give them their food in due time.[60] By your merciful providence our worldly behavior always brought bitter disappointments, but whenever we sought to discern the reason why we should suffer them, we met with only darkness. So we would turn away, moaning, "How long are we to go on like this?" We were perpetually asking this question, but even as we asked it we made no attempt to change our ways, because we had no light to see what we should grasp instead, if we were to let go of them.

Perplexities and plans: philosophy and the problem of continence

11, 18. For my own part I was reflecting with anxiety and some perplexity how much time had elapsed since my nineteenth year, when I had first been fired with passion for the pursuit of wisdom, resolving that once I had found it I would leave behind all empty hopes and vain desires and the follies that deluded me.[61] Yet here I was in my thirtieth year

---

58. Lk 16:11-12.
59. See Horace, *Epodi* II,3; Mt 19:29.
60. See Pss 103(104):27; 144(145):15.
61. See Ps 39:5(40:4).

sticking fast in the same muddy bog[62] through my craving to enjoy the good things of the present moment, which eluded and dissipated me. "Tomorrow," I had been saying to myself, "tomorrow I will find it; it will appear plainly and I will grasp it....

"Faustus will be coming and he will explain everything....

"Fine fellows, you Academics! So nothing that we need for living our lives can be known with certainty? Nonsense! Let us seek energetically and not give up hope. The passages which used to seem ridiculous in the Church's holy books are not so ridiculous after all, but can be understood in a different and quite acceptable way. I will plant my feet on that step where my parents put me as a child, until self-evident truth comes to light.

"But where is it to be sought? When, even? Ambrose is not available and we have no time to read. Where are we even to look for the right books? Where and when are we to buy them? From whom borrow them?

"Let us plan our day and reserve definite periods of time in the interest of our souls' salvation. A great hope has dawned, for the Catholic faith does not teach what we thought it did when we found fault with it in our vanity; its learned exponents reject as impious any suggestion that God is confined within the shape of a human body. Can we, then, hesitate to knock[63] where other truths may be opened? Our pupils occupy our morning hours, but what are we doing with the rest? Why do we not get on with it?

"Ah, but in that case, when are we to pay court to our important friends, whose patronage we need? When prepare the lessons we sell to our students? When refresh ourselves and relax our minds from concentrating on these problems?

19. "Devil take the lot of them; let us get rid of all these empty, meaningless occupations and devote ourselves solely to the quest for truth. Life is a wretched business and death unpredictable; suppose it takes us by surprise: in what condition shall we depart? Where shall we then have the chance to learn what we have neglected here? Shall we not rather suffer punishment for our negligence?

"But what if death cuts off all anxious searching, along with the power of thought itself, and puts an end to it all? Perhaps we should consider that?

---

62. See Terence, *Phormio* 780.
63. See Mt 7:7-8.

"No, perish the thought! It cannot be so. It is not meaningless, not without purpose, that the eminent and lofty authority of the Christian faith is spread throughout the world. Such great and wonderful provision would not have been made for us from above if bodily death meant the destruction of the soul's life as well. Why are we so slow, then, to abandon worldly ambition and apply ourselves singlemindedly to the search for God and a life of happiness?

"Wait a little, for those things are very pleasant too; they hold no slight sweetness. We should not be too ready to shrug them off, for to return to them later would be ignoble. Consider what a fine thing it is for a person to win a reputation. What prize could be more desirable? We have plenty of influential friends: without setting our sights unduly high, one may expect at least a governorship to come one's way. And one might marry a wife who is reasonably well off, and so will not be a heavy expense, and let this be the limit of one's ambitions. Many great men have been dedicated to the pursuit of wisdom in company with their wives, and one would do well to imitate them."

20. All the while, as I talked to myself like this and the wind blew now from this quarter, now from that, hurling my heart hither and thither, time was slipping by. I put off being *converted to the Lord* and from day to day[64] pushed away from me the day when I would live in you, though I could not postpone a daily dying in myself. Though I was so enamored of a happy life I feared to find it in its true home, and fled from it even as I sought it. For I thought I would be exceedingly miserable if deprived of a woman's embrace, and gave no thought to the medicine prepared by your mercy for the healing of this infirmity,[65] since I had no experience of it and believed that continence must be achieved by one's own strength, a strength of which I was not conscious in my own case. I was too stupid to realize that, as scripture testifies,[66] no one can be continent except by your gift. Yet you would certainly have given me the gift if I had beaten[67] upon your ears with my inward groans and cast my care upon you[68] with resolute faith.

2, 21. Alypius, however, dissuaded me from taking a wife. He repeatedly played on the fact that once I had done so it would be impossible for

---

64. See Sir 5:8.
65. See Ps 102(103):3; Mt 4:23.
66. See Wis 8:21.
67. See Mt 7:7.
68. See Ps 54:23(55:22).

us to live together in carefree leisure and devote ourselves to philosophy as we had long desired, and still desired, to do. With regard to this matter he was himself, even now as a grown man, thoroughly chaste, indeed remarkably so, perhaps because he had had an initial experience of sexual intercourse in early adolescence, but had not continued in it; he had been hurt and had felt ashamed, and thereafter lived in complete continence. I opposed his view, reminding him of the examples of people who, though married, had cultivated wisdom and found favor with God,[69] and had faithfully kept their friends and loved them dearly. Not that I could myself match their nobility of mind: I was shackled by weakness of the flesh and was dragging along with me a chain forged of deadly sweetness, fearing to be freed from it and beating away his words of sound advice as though from a touchy wound, for that advice was a hand that might have set me free. Worse still, the serpent[70] was speaking through me even to Alypius, attempting to bind him too and using my tongue to scatter sweet snares in his path[71] to trap those honorable, nimble feet.

22. He was in no sense overcome by lust for pleasure like mine; what lured him toward a tentative desire for marriage was curiosity. It came about like this. He looked on with astonishment that I, for whom he had no small regard, was so deeply mired in the sticky morass of sensual pleasure that whenever the subject came up for discussion between us I declared that I was utterly incapable of living a celibate life, and defended myself in the face of his obvious astonishment by pointing out the vast difference between that hasty, furtive experience of his, which by now he scarcely remembered and could therefore easily disdain with no trouble at all, and the delights of my habitual way of life. If only the honorable name of matrimony were conferred upon these pleasures, I told him, he would have no right to be astonished that I felt unable to despise the way I lived. He replied that he was most interested to know what this element was, without which my life, which to him appeared so attractive, would be to me a punishment. His mind, free from that fetter, was amazed at my servitude, and through amazement was drawn toward a hankering to experience it. He might have found his way into the same experience and perhaps have fallen from there into the very servitude which had provoked his amaze-

---

69. See Heb 13:16.
70. See Gn 3:1.
71. See Ps 141:4(142:3).

ment, for what he was bent upon was a pact with death,[72] and anyone who falls in love with danger will fall into it.[73] Neither of us considered, except feebly, what the glory of wedlock could be in terms of guiding the course of a marriage and bringing up children. It was my habitual attempt to sate an insatiable concupiscence that for the most part savagely tormented me and held me captive, while for him it was wonder that dragged him along toward captivity.

Such was our condition until you, O Most High, who forsake not our clay,[74] mercifully came to aid our misery in marvelous, hidden ways.

Projected marriage

13, 23. Insistent pressure was on me to marry a wife. Already I was asking for it myself, and a marriage was being arranged for me, thanks especially to my mother's efforts. She expected to see me washed in the saving waters of baptism after marriage, and she rejoiced to see me being daily shaped toward this end, observing that her prayers were beginning to be answered and your promises with regard to my faith fulfilled. In the light of my request and her own desire she besought you daily, with powerful, heartfelt cry, to show her in a vision something of my future marriage; but you never consented. She did have some illusory, fantastic dreams, brought on by the activity of her own human spirit as she busied herself about this matter, and these she related to me, but without the confidence she usually showed when you revealed something to her: to these dreams she attached little importance. She claimed that by something akin to the sense of taste, a faculty she could not explain in words, she was able to distinguish between your revelations to her and the fantasies of her own dreaming soul.

All the same, the pressure on me was kept up, and an offer for a certain girl was made on my behalf; but she was about two years below marriageable age.[75] I liked her, though, so we decided to wait.

---

72. See Wis 1:16; Is 28:18.
73. See Sir 3:27.
74. See Gn 2:7.
75. According to Justinian's Code (*Inst.* 1,22) girls could marry at twelve.

Dream of an ideal community

14, 24. Many of my friends and I were greatly exercised in mind as we talked together and shared our loathing of the annoying upheavals inseparable from human life; and we almost made up our minds to live a life of leisure,[76] far removed from the crowds. We would set up this place of leisurely retirement in such a way that any possessions we might have would be made available to the community and we would pool our resources in a single fund. The sincerity of our friendship should ensure that this thing should not belong to one person and that to another: there would be one single property formed out of many; the whole would belong to each of us, and all things would belong to all. It seemed to us that about ten people would be able to live like this in the same community and that there would be some exceptionally rich men among us, particularly our fellow-townsman Romanianus; he had been very well known to me since childhood and had now been drawn to the court by the serious complexities of his business affairs. He was the most enthusiastic of all for this project, and his persuasion carried special weight inasmuch as he was far more wealthy than the rest.[77] We agreed that two of us should be appointed as officials each year to see to necessary provisions, so that the others could be undisturbed.[78]

But some of us were already married and others hoped to be, and as soon as we began to consider whether our womenfolk[79] would consent to these arrangements the whole elaborate plan fell apart, came to pieces in our hands and had to be discarded. The sequel was sighs and groans and the redirection of our steps into the broad paths of the world,[80] because though our hearts were full of schemes, your design lasts for ever.[81] In the light of that design of yours you laughed at our plans while preparing your own, for you meant to give us our food in due time; you were to open your hand and fill our souls with your blessing.[82]

---

76. The ideal of *otium*, leisure, for the educated of the ancient world implied studious devotion to philosophy, literature, or the arts.

77. Romanianus of Thagaste, Augustine's financial benefactor, a Manichee, whom Augustine later attempted to lead to baptism.

78. Pythagorean, as well as Christian, models have been suggested as the inspiration for this commune. The scheme fell apart immediately, as Augustine goes on to relate, but was to some extent realized later at Cassiciacum; see IX,3.5.

79. *Mulierculae*, diminutive, as in I,6,10: possibly an ironic comment by Augustine on the fragility of the scheme.

80. See Mt 7:13.

81. See Prv 19:21; Ps 32(33):11.

82. See Ps 144(145):15-16.

Dismissal of Augustine's common-law wife; his grief

15, 25. Meanwhile my sins were multiplying,[83] for the woman with whom I had been cohabiting was ripped from my side, being regarded as an obstacle to my marriage. So deeply was she engrafted into my heart that it was left torn and wounded and trailing blood.[84] She had returned to Africa, vowing to you that she would never give herself to another man, and the son I had fathered by her was left with me. But I was too unhappy to follow a woman's example: I faced two years of waiting before I could marry the girl to whom I was betrothed, and I chafed at the delay, for I was no lover of marriage but the slave of lust. So I got myself another woman, in no sense a wife, that my soul's malady might be sustained in its pristine vigor or even aggravated, as it was conducted under the escort of inveterate custom into the realm of matrimony.

The wound inflicted on me by the earlier separation did not heal either. After the fever and the immediate acute pain had dulled, it putrefied, and the pain became a cold despair.

16, 26. Praise be to you, glory be to you,[85] O fount of all mercy! As I grew more and more miserable, you were drawing nearer. Already your right hand was ready to seize me and pull me out of the filth,[86] yet I did not know it. The only thing that restrained me from being sucked still deeper into the whirlpool of carnal lusts was the fear of death and of your future judgment, which throughout all the swings of opinion had never been dislodged from my heart. With my friends Alypius and Nebridius I argued about the fate of the good and the wicked: I maintained that, as I saw it, Epicurus would have won the debate had I not believed that after death life remains for the soul, and so do the consequences of our moral actions; this Epicurus refused to believe. I posed this question: if we were immortal, and lived in a state of perpetual bodily pleasure without any fear of losing it, why

---

83. See Sir 23:3.
84. It had been a faithful common-law marriage and had lasted about fourteen years. Such unions were considered normal and acceptable by Augustine's contemporaries and even countenanced (for the unmarried) by the Church: see Council of Toledo (400), canon 17. Augustine considered this situation himself in *The Excellence of Marriage* 5,5, written a few years later than *The Confessions*, and held that it approximated to true marriage. He was probably under pressure from Monica, and possibly from Ambrose, to break it off, but commentators tend to judge him severely.
85. See 1 Chr 29:11-12.
86. Or, reading *ablutura* with some manuscripts instead of *ablatura*, "to pull me out of the filth and wash me clean," that is, by baptism.

should we not be happy? Would there be anything else to seek?[87] I did not know that it was symptomatic of my vast misery that I had sunk so low, and was so blind, as to be incapable of even conceiving the light of a goodness, a beauty, which deserved to be embraced for its own sake, which the bodily eye sees not, though it is seen by the spirit within. Nor did I in my wretchedness consider what stream it was whence flowed to me the power to discuss even these distasteful things with my friends and still find sweetness in our talk, or whence came my inability to be happy, even in the sense in which I then understood happiness, without my friends, however lavishly supplied I might be with carnal luxuries. I loved these friends for their own sake, and felt myself loved by them for mine.

Oh, how tortuous were those paths! Woe betide the soul which supposes it will find something better if it forsakes you! Toss and turn as we may, now on our back, now side, now belly—our bed is hard at every point, for you alone are our rest.[88] But lo! Here you are;[89] you rescue us from our wretched meanderings and establish us on your way;[90] you console us and bid us, "Run:[91] I will carry you, I will lead you and I will bring you home."[92]

87. This doctrine of Epicurus is set out in Cicero, *De finibus* I,12,40.
88. Augustine's favorite theme of restlessness and rest in God is here given special poignancy by the evocation of insomnia.
89. See Ps 138(139):8.
90. See Pss 31(32):8; 85(86):11.
91. See 1 Cor 9:24.
92. See Is 46:4.

Book VII

Neo-Platonism Frees
Augustine's Mind

1, 1. By now my misspent, impious adolescence was dead, and I was entering the period of youth,[1] but as I advanced in age I sank ignobly into foolishness, for I was unable to grasp the idea of substance except as something we can see with our bodily eyes. I was no longer representing you to myself in the shape of a human body, O God, for since beginning to acquire some inkling of philosophy I always shunned this illusion, and now I was rejoicing to find a different view in the belief of our spiritual mother, your Catholic Church. Yet no alternative way of thinking about you had occurred to me; and here was I, a mere human, and a sinful one at that, striving to comprehend you, the supreme, sole, true God.[2]

Materialistic notions of God insufficient

From the core of my being I believed you to be imperishable, inviolable and unchangeable, because although I did not understand why or how this could be, I saw quite plainly and with full conviction that anything perishable is inferior to what is imperishable, and I unhesitatingly reckoned the inviolable higher than anything subject to violation, and what is constant and unchanging better than what can be changed.[3] My heart cried out in vehement protest against all the phantom shapes that thronged my imagination, and I strove with this single weapon to beat away from the gaze of

---

1. *Iuventus* is associated in Augustine's mind with Milan. *Adulescentia* lasted from 15 to 30.
2. See Jn 17:3.
3. The immutability of God was a key idea for Augustine, as becomes clear especially in this book.

my mind the cloud of filth that hovered round me,[4] but hardly had I got rid of it than in another twinkling of an eye[5] it was back again, clotted together, invading and clogging my vision, so that even though I was no longer hampered by the image of a human body, I was still forced to imagine something corporeal spread out in space, whether infused into the world or even diffused through the infinity outside it. This was still the case even though I recognized that this substance was imperishable, inviolable and immutable (necessarily so, being superior to anything perishable, subject to violation or changeable); because anything to which I must deny these spatial dimensions seemed to me to be nothing at all, absolutely nothing, not even a void such as might be left if every kind of body—earthly, watery, aerial or heavenly—were removed from it, for though such a place would be a nothingness, it would still have the quality of space.

2. Whatever was not stretched out in space, or diffused or compacted or inflated or possessed of some such qualities, or at least capable of possessing them, I judged to be nothing at all. Yet in so thinking I was gross of heart[6] and not even luminous to myself; for as my eyes were accustomed to roam among material forms, so did my mind among the images of them, yet I could not see that this very act of perception, whereby I formed those images, was different from them in kind. Yet my mind would never have been able to form them unless it was itself a reality, and a great one.

Hence I thought that even you, Life of my life, were a vast reality spread throughout space in every direction: I thought that you penetrated the whole mass of the earth and the immense, unbounded spaces beyond it on all sides, that earth, sky and all things were full of you, and that they found their limits in you, while you yourself had no limit anywhere. Since material air—I mean the atmosphere above the earth—posed no barrier to the sun's light, which was able to penetrate and pass through it, filling it entirely without bursting it apart or tearing it, I assumed that not only the material sky, air and sea, but even the material earth, were similarly traversable by you, penetrable and open in all their greatest and tiniest

---

4. See Virgil, *Aeneid* III,233, of the Harpies who harassed the Trojan refugees.
5. See 1 Cor 15:52.
6. See Mt 13:15; Acts 28:27.

parts to your presence, which secretly breathes through them within and without, controlling all that you have made.

I held this view only because I was unable to think in any other way; it was false, because on that showing a larger part of the earth would contain a larger portion of you, and a smaller a lesser portion, and all things would be full of you in such a way that an elephant's body would contain a larger amount of you than a sparrow's, because it is bigger and takes up more space. You would be distributed piecemeal throughout the elements of the world, with greater parts of yourself present where there is plenty of room, and smaller parts in more cramped places. Obviously this is not the case. You had not yet illumined my darkness.[7]

2, 3. I had a sufficient argument, Lord, against those self-deceived deceivers[8] who, though so talkative, were dumb because your word did not sound forth from them. Yes, I had a sufficient argument, one which Nebridius had been wont to propose ever since our days in Carthage, which left us all shaken who heard it. Those so-called powers of darkness, whom they always postulate as a horde deployed in opposition to you: what would they have done to you if you had refused to fight? If the reply is that they could have inflicted some injury on you, it would imply that you are subject to violation and therefore destructible. If, on the other hand, it is denied that they had power to injure you, there would have been no point in fighting.[9] Yet the fighting is alleged to have been so intense that some portion of yourself, a limb perhaps, or an offspring of your very substance, became entangled with hostile powers and with the natures of beings not created by you, and was by them so far corrupted and changed for the worse that its beatitude was turned to misery, and it could be rescued and purified only with help; and this portion is supposed to be the soul, enslaved, defiled, corrupt, and in need of aid from your Word, which must necessarily be free, pure and unscathed if it is to help, and yet, since it is of the same nature as the soul, must be equally corrupt itself!

---

7. See Ps 17:29(18:28).
8. The Manichees.
9. The battle between light and darkness was a primary postulate of the Manichees. In the fight some portion of the light-realm had been trapped in matter and darkness; it pervaded all nature but found its highest manifestation in the human soul. The contradiction in which the Manichees thereby involved themselves, spelled out by Augustine here, was used by him in a public disputation with the Manichee Felix, who recanted.

It follows that if they admitted that, whatever you are, you are incorruptible (your substance, that is, by which you exist), this whole rigmarole would be shown up as untrue and to be rejected with loathing; but if they alleged that you are corruptible, their position would already be false and no sooner stated than be condemned. The foregoing argument was therefore quite sufficient, and I ought to have squeezed these people from my gullet and vomited them out, for no escape was left them from the horrible sacrilege of heart and tongue they were committing by thinking and speaking of you in this fashion.

The problem of evil

3, 4. I declared and firmly believed that you, our God, our true God, who made not only our souls but our bodies too, and not only our souls and bodies but people everywhere and all things, are subject to no defilement or alteration, and are in all respects unchangeable; yet even so I was still convinced that the cause of evil had not been clarified or disentangled. Nonetheless I saw that, whatever it might be, I must beware of looking for it in such a way as to be forced into believing that the immutable God was changeable, lest I become myself the very thing I was trying to trace. Accordingly I conducted my search without anxiety, certain that those whom I now wholeheartedly shunned were not speaking the truth, because I saw that through their inquiry into the origin of evil they had waxed full of malice,[10] more ready to claim that your substance was vulnerable to evil than that their own perpetrated it.

5. I strained to see for myself the truth of an explanation I had heard: that the cause of evil is the free decision of our will, in consequence of which we act wrongly and suffer your righteous judgment; but I could not see it clearly. I struggled to raise my mental gaze from the depths, but sank back again; I strove repeatedly, but again and again sank back. I was as sure of having a will as I was of being alive, and this it was that lifted me into your light. When I wanted something, or did not want it, I was absolutely certain that no one else but I was wanting or not wanting it, and I was beginning to perceive that the root of my sin lay there. Any involuntary act I regarded as something I suffered rather than as something I did, and I

---

10. See Sir 9:3; Rom 1:29.

judged it to be a penalty rather than a fault, being quick to acknowledge that I was not unjustly punished in this way, since I held you to be just. But then I was forced to ask further, "Who made me? Was it not my God, who is not merely good, but Goodness itself? Whence, then, did I derive this ability to will evil and refuse good? Is it in me simply so that I should deserve the punishment I suffer? Who established that ability in me, who planted in me this bitter cutting,[11] when my whole being is from my most sweet God? If the devil is responsible, where did the devil come from? If he was a good angel who was transformed into a devil by his own perverted will, what was the origin of this evil will in him that turned him into a devil, when an angel is made entirely by the supremely good creator?"[12]

I was pushed down again by these thoughts and nearly choked; but never was I sucked into that pit of error where no one confesses to you, because people would rather hold that you suffer evil than that we commit it.

4, 6. My efforts were directed toward discovering more of the truth, on the basis of the discovery already made that what is indestructible is better than anything liable to be destroyed. Accordingly I confessed that, whatever you might be, you must be indestructible. No intelligence has ever conceived of anything better than you, or ever will, for you are the supreme and all-surpassing good; but since the indestructible is most truly and certainly to be esteemed above what is destructible, as I already knew, it followed that you must be indestructible, because otherwise my mind would have been able to attain something better than my God.

From this point, then, where I saw that the indestructible must be superior to what can be destroyed, I should have begun my inquiry by trying to understand where evil resides: that is, whence springs the corruption to which your nature is totally immune. For corruption can touch our God in no way whatever: neither by will, nor by necessity, nor by any unexpected misfortune. He is God, and what he wishes for himself is good, and he is himself the very nature of goodness, whereas to be corrupted is not good. Nor are you forced unwillingly into anything, because your will is not greater than your power: it could be greater only if you were greater than

---

11. See Heb 12:15.
12. Augustine will examine this question again in *The City of God* XII:1-9, but will find it insoluble.

yourself, for God's will and God's power are identical with God himself. And what unexpected chance can overtake you, who know everything? No nature exists, except because you know it. What need is there to prove at length why that substance which is God cannot be corruptible? If it were, it would not be God.

5, 7. So I was seeking the origin of evil, but seeking in an evil way, and failing to see the evil inherent in my search itself. I conjured up before my mind's eye[13] the whole of creation: all the things in it that we can see, such as earth and sea and stars and trees and living things that are mortal, and all that we do not see in it, such as the heavenly firmament overhead and all the angels and all its spiritual inhabitants; and my imagination gave form to them also, and arranged them in their due places as though they had been corporeal. And I envisaged your creation as one huge mass in which all were arrayed according to bodily kinds, both those things which were really bodily in nature and the bodies I had myself attributed to spirits. I pictured it as enormous, not of such size as it really was, of course, for that I could not know, but as large as my fancy stretched, yet finite on all sides. I imagined you, Lord, who are infinite in every possible respect, surrounding and penetrating it in its every part, like a sea extending in all directions through immense space, a single unlimited sea which held within itself a sponge as vast as one could imagine but still finite, and the sponge soaked in every fibre of itself by the boundless sea.[14]

This was how I pictured your creation filled with your infinite being, and I reflected, "Look, this is God, and these are the things God has created. God is good, and though he is far more wonderful than they in every respect, still he who is good has created them good; see too how he surrounds and pervades them. Where, then, is evil; where does it come from and how did it creep in? What is its root, its seed? Or does it not exist at all? But in that case, why do we fear and avoid something that has no reality? If we say that our fear is meaningless, then the fear itself is unde-niably evil, for it goads and tortures our heart to no purpose, and so the evil is all the greater inasmuch as the object of our fear is non-existent, yet we fear all the same. Either the evil we fear exists, or our fear itself is the evil.

---

13. See Ps 15(16):8.
14. Plotinus has a similar image in *Enneads* IV,3,9.

So where does it come from, if the good God made all things good?[15] He is the greater good, to be sure, the supreme good, and the things he has made are lesser goods; nonetheless creator and creatures are all good. Whence, then, comes evil? Was something bad in the material he used, so that though he formed it and disposed it in order[16] he left in it some element that was not turned to good? But why? Did he lack the power so to convert and change it all that no evil would remain, he who is omnipotent? In any case, why would he have chosen to use it for making things, rather than using this same almighty power to destroy it entirely? Or could it have existed against his will? Or again, if matter was eternal, why did he allow it to exist so long, from infinite ages past, and then at last decide to make things out of it? Or, if he suddenly decided to act, surely he, being almighty, could have acted in such a way that it should cease to be, and he alone should exist, he, the complete, true, supreme, infinite Good? Or, supposing that it was unseemly for him who is good not to fashion and build something good as well, ought he not to have done away with all the bad material and destroyed it, and himself originated some good matter instead, which he could use to create everything? If he were able to construct good things only with the help of material he had not himself constructed, he would not be omnipotent."

Such thoughts as these was I turning over in my miserable soul, weighed down as it was by the gnawing anxieties that flowed from my fear that death might overtake me before I had found the truth. Faith in your Christ, our Lord and Savior, as I found it in the Catholic Church, still persisted steadfastly in my heart, though it was a faith still in many ways unformed, wavering and at variance with the norm of her teaching. Yet my mind did not abandon it, but drank it in ever more deeply as the days passed.

He finally rejects astrology

6, 8. It was some time since I had rejected the misleading divinations and impious ravings of astrologers. On this score too let your merciful dealings themselves sing praise to you from the innermost depths of my

---

15. See Gn 1:31.
16. *Fecit ... formavit atque ordinavit*: probably a trinitarian pattern.

soul,[17] O my God! In my obstinacy you took care of me by providing[18] me with a friend: you it was, you and no other, for who else calls us back from our every death-dealing error but the Life that cannot die, the Wisdom who enlightens our needy minds but needs no borrowed light itself, the Wisdom who governs the whole world, even to the fluttering leaves on the trees? Obstinately indeed had I struggled against the shrewd old man, Vindicianus,[19] and against Nebridius, a youth of wonderful insight. The former had declared with emphasis, the latter admittedly with more hesitation, but frequently, that the art of foretelling the future is bogus, that human guesswork is often lucky, and that when people talk a great deal many truths about future events are likely to be uttered, not because the speakers know but because they stumble upon them by not keeping their mouths shut. So you provided for me a friend who was keen to consult astrologers, but not well versed in their lore. Having sought answers from them out of curiosity, as I have indicated, he already knew a certain amount, which he had heard, he said, from his father. Little did he know how efficacious it was to prove in giving the lie to that superstition.

His name was Firminus. He had been educated in the liberal arts and was a well-spoken man, and since he regarded me as a dear friend he consulted me about certain of his business affairs of which he had high hopes, inquiring how I interpreted his birth horoscope, as they call it. Now I was already inclined toward Nebridius' view of the practice; however, I did not refuse to offer an interpretation or say what came into my mind, doubtful though I was; but I remarked that I was almost persuaded that divination was absurd and meaningless.

Then he told me that his father had been an avid student of books dealing with such matters, and had had a friend who was equally a devotee. As the two men collaborated in research and discussion they became more and more ardently enthusiastic for this nonsense. If even dumb animals in their households were due to produce young, these men would record the exact moments of birth and note the position of the stars at the time, on the pretext of collecting experimental data for what claimed to be a science. Firminus went on to say that he had heard his father tell

---

17. See Ps 106 (107):8 and recurrently.
18. *Procurasti:* this friend Firminus was "procured" for Augustine by God, as the "books of the Platonists" will be in VII,9,13.
19. See IV,3,5.

how, when his mother was pregnant with him, Firminus, a certain slave-girl in the house of his father's friend was expecting a baby at the same time. This fact could not escape the girl's master, who took the utmost care to calculate even the whelping-times of his dogs. So while one man was observing and counting with meticulous precision the days, hours and smaller fractions of hours in his wife's case, the other was doing the same in respect of his maid-servant.

The two women gave birth simultaneously, forcing them to assign exactly the same horoscope, even in the finest detail, to both babies, the one to his son, the other to his slave. It happened like this. As the women went into labor the two friends sent word to each other to let each know what was happening at the other's house, and held messengers in readiness who would announce to each the birth of the child as soon as it occurred. It was easy for them to arrange for instantaneous announcement, since each was master in his own domain. So, Firminus related, the two sets of messengers were dispatched, and met at a point exactly halfway between the two houses, which meant that neither of the friends could assign a different position of the stars, or record any different moment of time. Yet Firminus was born in easy circumstances among his own relatives, and pursued quite a brilliant career in the world[20] making money and advancing in rank, while that slave-boy went on serving his masters, with no alleviation whatever of the yoke his status imposed on him. Firminus, who knew him, testified to the fact.

9. As soon as I heard this story, which, in view of the narrator's character, I believed, my obstinate resistance was completely overcome and dropped away. I attempted first of all to rescue Firminus himself from his curiosity about the occult by pointing out to him that if, after inspecting his birth horoscope, I had to make a prediction that accorded with the facts, I would have to say that I read in it that his parents were of excellent standing among his kinsfolk, that his family was a noble one in his home town, and that having been born a gentleman he would receive a good education in the liberal arts; whereas if the slave had consulted me about the indications of his birth horoscope—and his had been precisely the same—I would have to say, if my answer were to match reality, that what I saw in it was a family of the lowest class, a servile status, and all the rest of

---

20. Or "pursued a career along the world's highways," literally "whitened roads," possibly an allusion to the white surface on Roman roads, where chalk was used.

those very different conditions which marked off his lot from the other man's. The realization that after inspecting the same data I would either have to make divergent predictions in order to give a true answer, or else make the same prediction in the two cases and thereby speak falsely, was to me most certain evidence that when true predictions were offered by diviners who studied horoscopes, such things were the product of luck, not skill; but when false predictions were made, they resulted not from the practitioner's lack of skill, but from his luck letting him down.[21]

10. Approaching the subject from this aspect and pondering these points, I now turned my attention to the case of twins. I hoped to attack and refute and make a laughing-stock of the demented people who make a living by astrology, and I wanted to make sure that none of them would be in a position to retort that either Firminus had lied to me or his father had lied to him. At the birth of twins, then, it usually happens that both are delivered from the womb with only a short interval of time between them; and however great the influence this space of time may be alleged to have in the course of nature, it cannot be measured by human observation and certainly cannot be registered in the charts which an astrologer will later study with a view to making a true forecast. And true it will not be, because anyone who had examined the one same birth horoscope that applied to Esau and Jacob would have been obliged to foretell the same fate for both of them, whereas in fact their destinies were different. The astrologer would therefore have been wrong; or, if he spoke truly and foretold different things for each, he would have done so on the basis of the same data. He could speak the truth only by chance, then, not by skill.

For in truth it is you, Lord, who are at work, you, the supremely just ruler of the universe, though those who consult astrologers and those who are consulted know it not. By your secret inspiration you make each inquirer hear what befits him, as your unfathomable judgment shall justly assess our souls' secret deserving. Let no human being challenge you, "What is this?" or "Why that?" Let him not ask; no, let him not ask, for he is but human.

---

21. See IV,3,5.

Still searching

7, 11. So it was that you, my helper,[22] had already freed me from those bonds, but I was still trying to trace the cause of evil, and found no way out of the difficulty. Yet you allowed no flood of thoughts to sweep me away from the faith whereby I believed that you exist, that your essence is unchangeable, that you care for us humans and judge our deeds, and that in your Son, Christ our Lord, and in the holy scriptures which the authority of your Catholic Church guarantees, you have laid down the way for human beings to reach that eternal life[23] which awaits us after death. These beliefs were unaffected, and persisted strong and unshaken in me as I feverishly searched for the origin of evil.

What agonizing birth-pangs tore my heart, what groans it uttered, O my God! And there, unknown to me, were your hearkening ears, for as I labored hard in my silent search the mute sufferings of my mind reached your mercy as loud cries. You alone knew my pain, no one else; for how little of it could I express in words to my closest friends! Could their ears have caught all the tumult that raged in my soul, when even I had neither time enough nor eloquence to articulate it? Yet even as my heart roared its anguish my clamor found its way to your hearing, and all my longing lay before you, for the light of my eyes was not there at my command:[24] it was within, but I was outside;[25] it occupied no place, but I had fixed my gaze on spatially positioned things, and so I found in them nowhere to rest. Nor did they welcome me or afford me the chance to say, "This is enough, now all is well," nor did they even release me to return to where I could well have found what was enough. I was nobler than they, but lowlier than you; and as long as I was subject to you my true joy was your very self, and you had subjected to me all those things which you created below me. The happy mean, the central region[26] where I would find salvation, was to preserve your image in me, serving you and subduing my body; but because I was rearing up against you in my pride, charging head-high against the Lord and crassly presuming on my own strength,[27] even those inferior things gained the upper hand and pressed me down, so that nowhere could I

---

22. See Pss 17:3(18:2); 29:11(30:10); 58:18(59:17); 62:8(63:7).
23. *Viam ... vitam,* both titles of Christ; see Jn 14:6. Allusions to "the Way," implicitly Christ, are frequent in this book.
24. See Ps 37:9-11(38:8-10).
25. See X,27,38; the language is reminiscent of Porphyry.
26. In this central position the soul was poised between God and creatures. In XIII,9,10 Augustine will develop the idea that love is a weight that drags it up or down.
27. See Jb 15:26 (Old Latin).

find respite or relief. When I looked outward they crowded upon me thick and fast; when I tried to think the images of these material things blocked my path of return, as though demanding, "Where are you off to, you unworthy, degraded fellow?" All this had sprung from my wounded condition, for you humbled this proud man with a wounding blow.[28] My swollen pride got in the way and kept me from you, and my face was so puffy that my eyes were closed.

8, 12. But you, Lord, abide for ever[29] and will not for ever be angry with us,[30] for you have taken pity on us who are earth and ashes;[31] and so it was pleasing in your sight[32] to give new form to my deformity.[33] You goaded me within[34] to make me chafe impatiently until you should grow clear to my spiritual sight. At the unseen touch of your medicine[35] my swelling subsided, while under the stinging eye-salve[36] of curative pain the fretful, darkened vision of my spirit began to improve day by day.

He reads "the books of the Platonists"

9, 13. You wanted to show me first and foremost how you thwart the proud but give grace to the humble,[37] and with what immense mercy on your part the way of humility was demonstrated to us when your Word was made flesh and dwelt among men and women;[38] and so through a certain man grossly swollen with pride you provided me[39] with some books by the Platonists, translated from the Greek into Latin.[40] In them I read (not that the same words were used, but precisely the same doctrine was taught, buttressed by many and various argu-

---

28. See Ps 88:11(89:10).
29. See Ps 101:13(102:12).
30. See Pss 84:6(85:5); 102(103):9.
31. See Jb 42:6; Sir 17:31.
32. See Ps 18:15(19:14); Dn 3:40.
33. See X,27, 38; I,7,12, the special work of the second person of the Trinity.
34. See Virgil, *Aeneid* XI,337; Eccl 12:11; Acts 9:5.
35. That is, Christ. At IX,13,35 Augustine speaks of the medicine that hung on the cross, and at IX,8,18 of the medicine that watches over us.
36. See Rv 3:18. Augustime uses this word *collyrium* of the incarnate Christ in his *Homilies on the Gospel of John* 2, 16, and elsewhere.
37. See Prv 3:34; Jas 4:6; 1 Pt 5:5.
38. See Jn 1:14.
39. *Procurasti* as in VII,6,8.
40. The translator was Marius Victorinus. It may be significant that Augustine does not identify them more precisely, but commentators have not left it at that. He certainly knew some of Plotinus' treatises; probably he read some Porphyry at Milan, perhaps in the form of maxims. In *The City of God* VIII,12 he mentions Plotinus, Iamblichus, Porphyry, and Apuleius Afer as "very noble." He would in any case have imbibed some Neo-Platonism from Ambrose's teaching, to which he continued to listen, and from educated friends.

ments) that *in the beginning was the Word, and the Word was with God; he was God. He was with God in the beginning. Everything was made through him; nothing came to be without him. What was made is alive with his life, and that life was the light of humankind. The Light shines in the darkness, and the darkness has never been able to master it;* and that the human soul, even though it bears *testimony about the Light,* is not itself the Light, but that God, the Word, is *the true Light, which illumines every human person who comes into this world;* and that he was in this world, *a world made by him, but the world did not know him.* But that *he came to his own home, and his own people did not receive him; but to those who did receive him he gave power to become children of God: to those, that is, who believe in his name*[41]—none of this did I read there.

14. I also read in them that God, the Word, was born not of blood nor man's desire nor lust of the flesh, but of God;[42] but that *the Word was made flesh and dwelt among us,*[43] I did not read there. I certainly observed that in these writings it was often stated, in a variety of ways, that the Son, being *in the form of God* the Father, *deemed it no robbery to be equal to God,* because he is identical with him in nature. But that *he emptied himself and took on the form of a slave, and being made in the likeness of men was found in human form,* that *he humbled himself and was made obedient to the point of death, even death on a cross, which is why God raised him* from the dead, and *gave him a name above every other name, so that at the name of Jesus every knee should bow, in heaven, on earth, or in the underworld, and every tongue confess that Jesus Christ is Lord, in the glory of God the Father,*[44] of this no mention was made in these books.

I did read in them that your only-begotten Son, coeternal with you, abides before all ages and above all ages, and that *of his fullness*[45] our souls receive, to become blessed thereby, and that by participation in that Wisdom which abides in itself[46] they are made new in order to become wise;[47] but that *at the*

---

41. Jn 1:1-12.
42. See Jn 1:13.
43. Jn 1:14.
44. Phil 2:6-11.
45. Jn 1:16.
46. See Wis 7:27.
47. He would have found a kind of trinity in Plotinus: the one, or primordial unity from which everything else derived; the realm of intellect or pure intelligence, in which there was knowledge of differentiated reality; and the realm of soul, where knowledge was grasped for. The two latter are emanations from the one and effect the transition to multiplicity. But they are not equal, and the term logos is not appropriated to the second element.

who knows truth knows it, and whoever knows it knows eternity.[69] Love knows it.

O eternal Truth, true Love, and beloved Eternity, you are my God, and for you I sigh day and night.[70] As I first began to know you you lifted me up[71] and showed me that while that which I might see exists indeed, I was not yet capable of seeing it. Your rays beamed intensely upon me, beating back my feeble gaze, and I trembled with love and dread. I knew myself to be far away from you in a region of unlikeness,[72] and I seemed to hear your voice from on high: "I am the food of the mature; grow then, and you will eat me. You will not change me into yourself like bodily food: you will be changed into me."[73] And I recognized that you have chastened man for his sin and caused my soul to dwindle away like a spider's web,[74] and I said, "Is truth then a nothing, simply because it is not spread out through space either finite or infinite?" Then from afar you cried to me, "By no means, for *I am who am*."[75]

I heard it as one hears a word in the heart, and no possibility of doubt remained to me; I could more easily have doubted that I was alive than that truth exists, truth that is seen and understood through the things that are made.

New light on the problem of evil

11, 17. Contemplating other things below you, I saw that they do not in the fullest sense exist, nor yet are they completely non-beings: they are real because they are from you, but unreal inasmuch as they are not what

---

69. An echo of Christ's declaration in Jn 14:7. Augustine immediately goes on to "love" in the next two sentences. These clearly trinitarian terms presumably derive from his subsequent, Christian, reflection on the original experience.
70. See Ps 1:2; Jer 9:1; Ps 41:4(42:3).
71. See Ps 26(27):10.
72. The formula is from Plotinus, *Enneads* I,8,13, who derived it from Plato's "bottomless sea of unlikeness" in *Politics* 273 D6-E1. But Lk 15:13 is perhaps equally in Augustine's mind. In his *Exposition of Psalm* 99,5 he says, "In your unlikeness to God you have gone far from him; as you become like him you draw near." The idea that distance from God is equivalent to unlikeness became very influential and recurs in many Christian writers and mystics.
73. He uses eating as a metaphor for assimilating the truth of God in III,1,1; IV,1,1; X,6. 8; XIII, 18,23; but here there may be eucharistic overtones as well.
74. See Ps 38:12(39:11). In his *Exposition* of this psalm (38, 18) he explains, "What is frailer than a spider's web? You have only to lay a finger lightly on it, and it is a wreck ... and this is what you do to my soul ... when you chasten me for my sin."
75. Ex 3:14.

you are. For that alone truly is, which abides unchangingly. As for me, my good is to hold fast to God,[76] for if I do not abide in him, I shall not be able to in myself; whereas he, abiding ever in himself, renews all things.[77] You are my Lord, for you need no goods of mine.[78]

12, 18. It was further made clear to me that things prone to destruction are good,[79] since this destructibility would be out of the question if they were either supremely good or not good at all; because if they were supremely good they would be indestructible, whereas if they were not good at all there would be nothing in them that could be destroyed. Destruction is obviously harmful, yet it can do harm only by diminishing the good. It follows, then, that either destruction harms nothing, which is impossible, or that all things which suffer harm are being deprived of some good; this conclusion is beyond cavil. If, however, they lose all their good, they will not exist at all, for if they were to continue in existence without being any longer subject to destruction, they would be better, because permanently indestructible; and what could be more outrageous than to declare them better for having lost everything that was good in them? Hence if they are deprived of all good, they will be simply non-existent; and so it follows that as long as they do exist, they are good.

Everything that exists is good, then; and so evil, the source of which I was seeking, cannot be a substance, because if it were, it would be good. Either it would be an indestructible substance, and that would mean it was very good indeed, or it would be a substance liable to destruction—but then it would not be destructible unless it were good.

I saw, then, for it was made clear to me, that you have made all good things, and that there are absolutely no substances that you have not made. I saw too that you have not made all things equal. They all exist because they are severally good but collectively very good, for our God has made all things *exceedingly good.*[80]

13, 19. For you evil has no being at all, and this is true not of yourself only but of everything you have created, since apart from you there is nothing that could burst in and disrupt the order you have imposed on it. In some parts of it certain things are regarded as evil because they do not suit

---

76. See Ps 72(73):28.
77. See Wis 7:27.
78. See Ps 15(16):2.
79. See Plotinus, *Enneads* III,2,5.
80. Gn 1:31; Sir 39:21.

certain others; but these same things do fit in elsewhere, and they are good there, and good in themselves. All these things that are at odds with each other belong to the lower part of creation that we call earth, which has its own cloudy, windy sky, as befits it. Far be it from me ever to say, "These things ought not to be"; because even if I could see these things alone, and longed, certainly, for something better, it would already be incumbent on me to praise you for them alone; for on earth the dragons and all the depths proclaim you worthy of praise, as do the fire, hail, snow, ice and stormy winds that obey your word, the mountains and hills, fruit-bearing trees and all cedars, wild beasts and tame, creeping creatures and birds on the wing. Earth's kings and all its peoples, rulers and the world's judges, young men and maidens, old men and youths, all praise your name.[81] But since in heaven too your creatures praise you, our God, let all your angels tell your praises on high, let all your powers extol you, sun and moon, all stars and the light, the empyrean and the waters above the heavens: let them too praise your name.[82] No longer was I hankering for any elements to be better than they were, because I was now keeping the totality in view; and though I certainly esteemed the higher creatures above the lower, a more wholesome judgment showed me that the totality was better than the higher things on their own would have been.

14, 20. There is no wholesomeness[83] for those who find fault with anything you have created, as there was none for me when many of the things you have made displeased me. Since my soul did not dare to find my God displeasing, it was unwilling to admit that anything that displeased it was truly yours. This was why it had strayed away into believing in a duality of substances, but there it found no rest, and only mouthed the opinions of others. Turning back again it had made for itself a god extended through infinite space, all-pervasive, and had thought this god was you, and had set him up in its heart;[84] so it became yet again a temple for its own idol and an abomination in your sight. But when you cradled my stupid head and closed my eyes to the sight of vain things[85] so that I could absent me from myself awhile, and my unwholesome madness was

---

81. See Ps 148:7-12.
82. See Ps 148:1-5.
83. See Ps 37:4(38:3).
84. See Ez 14:7.
85. See Ps 118(119):37.

lulled to sleep, then I awoke in you and saw you to be infinite, but in a different sense; and that vision in no way derived from the flesh.

15, 21. I turned my gaze to other things and saw that they owe their being to you and that all of them are by you defined, but in a particular sense: not as though contained in a place, but because you hold all things in your Truth as though in your hand; and all of them are true insofar as they exist, and nothing whatever is a deceit unless it is thought to be what it is not. I saw, further, that all things are set not only in their appropriate places but also in their proper times, and that you, who alone are eternal, did not set to work after incalculable stretches of time, because no stretches of time, neither those which have passed away nor those still to come, would pass or come except because you are at work and you abide eternally.

16, 22. Drawing on my own experience I found it unsurprising that bread, which is pleasant to a healthy palate, is repugnant to a sick one, and that diseased eyes hate the light which to the unclouded is delightful. Villains find even your justice disagreeable, and snakes and maggots far more so, yet you have created these things good, and fit for the lower spheres of your world. Indeed, the villains themselves are fit only for these lower regions in the measure that they are unlike you, but for the higher when they come to resemble you more closely.

I inquired then what villainy might be, but I found no substance, only the perversity of a will twisted away from you, God, the supreme substance, toward the depths—a will that throws away its life within[86] and swells with vanity abroad.

Fresh attempt at mounting to God; he attains That Which Is

17, 23. I found it amazing that though I now loved your very self, and not some figment of imagination in place of you, I could not continue steadfastly in the enjoyment of my God. I was drawn toward you by your beauty but swiftly dragged away from you by my own weight, swept back headlong and groaning onto these things below myself; and this weight was carnal habit. Nonetheless the memory of you stayed with me, and I had no doubt whatever whom I ought to cling to, though I knew that I was not yet capable of clinging, because the perishable body weighs down the soul,

---

86. See Sir 10:10.

and its earthly habitation oppresses a mind teeming with thoughts.[87] I was
fully persuaded that your invisible reality is plainly to be understood
through created things, your everlasting power also, and your divinity;[88]
for I had been trying to understand how it was possible for me to appreciate the beauty of material things in the sky or on earth, and why the
power to make sound judgments about changeable matters was readily
available to me, so that I could say, "This thing ought to be like this, but
that other different"; and in seeking the reason why I was able to judge as I
did I realized that above my changeable mind soared the real, unchangeable truth, which is eternal.[89]

Thus I pursued my inquiry by stages, from material things to the soul
that perceives them through the body, and from there to that inner power
of the soul[90] to which the body's senses report external impressions. The
intelligence of animals can reach as far as this.

I proceeded further and came to the power of discursive reason, to
which the data of our senses are referred for judgment. Yet as found in me
even reason acknowledged itself to be subject to change, and stretched
upward to the source of its own intelligence, withholding its thoughts
from the tyranny of habit[91] and detaching itself from the swarms of noisy
phantasms. It strove to discover what this light was that bedewed it when it
cried out unhesitatingly that the Unchangeable is better than anything
liable to change; it sought the fount whence flowed its concept of the
Unchangeable—for unless it had in some fashion recognized Immutability, it could never with such certainty have judged it superior to things
that change.

And then my mind attained to *That Which Is*, in the flash of one tremulous
glance.[92] Then indeed did I perceive your invisible reality through created
things,[93] but to keep my gaze there was beyond my strength. I was forced back
through weakness and returned to my familiar surroundings, bearing with me

87. See Wis 9:15, frequently quoted by Augustine in connection with his image of *pondus*,
    weight.
88. See Rom 1:20.
89. See Plotinus, *Enneads* V,1,11, where it is argued that the abiding principles of beauty and
    goodness cannot be the property of the individual soul as such, since our rational mind is only
    intermittently aware of them: they must derive from mind, or the divine source of mind,
    residing in us.
90. That is, the "inner sense" he referred to in I, 20, 31, which coordinates sense-impressions and
    relates them to the perspective self.
91. See Cicero, *Tusculan Disputations* I,6,38.
92. The goal of the Plotinian ascent of the mind to God, but the last phrase echoes 1 Cor 15:52.
93. See Rom 1:20.

only a loving memory, one that yearned for something of which I had caught the fragrance, but could not yet feast upon.

He realizes the need for Christ the Mediator

18, 24. Accordingly I looked for a way to gain the strength I needed to enjoy you, but I did not find it until I embraced the mediator between God and humankind, the man Christ Jesus,[94] who also is God, supreme over all things and blessed for ever.[95] Not yet had I embraced him, though he called out, proclaiming, *I am the Way and the Truth and the Life,*[96] nor had I known him as the food which, though I was not yet strong enough to eat it, he had mingled with our flesh; for the Word became flesh so that your Wisdom, through whom you created all things,[97] might become for us the milk adapted to our infancy.[98] Not yet was I humble enough to grasp the humble Jesus as my God, nor did I know what his weakness had to teach. Your Word, the eternal Truth who towers above the higher spheres of your creation, raises up to himself those creatures who bow before him; but in these lower regions he has built himself a humble dwelling[99] from our clay,[100] and used it to cast down from their pretentious selves those who do not bow before him, and make a bridge to bring them to himself. He heals their swollen pride and nourishes their love, that they may not wander even further away through self-confidence, but rather weaken as they see before their feet the Godhead grown weak[101] by sharing our garments of skin,[102] and wearily fling themselves down upon him, so that he may arise and lift them up.

19, 25. I took a different view at the time, regarding Christ my Lord as no more than a man, though a man of excellent wisdom and without peer. I

---

94. See 1 Tm 2:5.
95. See Rom 9:5.
96. Jn 14:6. This verse implicitly underlines Augustine's whole story, though he explicitly cites it only here.
97. See Col 1:16.
98. In I,6,7 the infant Augustine sought from God the milk provided through his nurses; now as a grown man he stands in need of the milk supplied through another infancy, that of the speechless Word, in order to grow strong enough to eat the "food of the mature" mentioned in VII,10,16. The reference is primarily to the divine nature, but eucharistic overtones are strong.
99. See Prv 9:1.
100. See Gn 2:7.
101. See 1 Cor 1:25.
102. See Gn 3:21. In his *Exposition of Psalm* 103,1,8, Augustine interprets these as mortality, following Origen and Ambrose. A rich symbolism developed around this "old" clothing and the "putting on of Christ" in baptism.

was the more firmly persuaded of this because he had been born of a virgin and made plain to us by his own example that disdain for temporal goods is a condition for winning immortality; and it seemed to me that through God's solicitude for us in this respect Christ's teaching had acquired incomparable authority. But I could not even begin to guess what a mystery was concealed in the Word made flesh. All I had understood from the facts about him handed down in the scriptures—as, for instance, that he ate, drank, slept, walked, experienced joy and sorrow and spoke to the people—was that his flesh was united to your Word only in conjunction with a human soul and a human consciousness. This must be obvious to anyone who has recognized the immutability of your Word, as I had insofar as I was able, and on this score I had no doubt. It is characteristic of the instability of our soul or mind that it can move its bodily limbs at one moment and not move them at another, can be affected now by some emotion and now again be unaffected, can give expression to wise sentiments at one time and at another remain silent. If these actions were reported of him falsely it would lay the entirety of the scriptures open to suspicion of lying, and then these writings would afford no possibility of saving faith to the human race. In fact, however, the scriptures are trustworthy; and so I acknowledged Christ to be a perfect man: not a human body only, nor a body with a human soul but lacking intelligence. Yet I held that this same man was to be preferred to others not because he was Truth in person, but on account of the outstanding excellence of his human nature and his more perfect participation in wisdom.

Alypius thought that Catholics believed God to be clothed in flesh in such a way that there was in Christ nothing else but godhead and flesh; he did not think their preaching assigned to him a human soul or a human consciousness. Being firmly convinced that the actions Christ was remembered to have performed would have been impossible in the absence of a principle of created, rational life, Alypius was little disposed to Christian faith; but later on he recognized this error to be that of the Apollinarian heretics,[103] and so he came to rejoice with Catholics in their faith and to acquiesce in it.

---

103. Apollinaris of Laodicea, whose theories were condemned in 374, 380, and 381, held that there was no human soul in Christ, its functions being assumed by the Word.

For my own part I admit that it was later still that I learned how sharply divergent is Catholic truth from the falsehood of Photinus[104] with respect to the teaching that the Word was made flesh. Indeed, the discrediting of heretics serves to throw into high relief the mind of your Church and the content of sound doctrine,[105] for it was necessary for heresies to emerge in order to show up the people of sound faith among the weak.[106]

Christ the Way

20, 26. But in those days, after reading the books of the Platonists and following their advice to seek for truth beyond corporeal forms, I turned my gaze toward your invisible reality, trying to understand it through created things,[107] and though I was rebuffed I did perceive what that reality was which the darkness of my soul would not permit me to contemplate. I was certain that you exist, that you are infinite but not spread out through space either finite or infinite, and that you exist in the fullest sense because you have always been the same,[108] unvarying in every respect and in no wise subject to change. All other things I saw to have their being from you[109] and for this I needed but one unassailable proof—the fact that they exist. On these points I was quite certain, but I was far too weak to enjoy you. Yet I readily chattered as though skilled in the subject, and had I not been seeking your way in Christ our Savior[110] I would more probably have been killed than skilled.[111] For I had already begun to covet a reputation for wisdom, and though fully punished I shed no tears of compunction; rather was I complacently puffed up with knowledge. Where was that charity which builds[112] on the foundation of humility that is Christ Jesus?[113] And when would those books have taught it to me? I believe that you willed me to stumble upon them before I gave my mind to your scriptures, so that the memory of how I had been affected by them might be impressed upon

---

104. Photinus, Bishop of Sirmium c. 340, denied the pre-existence of Christ, holding that he first came to exist in the Virgin's womb; hence he was only man, though illuminated by special divine influence.
105. See 1 Tm 1:10; 2 Tm 4:3-4; Ti 1:9; 2:1.
106. See 1 Cor 11:19. For "the weak" see Rom 14:1, to which Alypius will appeal in the garden scene, VIII, 12, 30.
107. See Rom 1:20.
108. See Ps 101:28(102:27); Heb 1:12.
109. See Rom 11:36.
110. See Ti 1:4.
111. *Non peritus sed periturus.*
112. See 1 Cor 8:1; 13:4.
113. See 1 Cor 3:11.

me when later I had been brought to a new gentleness through the study of your books, and your fingers were tending my wounds; thus insight would be mine to recognize the difference between presumption and confession, between those who see the goal but not the way to it and the Way to our beatific homeland, a homeland to be not merely descried but lived in.[114] If I had first become well informed about your holy writings and you had grown sweet to me through my familiarity with them, and then I had afterward chanced upon those other volumes, they might perhaps have torn me loose from the strong root of piety, or else, if I had held firm in the salutary devotion I had absorbed, I might have supposed that it could be acquired equally well from those books, if everyone studied them and nothing else.

Augustine discovers Saint Paul

21, 27. It was therefore with intense eagerness that I seized on the hallowed calligraphy of your Spirit, and most especially the writings of the apostle Paul. In earlier days it had seemed to me that his teaching was self-contradictory, and in conflict with the witness of the law and the prophets,[115] but now as these problems melted away your chaste words[116] presented a single face to me, and I learned to rejoice with reverence.[117]

So I began to read, and discovered that every truth I had read in those other books was taught here also, but now inseparably from your gift of grace, so that no one who sees can boast as though what he sees and the very power to see it were not from you—for who has anything that he has not received?[118] So totally is it a matter of grace that the searcher is not only invited to see you, who are ever the same,[119] but healed as well, so that he can possess you. Whoever is too far off to see may yet walk in the way that will bring him to the place of seeing and possession; for even though a person may be delighted with God's law as far as his inmost self is concerned, how is he to deal with that other law in his bodily members which strives against the law approved by his mind, delivering him as prisoner to the law of sin dominant in his body?[120] You are

---

114. This heavenly *patria* is the counter-image to the "region of unlikeness" in which he found himself; see VII,10,16.
115. See Mt 5:17; 7:12; Lk 16:16.
116. See Ps 11:7(12:6).
117. See Ps 2:11.
118. See 1 Cor 4:7.
119. See Ps 101:28(102:27); Heb 1:12.
120. See Rom 7:22-23.

just, O Lord;[121] but we have sinned, and done wrong, and acted impiously,[122] and your hand has lain heavy upon us.[123] With good reason were we assigned to that ancient sinner who presides over death,[124] for he had seduced our will into imitating that perverse will of his by which he refused to stand fast in your truth.[125]

What is a human wretch to do? Who will free him from this death-laden body, if not your grace, given through Jesus Christ our Lord,[126] whom you have begotten coeternal with yourself and created at the beginning of all your works?[127] In him the ruler of this world found nothing that deserved death,[128] yet slew him all the same; and so the record of debt that stood against us was annulled.[129]

None of this is to be found in those other books. Not in those pages are traced the lineaments of such loving kindness, or the tears of confession, or the sacrifice of an anguished spirit offered to you from a contrite and humbled heart,[130] or the salvation of a people, or a city chosen to be your bride[131] or the pledge of the Holy Spirit,[132] or the cup of our ransom. Not there is anyone heard to sing, *Shall not my soul surrender itself to God? For my salvation comes from him. He is my very God, my Savior, my protector, and I shall waver no more.*[133] No one there hearkens to a voice calling, *Come to me, all you who struggle.* They are too scornful to learn from him, because he is gentle and humble of heart,[134] and you have hidden these things from the sagacious and shrewd, and revealed them to little ones.[135]

It is one thing to survey our peaceful homeland from a wooded height[136] but fail to find the way there, and make vain attempts to travel through impassable

---

121. See Tb 3:2; Ps 118(119):137.
122. See Dn 3:27.29; 1 Kgs 8:47.
123. See Ps 31(32):4.
124. See Heb 2:14.
125. See Jn 8:44.
126. See Rom 7:24-25.
127. See Prv 8:22. The Arians had appealed to this verb "created" in support of their doctrine of the subordination of the Son; Augustine in common with Athanasius, Ambrose, and others interprets it of Christ's humanity.
128. See Lk 23:14-15; Jn 14:30.
129. See Col 2:14.
130. See Ps 50:19(51:17).
131. See Rv 21:2.
132. See 2 Cor 5:5; 1:22.
133. Ps 61:2-3(62:1-2).
134. See Mt 11:28-29.
135. See Mt 11:25.
136. As Moses saw the promised land from afar, Dt 32:49.

terrain, while fugitive deserters marshaled by the lion and the dragon[137] obstruct and lurk in ambush; and quite another to walk steadily in the way that leads there, along the well-built road opened up by the heavenly emperor, where no deserters from the celestial army dare commit robbery, for they avoid that way like torment.

In awe-inspiring ways these truths were striking deep roots within me as I read the least of your apostles;[138] I had contemplated your works and was filled with dread.[139]

---

137. See Ps 90(91):13.
138. See 1 Cor 15:9.
139. See Hab 3:2.

Book VIII

Conversion

1, 1. In a spirit of thankfulness let me recall the mercies you lavished on me, O my God; to you let me confess them.[1] May I be flooded with love for you until my very bones cry out, "Who is like you, O Lord?"[2] Let me offer you a sacrifice of praise, for you have snapped my bonds.[3] How you broke them I will relate, so that all your worshipers who hear my tale may exclaim, "Blessed be the Lord, blessed in heaven and on earth, for great and wonderful is his name."[4]

Your words were now firmly implanted in my heart of hearts, and I was besieged by you on every side.[5] Concerning your eternal life I was now quite certain, though I had but glimpsed it like a tantalizing reflection in a mirror;[6] this had been enough to take from me any lingering doubt concerning that imperishable substance from which every other substance derives its being. What I now longed for was not greater certainty about you, but a more steadfast abiding in you. In my daily life everything seemed to be teetering, and my heart needed to be cleansed of the old leaven.[7] I was attracted to the Way, which is our Savior himself, but the narrowness of the path daunted me and I still could not walk in it.[8]

You inspired in me the idea that I ought to go to Simplicianus, and even I could see the sense of this. I regarded him as your good servant, a man

---

1. See Ps 85(86):13; Is 63:7.
2. See Ps 34(35):10.
3. See Ps 115(116):16-17.
4. See Pss 134(135):6; 75:2(76:1); 8:2(1).
5. See Is 29:2.
6. See 1 Cor 13:12.
7. See 1 Cor 5:7-8.
8. See Mt 7:14.

from whom grace radiated.[9] Moreover I had heard how from his youth he had lived for you in complete dedication, and since he was an old man by now I assumed that after following your way of life for long years and with such noble zeal he must be rich in experience and deeply learned. And so indeed he was. I hoped, therefore, that if I could discuss my perplexities with him he would bring out from his storehouse[10] appropriate advice as to how a man in my condition might walk in your way.

2. Surveying the full assembly of the Church I observed that people's lifestyles varied. For my own part I was irked by the secular business I was conducting, for no longer was I fired by ambition, and prepared on that account to endure such heavy servitude in the hope of reputation and wealth, as had formerly been the case. Those prospects held no charm for me now that I was in love with your tender kindness and the beauty of your house;[11] but I was in tight bondage to a woman. The apostle did not forbid me to marry, although he did propose a better choice, earnestly wishing that everyone might live as he did himself;[12] but I was too weak for that and inclined to an easier course. For this reason alone I was vacillating, bored and listless amid my shriveled cares because I was forced to adapt myself to other aspects of conjugal life to which I had pledged and constrained myself, though they were little to my liking. From the lips of your Truth I had heard that *there are eunuchs who have castrated themselves for love of the kingdom of heaven*, but the saying continues, *Let anyone accept this who can.*[13]

How foolish are they who know not God! So many good things before their eyes, yet *Him Who Is* they fail to see.[14] I was trapped in that foolishness no longer, for I had left it behind by hearkening to the concerted witness of your whole creation, and had discovered you, our creator, and your Word, who dwells with you and is with you the one sole God, through whom you have created all things.[15] But there are impious people of another type, who do recognize God yet have not glorified him as God, nor

---

9. Theological mentor for many years to Ambrose and later to Augustine, Simplicianus in spite of his advanced age succeeded Ambrose as bishop of Milan in 397.
10. See Mt 13:52.
11. See Ps 25(26):8.
12. See 1 Cor 7:7-8, where Paul discusses marriage and celibacy within the Christian calling, an issue which was becoming crucial for Augustine.
13. Mt 19:12.
14. See Wis 13:1.
15. See Jn 1:1-3.

given him thanks.[16] Into that error too I had formerly blundered, but your right hand grasped me,[17] plucked me out of it and put me in a place where I could be healed, for you have told us that *reverence for God—that is wisdom,*[18] and warned us, *Do not give yourself airs for wisdom,* because *those who believed themselves wise have sunk into folly.*[19] I had found a precious pearl, worth buying at the cost of all I had;[20] but I went on hesitating.

Conversation with Simplicianus

2, 3. Accordingly I made my way to Simplicianus. When Ambrose, then bishop, had been baptized, Simplicianus had stood as father to him, and Ambrose regarded him with affection as a father indeed. To him I described the winding paths of my wayward life. When I mentioned that I had read certain Platonist books, translated into Latin by Victorinus, who had formerly been a rhetorician in Rome but had, as I had heard, died a Christian, Simplicianus told me how fortunate I was not to have stumbled on the writings of other philosophers, works full of fallacies and dishonesty that smacked of the principles of this world,[21] whereas those Platonist writings conveyed in every possible way, albeit indirectly, the truth of God and his Word.

Story of Victorinus' conversion

He went on to reminisce about this Victorinus[22] with the object of inculcating in me that humility of Christ which is hidden from the sagacious but revealed to little ones.[23] He knew him intimately in Rome, and he told me a story about Victorinus which I will not pass over in silence, since it power-

---

16. See Rom 1:21.
17. See Ps 117:36(118:35).
18. Jb 28:28.
19. Prv 26:5; Rom 1:22.
20. See Mt 13:46; 19:21.
21. See Col 2:8.
22. Gaius Marius Victorinus Afer, thought to have been born sometime between 281 and 291, a highly cultured author and later a theologian. The parallel between this philosophically-inclined rhetorician hesitating on the threshold of the Church, and the young Augustine, must have been evident to Simplicianus.
23. See Mt 11:25.

fully redounds to the praise of your grace and moves me to confession, this story of a deeply learned old man.

Thoroughly conversant with all the liberal arts, Victorinus had also read widely and with discrimination in philosophy and had taught many a noble senator; in recognition of his distinction as a teacher a statue had been erected to him in the Roman forum, which was a very high honor in the eyes of worldly people, and one he well deserved. Until this period of his life he had been a worshiper of idols and shared the abominable super-stitions which at that time blew like an ill wind through almost the whole of the Roman nobility, who were agog for Pelusium[24] and for

> Anubis, dog-voiced god, and monstrous deities
> of many a hue, who warred in days gone by
> against Minerva, Neptune, Venus....[25]

These gods Rome had once vanquished, but now worshiped, and the elderly Victorinus with his terrible thunders had habitually defended their cults; yet he was not ashamed to become a child of your Christ and be born as an infant from your font, bending his neck to the yoke of humility[26] and accepting on his docile brow the sign of the ignominious cross.[27]

4. O Lord, Lord, who bade your heavens stoop, who touched the moun-tains and set them smoking,[28] by what means did you make your hidden way into that man's breast? The story as Simplicianus told it to me was this. Victorinus was in the habit of reading holy scripture and intensively studying all the Christian writings, which he subjected to close scrutiny; and he would say to Simplicianus, not openly but in private, intimate conversation, "I am already a Christian, you know." But the other always replied, "I will not believe that, nor count you among Christians, until I see you in Christ's Church." Victorinus would chaff him: "It's the walls that make Christians, then?" He would often talk like this, claiming that he was a Christian. Simplicianus often responded in the same way, and Victorinus would frequently repeat his joke about walls.

---

24. A city in Egypt. The text is corrupt here and conjectures abound, but the context suggests an Eastern or Egyptian deity. The Romans had deserted their traditional gods in favor of those of the conquered peoples.
25. Virgil, *Aeneid* VIII,698-700.
26. See Sir 51:34; Jer 27:12; Mt 11:29.
27. See Gal 5:11.
28. See Ps 143(144):5.

The fact was that he was sorely afraid of upsetting the proud demon-worshipers who were his friends, fearing that the weight of their resentment might come storming down on him from the peak of their Babylonian grandeur,[29] as though from lofty cedars on Lebanon not yet felled by the Lord.[30] But later he drank in courage from his avid reading and came to fear that he might be disowned by Christ before his holy angels if he feared to confess him before men and women.[31] In his own eyes he was guilty of a great crime in being ashamed of the holy mysteries instituted by your humble Word, while feeling no shame at the sacrilegious rites of proud demons, whose likeness he had been proud to assume himself. Accordingly he threw off the shamefacedness provoked by vanity and became modest in the face of truth: suddenly and without warning he said to Simplicianus, who told this tale, "Let us go to church: I want to become a Christian."

Hardly able to contain his joy, Simplicianus went with him. He was initiated into the first stage of the catechumenate,[32] and not long afterward he gave in his name, asking for rebirth in baptism.[33] Rome stood amazed, while the Church was jubilant. The proud looked on and fumed with anger; they ground their teeth in impotent fury;[34] but as for your servant, the Lord God was his hope, and he had no eyes for vanities or lying follies.[35]

5. Eventually the time came for him to make his profession of faith. Custom decrees that those who are approaching your grace in baptism make their profession in the presence of the baptized community of Rome, standing on a raised platform and using a set form of words which has been

---

29. For Babylon as a symbol of pride, see Is 14:4.12.13; and, identified with pagan Rome, Rv 17:5; 18:2.
30. See Ps 28(29):5.
31. See Mk 8:38 and par.
32. This comprised exorcism, the signing of the catechumen's forehead with the cross, the laying on of hands and the giving of salt. In this first stage the catechumens were *audientes*, hearers during the liturgy of the word.
33. The giving in of one's name, usually at the beginning of Lent, marked the transition to the second stage, that of the *competentes*, during which intensive instruction and the entrusting of the Lord's Prayer and the Creed to the catechumens prepared them for baptism at Easter.
34. See Ps 111(112):10.
35. See Ps 39:5(40:4).

entrusted to them and committed to memory.[36] Simplicianus told me that Victorinus had been offered by the priests the option of making his statement more privately, for it was customary to offer this concession to people who were likely to lose their nerve through shyness, but that he had chosen rather to proclaim his salvation before the holy company. What he taught in rhetoric was not salvation, he said, yet he had professed that publicly enough. If he was not afraid to address crowds of crazy people in his own words, how much less ought he to fear your peaceable flock as he uttered your word?

As he climbed up to repeat the Creed they all shouted his name to one another in a clamorous outburst of thanksgiving—everyone who knew him, that is; and was there anyone present who did not? Then in more subdued tones the word passed from joyful mouth to joyful mouth among them all: "Victorinus, Victorinus!" Spontaneous was their shout of delight as they saw him, and spontaneous their attentive silence to hear him. With magnificent confidence he proclaimed the true faith, and all the people longed to clasp him tenderly to their hearts. And so they did, by loving him and rejoicing with him, for those affections were like clasping hands.

3, 6. O God, who are so good, what is it in the human heart that makes us rejoice more intensely over the salvation of a soul which is despaired of but then freed from grave danger, than we would if there had always been good prospects for it and its peril slighter? You too, merciful Father, yes, even you are more joyful over one repentant sinner than over ninety-nine righteous people who need no repentance.[37] And we likewise listen with overflowing gladness when we hear how the shepherd carries back on exultant shoulders the sheep that had strayed,[38] and how the coin is returned to your treasury as neighbors share the glee of the woman who found it,[39] while the joy of your eucharistic assembly wrings tears from us when the story is read in your house of a younger son who *was dead, but has come back to life, was lost but is found.*[40] You express your own joy through ours, and through the joy of your angels who are made holy by

---

36. This is the *redditio symboli*, the "handing back" of the words of the Creed that the catechumens had been taught. The "discipline of secrecy," still in force in the mid-fourth century, forbade them to write it down.
37. See Lk 15:4-7.
38. See Lk 15:4-6; Ps 118(119):176.
39. See Lk 15:8-9.
40. Lk 15:24.32.

their holy charity; for you yourself are ever the same,[41] and all transient things, things which cannot abide constantly in their mode of being, are known to your unchanging intelligence.

7. What is going on in our minds, then, that we should be more highly delighted at finding cherished objects, or having them restored to us, than if we had always kept them safe? Other instances bear this out, and all our experience shouts its corroboration, "Yes, truly this is so." A victorious emperor celebrates his triumph. He would not have been victorious had there been no war, and the more imperiled he has been in battle, the more elated he is in his triumph. Or a storm batters mariners and threatens them with shipwreck. Every face pales at the prospect of death,[42] but sky and sea grow calm, and the sailors' joy is as intense as lately was their fear. Or someone we love falls sick. His pulse betrays the gravity of his condition, and all who long for his recovery are equally tormented in their minds. Then he takes a turn for the better, and although he is not yet walking with his pristine vigor there is already such joy as never there was when in earlier days he strode about well and strong.

Even the natural pleasures of human life are attained through distress, not only through the unexpected calamities that befall against our will but also through deliberate and planned discomfort. There is no pleasure in eating and drinking unless the discomfort of hunger and thirst have preceded them. Drunkards eat somewhat salty food to induce a searing, parched sensation, which will be deliciously quenched by a drink. Then again, custom requires that after betrothal brides shall not be handed over immediately, lest after marriage a man hold cheap the woman for whom he did not as a bridegroom have to sigh and wait.

8. This law holds for shameful, demeaning pleasure, but the same is true for what is permitted and lawful, the same for the most sincere and honorable friendship, and the same for that young man who had died but come back to life, had perished but was found. In every case greater sorrow issues in greater joy. How can this be, O Lord my God, when you are yourself your own eternal joy, and all around you heaven rejoices in you eternally? Why is it that our part of creation swings between decay and growth, pain and reconciliation? Perhaps because this is the proper mode of being for these things and with this alone you endowed them

---

41. See Ps 101:28 (102:27).
42. See Virgil, *Aeneid* IV,644.

when from highest heaven to the lowest places of the earth, from the dawn of the ages to their end, from angel to tiny worm, from the first stirring of change to the last, you assigned all classes of good things and all your righteous works to their appropriate places, and activated them at their proper times?

Ah, how high you are in the heights of heaven,[43] how deep in the depths! From no place are you absent, yet how tardily do we return to you!

4, 9. Come, Lord, arouse us and call us back, kindle us and seize us, prove to us how sweet you are in your burning tenderness; let us love you and run to you.[44] Are there not many who return to you from a deeper, blinder pit than did Victorinus, many who draw near to you and are illumined[45] as they welcome the light, and in welcoming it receive from you the power to become children of God?[46] Yet if they are less well known to the populace, even people who do know them find less joy in their conversion, because whenever joy is shared among many, even the gladness of individuals is increased, for all are affected by the common enthusiasm and they catch the flame from one another. Moreover, the fact that these converts are generally known ensures that they become for many an authoritative example pointing toward salvation; they forge ahead of crowds that will follow. That is why many who have made the journey before them rejoice particularly, with an eye to others besides these lone individuals.

Forbid it, Lord, that rich personages should ever be more welcome in your tabernacle than the poor, or the nobility than lowly folk,[47] when your own preferential choice fell upon the weak things of this world in order to shame the strong, upon lowly things, contemptible things and nonentities, as though they really were, to set at nought the things that are.[48] Nevertheless the least of your apostles,[49] through whose tongue you sent those words re-echoing, loved to be called not by his former name, "Saul," but "Paul," to commemorate that glorious victory when the proconsul

43. See Ps 112(113):4-5; Is 33:5.
44. See Sg 1:2-3.
45. See Ps 33:6(34:5).
46. See Jn 1:9,12.
47. See Dt 1:17; 16:19; Sir 42:1; Acts 10:34; Jas 2:1-9.
48. See 1 Cor 1:27-28; Rom 4:17.
49. See 1 Cor 15:9.

Paulus,[50] his pride beaten down[51] by the apostle's arms, was brought under Christ's lenient yoke to become a common subject of the great King.[52] The enemy is more thoroughly trounced in a person over whom he had a more powerful hold, or through whom he had a hold over a greater number of others; and stronger is his grip over those who on pretext of nobility are proud, stronger too his hold over many another on pretext of their authority.

The higher, then, the value set on the soul of Victorinus, which the devil had captured as an impregnable stronghold, and on Victorinus' tongue, which the devil had wielded like a huge, sharp weapon to destroy many, the greater was the gladness with which your children rightly rejoiced on seeing the powerful foe bound by our King[53] and his weaponry seized, cleaned, and made fit to serve in your honor as equipment useful to the Master for every good purpose.[54]

Augustine longs to imitate him, but is hindered by lustful habit

5, 10. On hearing this story I was fired to imitate Victorinus; indeed it was to this end that your servant Simplicianus had related it. But he added a further point. When in the reign of the Emperor Julian a law was passed which forbade Christians to teach literature and rhetoric, Victorinus willingly complied, for he preferred to abandon his school of talkativeness rather than forsake your word, through which you impart eloquence to the tongues of speechless babes.[55] In my eyes he appeared not so much heroic as all the happier for having taken this step, since it afforded him the opportunity to be at leisure for you. I ached for a like chance myself, for it was no iron chain imposed by anyone else that fettered me, but the iron of my own will. The enemy had my power of willing in his clutches, and from it had forged a chain to bind me. The truth is that disordered lust springs from a perverted will; when lust is pandered to, a habit is formed; when

---

50. See Acts 13:7-12.
51. See Virgil, *Aeneid* VI,853.
52. *Provincialis* originally meant a civilian as opposed to a soldier. Augustine uses it elsewhere to mean a "layperson" as distinct from a monk or cleric. Here the point is that from being a great man in the imperial system Sergius Paulus became an obscure private citizen in Christ's kingdom.
53. See Mt 12:29.
54. See 2 Tm 2:21.
55. See Wis 10:21.

habit is not checked, it hardens into compulsion. These were like interlinking rings forming what I have described as a chain, and my harsh servitude used it to keep me under duress.

A new will had begun to emerge in me, the will to worship you disinterestedly[56] and enjoy you, O God, our only sure felicity; but it was not yet capable of surmounting that earlier will strengthened by inveterate custom. And so the two wills fought it out—the old and the new,[57] the one carnal, the other spiritual—and in their struggle tore my soul apart.

11. I thus came to understand from my own experience what I had read, how the flesh lusts against the spirit and the spirit strives against the flesh.[58] I was aligned with both, but more with the desires I approved in myself than with those I frowned upon, for in these latter I was not really the agent, since for the most part I was enduring them against my will rather than acting freely.[59] All the same, the force of habit that fought against me had grown fiercer by my own doing, because I had come willingly to this point where I now wished not to be. And who has any right to object, when just punishment catches up with a sinner?

I had grown used to pretending that the only reason why I had not yet turned my back on the world to serve you was that my perception of the truth was uncertain, but that excuse was no longer available to me, for by now it was certain. But I was still entangled by the earth and refused to enlist in your service,[60] for the prospect of being freed from all these encumbrances frightened me as much as the encumbrances themselves ought to have done.

12. I was thus weighed down by the pleasant burden of the world in the way one commonly is by sleep, and the thoughts with which I attempted to meditate upon you[61] were like the efforts of people who are trying to wake up, but are overpowered and immersed once more in slumberous deeps. No one wants to be asleep all the time, and it is generally agreed among sensible people that being awake is a better state, yet it often happens that a person puts off the moment when he must shake himself out of sleep because his limbs are heavy with a lassitude that pulls him toward the

---

56. See Jb 1:9 (Old Latin).
57. See Eph 4:22.24; Col 3:9-10.
58. See Gal 5:17.
59. See Rom 7:16-17.
60. See 2 Tm 2:4.
61. See Ps 62:7(63:6), a psalm of early-morning imagery, like this paragraph.

more attractive alternative, even though he is already trying to resist it and the hour for rising has come; in a similar way I was quite sure that surrendering myself to your love would be better than succumbing to my lust, but while the former course commended itself and was beginning to conquer, the latter charmed and chained me. I had no answer to give as you said to me, *Arise, sleeper, rise from the dead: Christ will enlighten you,*[62] and plied me with evidence that you spoke truly; no, I was convinced by the truth and had no answer whatever except the sluggish, drowsy words, "Just a minute," "One more minute," "Let me have a little longer." But these "minutes" never diminished, and my "little longer" lasted inordinately long.

To find my delight in your law as far as my inmost self was concerned was of no profit to me when a different law in my bodily members was warring against the law of my mind, imprisoning me under the law of sin which held sway in my lower self. For the law of sin is that brute force of habit whereby the mind is dragged along and held fast against its will, and deservedly so because it slipped into the habit willingly. In my wretched state, who was there to free me from this death-doomed body, save your grace through Jesus Christ our Lord?[63]

Conversation with Ponticianus

6, 13. Now I will relate how you set me free from a craving for sexual gratification which fettered me like a tight-drawn chain, and from my enslavement to worldly affairs: I will confess to your name, O Lord,[64] my helper and redeemer.

I continued to attend to my accustomed duties, but with mounting anxiety. I longed for you every day and spent as much time in your church as could be spared from my business, under the weight of which I was groaning. With me was Alypius, who since his third stint as assessor[65] had been without legal advisory work, and was now looking round for clients to whom he might once more sell his counsel, just as I was trying to sell the art of speaking, insofar as it ever can be imparted by teaching. Nebridius,

---

62. Eph 5:14.
63. See Rom 7:24-25.
64. See Ps 53:8(54:6).
65. See VI,10,16.

however, yielding to our friendly persuasion, had consented to act as assistant teacher to Verecundus, a citizen and schoolmaster of Milan who was very well known to us all. This man had most earnestly desired reliable help from someone of our company, for he stood in sore need of it, and he had reinforced his insistent plea by appealing to his close association with us. Nebridius was not, therefore, attracted to this post by ambition for the advantages it might bring him, for he could have done better by the profession of literature, had he willed; he undertook it simply as a kindly service because, being such a very gentle and accommodating friend, he was unwilling to set our request aside. He carried out his duties with the utmost discretion, taking care not to attract the attention of persons whom the world regarded as important. He thus steered clear of any mental disturbance they might have caused him, for he wanted to keep his mind free and disengaged for as much of his time as he possibly could, with a view to research and to reading or listening to anything connected with wisdom.

14. On a certain day when Nebridius was absent (I forget why), something happened. A man named Ponticianus, who held an important post at court, came to our house to visit Alypius and me; being an African he was our compatriot, and he wanted something or other from us. We sat down together and talked. His eye happened to light upon a book that lay on a gaming table nearby;[66] he picked it up, opened it and found it to be the letters of the apostle Paul. This was certainly unexpected, for he had supposed it to be the kind of thing I exhausted myself in teaching. But then he smiled, looked up at me and offered his congratulations, surprised by his sudden discovery that those writings, and those alone, were under my eye. He was himself a baptized Christian and made a practice of prostrating himself in church before you, our God, in frequent and prolonged prayers. When I remarked that I was applying myself to intensive study of those scriptures, he began to tell us about the monk Antony of Egypt, whose name was illustrious and held in high honor among your servants, though we had never heard it until this moment.[67] When Ponticianus learned this he dwelt more fully on the subject, enlightening us about the great man; he was astonished at our ignorance. But we were stupefied as

---

66. The juxtaposition of these two objects, representing respectively Augustine's future and his past, may be intended to heighten the dramatic effect.
67. Antony of Egypt, c. 250-356, called "the father of monks."

we listened to the tale of the wonders you had worked within the true faith of the Catholic Church, especially as they were most firmly attested by recent memory and had occurred so near to our own times. So all of us were amazed: we because they were so tremendous, and he because we had never heard of them.

15. His discourse led on from this topic to the proliferation of monasteries, the sweet fragrance rising up to you from the lives of monks, and the fecund wastelands of the desert. We had known nothing of all this.[68] There was even a monastery full of good brothers at Milan, outside the city walls, under Ambrose's care, yet we were unaware of it.

Story of conversion of two court officials at Trier

Ponticianus went on talking and developing the theme, while we listened, spellbound. So it came about that he told us that one day when the court was at Trier[69] he and three of his colleagues went out for a walk in the gardens abutting on the walls,[70] while the emperor was occupied with the morning show at the circus. Now it happened that as they strolled about they split into pairs, one companion staying with Ponticianus while the other two went off by themselves. In their wandering these latter chanced upon a cottage where some servants of yours were living, men poor in spirit, the kind of people to whom the kingdom of heaven belongs.[71] There they found a book which contained *The Life of Antony*.[72] One of them began to read it. His admiration and enthusiasm were aroused, and as he read he began to mull over the possibility of appropriating the same kind of life for himself, by renouncing his secular career to serve you alone. (He belonged to the ranks of so-called administrative officers.[73]) Then quite suddenly he was filled with a love of

---

68. Though monasticism was already flourishing in Egypt and Cappadocia, there were few monasteries in Africa before Augustine's time, which may account for his ignorance.
69. Trier had been the capital of the Western Empire since Diocletian's time, but the court removed thence to Milan in 381. Bishop Athanasius of Alexandria had been in exile at Trier from 335 to 337; some lingering memory of him may explain the following episode.
70. The setting of this scene in a garden anticipates the experience of Augustine and Alypius in another garden, soon to be related; the parallel is reinforced by many verbal similarities.
71. See Mt 5:3.
72. Attributed to Athanasius and translated into Latin by Jerome's friend Evagrius.
73. These were inspectors in the imperial bureaucracy, sometimes used like secret police or intelligence agents, but more often in communications.

holiness and a realistic sense of shame and disgust with himself;[74] he turned his gaze toward his friend and demanded, "Tell me: where do we hope all our efforts are going to get us? What are we looking for? In whose cause are we striving? Does life at court promise us anything better than promotion to being Friends of the Emperor?[75] And once we are, will that not be a precarious position, fraught with perils? Will it not mean negotiating many a hazard, only to end in greater danger still? And how long would it take us to get there? Whereas I can become a friend of God[76] here and now if I want to."

Even as he spoke he was in labor with the new life that was struggling to birth within him. He directed his eyes back to the page, and as he read a change began to occur in that hidden place within him where you alone can see; his mind was being stripped of the world, as presently became apparent. The flood-tide of his heart leapt on, and at last he broke off his reading with a groan as he discerned the right course and determined to take it. By now he belonged to you. "I have already torn myself away from the ambitions we cherished, and have made up my mind to serve God," he told his friend. "I am going to set about it this very moment and in this place. If you have no stomach to imitate me, at least don't stand in my way." The other replied that he would bear him company, both in the noble reward and in the glorious combat. And both of them, now enlisted in your service, began to build their tower, knowing the cost full well: they abandoned all their possessions and followed you.[77]

Meanwhile Ponticianus was walking with his companion through other parts of the garden. In search of their friends they arrived at the place, and on finding them there urged them to return, for it was growing late. They, however, told their story, announcing the plan on which they had resolved and describing how the will to take this course had arisen within them and grown firm; and they begged their friends at least to place no obstacles in their way, if they had no mind to join them. Ponticianus and his companion shed tears on their own account, as he related, even though they were in no way altered from the men they had been. They offered devout congratulations to their friends and commended themselves to their prayers; then they went back to the palace, dragging heavy hearts along the ground, while their friends stayed in the cottage with hearts set on heaven. Both

---

74. See Ps 4:5(4).
75. People of senatorial or equestrian rank who formed the emperor's entourage and acted as advisors.
76. See Jas 2:23; Jdt 8:22.
77. See Lk 14:28; Mt 19:27; Lk 5:11.28.

were engaged to be married, and when their fiancées later heard of their decision, they likewise dedicated their virginity to you.

7, 16. Ponticianus went on with his story; but, Lord, even while he spoke you were wrenching me back toward myself, and pulling me round from that standpoint behind my back[78] which I had taken to avoid looking at myself. You set me down before my face,[79] forcing me to mark how despicable I was, how misshapen and begrimed, filthy and festering. I saw and shuddered. If I tried to turn my gaze away, he went on relentlessly telling his tale, and you set me before myself once more, thrusting me into my sight that I might perceive my sin and hate it.[80] I had been aware of it all along, but I had been glossing over it, suppressing it and forgetting.

17. But now self-abhorrence possessed me, all the harsher as my heart went out more ardently to those young men, and I heard of the blessed impulsiveness with which they had without reserve handed themselves over to you for healing. By contrast with them I felt myself loathsome, remembering how many of my years—twelve, perhaps—had gone to waste, and I with them, since my nineteenth year when I was aroused to pursue wisdom by the reading of Cicero's *Hortensius*.[81] I had been putting off the moment when by spurning earthly happiness I would clear space in my life to search for wisdom; yet even to seek it, let alone find it, would have been more rewarding than discovery of treasure or possession of all this world's kingdoms, or having every bodily pleasure at my beck and call. I had been extremely miserable in adolescence, miserable from its very onset, and as I prayed to you for the gift of chastity I had even pleaded, "Grant me chastity and self-control, but please not yet." I was afraid that you might hear me immediately and heal me forthwith of the morbid lust which I was more anxious to satisfy than to snuff out. So I had wandered off into the crooked paths[82] of a sacrilegious superstition, not because I had any certainty about it but because I preferred it to other beliefs—not that I was investigating these in any spirit of reverence: rather was I opposing them with malicious intent.

---

78. See Jer 2:27.
79. See Ps 49(50):21.
80. See Ps 35:3(36:2).
81. See III,4,7. We are now in 386; the following scene occurs in August.
82. See Sir 2:16.

18. I had been telling myself that my reason for putting off day after day[83] the decision to renounce worldly ambition and follow you alone was that I could as yet see no certain light by which to steer my course. But the day had dawned when I was stripped naked in my own eyes and my conscience challenged me within: "Where is your ready tongue now? You have been professing yourself reluctant to throw off your load of illusion because truth was uncertain. Well, it is certain now, yet the burden still weighs you down, while other people are given wings on freer shoulders,[84] people who have not worn themselves out with research, nor spent a decade and more reflecting on these questions."

My conscience gnawed away at me in this fashion, and I was fiercely shamed and flung into hideous confusion while Ponticianus was relating all this. Having brought the conversation to a close and settled his business with us, he returned to his place, and I to myself.

Was anything left unsaid in my inner debate? Was there any whip of sage advice I left unused to lash my soul into coming with me, as I tried to follow you? It fought and resisted, but could find no excuse. All its arguments had been used up and refuted, but there remained a dumb dread: frightful as death seemed the restraining of habit's oozy discharge, that very seepage which was rotting it to death.

Struggle in the garden

8, 19. Within the house of my spirit the violent conflict raged on, the quarrel with my soul that I had so powerfully provoked in our secret dwelling, my heart,[85] and at the height of it I rushed to Alypius with my mental anguish plain upon my face. "What is happening to us?" I exclaimed. "What does this mean? What did you make of it? The untaught are rising up and taking heaven by storm,[86] while we with all our dispassionate teachings are still groveling in this world of flesh and blood![87] Are we ashamed to follow, just because they have taken the lead, yet not ashamed of lacking the courage even to follow?" Some such words as these I spoke, and then my frenzy tore me away from him, while he

---

83. See Sir 5:8.
84. See Ps 54:7(55:6).
85. See Mt 6:6.
86. See Mt 11:12.
87. See 1 Cor 15:50; Mt 16:17; Gal 1:16.

regarded me in silent bewilderment. Unusual, certainly, was my speech, but my brow, cheeks and eyes, my flushed countenance and the cadences of my voice expressed my mind more fully than the words I uttered.

Adjacent to our lodgings was a small garden. We were free to make use of it as well as of the house, for our host, who owned the house, did not live there. The tumult in my breast had swept me away to this place, where no one would interfere with the blazing dispute I had engaged in with myself until it should be resolved. What the outcome would be you knew, not I. All I knew was that I was going mad, but for the sake of my sanity, and dying that I might live, aware of the evil that I was but unaware of the good I was soon to become. So I went out into the garden and Alypius followed at my heels; my privacy was not infringed by his presence, and, in any case, how could he abandon me in that state? We sat down as far as possible from the house. I was groaning in spirit[88] and shaken by violent anger because I could form no resolve to enter into a covenant with you, though in my bones I knew that this was what I ought to do,[89] and everything in me lauded such a course to the skies. It was a journey not to be undertaken by ship or carriage or on foot,[90] nor need it take me even that short distance I had walked from the house to the place where we were sitting; for to travel—and more, to reach journey's end—was nothing else but to want to go there, but to want it valiantly and with all my heart, not to whirl and toss this way and that a will half crippled by the struggle, as part of it rose up to walk while part sank down.

20. While this vacillation was at its most intense many of my bodily gestures were of the kind that people sometimes want to perform but cannot, either because the requisite limbs are missing, or because they are bound and restricted, or paralyzed through illness, or in some other way impeded. If I tore out my hair, battered my forehead, entwined my fingers and clasped them round my knee, I did so because I wanted to. I might have wanted to but found myself unable, if my limbs had not been mobile enough to obey. So then, there were plenty of actions that I performed where willing was not the same thing as being able; yet I was not doing the one thing that was incomparably more desirable to me, the thing that I would be able to do as soon as I willed, because as soon as I willed—why,

---

88. See Jn 11:33.
89. See Ps 34(35):10.
90. See I,18,28.

then, I would be willing it! For in this sole instance the faculty to act and the will to act precisely coincide, and the willing is already the doing. Yet this was not happening. My body was more ready to obey the slightest whim of my soul in the matter of moving my limbs, than the soul was to obey its own command in carrying out this major volition, which was to be accomplished within the will alone.

9, 21. How did this bizarre situation arise, how develop? May your mercy shed light on my inquiry, so that perhaps an answer may be found in the mysterious punishments meted out to humankind, those utterly baffling pains that afflict the children of Adam. How then did this bizarre situation arise, how develop? The mind commands the body and is instantly obeyed; the mind commands itself, and meets with resistance. When the mind orders the hand to move, so smooth is the compliance that command can scarcely be distinguished from execution; yet the mind is mind, while the hand is body. When the mind issues its command that the mind itself should will something (and the mind so commanded is no other than itself), it fails to do so. How did this bizarre situation arise, how develop? As I say, the mind commands itself to will something: it would not be giving the order if it did not want this thing; yet it does not do what it commands.

Evidently, then, it does not want this thing with the whole of itself, and therefore the command does not proceed from an undivided mind. Inasmuch as it issues the command, it does will it, but inasmuch as the command is not carried out, it does not will it. What the will is ordering is that a certain volition should exist, and this volition is not some alien thing, but its very self. Hence it cannot be giving the order with its whole self. It cannot be identical with that thing which it is commanding to come into existence, for if it were whole and entire it would not command itself to be, since it would be already.

This partial willing and partial non-willing is thus not so bizarre, but a sickness of the mind, which cannot rise with its whole self on the wings of truth because it is heavily burdened by habit. There are two wills, then, and neither is the whole: what one has the other lacks.

10, 22. Some there are who on perceiving two wills engaged in deliberation assert that in us there are two natures, one good, the other evil, each with a mind of its own.[91] Let them perish from your presence, O God,[92] as

---

91. Throughout this chapter Augustine attacks Manichean views.
92. See Ps 67:3(68:2).

perish all who talk wildly and lead our minds astray.[93] They are evil themselves as long as they hold these opinions, yet these same people will be good if they embrace true opinions and assent to true teaching, and so merit the apostle's commendation, *You were darkness once, but now you are light in the Lord.*[94] The trouble is that they want to be light not in the Lord but in themselves, with their notion that the soul is by nature divine, and so they have become denser darkness still, because by their appalling arrogance they have moved further away from you, the true Light, who enlighten everyone who comes into the world.[95] I warn these people, Take stock of what you are saying, and let it shame you; but once draw near to him and be illumined, and your faces will not blush with shame.[96]

When I was making up my mind to serve the Lord my God[97] at last, as I had long since purposed, I was the one who wanted to follow that course, and I was the one who wanted not to. I was the only one involved. I neither wanted it wholeheartedly nor turned from it wholeheartedly. I was at odds with myself, and fragmenting myself. This disintegration was occurring without my consent, but what it indicated was not the presence in me of a mind belonging to some alien nature but the punishment undergone by my own. In this sense, and this sense only, it was not I who brought it about, but the sin that dwelt within me[98] as penalty for that other sin committed with greater freedom;[99] for I was a son of Adam.

23. Moreover, if we were to take the number of conflicting urges to signify the number of natures present in us, we should have to assume that there are not two, but many. If someone is trying to make up his mind whether to go to a Manichean conventicle or to the theater, the Manichees declare, "There you are, there's the evidence for two natures: the good one is dragging him our way, the bad one is pulling him back in the other direction. How else explain this dithering between contradictory wills?" But I regard both as bad, the one that leads him to them and the one that lures

---

93. See Ti 1:10.
94. Eph 5:8.
95. See Jn 1:9.
96. See Ps 33:6(34:5).
97. See Dt 6:13; Mt 4:10; Jer 30:9.
98. See Rom 7:17,20.
99. That is, by Adam. Augustine uses the comparative to suggest a relative freedom enjoyed by Adam, superior to our own but short of perfect freedom. He was to spell out the distinction later in *Correction and Grace* XII,33 between *posse non peccare* (the ability not to sin, Adam's privilege), and *non posse peccare* (the perfection of freedom in heaven).

him back to the theater. They, on the contrary, think that an inclination toward them can only be good.

But consider this: suppose one of our people is deliberating, and as two desires clash he is undecided whether to go to the theater or to our church, will not our opponents too be undecided what attitude to take? Either they will have to admit that it is good will that leads a person to our church, just as good as that which leads to theirs the people who are initiated into their sacred rites and trapped there—and this they are unwilling to admit; or they will conclude that two evil natures and two bad minds are pitted against each other within one person, in which case their habitual assertion of one good and one evil nature will be erroneous; or, finally, they will be brought round to the truth and no longer deny that when a person is deliberating there is but one soul, thrown into turmoil by divergent impulses.

24. When, therefore, they observe two conflicting impulses within one person, let them stop saying that two hostile minds are at war, one good, the other evil, and that these derive from two hostile substances and two hostile principles. For you are true, O God, and so you chide and rebuke them and prove them wrong. The choice may lie between two impulses that are both evil, as when a person is debating whether to murder someone with poison or a dagger; whether to annex this part of another man's property or that, assuming he cannot get both; whether to buy himself pleasure by extravagant spending or hoard his money out of avarice; whether to go to the circus or the theater if both performances are on the same day—and I would even add a third possibility: whether to go and steal from someone else's house while he has the chance, and a fourth as well: whether to commit adultery while he is about it. All these impulses may occur together, at exactly the same time, and all be equally tempting, but they cannot all be acted upon at once. The mind is then rent apart by the plethora of desirable objects as four inclinations, or even more, do battle among themselves; yet the Manichees do not claim that there are as many disparate substances in us as this.

The same holds true for good impulses. I would put these questions to them: Is it good to find delight in a reading from the apostle? To enjoy the serenity of a psalm? To discuss the gospel? To each point they will reply, "Yes, that is good." Where does that leave us? If all these things tug at our will with equal force, and all together at the same time, will not these divergent inclinations put a great strain on the human heart, as we deliberate which to select? All are good, but they compete among themselves until one is chosen, to which the will, hitherto distracted between many options, may move as a united whole. So too when the joys of eternity call us from above, and pleasure in temporal prosperity holds us fast below, our one soul is in no state to embrace either with its entire will. Claimed by truth for the one, to the other clamped by custom, the soul is torn apart in its distress.

11, 25. Such was the sickness in which I agonized, blaming myself more sharply than ever, turning and twisting in my chain[100] as I strove to tear free from it completely, for slender indeed was the bond that still held me. But hold me it did. In my secret heart you stood by me, Lord, redoubling the lashes of fear and shame in the severity of your mercy, lest I give up the struggle and that slender, fragile bond that remained be not broken after all, but thicken again and constrict me more tightly. "Let it be now," I was saying to myself. "Now is the moment, let it be now," and merely by saying this I was moving toward the decision. I would almost achieve it, but then fall just short; yet I did not slip right down to my starting-point, but stood aside to get my breath back. Then I would make a fresh attempt, and now I was almost there, almost there.... I was touching the goal, grasping it ... and then I was not there, not touching, not grasping it. I shrank from dying to death and living to life, for ingrained evil was more powerful in me than new-grafted good. The nearer it came, that moment when I would be changed, the more it pierced me with terror. Dismayed, but not quite dislodged, I was left hanging.

26. The frivolity of frivolous aims, the futility of futile pursuits,[101] these things that had been my cronies of long standing,[102] still held me back, plucking softly at my garment of flesh and murmuring in my ear, "Do you mean to get rid of us? Shall we never be your companions again after that moment ... never ... never again? From that time onward so-and-so will be forbidden to you, all your life long." And what was it that they were reminding me of by those words, "so-and-so," O my God, what were they bringing to my mind? May your mercy banish such memories far from me!

---

100. A possible echo of Persius, *Satire* V,127, from which he quotes in the following chapter.
101. See Eccl 1:2; 12:8.
102. *Antiquae amicae meae*: not former female friends, as translators have sometimes taken it. This is the beginning of the personification he uses to make the struggle vivid; see "Continence" in VIII,11,27.

What foul deeds were they not hinting at, what disgraceful exploits! But now their voices were less than half as loud, for they no longer confronted me directly to argue their case, but muttered behind my back and slyly tweaked me as I walked away, trying to make me look back. Yet they did slow me down, for I could not bring myself to tear free and shake them off and leap across to that place whither I was summoned, while aggressive habit still taunted me: "Do you imagine you will be able to live without these things?"

27. The taunts had begun to sound much less persuasive, however; for a revelation was coming to me from that country toward which I was facing, but into which I trembled to cross. There I beheld the chaste, dignified figure of Continence. Calm and cheerful was her manner, though modest,[103] pure and honorable her charm as she coaxed me to come and hesitate no longer, stretching kindly hands to welcome and embrace me, hands filled with a wealth of heartening examples. A multitude of boys and girls were there, a great concourse of youth and persons of every age, venerable widows and women grown old in their virginity, and in all of them I saw that this same Continence was by no means sterile, but the fruitful mother of children[104] conceived in joy from you, her Bridegroom. She was smiling at me, but with a challenging smile, as though to say, "Can you not do what these men have done, these women? Could any of them achieve it by their own strength, without the Lord their God? He it was, the Lord their God, who granted me to them. Why try to stand by yourself, only to lose your footing? Cast yourself on him and do not be afraid: he will not step back and let you fall. Cast yourself upon him trustfully; he will support and heal you." And I was bitterly ashamed, because I could still hear the murmurs of those frivolities, and I was still in suspense, still hanging back. Again she appealed to me, as though urging, "Close your ears against those unclean parts of you which belong to the earth[105] and let them be put to death. They tell you titillating tales, but have nothing to do with the law of the Lord your God."[106]

All this argument in my heart raged only between myself and myself. Alypius stood fast at my side, silently awaiting the outcome of my unprecedented agitation.

---

103. Compare the cheerful young man in III,11,19.
104. See Ps 112(113):9.
105. See Col 3:5; the unquoted part of the context lists the relevant vices.
106. See Ps 118(119):85.

12, 28. But as this deep meditation dredged all my wretchedness up from the secret profundity of my being and heaped it all together before the eyes of my heart, a huge storm blew up within me and brought on a heavy rain of tears. In order to pour them out unchecked with the sobs that accompanied them I arose and left Alypius, for solitude seemed to me more suitable for the business of weeping. I withdrew far enough to ensure that his presence—even his—would not be burdensome to me. This was my need, and he understood it, for I think I had risen to my feet and blurted out something, my voice already choked with tears. He accordingly remained, in stunned amazement, at the place where we had been sitting. I flung myself down somehow under a fig-tree[107] and gave free rein to the tears that burst from my eyes like rivers, as an acceptable sacrifice to you.[108] Many things I had to say to you, and the gist of them, though not the precise words, was: "O Lord, how long?[109] How long? Will you be angry for ever? Do not remember our age-old sins."[110] For by these I was conscious of being held prisoner. I uttered cries of misery: "Why must I go on saying, 'Tomorrow ... tomorrow'?[111] Why not now? Why not put an end to my depravity this very hour?"

"Pick it up and read"

29. I went on talking like this and weeping in the intense bitterness of my broken heart.[112] Suddenly I heard a voice from a house nearby—perhaps a voice of some boy or girl, I do not know—singing over and over again, "Pick it up and read, pick it up and read." My expression immediately altered and I began to think hard whether children ordinarily repeated a ditty like this in any sort of game, but I could not recall ever having heard it anywhere else. I stemmed the flood of tears and rose to my feet, believing that this could be nothing other than a divine command to

---

107. Did he really note the species? It is more likely that he calls it a fig-tree for the sake of the symbolism: in Gn 3:7 Adam and Eve in the newly-discovered shame of their sin use fig-leaves to make loincloths; in Mt 21:19 (=Mk 11:13-14) Jesus curses a sterile fig-tree, which withers away. Hence the fig-tree can stand for the sinful, carnal condition condemned to die. But in Jn 1:47-48 Jesus sees Nathanael under a fig-tree, and calls him thence to grace and ultimate vision.
108. See Ps 50:19(51:17).
109. See Ps 6:4(3).
110. See Ps 78(79):5,8.
111. This seems to be an allusion to Persius, *Satire* V,66-69, but the Latin sound, *cras, cras,* resembled the raucous cry of a crow, as Augustine remarks in his *Exposition of Psalm* 102, 16; see Sermon 224,4,4.
112. See Ps 50:19(51:17).

open the Book and read the first passage I chanced upon; for I had heard the story of how Antony had been instructed by a gospel text. He happened to arrive while the gospel was being read, and took the words to be addressed to himself when he heard, *Go and sell all you possess and give the money to the poor: you will have treasure in heaven. Then come, follow me.*[113] So he was promptly converted to you by this plainly divine message. Stung into action, I returned to the place where Alypius was sitting, for on leaving it I had put down there the book of the apostle's letters. I snatched it up, opened it and read in silence the passage on which my eyes first lighted: *Not in dissipation and drunkenness, nor in debauchery and lewdness, nor in arguing and jealousy; but put on the Lord Jesus Christ, and make no provision for the flesh or the gratification of your desires.*[114] I had no wish to read further, nor was there need. No sooner had I reached the end of the verse than the light of certainty flooded my heart and all dark shades of doubt fled away.

Conversion of Augustine and Alypius; Monica's joy

30. I closed the book, marking the place with a finger between the leaves or by some other means, and told Alypius what had happened. My face was peaceful now. He in return told me what had been happening to him without my knowledge. He asked to see what I had read: I showed him, but he looked further than my reading had taken me. I did not know what followed, but the next verse was *Make room for the person who is weak in faith.*[115] He referred this text to himself and interpreted it to me. Confirmed by this admonition he associated himself with my decision and good purpose without any upheaval or delay, for it was entirely in harmony with his own moral character, which for a long time now had been far, far better than mine.

We went indoors and told my mother, who was overjoyed. When we related to her how it had happened she was filled with triumphant delight

---

113. Mt 19:21; see Athanasius, *Life of Antony* 2.
114. Rom 13:13-14. Since Book VII the central issue for Augustine has been acceptance of Christ; this now crystallizes into the "putting on" of Christ in baptism, sacramentally symbolized by the clothing in the new robe.
115. Rom 14:1.

and blessed you, who have power to do more than we ask or understand,[116] for she saw that you had granted her much more in my regard than she had been wont to beg of you in her wretched, tearful groaning. Many years earlier you had shown her a vision of me standing on the rule of faith;[117] and now indeed I stood there, no longer seeking a wife or entertaining any worldly hope, for you had converted me to yourself. In so doing you had also converted her grief into a joy[118] far more abundant than she had desired, and much more tender and chaste than she could ever have looked to find in grandchildren from my flesh.

---

116. See Eph 3:10.
117. See III,11,19.
118. See Ps 29:12(30:11).

Book IX

Death and Rebirth

1, 1. O Lord, I am your servant, I am your servant and your handmaid's son. You burst my bonds asunder, and to you will I offer a sacrifice of praise.[1] May my heart and tongue give praise to you, and all my bones cry out their question, "Who is like you, O Lord?"[2] Yes, let them ask, and then do you respond and say to my soul, "I am your salvation."[3]

But who am I, what am I? Is there any evil I have not committed in my deeds, or if not in deeds, then in my words, or if not in words, at least by willing it? But you, Lord, are good and merciful,[4] and your right hand plumbed the depths of my death, draining the cesspool of corruption in my heart, so that I ceased to will all that I had been wont to will, and now willed what you willed.[5] But where had my power of free decision been throughout those long, weary years, and from what depth, what hidden profundity, was it called forth in a moment, enabling me to bow my neck to your benign yoke and my shoulders to your light burden,[6] O Christ Jesus, my helper and redeemer?[7] How sweet did it suddenly seem to me to shrug off those sweet frivolities, and how glad I now was to get rid of them—I who had been loath to let them go! For it was you who cast them out from me, you, our real and all-surpassing sweetness. You cast them out and entered yourself to take their place, you who are lovelier than any pleasure, though not to flesh and blood, more lustrous than any light, yet more inward than is any secret intimacy, loftier than all honor, yet not to those

---

1. See Pss 115(116):16-17; 85(86):15-16.
2. See Ps 34(35):10.
3. See Ps 34(35):3.
4. See Ex 34:6; Ps 85(86):15.
5. See Mt 26:39; Mk 14:36.
6. See Mt 11:30.
7. See Ps 18:15(19:14). Here, so soon after his mention of the crucial text, *Put on the Lord Jesus Christ*, Augustine addresses Christ by this name for the only time in *The Confessions*.

209

who look for loftiness in themselves.[8] My mind was free at last from the gnawing need to seek advancement and riches, to welter in filth and scratch my itching lust. Childlike, I chattered away to you, my glory, my wealth, my salvation, and my Lord and God.

Augustine decides to renounce his career

2, 2. I believed it to be pleasing in your sight that I should withdraw the service of my tongue from the market of speechifying, so that young boys who were devoting their thoughts not to your law,[9] not to your peace, but to lying follies and legal battles, should no longer buy from my mouth the weapons for their frenzy; but I thought it better to retire unobtrusively rather than make an abrupt and sensational break. Fortunately there were now only a few days left before the vintage holidays,[10] and I decided to put up with this delay. I would then resign in the regular way, but return no more to offer myself for sale, now that you had redeemed me.

Our plan was therefore kept between ourselves and you, and not made known to other people outside our own company. We had agreed that it should not be divulged to all and sundry, even though as we climbed up from the valley of weeping[11] singing our pilgrim-song,[12] you had armed us with sharp arrows and burning coals[13] with which to fight the guileful tongues of any who opposed our project while pretending to promote it, and devoured us as they might food on pretense of liking.

3. With the arrows of your charity you had pierced our hearts,[14] and we bore your words within us like a sword penetrating us to the core. The examples of your servants, whom you had changed from murky to luminous beings, from dead to living men, were crowding in upon our thoughts, where they burned and consumed the heavy torpor that might

---

8. Probably a trinitarian allusion: Spirit-Word-Father; but also the antithesis of the three temptations of 1 Jn 2:16.

9. See Ps 118(119):70.77.

10. 23 August to 15 October, a holiday period fixed for the imperial law-courts and probably the schools by Theodosius (*Cod. Theod.* II,8,19) to provide a respite from the summer heat and an opportunity for gathering autumn crops. This book is Augustine's book of vintage and harvest in the spiritual world.

11. See Ps 83:7(84:6).

12. Pss 119-133(120-134) were traditionally associated with the pilgrims going up to Jerusalem.

13. See Ps 119(120):3-4. In his *Exposition of Psalm* 119,5, Augustine explains that the sharp arrows are God's words and the burning coals salutary examples.

14. This imagery inspired the traditional icon for Augustine, a pierced and burning heart.

have pulled us down again. So powerfully did they ignite us that every breath of guileful opposition blew our flame into fiercer heat, rather than extinguishing us.

We could be certain, however, that there would be some who would admire the course we had resolved to follow, since you had spread the knowledge of your holy name throughout the world.[15] It therefore seemed like boastfulness to refuse to wait for a holiday period so close at hand, and instead to quit a professional post where I was in the public eye in such a fashion that, as everyone's attention was drawn to what I was doing, and they noted how little time was left before the first day of the holidays, which I had nevertheless chosen to forestall, they might have plenty to say about it, concluding that I merely wished to look important. And what was the point of arousing conjecture and contention over my state of mind, and letting this good thing that had come our way provide an occasion for slanderous gossip?[16]

4. It happened by coincidence that in that same summer my lungs had begun to fail under the severe strain of teaching, making it difficult for me to draw breath and giving proof of their unhealthy condition by pains in my chest. My tone was husky and I could not manage any sustained vocal effort. These symptoms had worried me when they first appeared, because they were forcing upon me the necessity of either giving up my professorial career or, if there were any prospect of my being cured and recovering my strength, at least of taking some rest. But now that a wholehearted desire to be still and see that you are the Lord[17] had arisen within me and grown strong, as you know, my God, I began even to rejoice that a genuine excuse lay to hand which I could use to appease those parents who for their children's sake were unwilling ever to allow me freedom.[18] Full of this joy I endured the interval of time until it had run its course—it lasted perhaps twenty days or so—yet this took fortitude, because the desire for gain that had customarily helped me to sustain the heavy burden of work had now left me, and had not patience taken its place I should have been crushed by the load.

---

15. See Ez 36:23.
16. See Rom 14:16.
17. See Ps 45:11(46:10). Augustine evokes the ultimate "letting go," the Sabbath of rest with no evening, in the last chapter of *The City of God* (XXII,30).
18. An untranslatable Augustinian pun on *liberi* ("children") and *liber* ("free").

It may be that someone among your servants, my brethren in the faith, will judge that I sinned in this matter by allowing myself to remain even for an hour in a professorial chair of lying[19] once my heart was fully intent on your service. I will not argue. But have you not pardoned this sin, most merciful Lord, along with all the rest of my hideous, dismal sins, in the water of baptism, and forgiven me?

3, 5. Verecundus was racked with anxiety over this good thing that had befallen us, because he saw himself being distanced from our fellowship by the bonds that unbreakably held him. He was not yet a Christian, and though his wife was a believer, it was precisely she who trammeled him most rigidly and restrained him from the path on which we had set out; for he declared that he was unwilling to be a Christian in any way other than that from which he was debarred. In spite of this he kindly suggested that as long as we were there we should stay on his estate. At the resurrection of the just you will surely reward him, Lord,[20] since you have granted him already his allotted place among the just,[21] for later on, when we had gone to Rome, he was overtaken by an illness, in the course of which he became a believing Christian in our absence, and in that state departed this life. So it was that you showed mercy not only to him but to us as well, sparing us the unbearable grief of being forced to recall his outstanding kindliness toward us while at the same time regarding him as an outsider to your flock. Thanks be to you, our God! We belong to you. You prove it by the exhortations and consolations you provide for us. Because you are faithful to your promises you are even now rewarding Verecundus for that country house of his at Cassiciacum, where we found rest in you from the hurly-burly of the world.[22] In exchange for his estate you now endow him with the delights of your verdant paradise for ever, since you pardoned him for his earthly sins by setting him on the mountain of rich pasture, your mountain, the mount of plenty.[23]

6. Verecundus was therefore full of anxiety at the time of which I speak, whereas Nebridius shared our joy. While not yet a Christian he, like us, had

---

19. See Ps 1:1.
20. See Lk 14:14.
21. See Ps 124(125):3.
22. Rest in God, Augustine's perpetual desire from I,1,1 to XIII,38,53, was achieved partially and temporarily at Cassiciacum, to which he and some others retired after the end of the vintage holidays. Its exact location is disputed. Some Augustinian dialogues took shape during the following weeks.
23. See Ps 67:16(68:15) (Old Latin). The first phrase literally means "cheesy mountain"; in his *Exposition of Psalm* 67,22, Augustine explains that the mountain is Christ, milk represents grace, and cheese is made from milk. The similarity of sound (*incaseato*) may have reminded him of the name of Cassiciacum.

fallen into a pit of very dangerous error,[24] believing that the flesh of your Son, who is the Truth, was mere make-believe; but he was beginning to emerge from this error, and was in the position of one who, though not yet initiated into any of the rites of your Church, was a most ardent seeker of the truth.

But not very long after our conversion and rebirth in baptism, when he too was a believing Catholic, when he was serving you in perfect chastity and continence among his own people in Africa, when his whole household had become Christian through his example, you released him from the flesh. And now he lives in Abraham's bosom.[25] Whatever that may be, whatever the gospel word "bosom" may mean, there my Nebridius is living, to me a friend most tenderly loved, to you, Lord, a freedman adopted as your son; yes, there he lives on. Where else could such a soul be at home? He is alive in that place about which he used to ask me so many questions, ignorant and paltry fellow that I am. No longer does he bend his ear to my mouth; rather does he lay the mouth of his spirit to your fountain and avidly slake his thirst as he drinks your wisdom to the uttermost of his capacity, in happiness without end. Yet I cannot believe that he is so inebriated as to forget me, since you, Lord, from whom he drinks, are mindful of us.

Such, then, was our situation. On the one hand we sought to console Verecundus who, though saddened by our conversion, continued to be our friend, urging him to be faithful to his own calling, namely married life; on the other we waited for Nebridius to follow us. He was very close to doing so, indeed on the point of making his decision, when the days of waiting expired at last. Slow and tedious they had seemed, so sharp was my longing for leisured freedom in which to sing with every fibre of my being, *To you my heart tells its love: I have sought your face, O Lord, for your face will I seek.*[26]

To Cassiciacum with his mother, son, and friends

4, 7. At last the day arrived which was to set me free in fact from the profession of rhetor, as I was free already in spirit. And so it was done; you

---

24. See Ps 7:16(15).
25. See Lk 16:22.
26. Ps 26(27):8.

detached my tongue from that bond whence you had already delivered my heart, and I blessed you as I joyfully set out for the villa with all my company.[27] The evidence of what I did there in the way of literary work is to be found in the books that record disputations held between those there present, and deliberations alone with myself in your sight; it was work unquestionably devoted by now to your service, but still with a whiff of scholastic pride about it, like combatants still panting in the interval.[28] What I wrote to Nebridius, who was absent, my letters to him testify.[29]

When could I ever find time enough to record all your generous favors to us during that period—especially now that I am hurrying on to greater matters still? My memory harks back to our sojourn there, and it is my delight, Lord, to acknowledge before you what inward goads you employed to tame me, how you laid low the mountains and hills of my proud intellect and made of me an even plain, how you straightened my winding ways and smoothed my rugged patches,[30] and how you also brought my heart's brother, Alypius, to submit to the name of your only-begotten Son, our Lord and Savior Jesus Christ. At first he disdained to admit it into our writings, for he wanted them to give off the tang of those lofty cedars of Lebanon, felled though these now were by the Lord,[31] rather than the scent of plants grown in your Church and efficacious against snakebite.

He lives with the psalms

8. How loudly I cried out to you, my God, as I read the psalms of David, songs full of faith, outbursts of devotion with no room in them for the breath of pride! Uncouth I was in real love for you, a catechumen on holiday in a country house with another catechumen, Alypius; but my mother kept us company, woman in outward form but endowed with virile faith, uniting the serenity of an elderly person with a mother's love and Christian devotion. How loudly I began to cry out to you in those psalms,

---

27. The party included Alypius, Monica, Augustine's brother Navigius, his son Adeodatus, two pupils (Licentius and Trygetius), and two cousins.
28. The three dialogues, *Answer to the Skeptics*, *The Happy Life*, and *Order*, and the two books of *Soliloquies* belong to this time.
29. Letters 3 and 4 were written from Cassiciacum.
30. See Is 40:4; Lk 3:4-5.
31. See Ps 28(29):5.

how I was inflamed by them with love for you and fired to recite them to the whole world, were I able, as a remedy against human pride! Yet in truth they are sung throughout the world, and no one can hide from your burning heat.[32] I felt bitterly angry with the Manichees, though my indignation was tinged with pity, because they knew nothing of this remedy and ranted against the very antidote which might have healed them. I could wish that they had been somewhere nearby, without my knowing it, and had gazed upon my face and listened to my voice as I read the fourth psalm in that place of peace. *When I called on him he heard me, the God of my vindication; when I was hard beset you led me into spacious freedom. Have mercy on me, Lord, and hearken to my prayer:*[33] would that they had heard what these words of the psalm did to me, but heard without my knowledge, lest they think that it was for their benefit that I uttered words of my own, interspersed with yours! I would surely not have spoken, or not in the same vein, had I felt myself exposed to their ears and eyes; and even if I had, they would not have taken those words I uttered for what they were, the intimate expression of my mind, as I conversed with myself and addressed myself in your presence.

9. I shuddered with awe, yet all the while hope and joy surged up within me at your mercy, Father.[34] It all found an outlet through my eyes and voice when your good Spirit turned to us, saying, *How long will you be heavy-hearted, human creatures? Why love emptiness and chase falsehood?*[35] I, certainly, had loved emptiness and chased falsehood, and you, Lord, had already glorified your Holy One,[36] raising him from the dead and setting him at your right hand, whence he could send the Paraclete, the Spirit of Truth[37] from on high, as he had promised.[38] He had sent him already, but I did not know it. Yes, he had sent the Spirit, for already he had been glorified in his resurrection from the dead[39] and ascension to heaven. Before that time the Spirit was not given, because Jesus had not been glori-

---

32. See Ps 18:7(19:6).
33. Ps 4:2(1).
34. See Ps 30:7-8(31:6-7).
35. Ps 4:3(2). Not only is this a harvest/vintage psalm, in tune with Augustine's mood in the present peaceful interlude; its structure also corresponds to the stages of his life so far, which explains its powerful appeal to him.
36. Ps 4:3(2).
37. See Jn 14:16-17.
38. See Lk 24:49.
39. See Rom 6:9; 7:4; 1 Cor 15:20.

fied.[40] This is why the prophecy cries out, *How long will you be heavy-hearted? Why love emptiness and chase falsehood? Be sure of this: the Lord has glorified his Holy One.*[41] It demands, *How long?* It cries, *Be sure of this;* yet for so long I had been anything but sure, and had loved emptiness and chased falsehood, and so I trembled as I heard these words, for they are addressed to the kind of person I remembered myself to have been. In the fables which I had taken for truth there was emptiness and falsehood; loud and strong I bewailed many an episode among my painful memories. Oh, that they could have heard me, those who still love emptiness and chase falsehood! They might perhaps be so shaken as to spew it out, and then you would hear them when they cried to you,[42] because he who for us died a true death in the flesh now intercedes with you on our behalf.

10. Then I read, *Let your anger deter you from sin,*[43] and how these words moved me, my God! I had already learned to feel for my past sins an anger with myself that would hold me back from sinning again. With good reason had I learned this anger, since it was no alien nature from a tribe of darkness that had been sinning through me, as they maintain who, though not angry with themselves, are accumulating a fund of anger that will overwhelm them on the day of anger, the day when your righteous judgment is to be revealed.[44]

For me, good things were no longer outside, no longer quested for by fleshly eyes in this world's sunlight. Those who want to find their joy in externals all too easily grow empty themselves. They pour themselves out on things which, being seen, are but transient,[45] and lick even the images of these things with their famished imagination. If only they would weary of their starvation and ask, *Who will show us good things?*[46] Let us answer them, and let them hear the truth: *The light of your countenance has set its seal upon us, O Lord.*[47] We are not ourselves that Light which illumines every human being,[48] but by you we are illumined, so that we who were

40. See Jn 7:39.
41. Ps 4:3-4(2-3).
42. See Ps 4:4(3).
43. Ps 4:5(4).
44. See Rom 2:5.
45. See 2 Cor 4:18.
46. Ps 4:6(5).
47. Ibid.
48. See Jn 1:9.

once darkness may become light in you.[49] Ah, if only they could see the eternal reality within! I had tasted it,[50] and was frantic at my inability to show it to them; if only they would bring to me those hearts of theirs which lived in their outward-gazing eyes, outside and away from you; if only they would say, *Who will show us good things?* There within, where I had grown angry with myself, there in the inner chamber where I was pierced with sorrow,[51] where I had offered sacrifice, slaying my old nature[52] and hoping in you as I began to give my mind to the new life,[53] there you had begun to make me feel your sweetness and had given me *joy in my heart.*[54]

As I read these words outwardly and experienced their truth inwardly I shouted with joy, and lost my desire to dissipate myself amid a profusion of earthly goods, eating up time as I was myself eaten by it; for in your eternal simplicity I now had a different *wheat and wine and oil.*[55]

11. The next verse wrung a cry from the very depths of my heart: *In peace!* Oh, *In Being itself!* What did it say? *I will rest and fall asleep.*[56] Yes, for who shall make war against us when that promise of scripture is fulfilled, *Death is swallowed up into victory?*[57] In truth you are Being itself, unchangeable, and in you is found the rest that is mindful no more of its labors, for there is no one else beside you, nor need our rest concern itself with striving for a host of other things that are not what you are; rather it is you, *you, Lord, who through hope establish me in unity.*[58]

I read on and on, all afire, but I could find no way to help those deaf, dead folk among whom I had once been numbered. I had been a lethal nuisance, bitter and blind and baying against honey-sweet scriptures

---

49. See Eph 5:8.
50. See Ps 33:9(34:8).
51. See Ps 4:5(4).
52. See Eph 4:22; Col 3:9.
53. See Col 3:10; 2 Cor 4:16.
54. Ps 4:7.
55. Ps 4:8(7).
56. Ps 4:9(8). The word *idipsum* ("the selfsame") in the Latin of the psalm is for Augustine a mysterious name for God, the infinite, immutable Being. It evokes for him the revelation of the divine name to Moses in Ex 3:14. Parallels within *The Confessions* are VII,17,23; IX,10, 24; XII,7,7.
57. 1 Cor 15:54.
58. Ps 4:10(8). *Singulariter*, here translated as *in unity*, could be an adverb applied to God's action: *You alone establish ...* ; but Augustine takes it to be the antithesis of the dispersion, multiplicity, evoked at the end of the preceding paragraph.

distilled from heaven's honey, scriptures luminous by your light;[59] but now to think of the enemies of that scripture[60] caused me anguish.

12. How shall I ever remember all that happened during that holiday? But one thing I cannot forget and will not omit, a harsh chastisement you laid on me, which was followed with amazing swiftness by your mercy. At that time you tortured me with a toothache, and when it had grown so severe that I could not speak, the thought entered my heart that I should urge all my own people who were there to pray for me to you, the God of every kind of healing. I wrote this on a wax tablet and gave it to one of them to read out to the rest. The moment we knelt down and begged this favor from you, the pain vanished. What was that pain? Where did it go? I must admit that I was terrified, my Lord and my God,[61] for I had never in all my life experienced anything like it. It came home to me most deeply that this was a sign of your powerful will, and I rejoiced in my faith as I praised your name;[62] yet this same faith did not allow me to be complacent about my past sins, which had not yet been forgiven me through baptism.

5, 13. When the holidays were over I announced my retirement. The citizens of Milan would have to provide another word-peddler for their students, because I had made up my mind to give myself to your service, and in any case I was unequal to that profession now that I had difficulty in breathing and pains in the chest. I wrote to the holy man Ambrose, your bishop, notifying him of my past errors and present intention, and asking his advice as to which of your books in particular I ought to read, the better to prepare myself for so great a grace and render me more fit to receive it. He recommended the prophet Isaiah, I think because he more plainly than all others foretold the gospel and the call of the Gentiles. The first part I read of this book was incomprehensible to me, however, and, assuming that all the rest would be the same, I put it off, meaning to take it up again later, when I was more proficient in the word of the Lord.

---

59. See Ps 118(119):103.105.
60. See Ps 138(139):21.
61. See Jn 20:28.
62. See Ps 144(145):2; Sir 51:15.

They return to Milan and are baptized

6, 14. The time arrived for me to give in my name for baptism, so we left the country and moved back to Milan.[63] Alypius had decided to join me in being reborn in you, and was already clothed with the humility[64] that befitted your mysteries. He was also extremely courageous in subduing his body, even to the point of walking barefoot on the icy soil of Italy, a thing few dared to do. We associated the boy Adeodatus with us as well, my son according to the flesh, born of my sin. Very fair had you fashioned him. He was then about fifteen, but surpassed many educated men of weighty learning. I am acknowledging that these were your gifts, O Lord my God, creator of all things,[65] who are more than powerful enough to give fair form to our deformities, for nothing did I contribute to that boy's making except my fault. It was you, and you alone, who had inspired us to instruct him in your truth as he grew up, and so it is your own gifts that I acknowledge to you. There is a book of ours entitled *The Teacher*, in which he converses with me. You know that all the thoughts there attributed to my interlocutor were truly his, although he was only about sixteen years old. Many other things even more wonderful did I observe in him. The brilliance he evinced filled me with awe, for who else but you could be the artificer of such prodigies? Very soon you took him away from this life on earth, but I remember him without anxiety, for I have no fear about anything in his boyhood or adolescence; indeed I fear nothing whatever for that man. We included him in the group as our contemporary in the life of your grace, to be schooled along with us in your doctrine.

And so we were baptized, and all our dread about our earlier lives dropped away from us.[66] During the days that followed[67] I could not get enough of the wonderful sweetness that filled me as I meditated upon your

---

63. About six months have elapsed since the preceding chapter; Augustine and his little group spent the winter of 386-387 at Cassiciacum. We have now reached the early days of Lent, around the beginning of March 387.

64. See Col 3:12.

65. See 2 Mc 1:24; Ambrose, Hymn 1,2, quoted more extensively at IX,12,32.

66. They were baptized by immersion, confessing faith in the Trinity, at the Easter Vigil during the night of 24-25 April 387. Augustine himself (at least) was baptized by Ambrose, as he later testified. A description of the whole ceremony as observed at that time has survived in two works by Ambrose, *On the Sacraments* and *On the Mysteries*. After baptism the white-clad neophytes were led from baptistery to church, were they were present at the full eucharist for the first time and received communion.

67. That is, from Easter until the following Sunday. During this week the neophytes kept on the white garments received at baptism and attended daily liturgies at which fuller instruction about the faith and the sacraments was given to them. Many of the sermons later preached by Augustine as a bishop to the neophytes in Easter week have survived.

deep design for the salvation of the human race. How copiously I wept at your hymns and canticles, how intensely was I moved by the lovely harmonies of your singing Church! Those voices flooded my ears, and the truth was distilled into my heart until it overflowed in loving devotion; my tears ran down, and I was the better for them.

Use of hymns in liturgy

7, 15. Not long since, the faithful of the church in Milan had begun to find mutual comfort and encouragement in the liturgy through the practice of singing hymns, in which everyone fervently joined with voice and heart. It was about a year earlier, or not much more, that Justina, mother of the boy-emperor Valentinian, had been persecuting your faithful Ambrose, in the interests of the Arian heresy by which she had been led astray. His God-fearing congregation, prepared to die with their bishop, your servant, stayed up all night in the church. Your maidservant, my mother, was among them, foremost in giving support and keeping vigil, and constant in her life of prayer. As for us, we were still cold, not being yet warmed by the fire of your Spirit, yet we too were stirred as alarm and excitement shook the city.[68]

It was then that the practice was established of singing hymns and psalms[69] in the manner customary in regions of the East, to prevent the people losing heart and fainting from weariness. It has persisted from that time until the present, and in other parts of the world also many of your churches imitate the practice: indeed, nearly all of them.[70]

---

68. The events are related in Ambrose's Letters 20 and 21, and in Paulinus' *Life of Ambrose*. Justina, from a senatorial family, had married Valentinian I as her second husband and bore him four children. She had, as Ambrose relates, demanded that he make a church available within the walls of the city for the use of the Arian heretics. Ambrose refused; he and the people stayed all night in the church to prevent its annexation, and he introduced hymn-singing to keep up their spirits. This led to its adoption into the liturgy of the Western Church. The siege of the church was in February 386.

69. See Col 3:16.

70. Ambrose explains (Letters 20,24; 21a,34) that, by learning to sing hymns to the Father, the Son and the Spirit, people who before were scarcely disciples became teachers, that is, they preached the faith to one another by this means. More than ninety hymns are attributed to Ambrose personally, though not all are authentic.

Discovery of the bodies of two saints

16. At this same time you revealed in a vision to the aforementioned Ambrose, your bishop, where the bodies of the martyrs Gervasius and Protasius were hidden. You had for many years treasured them, incorrupt and concealed in a secret place of your own, until the right moment came when you could bring them out into the open to check a certain person's ferocity—a woman's rage only, yet a queen's. When they had been exposed to the light of day and dug up, and were being transported with due honor to the Ambrosian basilica, some people hitherto tormented by unclean spirits were restored to health[71] as confession was wrung from these same demons. But that was not all. A certain citizen of Milan, very well known in the city, who had been blind for several years, became aware of the riotous joy of the people and inquired the reason for it; on hearing what was happening he leapt up and asked his guide to take him there. He was led to the basilica and begged to be admitted, so that he might touch with his handkerchief the funeral bier of your holy ones, whose death was precious in your sight.[72] He did so, and applied the handkerchief to his eyes: they were immediately opened.[73] The consequences of this were the wide diffusion of the story, fervent praise offered to you, and a change of mind on the part of our enemy, for although she was not brought to the healthy state of believing, her persecuting fury was at least curbed. Thanks be to you, O my God!

From what point, by what path, have you led my memory to this, so that I can include in my confession to you these great happenings, which I had forgotten and passed over? Yet at that time, though the fragrance of your ointments blew so freely abroad, we did not run after you;[74] and that was why I wept the more abundantly later on when your hymns were sung: once I had gasped for you, but now at last I breathed your fragrance, insofar as your wind can blow through our house of straw.[75]

---

71. See Lk 6:18.
72. See Ps 115(116):16.
73. These events occurred from 17 to 19 June 386. Ambrose says that the blind man was named Severus and had been a butcher.
74. See Sg 1:3.
75. Contrast the "breath of pride" in IX,4,8. For the "flesh is grass" motif see Is 40:6; for the earthly habitation see 2 Cor 5:1. He has now brought the narrative back to his post-baptismal period, April-May 387.

Monica's story

8, 17. You gather like-minded people to dwell together,[76] and so you brought into our fellowship a young man named Evodius, who was from our home town.[77] While serving as an administrative officer in the Special Branch he had been converted to you before we were; he was then baptized and abandoned his secular career to enlist in your service. We stayed together, and made a holy agreement to live together in the future. In search of a place where we could best serve you, we made arrangements to return as a group to Africa. And while we were at Ostia on the Tiber[78] my mother died.[79]

I am passing over many things because time is short: accept my confessions and thanks for mercies without number, O my God, though I offer them in silence. But I will not pass over anything that my soul brings forth concerning that servant of yours who brought me forth from her flesh to birth in this temporal light, and from her heart to birth in light eternal. I will speak not of her gifts, but of the gifts with which you endowed her; for she did not fashion herself or bring herself up: you created her, and not even her father or mother knew what kind of child would be born from them. She was brought up to reverence you,[80] schooled by the crook of your Christ,[81] the shepherd's care of your only Son, in a faithful family that was a sound limb of your Church. She used to speak less, though, of her mother's discipline than of the training she received from a certain aged servant who had carried her father in his childhood, as is often the way with little girls who carry smaller children on their backs. In consideration of this, and of her advanced age and excellent character, the servant was held in high respect by her master and mistress in this Christian household. The care of her master's daughters was therefore entrusted to her, and she carried out her duty conscientiously, drastic with a holy severity in controlling them as occasion required, discreet and sensible in teaching them. An example of this was her refusal to allow them so much as a drink

---

76. See Ps 67:7(68:6).
77. A Thagastan by birth, Evodius was an interlocutor in Augustine's dialogues *The Greatness of the Soul* and *Free Will*. He later became bishop of Uzalis and was energetic in controversy against Manichees and Pelagians.
78. See Virgil, *Aeneid* I,13-14.
79. In the summer or early autumn of 387, before Augustine's thirty-third birthday on 13 November.
80. See Pss 5:8(7); 118(119):138.
81. See Ps 22(23):4.

of water outside the hours when they were sufficiently provided for at their parents' table, even if they were burning with thirst. She was taking precautions against the development of harmful habits, and made the point with her wise counsel: "It is water that you are drinking now, because wine is not within your reach; but the day will come when you are married and find yourselves in charge of storerooms and cellars, and then water will not seem good enough; yet the habit of tippling will be too strong for you." By this policy of advising the girls and exercising authority over them she reined in their childish greed and imposed a reasonable measure on their very thirst, with the result that they lost even the desire for what was unbecoming.

18. In spite of this, something had stealthily snared your handmaid, as she told me, her son—a furtive fondness for wine: for whenever, in accord with custom, her parents sent this responsible daughter of theirs to draw wine from the cask by dipping a cup in through an opening near the head, she would take a tiny sip by brushing it with her lips before pouring it into the decanter. Repugnance prevented her from taking more, for she was acting not from any real craving for drink, but from a certain exuberance of youthful naughtiness, which is apt to erupt in playful behavior, and is usually curbed when it appears in children by the authority of their elders. But by adding to that modest allowance daily modest allowances—for one who allows himself license in little things is ruined little by little[82]—she had fallen at length into the habit of avidly quaffing near goblets-full of wine.

What had become of the wise old woman and her stern prohibition? Would anything have been efficacious against that sly sickness, had your medicine[83] not been watching over us, Lord? Father, mother and guardians may all be absent, but you are present, you who created us and called us and even through those set over us work for our good and the saving of souls. How did you work then, O my God? How did you cure her, how bring her back to health? Did you not elicit a hard, sharp reproof from another soul, and use it like a surgeon's knife drawn from your hidden, providential resources to cut away that diseased tissue in a single sweep? The maid who usually accompanied her to the cask was one day quarreling with her young mistress—a thing that sometimes happens—and flung an accusation against her when the two of them were alone, calling her in the

---

82. See Sir 19:1.
83. That is, implicitly Christ.

most bitterly insulting language a wine-swiller.[84] This shaft went home, and my mother took heed to her disgraceful conduct, condemned it and threw it off at once.

Just as flattering friends pervert, so quarrelsome foes may often correct us, though you requite them not for what you effect through their means but for their intention. That angry maid meant to upset her little mistress, not heal her, so she spoke up in private, either because the quarrel happened to break out in a place and at a time when they were alone, or because she might have exposed herself to danger if it emerged that she had delayed so long in reporting the matter. But you, Lord, are the ruler of all things in heaven and on earth, and as worldly events flow on their tumultuous way you dispose them in due order, diverting the course of that deep torrent to serve your purposes. Through one unwholesome soul you brought wholesomeness to another, so that no one who takes note of this episode may ascribe it to his own power if another person, who, in his opinion, stands in need of correction, is put right by some word of his.

9, 19. She was thus nurtured in an atmosphere of purity and temperance, and was subjected by you to the authority of her parents rather than by them to yours. When she attained full marriageable age she was entrusted to a husband; she served him as her lord,[85] but she made it her business to win him for you[86] by preaching you to him through her way of life, for by her conduct you made her beautiful in her husband's eyes, as a person to be respected, loved and admired. So gently did she put up with his marital infidelities that no quarrel ever broke out between them on this score, for she looked to you to show him mercy, knowing that once he came to believe he would become chaste.[87] Although he was outstandingly generous, he was also hot-tempered, but she learned to offer him no resistance, by deed or even by word, when he was angry; she would wait for a favorable moment, when she saw that his mood had changed and he was calm again, and then explain her action, in case he had given way to wrath without due consideration. There were plenty of women married to

---

84. *Meribibulam.* Many years later Augustine's adversary Julian, the Pelagian bishop of Eclanum, taunted him with this weakness of his mother, of which Augustine had himself used the derogatory word. Augustine replied, "What wonder that you show yourself her enemy, since you are the enemy of that grace of God by means of which, as I stated, she was freed from her childish vice?" (*Unfinished Work in Answer to Julian* I, 68)
85. See Eph 5:22; 1 Pt 3:6.
86. See 1 Pt 3:1.
87. See 1 Jn 3:3.

husbands of gentler temper whose faces were badly disfigured by traces of blows, who while gossiping together would complain about their husbands' behavior; but she checked their talk, reminding them in what seemed to be a joking vein but with serious import that from the time they had heard their marriage contracts read out they had been in duty bound to consider these as legal documents which made slaves of them. In consequence they ought to keep their subservient status in mind and not defy their masters. These other wives knew what a violent husband she had to put up with, and were amazed that there had never been any rumor of Patricius's striking his wife, nor the least evidence of its happening, nor even a day's domestic strife between the two of them; and in friendly talk they sought an explanation. My mother would then instruct them in this plan of hers that I have outlined. Those who followed it found out its worth and were happy; those who did not continued to be bullied and battered.

20. By persevering in devoted service, and by patience and gentleness, she won over her mother-in-law, who had initially been provoked against her by the whispering of mischievous maids, but now of her own accord informed her son of the servants' meddling tongues that had troubled the domestic peace between herself and her daughter-in-law, and demanded that those responsible be punished. Minded to obey his mother, to enforce discipline in the household and to ensure concord between his relatives, he punished those reported to him with beatings, as she who had reported them judged fit; and she promised that anyone who in the future should say anything malicious to her concerning her daughter-in-law, with a view to currying favor, might hope for a like recompense from her. Since no one dared to do so again, the two lived in a remarkably sweet atmosphere of mutual goodwill.

21. There was another great gift with which you had endowed this bondswoman of yours, in whose womb you created me, O my God, my mercy,[88] and that was the gift of acting as peacemaker whenever she could if friction occurred between souls at variance. She would hear many a bitter accusation from each against the other, of the kind that lumpy, ill-digested discord is wont to belch forth when someone dyspeptic with hatred spews out acid talk to a present friend concerning an absent enemy; but never would she repeat to one anything the other had alleged, except what would be effective in reconciling them. This would have seemed to

---

88. See Ps 58:18(59:17).

me a boon of small account, did I not have sad experience of innumerable hordes of people, inspired by what rampant, grisly gangrene of sin I cannot conceive, who not only betray to angry people what their angry enemies have said, but add things unsaid as well, whereas it ought to be easy enough for any who have kindly feelings toward their own kind to avoid provoking or aggravating the enmity of others by reporting malicious gossip, except in cases where they have made sure they can extinguish it again by peaceable speech. Such was she, because you, her intimate teacher, instructed her in the school of her heart.

22. Eventually she won even her husband for you, toward the end of his life on earth,[89] and she had no cause for complaint about anything in him after his baptism that she had tolerated in him while unbaptized. Moreover she was the servant of your servants. Every one of them who knew her found ample reason to praise, honor and love you as he sensed your presence in her heart, attested by the fruits of her holy way of life.[90] She had been married to one man only, had loyally repaid what she owed to her parents, had governed her household in the fear of God, and earned a reputation for good works.[91] She had brought up children, in labor anew with them[92] each time she saw them straying away from you. Finally, Lord, she took care of all of us who were your servants—for by your gift you permit us to speak—who before her death lived together as companions in you after receiving the grace of your baptism; she took care of us all as though all had been her children, and served us as though she had been the daughter of all.

Ostia

10, 23. But because the day when she was to quit this life was drawing near—a day known to you, though we were ignorant of it—she and I happened to be alone, through the mysterious workings of your will, as I believe. We stood leaning against a window which looked out on a

89. Patricius died c. 370/371, as appears from III,4,7.
90. See Mt 7:20; 2 Pt 3:11.
91. All this description closely corresponds to that of an authentic Christian widow in 1 Tm 5:4-10.
92. See Gal 4:19.

garden[93] within the house where we were staying at Ostia on the Tiber, for there, far from the crowds, we were recruiting our strength after the long journey, in preparation for our voyage overseas. We were alone, conferring very intimately. Forgetting what lay in the past, and stretching out to what was ahead,[94] we inquired between ourselves in the light of present truth, the Truth which is yourself,[95] what the eternal life of the saints would be like. Eye has not seen nor ear heard nor human heart conceived it,[96] yet with the mouth of our hearts wide open we panted thirstily for the celestial streams of your fountain, the fount of life which is with you,[97] that bedewed from it according to our present capacity we might in our little measure think upon a thing so great.

24. Our colloquy led us to the point where the pleasures of the body's senses, however intense and in however brilliant a material light enjoyed, seemed unworthy not merely of comparison but even of remembrance beside the joy of that life, and we lifted ourselves in longing yet more ardent toward *That Which Is*,[98] and step by step traversed all bodily creatures and heaven itself, whence sun and moon and stars shed their light upon the earth. Higher still we mounted by inward thought and wondering discourse on your works, and we arrived at the summit of our own minds; and this too we transcended, to touch that land of never-failing plenty[99] where you pasture Israel[100] for ever with the food of truth. Life there is the Wisdom through whom all these things are made,[101] and all others that have been or ever will be; but Wisdom herself is not made: she is as she always has been and will be for ever. Rather should we say that in her there is no "has been" or "will be," but only being, for she is eternal, but past and future do not belong to eternity. And as we talked and panted for it, we just

---

93. Gardens are significant for Augustine, as in Christian mythology more widely. The conversion of the two court officials occurs in one (VIII,6,15) and so does that of Augustine and Alypius (VIII,8,19). Now in Augustine's supreme mystical experience he and Monica are looking out into a garden. The paradisal overtones are evident.

94. See Phil 3:13.

95. See Jn 14:6; 2 Pt 1:12; Plotinus, *Enneads* V,1,4.

96. See Is 64:4; 1 Cor 2:9-10.

97. See Ps 35:10(36:9). The sheer physicality of the language which Augustine uses to describe this mystical experience is noteworthy. *Inhiare* (gape, gasp, pant, crave, thirst after) and the metaphor of avid drinking recall Monica's youthful wine-bibbing described a few paragraphs earlier: the two scenes, in which she is central, are intentionally paralleled and contrasted.

98. *In idipsum*, Ps 4:9(8); see note on IX,4,11.

99. See Ez 34:14.

100. See Ps 79:2(80:1).

101. See Prv 8:23-31.

touched the edge of it by the utmost leap of our hearts; then, sighing and unsatisfied, we left the first-fruits of our spirit[102] captive there, and returned to the noise of articulate speech, where a word has beginning and end. How different from your Word, our Lord, who abides in himself, and grows not old, but renews all things.[103]

25. Then we said,

"If the tumult of the flesh fell silent for someone,
and silent too were the phantasms of earth, sea and air,
silent the heavens,
and the very soul silent to itself,
that it might pass beyond itself by not thinking of its own being;
if dreams and revelations known through its imagination were
    silent,
if every tongue, and every sign, and whatever is subject to transience
were wholly stilled for him
—for if anyone listens, all these things will tell him,
'We did not make ourselves;[104]
he made us who abides for ever,'[105]—
and having said this they held their peace

---

102. The expression is directly quoted from Rom 8:23, but with a change of sense; here it means the offering made to God in faith of the highest part of the human spirit, pledge that the whole person will follow.

103. See Wis 7:27. The stress on hearing rather than seeing is insignificant. Augustine's language in describing this supreme experience is strongly reminiscent of Plotinus (see *Enneads* V,1,2 and I,6,7) and he certainly recognized that the goal of Plotinian ascent through creatures to God, the One, the Eternal, was the same as that to which he now aspired. But the differences between his earlier attempts (see IV,13, 20; VII,10,16;17,23) and his experience are vital. In between have come the whole journey of Books VII and VIII, his personal acceptance of Christ in the garden scene and in baptism, and the moral liberation associated with that. The allusion to Phil 3 strikes a clear Christian note as the description begins. The Word/Wisdom who is the object of Augustine and Monica's contemplation is he who is incarnate in Jesus Christ. Augustine's earlier experience at Milan was presented within a context of pride, his own and that of the man who gave him the Platonist books (see VII, 8,12;9,13-14;20,26), but now he has moved from presumption to confession, from pride to the humility which above all characterizes the incarnate Word. Moreover the experience at Ostia is shared: Augustine and Monica are aware of each other, they are together in it: this would be impossible in Plotinian ecstasy, where the visionary is no longer conscious of distinctions; Augustine's description is a far cry from Plotinus' "flight of the alone to the Alone" (see *Enneads* VI,9,11). Augustine and Monica discuss "the eternal life of the saints," a shared joy, and one promised to them as their own fulfillment. Monica has no philosophical training and would have been incapable of Plotinian ecstasy, but her faith in Christ gives her access to as full an experience here as Augustine's own, and the inclusion of this episode in the miniature "Life of Monica" in Book IX suggests that it is seen as the earthly culmination of the life of baptismal grace. Finally the body is no longer seen as an obstacle; on the contrary, Augustine looks to the final resurrection of the body as the precondition of permanent enjoyment of what is now transitory.

104. See Ps 99(100):3.

105. See Sir 18:1; Pss 32(33):11; 116(117):2; Is 40:8; Jn 12:34.

for they had pricked the listening ear to him who made them;
and then he alone were to speak,
not through things that are made, but of himself,
that we might hear his Word,
not through fleshly tongue nor angel's voice,
nor thundercloud,[106]
nor any riddling parable,[107]
hear him unmediated, whom we love in all these things,
hear him without them,
as now we stretch out[108] and in a flash of thought
touch that eternal Wisdom who abides above all things;
if this could last,
and all other visions, so far inferior, be taken away,
and this sight alone ravish him who saw it,
and engulf him and hide him away, kept for inward joys,
so that this moment of knowledge—
this passing moment that left us aching for more—
should there be life eternal,
would not *Enter into the joy of your Lord*[109]
be this, and this alone?
And when, when will this be?
When we all rise again, but not all are changed?"[110]

26. So did I speak, though not in this wise exactly, nor in these same words. Yet you know, O Lord, how on that very day amid this talk of ours that seemed to make the world with all its charms grow cheap, she said, "For my part, my son, I find pleasure no longer in anything this life holds. What I am doing here still, or why I tarry, I do not know, for all worldly hope has withered away for me. One thing only there was for which I desired to linger awhile in this life: to see you a Catholic Christian before I died. And this my God has granted to me more lavishly than I could have hoped, letting me see you even spurning earthly happiness to be his servant. What now keeps me here?"[111]

---

106. See Ps 76:18(77:17); Ex 19:19; Jn 12:29.
107. See 1 Cor 13:12; Nm 12:6-8.
108. See Phil 3:13.
109. Mt 25:21.
110. See 1 Cor 15:51.
111. The episode may have some literary affinity with the last meeting of Aeneas with his aged father Anchises in *Aeneid* VI. The garden here recalls the meadow of Hades *(Aeneid* VI,679. 703); Ostia is not far from Virgil's entrance to the underworld, and the name "Ostia" is itself suggestive.

Monica's death

11, 27. What I replied I do not clearly remember, because just about that time—five days afterward or not much more—she took to her bed with fever. One day during her illness she lapsed into unconsciousness and for a short time was unaware of her surroundings. We all came running, but she quickly returned to her senses, and, gazing at me and my brother[112] as we stood there, she asked in puzzlement, "Where was I?" We were bewildered with grief, but she looked keenly at us and said, "You are to bury your mother here." I was silent, holding back my tears, but my brother said something about his hope that she would not die far from home, but in her own country, for that would be a happier way. On hearing this she looked anxious and her eyes rebuked him for thinking so; then she turned her gaze from him to me and said, "What silly talk!" Not long afterward, addressing us both, she said, "Lay this body anywhere, and take no trouble over it. One thing only do I ask of you, that you remember me at the altar of the Lord wherever you may be." Having made her meaning clear to us with such words as she could muster, she fell silent, and travailed as the disease grew worse.

28. But my thoughts were upon the gifts you implant in the hearts of your faithful, O invisible God,[113] and the wondrous fruits they produce. I was rejoicing and thanking you[114] as I recalled what had earlier been well known to me: her constant preoccupation with the grave she had provided for herself beside the body of her husband. Since they had lived together in such harmony, she wanted this blessing also to be added to their happiness (so inept is the human mind at grasping divine reality), a blessing people would remember: that when her pilgrimage overseas was done, it had been granted to her that the earthly remains of husband and wife[115] should be covered by one same earth. When this frivolous wish had by your generous goodness left her heart I did not know, and I was filled with wondering joy that its departure had been signaled to me in this fashion; although in our conversation at the window her words, "What still keeps me here?" did not suggest that she desired to die in her own country. Later I heard that already during our stay at Ostia she was one day talking with

---

112. Navigius.
113. See Col 1:15.
114. See Col 1:3.
115. See Gn 2:7.

motherly openness with some of my friends, in my absence, about contempt for this life and the blessing of death. They were amazed at such courage in a woman—for it was you who had given it to her—and asked whether she was not afraid to leave her body so far from her own city. "Nothing is far from God," she replied. "There is no danger that at the end of the world he will not know where to find me and raise me up."

So on the ninth day of her illness, in the fifty-sixth year of her age, in my thirty-third year, that religious and godly soul was set free from her body.

Augustine's grief

12, 29. I closed her eyes, and a huge sadness surged into my heart; the tears welled up, but in response to a ferocious command from my mind my eyes held the fount in check until it dried up, though the struggle was intensely painful for me. But as she breathed her last the boy Adeodatus burst out crying; he was restrained by all of us and grew quiet. By this means something boyish in myself, which was sliding toward tears, was also restrained by the man's voice of my heart, and it too grew quiet. We judged it unfitting[116] to mark this death by plaintive protests and laments, since these are customarily employed to mourn the misery of the dying, or death as complete extinction. But she neither died in misery nor died altogether. The evidence of her virtues and her sincere faith[117] gave us good reason to hold this as certain.

30. What was it, then, that gave me such sharp inward pain? She and I had grown accustomed to living together; an exceedingly gentle and dear custom it was, and its sudden disruption was like a newly-inflicted wound. I found some solace in her commendation of me, for in that last illness she would at times respond with a caress to some little service I rendered her, calling me a devoted son, and with deep affection would declare that she had never heard from my lips any harsh or rough expression flung against her. But what is that, O my God, who have made us?[118] What common measure is there between the respect with which I treated her and the service she did to me? Being now bereft of her comfort, so great a comfort,

---

116. See 1 Thes 4:12.
117. See 1 Tm 1:5.
118. See Ps 99(100):3; Bar 4:7.

my soul was wounded; it was as though my life was rent apart, for there had been but one life, woven out of mine and hers.

31. As soon as we had persuaded the boy to stop weeping, Evodius took up the psalter and began to sing a psalm. All of us in the house joined in: *I will sing to you of your mercy and justice, O Lord.*[119] Many brethren and religious women assembled when they heard what was happening, and while those whose business it was prepared the body for burial, according to custom, I withdrew to where I could suitably engage in discussion on subjects appropriate to this occasion with those who felt I should not be left alone. With this salve of truth I soothed the agony that was known only to you; they were unaware of it, and though they listened attentively to my words, they believed that I felt no pain. Yet in your ears, where none of them could hear me, I chided myself with weakness for feeling as I did, and dammed up the flood of grief, so that for a little space it receded from me; but then a fresh wave swept over me, and though it was not enough to bring on an outburst of tears or even a change of expression, I knew myself what I was suppressing in my heart. And since I was gravely displeased to find how powerfully I could be affected by these human experiences, which in the due order of things and as a consequence of our natural condition are bound to occur, the woe I felt over my woe was yet another woe, and I was distressed by this double sadness.

32. Now came the moment when the body was borne away. We followed it, and returned again dry-eyed; for not even in the course of those prayers we poured out to you when the sacrifice of our redemption was offered for her beside the grave, where the body had been laid prior to burial, as is the custom there—no, not even during those prayers did I weep, but all day long I was secretly weighed down by sorrow, and in my mental turmoil I begged you as best I could to heal my hurt. You did not, and this because, as I believe, you were reminding me that any sort of habit is bondage, even to a mind no longer feeding on deceitful words.

I thought it a good idea to go and take a bath, because I had heard that baths derived their name from the Greeks, who called a bath *balaneion* because it banishes worry from the mind.[120] This too I must confess to your

---

119. Ps 100(101):1. The mention of the opening verse evokes the whole psalm, which could have been recited truthfully by Monica, and was doubtless chosen as particularly apposite in the circumstances.
120. A fanciful etymology from *ballō*, throw, and *ania*, grief.

mercy, O Father of orphans,[121] that I bathed, and afterward was quite unchanged, for I had not sweated the bitter sorrow out of my heart. But then I went to sleep, and on awakening felt a good deal better. As I lay in bed alone I remembered some lines by your servant Ambrose, which rang true for me:

Creator God, O Lord of all,
who rule the skies, you clothe the day
in radiant color, bid the night
in quietness serve the gracious sway
of sleep, that weary limbs, restored
to labor's use, may rise again,
and jaded minds abate their fret,
and mourners find release from pain.[122]

33. Little by little I recovered my earlier thoughts about your handmaid, remembering how devout had been her attitude toward you, and how full of holy kindness, how willing to make allowances, she had been in our regard; and now that I was suddenly bereft of this I found comfort in weeping before you about her and for her, about myself and for myself. The tears that I had been holding back I now released to flow as plentifully as they would, and strewed them as a bed beneath my heart. There it could rest, because there were your ears only, not the ears of anyone who would judge my weeping by the norms of his own pride.

And now, Lord, it is in writing that I confess to you. Let anyone read it who will, and judge it as he will, and if he finds it sinful that I wept over my mother for a brief part of a single hour—the mother who for a little space was to my sight dead, and who had wept long years for me that in your sight I might live—then let such a reader not mock, but rather, if his charity is wide enough, himself weep for my sins to you, who are Father to all whom your Christ calls his brethren.

13, 34. But now that my heart is healed of that wound, in which I was perhaps guilty of some carnal affection, I pour out to you tears of a very different kind for this servant of yours, O our God; they come gushing forth from a mind struck by the perils besetting every soul that dies in

---

121. See Ps 67:6(68:5).
122. From Ambrose's evening hymn, *Deus, Creator omnium*, which may have been a favorite with Augustine. It is quoted elsewhere in *The Confessions*, and in a dialogue at Cassiciacum (*The Happy Life* IV,35) Monica quotes another line from it. The verses quoted here are obviously suited to Augustine's immediate need, but also bring Ambrose to mind in association with Monica for a last time.

Adam. True, she had been brought to new life in Christ,[123] and even before her release from the body she so lived that her faith and conduct redounded to the glory of your name. Yet all the same I dare not assert that from the time you brought her to new birth in baptism[124] no word contrary to your commandment escaped her lips.[125] And by the Truth who is your Son[126] we are warned, *If anyone says to his brother, "You fool!"* he will be liable to hellfire,[127] so woe betide anyone, even one whose life is praiseworthy, if you should examine it without mercy![128] But since you are not ruthless in searching out our faults, we trustingly hope for a place in your house. If anyone were to give you an account of his real merits, what else would that be but a list of your gifts? If only humans would acknowledge that they are human, and anyone minded to boast would boast in the Lord![129]

35. This is why, O God of my heart,[130] my praise,[131] my life, I will for a little while disregard her good deeds, for which I joyfully give you thanks, and pray to you now for my mother's sins. Hear me through that healing remedy who hung upon the tree,[132] the medicine for our wounds who sits at your right hand and intercedes for us.[133] I know that she dealt mercifully with others and from her heart forgave her debtors their debts; do you then forgive her any debts[134] she contracted during all those years after she had passed through the saving waters. Forgive her, Lord, forgive, I beg you,[135] and do not arraign her before you.[136] Let mercy triumph over judgment,[137] for you, whose utterances are true, have to the merciful promised mercy.[138] Since their very power to be merciful was your gift to them in the first place, you will be showing mercy to those with whom you have yourself

---

123. See 1 Cor 15:22; Eph 2:5.
124. See Ti 3:5.
125. See Mt 12:36-37.
126. See Jn 14:6.
127. Mt 5:22.
128. See Ps 129(130):3.
129. See 1 Cor 1:31; 2 Cor 10:17.
130. See Ps 72(73):26.
131. See Pss 117(118):14; 21:4, 26 (22:3, 25); Jer 17:14; Ex 15:2; Is 12:2; Dt 10:21.
132. See Dt 21:23; Gal 3:13.
133. See Ps 109(110):1; Rom 8:34.
134. See Mt 6:12; 18:35.
135. See Nm 14:19.
136. See Ps 142(143):2.
137. See Jas 2:13.
138. See Mt 5:7.

dealt mercifully, and granting pity to those toward whom you have shown pity first.[139]

36. I believe you have already done what I am asking you, but look favorably, Lord, on this free offering of my lips.[140] On the day when her release was at hand[141] she gave no thought to costly burial or the embalming of her body with spices, nor did she pine for a special monument or concern herself about a grave in her native land; no, that was not her command to us. She desired only to be remembered at your altar, where she had served you with never a day's absence. From that altar, as she knew, the holy Victim is made available to us, he through whom the record of debt that stood against us was annulled.[142] He has triumphed over an enemy who does keep a tally of our faults and looks for anything to lay to our charge, but finds no case against him.[143] In him we win our victory. Who will reimburse him for that innocent blood?[144] Who will pay back to him the price he paid[145] to purchase us, as though to snatch us back from him?

To the sacrament of that ransom-price your handmaid made fast her soul with the bonds of faith. Let no one wrench her away from your protection. Let no lion or dragon[146] thrust in between by force or guile; for she will not claim that she has no debts to pay, lest she be convicted by the crafty accuser and fall into his power; she will reply only that her debts have been forgiven by him to whom no one can repay what he paid for us, though he owed us nothing.

Peace

37. May she then rest in peace[147] with her husband. She was married to no other man[148] either before or after him, and in serving him she brought

---

139. See Ex 33:19; Rom 9:15.
140. See Ps 118(119):108.
141. See 2 Tm 4:6.
142. See Col 2:14-15.
143. See Lk 23:4; Jn 14:30; 18:38; 19:4.
144. See Mt 27:4.
145. See 1 Cor 6:20; 7:23.
146. See Ps 90(91):13.
147. Peace is the keynote at the end of the narrative part of *The Confessions*, as it will be at the close of the whole work, XIII,15,50.
148. See 1 Tm 5:9.

forth fruit for you by patience,[149] to win him for you in the end. Inspire others, my Lord, my God,[150] inspire your servants who are my brethren, your children who are my masters, whom I now serve with heart and voice and pen, that as many of them as read this may remember Monica, your servant,[151] at your altar, along with Patricius, sometime her husband. From their flesh you brought me into this life, though how I do not know. Let them remember with loving devotion these two who were my parents in this transitory light, but also were my brethren under you, our Father, within our mother the Catholic Church, and my fellow-citizens in the eternal Jerusalem, for which your people[152] sighs with longing throughout its pilgrimage, from its setting out to its return. So may the last request she made of me be granted to her more abundantly by the prayers of many, evoked by my confessions, than by my prayers alone.

---

149. See Lk 8:15.
150. See Jn 20:28.
151. This is the only mention of her name in Augustine's writings. The spelling here given has the best manuscript support.
152. See Heb 11:10.13.14.

Book X

Memory

₁, 1. Let me know you, O you who know me; then shall I know even as I am known.[1] You are the strength of my soul; make your way in and shape it to yourself, that it may be yours to have and to hold, free from stain or wrinkle.[2] I speak because this is my hope,[3] and whenever my joy springs from that hope it is joy well founded. As for the rest of this life's experiences, the more tears are shed over them the less are they worth weeping over, and the more truly worth lamenting the less do we bewail them while mired in them. You love the truth[4] because anyone who does truth comes to the light. Truth it is that I want to do, in my heart by confession in your presence, and with my pen before many witnesses.[5]

Motives for confession

₂, 2. But the abyss of the human conscience lies naked to your eyes, O Lord,[6] so would anything in me be secret even if I were unwilling to confess to you? I would be hiding you from myself, but not myself from you. But now that my groans bear witness that I find no pleasure in myself, you shed light upon me and give me joy, you offer yourself, lovable and longed for, that I may thrust myself away in disgust and choose you, and

---

1. See 1 Cor 13:12; 8:2-3; Gal 4:9.
2. See Eph 5:27.
3. See Ps 115(116):10; 2 Cor 4:13.
4. See Ps 50:8(51:6).
5. See Jn 3:21; Eph 4:15. The phrase "to do truth" is awkward in English, but no other captures the root meaning of the biblical word. "Truth" is originally what is real, genuine, reliable, trustworthy; it is a moral quality, above all of God, and of human beings who are like him. Only by extension from this does it come to mean accuracy of statement, a quality of speech.
6. See Sir 42:18-20; Heb 4:13.

be pleasing no more either to you or to myself except in what I have from you.

To you, then, Lord, I lie exposed, exactly as I am. I have spoken of what I hope to gain by confessing to you. My confession to you is made not with words of tongue and voice, but with the words of my soul and the clamor of my thought, to which your ear is attuned; for when I am bad, confession to you is simply disgust with myself, but when I am good, confession to you consists in not attributing my goodness to myself, because though you, Lord, bless the person who is just, it is only because you have first made him just when he was sinful.[7] This is why, O my God, my confession in your presence is silent, yet not altogether silent: there is no noise to it, but it shouts by love. I can say nothing right to other people unless you have heard it from me first, nor can you even hear anything of the kind from me which you have not first told me.[8]

3, 3. What point is there for me in other people hearing my confessions? Are they likely to heal my infirmities?[9] A curious lot they are, eager to pry into the lives of others, but tardy when it comes to correcting their own. Why should they seek to hear from me what I am, when they are reluctant to hear from you what they are? And when they hear from me about myself, how do they know that I am speaking the truth, since no one knows what goes on inside a person except the spirit of that person within him?[10] If, on the contrary, they hear from you about themselves, they will be in no position to say, "The Lord is lying." Is hearing the truth about oneself from you anything different from knowing oneself? And can anyone have this self-knowledge and still protest, "It is not true," unless he himself is lying?

Yet charity believes without stint,[11] at least among those who are bonded together by charity,[12] and so I also confess to you, Lord, in such a way that people to whom I can offer no proof may discern whether I confess truthfully. I cannot prove it, but all whose ears are open to me by love will believe me.

4. All the same, my inward healer, make clear to me what advantage there is in doing this. When the confession of my past evil deeds is read and

---

7. See Ps 5:13(12); Rom 4:5.
8. This sentence goes to the heart of what Augustine understands by truth and confession.
9. See Ps 102(103):3; Mt 4:23.
10. See 1 Cor 2:11.
11. See 1 Cor 13:7.
12. See Col 3:14.

listened to—those evil deeds which you have forgiven and covered over[13] to make me glad in yourself, transforming my soul by faith and your sacrament—that recital arouses the hearer's heart, forbidding it to slump into despair and say, "I can't." Let it rather keep watch[14] for your loving mercy and your gentle grace, through which every weak soul that knows its own weakness grows strong.[15] It is cheering to good people to hear about the past evil deeds of those who are now freed from them: cheering not because the deeds were evil but because they existed once but exist no more.

But then what profit is there, O my Lord, to whom my conscience confesses every day, more secure in the hope of your mercy than in its own innocence—what profit is there, I ask, if through these writings I also confess to other people in your presence not what I have been, but what I still am? The desirability of confessing the past I have recognized and stated; but there are many people who desire to know what I still am at this time of writing my confessions, people who know me without really knowing me, people who have read my works or know me only by hearsay. None of these have laid their ears to my heart, though it is only there that I am whoever I am. They therefore want to hear from my own confession what I am within, where they can venture neither eye nor ear nor mind. They want to hear and are ready to believe me: will they really recognize me? Yes, because the charity that makes them good assures them that I am not lying when I confess about myself; that very charity in them believes me.

4, 5. But what do they hope to gain, those who want this? Do they wish to congratulate me when they hear how much progress I am making toward you by your gift, and to pray for me when they hear how badly I am dragged back by my own weight? To people like that I will disclose myself, for it is no small gain, O Lord my God, if thanks are offered to you by many people on our account[16] and many pray to you for us. Yes, let a fraternal mind love in me what you teach us to be worthy of love, and deplore in me what you teach us to be deplorable. But let it be a brotherly mind that does this, not the mind of a stranger, not the minds of alien foes

---

13. See Ps 31(32):1.
14. See Sg 5:2; Mt 25:1-13.
15. See 2 Cor 12:9-10.
16. See 2 Cor 1:11.

who mouth falsehood and whose power wreaks wickedness;[17] let it be a brotherly mind which when it approves of me will rejoice over me, and when it disapproves will be saddened on my account, because whether it approves or disapproves it still loves me. To such people I will disclose myself: let them sigh with relief over my good actions, but with grief over my evil deeds. The good derive from you and are your gift; the evil are my sins and your punishments. Let them sigh with relief over the one and with grief over the other, and let both hymns and laments ascend into your presence from the hearts of my brethren, which are your censers.[18] And then do you, Lord, in your delight at the fragrance which pervades your holy temple, have mercy on me according to your great mercy[19] for the sake of your name.[20] Do not, I entreat you, do not abandon your unfinished work, but bring to perfection all that is wanting in me.[21]

6. So then, when I confess not what I have been but what I am now, this is the fruit to be reaped from my confessions: I confess not only before you in secret exultation tinged with fear[22] and secret sorrow infused with hope, but also in the ears of believing men and women, the companions of my joy and sharers in my mortality, my fellow citizens still on pilgrimage with me, those who have gone before and those who will follow, and all who bear me company in my life. They are your servants and my brethren, but you have willed them to be your children and my masters, and you have ordered me to serve them if I wish to live with you and share your life. This command of yours would mean little to me if it were only spoken, and not first carried out in deed as well.[23] So I do likewise, and I do it in deeds and in words; I do it under your outstretched wings[24] and would do it in grave peril, were it not that under those wings my soul is surrendered to you[25] and to you my weakness known. I am a little child, but my Father lives for ever and in him I have a guardian suited to me. He who begot me is also he who

---

17. See Ps 143(144):11.
18. See Rv 8:3-4.
19. See Ps 50:3(51:1).
20. See Mt 10:22; 24:9; Jn 15:21.
21. See Phil 1:6.
22. See Ps 2:11.
23. See Jn 13:1-17.
24. See Pss 16(17):8; 35:8(36:7). This is possibly a reference to the outstretched arms of Christ, represented in Augustine's day as triumphant and glorious before the cross.
25. See Ps 61:2(62:1).

keeps me safe; you yourself are all the good I have, you are almighty and you are with me before ever I am with you.

To such people, then, the people you command me to serve, I will disclose myself not as I have been but as I am now, as I am still, though I do not judge myself.[26] In this way, then, let me be heard.

5, 7. For it is you, Lord, who judge me. No one knows what he himself is made of, except his own spirit within him,[27] yet there is still some part of him which remains hidden even from his own spirit; but you, Lord, know everything about a human being because you have made him. And though in your sight I may despise myself and reckon myself dust and ashes,[28] I know something about you which I do not know about myself. It is true that we now see only a tantalizing reflection in a mirror,[29] and so it is that while I am on pilgrimage far from you[30] I am more present to myself than to you; yet I do know that you cannot be defiled in any way whatever, whereas I do not know which temptations I may have the strength to resist, and to which ones I shall succumb. Our hope is that, because you are trustworthy, you do not allow us to be tempted more fiercely than we can bear, but along with the temptation you ordain the outcome of it, so that we can endure.[31] Let me, then, confess what I know about myself, and confess too what I do not know, because what I know of myself I know only because you shed light on me, and what I do not know I shall remain ignorant about until my darkness becomes like bright noon before your face.[32]

Looking for God in creatures

6, 8. I love you, Lord, with no doubtful mind but with absolute certainty. You pierced my heart with your word, and I fell in love with you. But the sky and the earth too, and everything in them—all these things around me are telling me that I should love you; and since they never cease to

---

26. See 1 Cor 4:3.
27. See 1 Cor 2:11.
28. See Jb 42:6; Sir 10:9; Gn 18:27.
29. See 1 Cor 13:12.
30. See 2 Cor 5:6.
31. See 1 Cor 10:13.
32. See Is 58:10; Ps 89(90):8.

proclaim this to everyone, those who do not hear are left without excuse.[33] But you, far above, will show mercy to anyone with whom you have already determined to deal mercifully, and will grant pity to whomsoever you choose.[34] Were this not so, the sky and the earth would be proclaiming your praises to the deaf.

But what am I loving when I love you? Not beauty of body nor transient grace, not this fair light which is now so friendly to my eyes, not melodious song in all its lovely harmonies, not the sweet fragrance of flowers or ointments or spices, not manna or honey, not limbs that draw me to carnal embrace: none of these do I love when I love my God. And yet I do love a kind of light, a kind of voice, a certain fragrance, a food and an embrace, when I love my God: a light, voice, fragrance, food and embrace for my inmost self, where something limited to no place shines into my mind, where something not snatched away by passing time sings for me, where something no breath blows away yields to me its scent, where there is savor undiminished by famished eating, and where I am clasped in a union from which no satiety can tear me away. This is what I love, when I love my God.

9. And what is this?
I put my question to the earth, and it replied, "I am not he";
I questioned everything it held, and they confessed the same.
I questioned the sea and the great deep,[35]
and the teeming live creatures that crawl,[36] and they replied,
"We are not God; seek higher."
I questioned the gusty winds,
and every breeze with all its flying creatures told me,
"Anaximenes was wrong: I am not God."[37]
To the sky I put my question, to sun, moon, stars,
but they denied me: "We are not the God you seek."
And to all things which stood around the portals of my flesh I said,
"Tell me of my God.
You are not he, but tell me something of him."
Then they lifted up their mighty voices and cried,

---

33. See Rom 1:20.
34. See Rom 9:15; Ex 33:19.
35. See Jb 28:14.
36. See Gn 1:20.
37. Anaximenes of Miletus, sixth century B.C., had taught that all things came from air.

"He made us."[38]
My questioning was my attentive spirit,
and their reply, their beauty.

Then toward myself I turned, and asked myself, "Who are you?"And I answered my own question: "A man." See, here are the body and soul that make up myself, the one outward and the other within. Through which of these should I seek my God? With my body's senses I had already sought him from earth to heaven, to the farthest place whither I could send the darting rays of my eyes;[39] but what lay within me was better, and to this all those bodily messengers reported back, for it controlled and judged the replies of sky and earth, and of all the creatures dwelling in them, all those who had proclaimed, "We are not God," and "He made us." My inner self[40] recognized them all through the service of the outer. I, who was that inmost self, I, who was mind, knew them through the senses of my body; and so I questioned the vast frame of the world concerning my God, and it answered, "I am not he, but he made me."[41]

10. Surely this beauty is apparent to all whose faculties are sound? Why, then, does it not speak the same message to all? Animals, both small and large, see the beauty, but they are not able to question it, for in them reason does not hold sway as judge over the reports of the senses. Human beings have the power to question, so that by understanding the things he has made they may glimpse the unseen things of God;[42] but by base love they subject themselves to these creatures, and once subject can no longer judge.[43] Creatures do not respond to those who question unless the questioners are also judges: not that they change their voice—that is, their beauty—if one person merely sees it, while another sees and inquires, as though they would appear in one guise to the former, and differently to the latter; no, the beauty appears in the same way to both beholders, but to one it is dumb, and to the other it speaks. Or rather, it speaks to all, but only they understand who test the voice heard outwardly against the truth

---

38. See Ps 99(100):3.
39. Sight, unlike hearing, is a very active sense for Augustine; see Sermon 277,10,10.
40. See Rom 7:22; 2 Cor 4:16; Eph 3:16.
41. Plotinus speaks similarly of an ascent to the archetype through the beauty of creatures; see *Enneads* V,1,4.
42. See Rom 1:20.
43. See Plotinus, *Enneads* V,1,1: to pursue a being alien to one's own nature is to admit oneself inferior to it. A slave cannot be judge.

within.[44] Truth tells me, "Neither earth nor sky nor any bodily thing is your God." Their own nature avers it. Do you not see, my soul? Nature is an extended mass, smaller in any one part than in the whole. Even you, my soul, are better than that, for you impart energy to the mass of your body and endow it with life, and no corporeal thing can do that for any other corporeal thing. But your God is to you the life of your life itself.[45]

7, 11. What is it, then, that I love when I love my God? Who is he who towers above my soul? By this same soul I will mount to him. I will leave behind that faculty whereby I am united to a body and animate its frame. Not by that faculty do I find my God, for horse and mule would find him equally, since the same faculty gives life to their bodies too, yet they are beasts who lack intelligence.[46]

There is another power by which I do more than give life to my flesh: with this I endow with senses the flesh that God has fashioned for me, commanding the eye not to hear and the ear not to see, giving to my organ of seeing and my organ of hearing and to all my other senses what is proper to them in their respective places and for their particular work. Their functions are diverse, but I, the one mind, act through them all. This power too I will leave behind, for horse and mule have it too, since they also have sensory organs throughout their bodies.

Looking for God in himself: the fields of memory

8, 12. So then, I will leave behind that faculty of my nature, and mount by stages toward him who made me.

Now I arrive in the fields and vast mansions of memory, where are treasured innumerable images brought in there from objects of every conceiv-

---

44. That is, probably Truth, the incarnate Word, present in the believer through faith and baptism. Plotinus also held that a mind, in us but not our own, enables us to discern truth; see *Enneads* V,1.10;3,3. Of the Neo-Platonists Augustine later said in *The City of God* VIII,7, "They declared that the light of our minds is God himself, through whom all things were made."

45. This chapter is not an "argument for the existence of God": Augustine takes as his premise that God created the universe. His interest is a moral one. To discern the beauty and nature of God through created beauty requires rightousness of heart and well-ordered love. Inordinate love of creatures debases them and deprives the human viewer of the power to judge rightly. Augustine speaks elsewhere of our power to endow an otherwise dumb creation with its voice, so that it too can praise its creator; see *Exposition of Psalm* 144,13-14.

46. See Ps 31(32):9.

able kind perceived by the senses.[47] There too are hidden away the modified images we produce when by our thinking we magnify or diminish or in any way alter the information our senses have reported. There too is everything else that has been consigned and stowed away, and not yet engulfed and buried in oblivion. Sojourning there I command something I want to present itself, and immediately certain things emerge, while others have to be pursued for some time and dug out from remote crannies. Others again come tumbling out in disorderly profusion, and leap into prominence as though asking, "Are we what you want?" when it is something different that I am asking for and trying to recall. With my mental hand I push them out of the way of my effort to remember, until what I want becomes clear and breaks from cover. Then there are remembered items that come to hand easily and in orderly sequence as soon as they are summoned, the earlier members giving way to those that follow and returning to their storage-places, ready to be retrieved next time I need them. All of which happens when I recite anything from memory.

13. Preserved there, classified and distinct, are all those impressions which have been admitted through the entrances proper to each: light, colors and bodily shapes through the eye; all kinds of sound through the ears; various odors through the gateways of the nostrils; flavors through the entrance of the mouth; and through the pervasive sense of touch whatever is felt as hard or soft, hot or cold, smooth or rough, heavy or light, external to the body or inside it. The huge repository of the memory, with its secret and unimaginable caverns, welcomes and keeps all these things, to be recalled and brought out for use when needed; and as all of them have their particular ways into it, so all are put back again in their proper places.

The sense-impressions themselves do not find their way in, however; it is the images of things perceived by the senses that are available there to the person who recalls them. Who can tell how these images are fashioned, obvious though it may be through which senses they were captured and stowed away within? For when I am sitting quietly in the dark I can bring up colors in my memory if I wish, and distinguish white from black and any others I select. No sounds burst in to intrude on these images acquired through my eyes, which I am considering, though sounds too are present

---

47. *Memoria* for Augustine connotes something vaster than what we mean by "memory," though it includes this. As the following chapters make clear, consideration of it is a vital part of his quest for authentic self-knowledge. See the Introduction.

there, lying hidden and stored in a place by themselves. I can summon them equally well, if I wish, and find them present at once, and though my tongue and throat are silent I sing as much as I like. Images of color, which are just as truly present, do not thrust themselves in on my song or interrupt it while I am enjoying this other treasure, which has flowed into me through my ears. Similarly I can recall at will anything drawn in and hoarded by way of my other senses. I can distinguish the scent of lilies from violets even though I am not actually smelling anything, and honey from grape-juice, smooth from rough, without tasting or feeling anything: I am simply passing them in review before my mind by remembering them.

14. This I do within myself in the immense court of my memory; for there sky and earth and sea are readily available to me, together with everything that I have ever been able to perceive in them, apart from what I have forgotten. And there I come to meet myself.[48] I recall myself, what I did, when and where I acted in a certain way, and how I felt about so acting. Everything is there which I remember having experienced for myself or believed on the assertion of others. Moreover, I can draw on this abundant store to form imaginary pictures which resemble the things I have myself experienced, or believed because my own experience confirmed them, and weave these together with images from the past, and so evoke future actions, occurrences or hopes; and on all these as well I can meditate as though they were present to me. In that same enormous recess of my mind, thronging with so many great images, I say to myself, "That's what I will do!" And the action I have envisaged follows. "Oh, if only this or that could be! Pray God this or that may not happen!" I say to myself, and even as I say it the images of all these things of which I speak pass before me, coming from the same treasure-house of memory. If they were not there, I would be quite unable to conjure up such possibilities.[49]

15. This faculty of memory is a great one, O my God, exceedingly great, a vast, infinite recess. Who can plumb its depth? This is a faculty of my mind, belonging to my nature, yet I cannot myself comprehend all that I am. Is the mind, then, too narrow to grasp itself, forcing us to ask where

---

48. That is, memory is the place of self-awareness.
49. The memory contributes images which can be combined in ever-new ways, the raw material for imaginative construction.

that part of it is which it is incapable of grasping? Is it outside the mind, not inside? How can the mind not compass it?

Enormous wonder wells up within me when I think of this, and I am dumbfounded. People go to admire lofty mountains, and huge breakers at sea, and crashing waterfalls, and vast stretches of ocean, and the dance of the stars, but they leave themselves behind out of sight. It does not strike them as wonderful that I could enumerate those things without seeing them with my eyes, and that I could not even have spoken of them unless I could within my mind contemplate mountains and waves and rivers and stars (which I have seen), and the ocean (which I only take on trust), and contemplate them there in spaces just as vast as though I were seeing them outside myself. But I did not suck them into myself when I looked at them with my eyes, for it was not these things themselves that entered me, but only the images of them; and I know which impressions were made on me through which of my bodily senses.

9, 16. The immense spaces of my memory harbor even more than these, however. Here too are all those things which I received through a liberal education and have not yet forgotten; they are stored away in some remote inner place, which yet is not really a place at all. However, in this case it is not images of the realities that I harbor, but the realities themselves; for everything I know about literature, or skill in debate, or how many kinds of questions can logically be formulated, lodges indeed in my memory, but not like an image which remains after I have turned away from some object perceived externally, nor like the trace of a sound that has faded, by means of which a voice that has penetrated my ears can still be recalled as though audible when it is audible no longer, nor like a fleeting scent that is blown away by the wind after affecting our nostrils, but leaves an image of itself in the memory which we can savor again later by remembering it, nor like food, which is certainly no longer present as a flavor in the stomach but can still be tasted in the memory, nor like anything which is felt by bodily touch and can still be touched by our memory when the object is no longer in contact with our bodies. None of these objects is admitted into the memory in its own right; only the images of them are captured with astonishing speed, put away in wonderful compartments, and brought out again in a wonderful way when we recall them.

10, 17. When I hear that there are three classes of questions—namely, whether something exists, what it is, and what qualities belong to it—I do, to be sure, retain images of the sounds by which these words are composed; and I know that those sounds were borne upon the breeze with some noise, but have now fallen silent. But through no bodily sense whatever have I made contact with the realities themselves, for I have never seen these realities anywhere except in my own mind. What I have stowed away in my memory is not the images of these things but the things themselves. Let them say how they found their way into me if they can, for when I check every physical gateway in myself I find none by which they can have entered. My eyes tell me, "If those things were colored, it was we who reported them"; my ears declare, "If they made some sound, we gave you the information"; my nostrils say, "If there was a smell to them, we let them through"; my sense of taste replies, "If they had no flavor, don't ask me"; touch says, "If they had no bodily substance, I did not handle them, and if I did not handle them, I told you nothing." From what source and by what route did they enter my memory? I do not know, for when I learned them I did not take them on trust from some stranger's intelligence but recognized them as present in my own, and affirmed them as true, and entrusted them to my memory for safekeeping so that I could bring them out again when I wished. This means that they were there even before I learned them, but not remembered. Where and why did I recognize them and say, "Yes, that's how it is; that is true," when these things were stated? Surely because they were already in my memory, but so remote, so hidden from sight in concealed hollows, that unless they had been dug out by someone who reminded me, I would perhaps never have been able to think about them.[50]

11, 18. We are therefore led to conclude that when we learn things which are not imbibed through the senses as images, but are known directly in their own reality inside the mind, as they are in themselves, and without the intervention of images, we are collecting by means of our thought those things which the memory already held, but in a scattered and disorderly way. By applying our minds to them we ensure that they are stacked ready-to-hand in the memory, where they may be easily available for habitual use, instead of lying hidden, dispersed and neglected, as

---

50. In *Meno* 81 D, Plato says that learning is simply remembering. Augustine seems to espouse the same view here; but in his *Revisions* I, 8, 2 (with reference to *The Greatness of the Soul* 20,34) he disclaims any theory of the soul's existence prior to its infusion into its particular body.

hitherto. How many things of this kind are carried in my memory! Such things have been found and placed ready-to-hand in the way I have described, and so it is said that we have learned them and now we know them. If I have ceased to recall them for a fair stretch of time they sink back again and slip away into distant caverns, and then they need to be pulled from the same places (for there is no other home for them) as though newly thought out, and herded together[51] to become knowable once more: that is to say they need to be collected again,[52] which is why we call this activity cogitating,[53] or collecting one's thoughts. *Cogo* is related to *cogito* as *ago* is to *agito* and *facio* to *factito*.[54] The mind, however, has claimed this verb as properly applicable to itself, so that only what is "collected," within the mind, what is "herded together" there, and there only, is properly said to be "thought."

12, 19. The memory also stores countless truths and laws of mathematics and mensuration, no single one of which was impressed upon it by bodily sense, for they have no color, sound or smell, nor have they been tasted or handled. I heard the sound of the words that indicated these truths when they were under discussion, but the sounds are one thing and the truths themselves something else. The words sound one way in Greek and differently in Latin, but the truths are neither Greek nor Latin, nor spoken entities of any kind. I have seen a draughtsman's geometric lines, and even though they are infinitely fine, like a spider's thread, the mathematical lines they represent are something quite different, not the images of those lines which my fleshly eye has observed. Everyone knows these truths, without a physical representation of any kind being involved. One recognizes them within oneself. With all my bodily senses I have apprehended the numbers of things as we count them; but the principle of number is something entirely different, and without it we could not think mathematically at all. This principle is not an image of the things counted, and there-

---

51. *Cogenda.*
52. *Conligenda.*
53. *Cogitare.*
54. The etymology is from Varro. The Latin suffix -*ito* signifies an intensification or frequent repetition of the action expressed by the simple verb. Augustine thus derives *cogito*, think, from *cogo*, force, drive, herd together, and associates them both with *colligo* or *conligo*, collect, gather.

fore has a much more real existence.[55] Let anyone who cannot see it laugh at me, but allow me to pity him for laughing.

13, 20. Not only do I retain all these things in my memory: I can also keep in my memory the way in which I learned them. I have heard many completely erroneous arguments urged against them, and these too I retain in my memory. Erroneous they were, yet my memory is not in error as I recall them. Further, I can remember discriminating between the truth and those erroneous arguments against it, and I see that my discrimination between them today is distinct from the discrimination I often practiced at various times in the past when I thought about them. So I remember that I have often understood these matters, and I also store in my memory what I discern and understand now, so that later on I may remember that I understood it today. It follows that I have the power to remember that I remembered, just as later, if I recall that I have been able to remember these things now, I shall undoubtedly be recalling it through the faculty of memory.

14, 21. The same memory also records emotions previously experienced in the mind, not in the same way as the mind experienced them at the time, but in the mode proper to the power of memory. I remember having been happy, without feeling happy now; I recall my past sadness but feel no sadness in so doing; I remember having been afraid once, but am not frightened as I remember; I summon the memory of how I once wanted something, but without wanting it today. Sometimes the opposite emotion is present: I can happily remember some sadness I suffered which is now over and done with, or sadly recall lost happiness. There is nothing strange about this where the previous experience was one that simply involved the body, for the mind is one thing and the body another; it is therefore unremarkable if in my mind I joyfully recall some former bodily pain. Mind and memory, however, are one and the same. This is why when we instruct someone to remember a point we say, "Be sure to bear that in mind"; and when we forget we say, "I didn't have my mind on it" or "It slipped my mind." So we call memory itself "mind." This being the case, how does it happen that when I happily recall my past sadness, my mind is experiencing joy while my memory is of sorrow, and yet while the mind is happy

---

55. The distinction between numbers as handled by the senses and ideal or intelligible numbers goes back to Pythagoras and is present in Plato and Plotinus. It was important to Augustine from his early works *Order* and *Answer to the Skeptics* and especially *Music* (VI,16), where he relates it to our sense of rhythm.

in the joy it contains, the memory is not saddened by the sadness in it? Does the memory not belong to the mind? Who would maintain that? It is truer to say that the memory is like the mind's stomach, while joy and sorrow are like delicious or bitter food. When they are committed to memory they are transferred to the stomach, as it were, and can be kept there, but cannot be tasted. It is absurd to think the operations of memory and stomach are really alike, yet they are not in all respects dissimilar.[56]

22. But now suppose I produce something else from my memory: I state that there are four passions that disturb the soul—desire, joy, fear and sadness; for purposes of disputation I state whatever analysis of them I have formulated by dividing each according to species and genus; I find in my memory what I am to say and it is from there that I produce my statement; yet when I run through these passions from memory I suffer no emotional disturbance from any of them. Before they were recalled and brought out for inspection they were there: that is why they could be fetched by the act of remembrance. Perhaps, then, these things are produced from the memory in the same way that cattle can bring food back from the stomach for chewing the cud. But in that case why does the disputant (that is, the person who remembers) not taste the sweetness of joy or the bitterness of grief in the mouth of his thought? Or is this precisely the point of difference between two activities, the point where the analogy breaks down? Who indeed would discuss these passions if every time we mentioned sadness or fear we were forced to mourn or feel frightened? And yet we would be in no position to discuss them unless we found in our memory not just the sound of their names, as images derived from sense-impressions, but the very notions of the things themselves. These we have received through no gateway of the flesh; the mind itself has become aware of them by undergoing its emotions and has committed them to memory, or else the memory has retained them of its own accord, though they were not expressly entrusted to it.

15, 23. It is not easy to say whether this process occurs with the help of images or not. I speak of a stone, or the sun, when these objects are not present to my senses, and unquestionably the images of them are available in my memory. I name a bodily pain: it is not present to me, because

---

56. Memory is mind engaged in particular activities. Augustine seems to come very close here to identifying memory with mind; probably he did not, but he thought of memory as both the focus of personal identity and our link between past, present and future.

nothing is hurting; but unless the image of it resided in my memory I would not know how to speak of it, nor would I be able in an argument to distinguish it from pleasure. I name bodily health when I am myself in a healthy condition; in this case the object itself is present to me, yet if its image were not also retained in my memory I would be quite unable to recall what the sound of its name signified; and similarly sick people would not know the meaning of any statement about health if the same image were not retained by the power of memory, even though the thing itself is lacking in their bodies.[57]

When I speak of "numbers"—ideal numbers in the light of which we count—it is not the images of them that are present in my memory but the numbers themselves. I speak of "the image of the sun," and this is precisely what is in my memory, for what I recall is not an image of that image, but the primary image itself: it is this which springs to mind immediately in my act of remembering. I name "memory," and recognize what I am naming; but where can this act of recognition take place, except in the memory? Does this mean that memory is present to itself through its image, and not in itself?

16, 24. Now when I name "forgetfulness" and similarly recognize the thing I am naming, whence comes my recognition, if not from an act of remembering? I do not mean recognition of the sound of its name, but of the thing signified, for if I forgot that, I would be unable to recognize the meaning of the word. So when I remember "memory," memory itself immediately makes itself available; but when I remember "forgetfulness," both memory and forgetfulness are promptly present: memory since by means of it I remember, and forgetfulness since that is what I am remembering. But what else is forgetfulness but loss of memory? How then can it be present so that I can remember it, when its very presence deprives me of the power to remember? What we remember, we retain in our memory. If we did not remember forgetfulness, we would never recognize the reality which is being referred to when we hear its name; hence forgetfulness is retained by the memory. It must be present, otherwise we would forget it, yet when it is present we forget! Are we to understand, then, that forgetfulness is not in itself present in the memory when we remember it, but present only through its image, since if it were immediately present in its reality it would make us

---

57. So it is in memory that we connect signs with the objects signified, and this holds whether the objects are present or not.

forget, not remember?[58] In the end, who can fathom this matter, who understand how the mind works?

25. This much is certain, Lord, that I am laboring over it, laboring over myself, and I have become for myself a land hard to till and of heavy sweat.[59] We are not in this instance gazing at the expanses of the sky[60] or calculating the distances between stars or the weight of the earth:[61] the person who remembers is myself; I am my mind.[62] It is not surprising that whatever is not myself should be remote, but what can be nearer to me than I am to myself? Yet here I am, unable to comprehend the nature of my memory, when I cannot even speak of myself without it. How am I to explain it, when I am quite certain that I remember forgetting? Am I to say that something I remember is not in my memory? Or am I to say that forgetfulness is in my memory for the very purpose of preventing me from forgetting? Either alternative is completely absurd.

Is there a third possibility? I might say that when I remember "forgetfulness" it is only the image of forgetfulness that is held in my memory, not forgetfulness itself. But what right have I to make that assertion, in view of the fact that when an image of something is imprinted upon the memory, the thing itself must have been present first, so that the image can be derived from it and imprinted? That is how I remember Carthage; that is how I remember all the places where I have been and the faces of people I have met, and that is how I remember all the information reported by my other senses, and the health or pain of my own body: when these objects were to hand my memory abstracted from them images which I would be able to contemplate as truly present and review in my mind, when later I remembered those objects in their absence. It would follow, then, that if "forgetfulness" is kept in the memory not in its own reality but by means of its image, it would need to have been present so that its image could be

58. The argument is not rigorous: the connotation of *oblivio* (forgetfulness) as Augustine here uses it shifts between a particular instance of forgetting something (which we can be well aware of when it has occurred, and be distressed about, and hence remember as we can other mental events) and a generalized, almost hypostatized, forgetting which would mean a complete blotting out of all memory. But the discussion serves his purpose of provoking himself and his readers to wonder at the mysteries of the human mind, through which he ascends to the mystery of God.

59. See Gn 3:17,19; and Augustine's discovery of himself as a land of famine, II,10,18, and a great enigma, IV,4,9.

60. Echo of Ennius, *Iphigeneia*, quoted by Cicero, *On Divination* II,30.

61. See Jb 28:25 (Old Latin).

62. Again he seems to identify memory, mind, and self.

abstracted. But when it was present, how did it inscribe its image in my memory, when its very presence blotted out even what it found already registered there?

Nonetheless in some way, some way which is incomprehensible and defies explanation, I am certain that I do remember forgetfulness—that very forgetfulness beneath which what we remember is submerged.

17, 26. O my God, profound, infinite complexity, what a great faculty memory is, how awesome a mystery! It is the mind, and this is nothing other than my very self. What am I, then, O my God? What is my nature? It is teeming life of every conceivable kind, and exceedingly vast. See, in the measureless plains and vaults and caves of my memory, immeasurably full of countless kinds of things which are there either through their images (as with material things), or by being themselves present (as is the knowledge acquired through a liberal education), or by registering themselves and making their mark in some indefinable way (as with emotional states which the memory retains even when the mind is not actually experiencing them, although whatever is in the memory must be in the mind too)—in this wide land I am made free of all of them, free to run and fly to and fro, to penetrate as deeply as I can, to collide with no boundary anywhere. So great is the faculty of memory, so great the power of life in a person whose life is tending toward death!

What shall I do, then, O my God, my true life? I will pass beyond this faculty of mine called memory, I will pass beyond it and continue resolutely toward you, O lovely Light.[63] What are you saying to me? See, I am climbing through my mind to you who abide high above me; I will pass beyond even this faculty of mine which is called memory in my longing to touch you from that side whence you can be touched, and cleave to you in the way in which holding fast to you is possible. For animals and birds also have memories; they would not otherwise return to their accustomed lairs and nests, rather than randomly to others, and indeed they would never be able to grow accustomed to anything without memory. I will therefore pass beyond memory and try to touch him who marked me out from the four-footed beasts and made me wiser than the birds in the sky;[64] yes, I will pass beyond even my memory that I may find you ... where? O my true good, O sweetness that will never fail me, that I may find you ... where? If I find you somewhere beyond my memory, that means that I shall be

---

63. See Eccl 11:7.
64. See Jb 35:11 (Old Latin).

forgetful of you. And how shall I find you, once I am no longer mindful of you?

18, 27. A woman had lost a coin; she searched for it with a lamp,[65] and unless she had had some memory of it she would not have found it, for when it was found, how could she have known that this was it, if she did not remember it? I remember losing many things myself, and looking for them and finding them, and this is how I know, because when I was searching for one or another of them, and someone said to me, "Perhaps this is it?" or "Is that it?" I went on saying, "No, that's not it," until what I was looking for was offered to me. Unless I had remembered that thing, whatever it was, I would not have found it even when it was handed to me, because I would not have recognized it. This is what always happens when we look for something we have lost and then find it. If some article chances to drop out of view, but not out of memory, such as any kind of visible object, the image of it persists within us and the thing is sought until it comes to light again; and when it has been found it is recognized by comparison with this inward image. We do not say that we have found the lost object unless we recognize it, and we cannot recognize it if we do not remember it. The thing had disappeared from our sight, but was held in our memory.

19, 28. What follows? When the memory itself loses some item, as for instance when we forget something and try to remember, where are we to search in the end but in the memory itself? And if some other thing is offered us there, we brush it aside, until the thing we are looking for turns up. When it does, we say, "That's it!" which we would not be in a position to say if we did not recognize the object, and we could not recognize it if we did not remember it. Yet we had undoubtedly forgotten. Is this the explanation: that the thing had not fallen out of the memory entirely? Can it be that the part which was retained gave a clue to the part which had vanished,[66] because the memory was aware that some item was absent from the full complement it was used to turning over and, feeling itself to be lame and lacking something that normally belonged to it, demanded that the missing element be restored? Suppose we see with our eyes or consider in our mind a certain person known to us, but cannot remember his name, and try to recall it. Any other name that presents itself will seem

---

65. See Lk 15:8.
66. As when we are trying to recall someone's name, and feel sure of the first letter.

quite irrelevant to him, because we are not used to associating him with that, and so we reject it. Then at last the right one comes up, and this fits satisfactorily with ... our habitual knowledge of the person. From where does it emerge, if not from the memory itself? This must be the case, because even if someone else reminds us, we recognize it again only because it springs from our memory: we do not believe what we are told as though this were a piece of fresh information, but remember and agree that what we have just been told is correct. If it has been entirely blotted out from the mind, we do not remember even when reminded. If we remember that we have forgotten something, we have not forgotten it entirely. But if we have forgotten altogether, we shall not be in a position to search for it.

Universal desire for happiness

20, 29. How then am I to seek you, Lord? When I seek you, my God, what I am seeking is a life of happiness.[67] Let me seek you that my soul may live,[68] for as my body draws its life from my soul, so does my soul draw its life from you. How, then, am I to seek a life of happiness? It is not mine until I can say, "This is all I want; here is happiness." I must know how to seek it. Should it be by way of remembering, as though it were something I have forgotten but am still aware of having forgotten? Or by thirsting for a life still strange to me, either because I have never known it or because I have so completely forgotten that I do not even remember that I have forgotten? What is a life of happiness? Surely what everyone wants, absolutely everyone without exception?[69] But if they all want it so badly, where did they come to know it? Where have they seen it, that they are so enamored of it? Evidently we possess it in some fashion. A person who possesses it is happy in one way, actually happy; in a different manner others are made happy by hoping for happiness. These latter possess happiness in a less perfect way than the former, who are happy in the reality itself, but they are better off than people who are happy neither in possessing the reality nor in hoping for it. Yet even these would not so

---

67. *The Happy Life* was the subject of a dialogue at Cassiciacum. The phrase comes from Cicero and is not directly biblical, but is close to the recurrent *Blessed is/are ...* of the scriptures, for example, Ps 1:1 and Mt 5:3-11.
68. See Ps 68:33(69:32); Is 55:3.
69. Cicero's *Hortensius* (fr. 36 M) began with this universal desire for happiness, and the idea recurs frequently in Augustine's writings.

strongly desire happiness[70] unless they possessed it in some degree, and there can be no doubt that they do desire it. In some mysterious way they must know it, therefore, and hence truly possess it through some kind of cognizance. What I am attempting to find out is whether this resides in the memory, because if it does, that must mean that we were happy once upon a time—though whether each of us was happy individually, or we were all happy in the man who committed the first sin, in whom we all died and from whom we are all born to misery,[71] I am not now inquiring. I am simply posing the question: Does the life of happiness exist in the memory? We should not love it if we had no acquaintance with it. When we hear the word we all acknowledge that what we want is the reality behind the name, for the sound in itself holds no attraction for us. If a Greek hears it mentioned in Latin he does not find it delightful, because he does not understand what has been said; we, on the contrary, are delighted, just as he would be if he heard it in Greek, because the reality itself is neither Greek nor Latin. Greek-speakers, Latin-speakers and peoples of every other tongue are all athirst with longing to gain it. This proves that it is known to everyone, and if they could all be asked in some common tongue whether they wish to be happy, they would undoubtedly all reply that they do. This affirmation would not be possible if the reality spoken of were not held in their memories.

21, 30. Do they retain it in their memories in the same way as someone remembers Carthage after visiting it? No: the happy life is not seen with the eye, since it is not a corporeal object. Perhaps in the way we remember numbers, then? No, for a person who has knowledge of these does not still seek to gain it; but while we have knowledge of the happy life and therefore love for it, we still long to obtain it in order to be happy. Then in the way we remember eloquence, perhaps? No again. It is true that on hearing the word "eloquence" even people who are not yet eloquent remember the reality, and many of them desire to make it their own; this proves that some knowledge of eloquence is in them, but that is only because they have been exposed through the medium of their bodily senses to eloquence in others, and have appreciated it and desire to be similarly eloquent (though to be sure they would not appreciate it unless some knowledge of it were in them already, and they would not want it for themselves if they had no

---

70. See Cicero, *Tusculan Disputations* V,28; *Hortensius* fr. 36 M.
71. See 1 Cor 15:22.

appreciation of it). But we do not experience the happy life in other people through any kind of bodily sense. Are we aware of it, then, in the way that we remember enjoyment? This may be the case, for even when sad I remember my earlier enjoyment, as I can remember leading a happy life even when I am miserable, yet I have never made contact with my enjoyment through any bodily sense: I have never seen, heard, smelled, tasted or touched it; in my mind alone I experienced being happy, and the knowledge of it stuck fast in my memory, so that I am able to remember it, sometimes with contempt and at other times with longing for the various things which I recall having enjoyed. I was formerly flooded with a kind of joy in depraved actions which I now recollect with loathing and disgust. Sometimes, though, it was good and honorable things that I enjoyed, and when I recall these I am stirred by desire for them, even if perhaps they are no longer present, and then it is in sadness that I recollect my earlier joy.

31. So where and when did I experience my life of happiness, so as to remember, love and desire it? This desire is not confined to me alone, nor to me and a few others; absolutely all of us want to be happy. Unless we had some sure knowledge of it, our wills would not be so firmly set on gaining it. But how can this be? If two men are asked whether they wish to undertake military service, it may happen that one of them will reply that he does, and the other that he does not, whereas if they are asked whether they wish to be happy, each of them will immediately say without hesitation that this is what he longs for; and in fact the choice of military service by the one and the refusal of it by the other are directed to no other end than happiness. Is this, perhaps, because one person finds enjoyment in one way and another differently? Thus all agree that they want to be happy, just as they would, if questioned, all agree that they want to enjoy life, and they think that a life of happiness consists of this enjoyment. One person pursues it in this way, another in that, but all are striving for the same goal, enjoyment. And since no one can claim never to have enjoyed anything, enjoyment is discovered in the memory and recognized there when the life of happiness is mentioned.

22, 32. Far be it, Lord, far be it from the heart of your servant who confesses to you, far be it from me to think that enjoyment of any and every kind could make me happy. A joy there is that is not granted to the godless,[72] but to those only who worship you without looking for reward, because you yourself are their joy. This is the happy life, and this alone: to

---

72. See Is 48:22.

rejoice in you, about you and because of you. This is the life of happiness, and it is not to be found anywhere else. Whoever thinks there can be some other is chasing a joy that is not the true one; yet such a person's will has not turned away from all notion of joy.

23, 33. We cannot therefore assert without qualification that everyone wants to be happy, because people who are unwilling to find joy in you, in which alone the happy life consists, obviously do not want the happy life. Perhaps, though, all men and women do want it, but by reason of the struggle of flesh against spirit and spirit against flesh, which hinders them from doing what they want to do,[73] they fall back on what their strength permits, and make do with that? But is this because they do not want that other thing, for which strength is lacking, ardently enough to find the necessary strength? I think so, because when I ask everybody which they prefer, joy over the truth or joy over what is false,[74] they are as unhesitating in their reply that they prefer to rejoice over the truth as in their declaration that they want to be happy. Now the happy life is joy in the truth; and that means joy in you, who are the Truth,[75] O God who shed the light of salvation on my face,[76] my God.

Everyone wants this happy life, this life which alone deserves to be called happy; all want it, all want joy in the truth. I have met plenty of people who would gladly deceive others, but no one who wants to be deceived. Where else, then, did they come to know this happy life, except where they also came to know about truth? Since they do not wish to be deceived, they must love truth; and when they love the happy life, which is nothing else but joy in the truth, they are unquestionably loving truth also; but they could not be loving the truth unless there was some knowledge of it in their memories. Why, in that case, do they not rejoice over it? Why are they not happy? Because they are more immediately engrossed in other things which more surely make them miserable than that other reality, so faintly remembered, can make them happy. For a little while yet there is light for human beings; let them walk in it, yes, let them walk, lest the darkness close over them.[77]

---

73. See Gal 5:17.
74. See 1 Cor 13:6.
75. See Jn 14:6.
76. See Pss 26(27):1; 41:12(42:11); 42(43):5.
77. See Jn 12:35.

34. Why, though, does "truth engender hatred,"[78] why does a servant of yours who preaches the truth make himself an enemy to his hearers,[79] if the life of happiness, which consists in rejoicing over the truth, is what they love? It must be because people love truth in such a way that those who love something else wish to regard what they love as truth and, since they would not want to be deceived, are unwilling to be convinced that they are wrong. They are thus led into hatred of truth for the sake of that very thing which they love under the guise of truth. They love truth when it enlightens them, but hate it when it accuses them.[80] In this attitude of reluctance to be deceived and intent to deceive others they love truth when it reveals itself but hate it when it reveals them. Truth will therefore take its revenge: when people refuse to be shown up by it, truth will show them up willy-nilly and yet elude them. Yes, this is our condition, this is the lot of the human soul, this is its case, as blind and feeble, disreputable and shabby, it attempts to hide, while at the same time not wishing anything to be hidden from it. It is paid back in a coin which is the opposite to what it desires, for while the soul cannot hide from truth, truth hides from the soul. Nonetheless, even while in this miserable state it would rather rejoice in truth than in a sham; and so it will be happy when it comes to rejoice without interruption or hindrance in the very truth, upon which depends whatever else is true.

In memory he knows God

24, 35. How widely I have ranged through my memory seeking you, Lord, and I have not found you outside it; for I have discovered nothing about you that I did not remember from the time I learned to know you. From that time when I learned about you I have never forgotten you, because wherever I have found truth I have found my God who is absolute Truth, and once I had learned that I did not forget it. That is why you have dwelt in my memory ever since I learned to know you, and it is there that I find you when I remember and delight in you. These are my holy delights, and they are your gift to me, for in your mercy you look graciously upon my poverty.

---

78. Terence, *Andria* 68: "Flattery wins friends, but truth engenders hatred."
79. See Jn 8:40; Gal 4:16.
80. See Jn 3:20; 5:35.

25, 36. But whereabouts in my memory do you dwell, Lord, in which part of it do you abide? What kind of couch have you fashioned for your repose, what manner of temple have you built yourself there? You have honored my memory by making it your dwelling-place, but I am wondering in what region of it you dwell. As I remembered you I left behind those parts of it which animals also possess, because I did not find you there amid the images of material things. I came to those regions of memory to which I had committed my emotional states, but I did not find you there either. Then I arrived at that place in my memory where my mind itself is enthroned, for indeed the mind must reside there, since it can remember itself; yet not even there were you to be found. Just as you are not any corporeal image, nor any of the emotions that belong to a living person, such as we experience when we are joyful or sad, when we desire or fear something, when we remember or forget or anything similar, so neither are you the mind itself: you are the Lord and God of the mind, and though all these things are subject to change you abide unchangeably[81] above them all. And yet you have deigned to dwell in my memory from the first day that I learned to know you. What am I doing, inquiring which place in it is your place, as though there were really places there? Most certain it is that you do dwell in it, because I have been remembering you since I first learned to know you, and there I find you when I remember you.

26, 37. If that is so, where did I find you in order to make acquaintance with you at the outset? You could not have been in my memory before I learned to know you. Where then could I have found you in order to learn of you, if not in yourself, far above me? "Place" has here no meaning: further away from you or toward you we may travel, but place there is none. O Truth, you hold sovereign sway over all who turn to you for counsel, and to all of them you respond at the same time, however diverse their pleas. Clear is your response, but not all hear it clearly. They all appeal to you about what they want, but do not always hear what they want to hear. Your best servant is the one who is less intent on hearing from you what accords with his own will, and more on embracing with his will what he has heard from you.

---

81. See Ps 101:27(102:26).

27, 38. Late have I loved you, Beauty so ancient and so new,
late have I loved you!
Lo, you were within,
but I outside, seeking there for you,
and upon the shapely things you have made I rushed headlong,
I, misshapen.
You were with me, but I was not with you.
They held me back far from you,
those things which would have no being
were they not in you.
You called, shouted, broke through my deafness;
you flared, blazed, banished my blindness;
you lavished your fragrance, I gasped, and now I pant for you;
I tasted you, and I hunger and thirst;
you touched me, and I burned for your peace.[82]

28, 39. When at last I cling to you[83] with my whole being there will be no more anguish or labor for me,[84] and my life will be alive indeed, because filled with you. But now it is very different. Anyone whom you fill you also uplift, but I am not full of you, and so I am a burden to myself. Joys over which I ought to weep do battle with sorrows that should be matter for joy, and I know not which will be victorious. But I also see griefs that are evil at war in me with joys that are good, and I know not which will win the day. This is agony, Lord, have pity on me! It is agony! See, I do not hide my wounds; you are the physician and I am sick; you are merciful, I in need of mercy. Is not human life on earth a time of testing?[85]

Who would choose troubles and hardships? You command us to endure them, but not to love them. No one loves what he has to endure, even if he loves the endurance, for although he may rejoice in his power to endure, he would prefer to have nothing that demands endurance. In adverse circumstances I long for prosperity, and in times of prosperity I dread adversity.

---

82. The idea of a beauty which the soul recognizes as from an ancient knowledge is found in Plotinus' Tractate on Beauty (*Enneads* I,6,2). Augustine has enumerated the five senses several times before; it may be significant that this time the usual order is changed, with hearing being mentioned first. He has listened to the Word, and so his eyes are opened to beauty; contrast IV,13,20; for tasting the sweetness, see Ps 33:9(34:8); 1 Pt 2:3; for hungering and thirsting, Mt 5:6.
83. See Ps 62:9(63:8).
84. See Ps 89(90):10.
85. See Jb 7:1(Old Latin).

What middle ground is there between the two, where human life might be free from trial? Woe and woe again betide worldly prosperity, from fear of disaster and evanescent joy! But woe, woe, and woe again upon worldly adversity, from envy of better fortune, the hardship of adversity itself, and the fear that endurance may falter. Is not human life on earth a time of testing without respite?

"Give what you command"

29, 40. On your exceedingly great mercy rests all my hope. Give what you command, and then command whatever you will.[86] You order us to practice continence. A certain writer tells us, *I knew that no one can be continent except by God's gift, and that it is already a mark of wisdom to recognize whose gift this is.*[87] By continence the scattered elements of the self are collected and brought back into the unity from which we have slid away into dispersion; for anyone who loves something else along with you, but does not love it for your sake, loves you less. O Love, ever burning, never extinguished, O Charity, my God, set me on fire! You command continence: give what you command, and then command whatever you will.

Concupiscence of the flesh: sense of touch

30, 41. Quite certainly you command me to refrain from concupiscence of the flesh and concupiscence of the eyes and worldly pride.[88] You commanded me to abstain from fornication, and recommended a course even better than the marital union you have sanctioned;[89] and because you granted me the grace, this was the course I took even before I was ordained as a dispenser of your sacrament.

---

86. This famous phrase, repeated here and in subsequent chapters, was later to annoy Pelagius, as Augustine records in *The Gift of Perseverance* 20,53.
87. Wis 8:21.
88. See 1 Jn 2:16, and a comparable analysis in Cicero, *De Officiis* I,4,11-13. This threefold pattern of temptation structures the rest of Book X as Augustine discusses his present difficulties. The three vices, comprehensively understood, are the antithesis and parody of the virtues which make the triadically-created soul like the triune God.
89. See 1 Cor 7:38.

Yet in my memory, of which I have spoken at length, sexual images survive, because they were imprinted there by former habit. While I am awake they suggest themselves feebly enough, but in dreams with power to arouse me not only to pleasurable sensations but even to consent, to something closely akin to the act they represent. So strongly does the illusory image in my mind affect my body that these unreal figments influence me in sleep in a way that the reality could never do while I am awake. Surely this cannot mean that I am not myself while asleep, O Lord my God? Yet the moment of passing from wakefulness to sleep or back again certainly marks a great change in me. What becomes then of my reason, which enables me to resist these suggestions in waking hours, and remain unshaken if the actions themselves intrude upon my attention? Is reason shut down along with my eyelids? Is it lulled to sleep with the body's senses? Surely not, for how can it happen that often we do resist even in dreams, remembering our commitment and standing firm in complete chastity, giving no consent to these seductions? There is, notwithstanding, so wide a difference between the two states that even when the opposite occurs we return to peace of conscience on awakening, for the very difference between sleep and waking is obvious enough to convince us that we did not really do the disgraceful thing, even though we are sorry that it was in some sense done in us.

42. Is your hand not powerful enough[90] to heal all my soul's ills,[91] all-powerful God, and by a still more generous grace to extinguish unruly stirrings even in my sleep? Yes, Lord, you will heap gift after gift upon me, that my soul may shake itself free from the sticky morass of concupiscence and follow me to you. As for those foul obscenities in my dreams, where bestial imagination drives the flesh to the point of polluting itself, grant that this soul of mine, through your grace rebellious against itself no more, may not even consent to, still less commit them. You are the Almighty, able to do more than we ask or understand,[92] and it is no great task for you to make provision that nothing of this kind shall arouse the least sensual pleasure—not even such slight titillation as may be easily restrained—in a person of chaste intention while he is asleep, and this even in the prime of life.

---

90. See Nm 11:23.
91. See Ps 102(103):3.
92. See Eph 3:20.

But now that I have declared what I still am in this area of my sinfulness, speaking to my good Lord and exulting with trepidation[93] in what your gift has achieved in me, while deploring my unfinished state, my hope is that you will bring your merciful dealings in me to perfection, until I attain that utter peace which all that is within me and all my outward being will enjoy with you, when death shall be swallowed up in victory.[94]

Taste

31, 43. During the day there is another trouble—and would that the day's troubles were limited to this![95] By eating and drinking we repair the daily wear and tear on our bodies, until such time as you consign both food and belly to destruction.[96] Then you will put an end to our penury with wondrous abundance, and clothe this corruptible flesh in everlasting incorruptibility.[97] For the present, however, this necessity is pleasant to me, and I fight against the pleasure in order not to be captivated by it. By fasting I wage a daily warfare, and habitually force my body to obey me,[98] yet the painfulness of this is outweighed by pleasure, for hunger and thirst are pains of a sort, which like a fever burn and even kill unless we have recourse to the medicine of food; and since this is ready-to-hand through your comforting provision, whereby earth and water and sky are at the service of our weakness, what could be a calamity for us becomes instead an occasion of enjoyment.

44. You have taught me to take food at mealtimes as though it were medicine. But when I pass from uncomfortable need to tranquil satisfaction, the snare of concupiscence lies waiting for me in the very passage from one to the other; for this transition itself is pleasurable, yet there is no other route for us to take if we are to arrive where necessity forces us to go. Preservation of health is our justification for eating and drinking, but perilous partiality comes hot on its heels, and indeed often tries to run ahead, and so becomes the real motive for what I profess to do (and hope I

---

93. See Ps 2:11.
94. See 1 Cor 15:54.
95. See Mt 6:34.
96. See 1 Cor 6:13.
97. See 1 Cor 15:53.
98. See 1 Cor 9:26-27.

am doing) in the interests of health. The same standard does not apply to both, for what suffices to maintain health appears meager to appetite, and it is frequently hard to tell whether proper care for the body indicates that further support is needed, or deceitful, pleasure-seeking greed is demanding what will gratify it. At this uncertainty the wretched soul cheers up and marshals excuses in its own defense, glad to take advantage of the ambiguity about what temperate preservation of health requires, and cloaks its self-indulgence under the pretense that health is being prudently provided for.

Every day I strive to withstand these temptations. I call upon your right hand[99] and submit my perplexity to you, because as yet I do not know where I stand in this matter.

45. I hear the voice of my God commanding us, *Let not your hearts become gross with gluttony and drunkenness.*[100] In my case, drunkenness is far away, and by your mercy it will not come near me. Gluttony is a different matter: sometimes it creeps up on your servant, and only your mercy will drive it away. For no one can be continent except by your gift. When we pray you grant us many things; whatever good we had before we prayed was ours because we received it from you; and even the grace to recognize this afterward is received from you as gift. I have never been a drunkard myself, but I have known drunkards turned sober by you. It is your doing, then, that those who have never been drunkards are not so, and your doing again that those who have been should not be permanently addicted, and finally your doing that both sorts know whose work this is.

I have also heard you telling us: *Go not after your unruly desires, and hold back from indulgence.*[101] Another admonition too I have heard from your Spirit, and this I greatly love: *If we eat we shall be none the better for it, and if we abstain, none the worse;*[102] this means that the one choice will not make me rich, nor the other miserable. Again, there is another saying that I have heard: *Whatever circumstances I am in, I have learned to be content with them; I know how to have enough and to spare, and also how to endure privation. I am capable of anything in him who strengthens*

---

99. That is, Christ.
100. Lk 21:34.
101. Sir 18:30.
102. 1 Cor 8:8.

me.[103] And the man who made that claim was a soldier of the heavenly army, not mere dust as we are.

But dust we are, Lord,[104] and remember that from this dust you made us,[105] and that our race, once lost, was found again.[106] I love Paul for saying what he did in response to the breath of your Spirit, but not even he could have spoken so by his own powers, for he was made of the same dust; but, he declared, *I am capable of anything in him who strengthens me.* Strengthen me too, that I may be capable, give what you command, and then command whatever you will. Paul acknowledges that he has received everything from you, and his boasting is boasting only in the Lord.[107] I have heard another man making a similar request to mine: *Take gluttony away from me*, he prays.[108] These texts make it clear, O holy God, my God, that when what you command is done, it is by your gift.

46. You have taught me, my good Father, that *to the pure all things are pure*,[109] but that *it is bad for anyone to eat in a way that gives scandal.*[110] You have taught that everything you have created is good, and *nothing is to be rejected, provided it is received with thankfulness*,[111] that *food does not commend us to God*,[112] that *no one should take us to task in the matter of food or drink.*[113] and that *a person who eats should not despise one who abstains, nor should a person who abstains pass judgment on another who eats.*[114] All this I have learned, and I give thanks and praise to you, my God, my teacher, for knocking at the door of my ears[115] and shedding your light into my heart. Pluck me free from all temptation. It is no uncleanness in food that I fear, but the uncleanness of greed. I know that Noah was given permission to eat any kind of flesh meat that was serviceable as food,[116]

103. Phil 4:11-13.
104. See Ps 102(103):14.
105. See Gn 3:19.
106. See Lk 15:24,32.
107. See 1 Cor 1:31; 2 Cor 10:17.
108. Sir 23:6.
109. Ti 1:15.
110. Rom 14:20.
111. 1 Tm 4:4.
112. 1 Cor 8:8.
113. Col 2:16.
114. Rom 14:3.
115. See Rv 3:20.
116. See Gn 9:2-3.

that Elijah was sustained with meat,[117] and that John, for all his marvelous grace of abstinence, was not defiled by animal food when he made use of locusts.[118] On the contrary, I am aware that Esau was led astray by craving for lentils,[119] that David condemned himself for his intemperate thirst for water[120] and that our King himself was tempted not by meat but by bread.[121] So too your people deserved rebuke in the desert not because they wanted meat, but because their hunger for food led them to murmur against the Lord.[122]

47. Beset by these temptations I struggle every day against gluttony, for eating and drinking are not something I can decide to cut away once and for all, and never touch again, as I have been able to do with sexual indulgence. The reins that control the throat must therefore be relaxed or tightened judiciously; and is there anyone, Lord, who is not sometimes dragged a little beyond the bounds of what is needful? If there is such a person, he is a great man, so let him tell out the greatness of your name.[123] I am not he, for I am a sinful man,[124] yet I will tell out the greatness of your name nonetheless; and may he who has overcome the world[125] intercede for my sins,[126] and count me among the frailer members of his body,[127] because your eyes rest upon my imperfections and in your book everyone will find a place.[128]

Smell

32, 48. I am not much troubled by sensuality in regard to pleasant smells: if they are absent I do not seek them, if present, I do not reject them, and I am prepared to do without them at all times. Or so it seems to me, though I may perhaps be deceived; for whatever discernment there is in me is shrouded by dismal darkness and hidden from my sight, so that when

---

117. See 1 Kgs 17:6.
118. See Mt 3:4.
119. See Gn 25:34.
120. See 2 Sm 23:15-17.
121. See Mt 4:3.
122. See Nm 11:1-20.
123. See Ps 68:31(69:30); Rv 15:4; Lk 1:46.
124. See Lk 5:8.
125. See Jn 16:33.
126. See Rom 8:34.
127. See Rom 12:5; 1 Cor 12:22.
128. See Ps 138(139):16.

my mind questions itself about its powers it can scarcely trust any reply it receives. What lies within is generally obscured unless brought to the light by experience. In this life, which is said to be one long temptation,[129] no one should be complacent, for we cannot tell whether someone who has perhaps made progress from a bad state to a better may not also degenerate from that better state to something worse. There is but one hope, one reliance, one solid promise, and that is your mercy.[130]

Hearing

33, 49. In earlier days the pleasures of the ear enthralled me more persistently and held me under their spell, but you broke my bonds and set me free. Nowadays I do admittedly find some peaceful contentment in sounds to which your words impart life and meaning, provided the words are sung sensitively by a tuneful voice; but the pleasure is not such as to hold me fast, for when I wish I can get up and go. These melodies, however, demand a place of some dignity in my heart, along with the ideas that are their life and in whose company they gain admittance, and I do not find it easy to determine what place is suitable for them. At times it seems to me that I am paying them more honor than is their due, because I am aware that our minds are more deeply moved to devotion by those holy words when they are sung, and more ardently inflamed to piety, than would be the case without singing. I realize that all the varied emotions of the human spirit respond in ways proper to themselves to a singing voice and a song, which arouse them by appealing to some secret affinity. Yet sensuous gratification, to which I must not yield my mind for fear it grow languid, often deceives me: not content to follow meekly in the wake of reason, in whose company it has gained entrance, sensuous enjoyment often essays to run ahead and take the lead. And so in this respect I sin inadvertently, and only realize it later.

50. On occasion, however, I stray into excessive rigor in my exaggerated caution against such a mistake. While this mood lasts I would dearly like all those sweet and tuneful strains which accompany David's psalter

---

129. See Jb 7:1.
130. This is the fundamental conviction underlying all of Augustine's analysis of temptation, and the entire rationale of *confessio* for him: the self not only discovers itself but essentially constitutes itself in relation to God.

to be banished from my ears, and indeed from the ears of the Church. It seems safer to me that we should follow the example of Athanasius, bishop of Alexandria, of which I have been frequently reminded: he permitted the reader of the psalm so slight an inflection of the voice that he seemed to be proclaiming it rather than singing. All the same, I remember the tears I shed at the Church's song in the early days of my newly-recovered faith,[131] and how even today I am moved not by the singing as such but by the substance of what is sung, when it is rendered in a clear voice and in the most appropriate melodies, and then I recognize once more the value of this custom.

Thus I vacillate between the danger of sensuality and the undeniable benefits. Without pretending to give a definitive opinion I am more inclined to approve the custom of singing in church, to the end that through the pleasures of the ear a weaker mind may rise up to loving devotion. Nonetheless when in my own case it happens that the singing has a more powerful effect on me than the sense of what is sung, I confess my sin and my need of repentance, and then I would rather not hear any singer. Such is my condition: weep with me, and weep for me, you who feel within yourselves that goodness from which kind actions spring! Any of you who do not have these feelings will not be moved by my experience. But do you hear me, O Lord my God: look upon me and see,[132] have mercy and heal me,[133] for in your eyes I have become an enigma to myself, and herein lies my sickness.

Sight

34. 51. If we are to conclude the account of these temptations of the flesh[134] that still beat upon me as I groan and long to have my heavenly tent put on over this earthly one,[135] I must confess in the tender, brotherly hearing of your temple[136] my weakness with regard to one more sense that remains to be discussed: over-indulgence of the eyes. Beautiful things and varied shapes appeal to them, vivid and well-matched colors attract; but

---

131. Especially in the week that followed his baptism; see IX,6,14.
132. See Ps 79:15(80:14).
133. See Pss 6:3(2); 12:4(13:3); 24(25):16-17; 102(103):3; Mt 4:23.
134. See 1 Jn 2:16.
135. See 2 Cor 5:2.
136. That is, his hearers among the faithful; see 1 Cor 3:16-17; 2 Cor 6:16.

let not these captivate my soul. Rather let God ravish it; he made these things exceedingly good,[137] to be sure, but he is my good, not they. Every day, all through the hours that I am awake, colors and shapes impinge upon me, and never is any respite from them allowed me, as it is from the sound of song, or sometimes from all sounds, when silence reigns. Light is the queen of colors and bathes everything we see, and wherever I am in the daytime it flows all around me, and caresses me even while I am doing something else and not thinking about it. So insistently does it make its way in that if it is suddenly withdrawn we long to get it back, and if we are deprived of it for any length of time we feel depressed.

52. O Light, Tobit saw you when despite the blindness of his carnal eyes he pointed out the path of life to his son, and strode unerringly ahead, borne by the feet of charity.[138] Isaac saw you, though his bodily eyes were dimmed and closed by age, when true insight was granted him in blessing his sons, notwithstanding his inability to tell one from the other as he uttered his blessing.[139] Jacob saw you when, likewise blinded by advanced age, he beheld by the radiant vision of his heart the tribes of the people that was to be, prefigured in his sons; and when, stretching out crossed hands in a gesture full of mystery, he laid them on his grandsons, Joseph's children, not in the way indicated by their father, who saw only the externals, but as he himself judged to be right by the vision that guided him within.[140] All these enjoyed the same Light, the Light that is one in itself and unites all who see and love it.

The case is different with earthly light, of which I was speaking. This imparts to the life of this world a seductive zest, dangerous to those whose love for it is blind. Yet once they have learned to praise you for light as well as for your other gifts, "Creator God, O Lord of all,"[141] they take it up in a hymn to your glory, instead of being sapped by it in somnolence of spirit,[142] and this is how I would wish to act. I resist alluring sights lest my feet, those feet with which I walk in your way, become entangled, and to you I lift the invisible eyes of my spirit that you may pluck my feet from

---

137. See Gn 1:31.
138. See Tb 4:2-20.
139. See Gn 27:1-40.
140. See Gn 48:3; 49:28.
141. From Ambrose's evening hymn; see IX,12,32.
142. As were the Manichees by their light doctrine.

the snare.[143] I know that you will pluck them free again and again, for enmeshed they often are. I am repeatedly caught in the traps scattered on every side, but you will never fail to free me, for you neither grow drowsy nor fall asleep, who guard Israel.[144]

53. How many things craftsmen have made, things without number, employing their manifold skills and ingenuity on apparel, footwear, pottery and artifacts of every conceivable kind, on pictures too, and various images; and how far they have in these matters exceeded what is reasonably necessary or useful, or serves some pious purpose! All of them increase the temptations to which our eyes are subject. People pursue outside themselves what they are making, but forsake the One within by whom they were made, and so destroy what they were made to be by driving it out of doors.

O my God, for me you are loveliness itself; yet for all these things too I sing a hymn and offer a sacrifice of praise[145] to you who sanctify me, because the beautiful designs that are born in our minds and find expression through clever hands derive from that Beauty which transcends all minds, the Beauty to which my own mind aspires day and night. Those who create beauty in material things, and those who seek it, draw from that source their power to appreciate beauty, but not the norm for its use. The norm is there, and could they but see it they would need to search no further. They could save their strength for you[146] rather than dissipate it on enervating luxuries.

As for me, I say all these things and recognize their truth, yet still I snag my steps on these beautiful objects; but you pluck me free, Lord, you pluck me free because my eyes are fixed on your mercy.[147] I am miserably caught, but you mercifully extricate me, sometimes without my being aware of it, when I am only lightly entangled, but sometimes painfully because I am already stuck fast.

---

143. See Ps 24(25):15.
144. See Ps 120(121):4.
145. See Ps 115(116):17.
146. See Ps 58:10(59:9).
147. See Ps 25(26):3.

Concupiscence of the eyes

35, 54. There is still another temptation, one more fraught with danger. In addition to the concupiscence of the flesh, which lures us to indulge in the pleasures of all the senses, and brings disaster on its slaves who flee far from you,[148] there is also concupiscence of the mind, a frivolous, avid curiosity. Though it works through these same senses it is a craving not for gratification of the flesh but for experience through the flesh. It masquerades as a zeal for knowledge and learning. Since it is rooted in a thirst for firsthand information about everything, and since the eyes are paramount among the senses in acquiring information, this inquisitive tendency is called in holy scripture *concupiscence of the eyes.*[149] Sight is, properly speaking, the eyes' business, but we use the word also of our other senses in their cognitive function. Thus we do not say, "Listen for anything red," or "Smell how shiny!" or "Taste how brilliant this is!" or "Feel the brightness of that!" For all such objects we speak of seeing. Yet we do say not only, "See how it shines," which the eyes alone can report; we also say, "Let's see how this sounds ... See how fragrant ... See what this tastes like ... Just look how hard that is!" So, as I have pointed out, general sense-experience is called lust of the eyes, because when the other senses explore an object in an effort to collect knowledge, they claim for themselves, by a certain analogy, the office of seeing, in which the eyes unquestionably hold the primacy.

55. From this consideration the distinction more clearly emerges between two kinds of activity on the part of the senses: pleasure-seeking and curiosity; for sensuality pursues the beautiful, the melodious, the fragrant, the tasty and the silky, whereas curiosity seeks the opposite to all these, not because it wants to undergo discomfort but from lust to experience and find out. What sensual pleasure is to be had in viewing a mangled corpse which sickens you? Yet if there is one lying anywhere, people congregate in order to experience ashen-faced horror. At the same time they are frightened that it may give them nightmares! Anyone would think they had been forced to look at the thing while awake, or had been persuaded to do so by some rumor of its beauty. The same holds for the other senses, but it would be tedious to pursue the point through them all.

---

148. See Ps 72(73):27.
149. 1 Jn 2:16, the second temptation.

To satisfy this morbid craving monstrous sights are exhibited at shows. From the same motive efforts are made to scrutinize the secrets of the natural world that lie beyond our sight; knowledge of these is of no profit, yet people want to know them simply for the sake of knowing. The same motive prompts some to seek perverted knowledge through magical practices. In religion itself people tempt God from the same motive, demanding signs and wonders[150] not for any salutary purpose but simply because they crave experience.

56. In this vast thicket full of snares and perils there are many temptations that I have by now lopped off and cleared out of my heart, as you have enabled me, O God of my salvation;[151] yet when dare I claim, with so many of these things besetting our daily life with their din—when dare I claim that by no such sight am I ever drawn to gaze, ever trapped into frivolous fascination? Theatrical shows, admittedly, have no hold on me now, nor do I care to trace the movements of the stars, nor has my mind ever sought answers through necromancy; I hate all unhallowed rites. But with what contrivances does the enemy work to persuade me to ask some sign of you, O Lord my God, to whom I owe humble and single-hearted service! I beg you through our King and through Jerusalem, our single-hearted, chaste homeland, that as consent to such suggestions is far from me, so may it be far always, and farther still. When I entreat you for the salvation of someone, the object of my prayer is quite different.[152] You grant me, and will continue to grant me, the grace to follow you freely, whatever you choose to do.

57. Be that as it may, the many minute, contemptible things that solicit our curiosity every day are past counting, as are our frequent falls. How often do we begin by putting up with gossips in order not to upset the vulnerable, and then gradually come to listen avidly? When a hound in pursuit of a hare is part of a show at the circus I will not watch, but when it happens in the country and I chance to be passing, the chase may distract me from some deep thought and attract me to itself. It is not the swerving of my horse's body that alters my course, but the inclination of my own heart; and unless you promptly show me my weakness and command me to use the spectacle as a means of lifting my mind to you by some suitable

---

150. See Lk 11:16; Jn 4:48.
151. See Pss 17:47(18:46); 37:23(38:22).
152. That is, his intercession has nothing to do with magical or astronomical practices employed by superstitious "healers."

reflection, or else to disregard the whole thing and pass on, I stand foolishly gaping. Even when I am sitting at home, why does a lizard catching flies, or a spider binding them when they blunder into its web, often have me gazing intently? Does the fact that these animals are so small make any difference to the situation? True, I pass from watching them to praising you, wonderful creator and dispenser of all that is, but it is not in that frame of mind that I begin to watch. To get up without delay is one thing, not to fall in the first place is another.

My life is full of such weaknesses, and my sole hope is your exceedingly great mercy. When our heart becomes a bin for things like this, stuffed with a load of idle rubbish, our prayers are often interrupted and disturbed by it, and though the pleading of our heart is addressed to your ears, worthless thoughts intrude from who knows where to cut short the great business on which we are engaged in your presence.

The third great temptation: pride

36, 58. Are we to regard this as a trivial fault? Can there be for us any route back to hope other than your mercy, of which we have proof already because you have begun to change us? You know how much you have changed me, for you began by healing me of the itch to justify myself, so that you could be compassionate to all my other iniquities as well, heal all my ailments, rescue my life from decay, crown me in pity and mercy and overwhelmingly satisfy my desire with good things.[153] You crushed my pride by inspiring in me reverential fear, and you made my neck submissive to your yoke. And now I wear it, and find it benign, as you have promised and as you have made it.[154] Indeed it was so before, when I was afraid to take it on me, but I did not know it then.

59. Is it possible, Lord—this I ask of you who alone hold sway without trace of pride, because you alone are the true Lord[155] who owe fealty to no other—is it possible that the third category of temptation[156] has left me in peace, or ever can leave me in peace throughout my life in this world? This is the temptation to want veneration and affection from others, and to want

---

153. See Ps 102(103):3.
154. See Mt 11:30.
155. See Is 37:20.
156. See 1 Jn 2:16: he has now reached "the pride of life."

them not for the sake of some quality that merits them, but in order to make such admiration itself the cause of my joy. It is no true joy at all, but leads only to a miserable life and shameful ostentation. This tendency is one of the chief impediments to loving you and revering you with chaste fear,[157] and therefore you thwart the proud but give your grace to the humble;[158] you thunder at this world's ambitions till the foundations of the mountains shudder.[159]

The enemy of our true happiness therefore lies in wait for those of us who by reason of our official positions in human society must of necessity be loved and honored by our fellows.[160] On every side he scatters popular plaudits to trap us, so that as we eagerly collect them we may be caught unawares, and abandon our delight in your truth to look for it instead in human flattery. So the affection and honor we receive come to be something we enjoy not for your sake but in your stead, and in this way that enemy who decided to set up his throne in the far recesses of the north[161] wins cronies in his own likeness, not to live with him in loving concord but to be tormented in his company, slaves in darkness and cold of him who imitates you in his perverse, distorted fashion.[162]

But as for us, Lord, remember that we are your little flock:[163] keep us as your own.[164] Spread your wings and let us flee to shelter beneath them. Be yourself our glory: let us be loved on your account, and let it be your word in us that is honored. Whoever touts for human praise that you reprehend will find no human champion when you judge, nor be reprieved when you condemn. It may not be the case that a sinner is praised for his cherished plans, or a wrongdoer commended;[165] even so, if a person is lauded for some gift that you have given him, and he derives more joy from being praised than for possessing the gift which earns the praise, he too is accepting praise which in your sight is a sham. Even the one who extols

---

157. See Ps 18:10(19:9).
158. See Jas 4:6; 1 Pt 5:5.
159. See Ps 17:14.8(18:13.7).
160. Here Augustine's own anxieties are apparent as he contemplates the role of bishop he must assume, particularly the large opportunities that preaching affords him.
161. See Is 14:13-15.
162. The derisory poem in Is 14 refers immediately to a king of Babylon, but was applied in Christian tradition to the devil. The north, as the region of cold and darkness most distant from the sun, came to symbolize the devil's realm; so Dante found the depths of hell cold.
163. See Lk 12:32.
164. See Is 26:13.
165. See Ps 9:24(10:3).

him is better off than the one so esteemed, for the former at least appreciates God's gift in a human being, whereas the other prizes what humans give him more than the gift of God.

37, 60. We are put to the test by these temptations every day, Lord, unceasingly are we tempted; and the crucible in which we are assayed is the human tongue.[166] In this respect too you lay upon us the injunction to continence: so give what you command, and then command whatever you will. You know how my heart groans to you[167] over this, and how my eyes stream with tears; for there is a dangerous infection here, and how far I am clear of it is not easy for me to discern. I am sorely afraid about my hidden sins,[168] which are plain to your eyes[169] but not to mine. In other areas of temptation I have some shrewdness in self-examination, but in this matter almost none. Where sensual desires or idle curiosity are concerned I can measure my progress in self-restraint by going without these pleasures either voluntarily or because opportunity for indulgence is lacking. In that situation I question myself as to whether I am more troubled by their absence, or less. The same applies to riches. People seek wealth in order to use it in the furtherance of one of the three concupiscences, or two of them, or all three; and anyone who lacks the insight to be certain whether he can despise wealth while still possessing it can test himself by getting rid of it. But what of praise? Are we to lead evil lives in order to be rid of it and so test our ability? Should we live in such an abandoned and brutal fashion that everyone who knows us will hate us? Can one imagine a crazier idea than this? If a good life characterized by noble works inevitably and rightly entails being commended, neither the good life nor the resultant commendation can be renounced. Yet only when something pleasant has been withdrawn can I be sure of my ability to live without it, either contentedly or perhaps with reluctance.

61. What then am I to confess to you, Lord, with regard to this kind of temptation? What indeed, except that I do enjoy being praised? But I take more delight in truth itself than in any eulogy; for if I were asked which I would prefer: to be a thief and crooked in every respect yet praised for it by other people, or to be steadfast and absolutely firm in the truth, but reviled by all, I know which I would choose. All the same I must admit that,

---

166. See Prv 27:21.
167. See Ps 37:9(38:8).
168. See Ps 18:13(19:12).
169. See Sir 15:20.

though I would not wish the satisfaction I take in anything good about myself to be enhanced by someone else's approbation, yet it is enhanced; and, what is more, criticism diminishes it.

And when this wretchedness on my part troubles me, an excuse sidles into my mind, the validity of which only you know, O God, for it leaves me perplexed. You have enjoined upon us not only continence, which means restraining our love from certain objects, but also justice, which requires us to bestow it on certain others; and you have willed that our charity should be directed not to you alone but also to our neighbor. Now, the idea often occurs to me that when I take pleasure in being spoken highly of by someone of good understanding, what I am pleased about is the progress, or the promise, shown by my neighbor, while on the contrary I am saddened by my neighbor's misfortune when I hear him finding fault with something good, or something he does not understand. In fact I am saddened at times by the adulation I receive when qualities of mine which I do not myself much like are eulogized, or even when good points which are of only slight importance are rated more highly than they deserve. I am reluctant, then, to have a person who speaks highly of me holding a different opinion from my own on the subject of myself; but how am I to know whether this reaction springs from concern for the other person's welfare? Might it not just as well be due to the fact that I get increased satisfaction from good features I like in my own character when they find favor with another person too? After all, it is no compliment to me if my opinion of myself does not commend itself to others, since this implies either that qualities displeasing to me are being applauded, or that features which I find less attractive are being accorded higher honor. Am I not justified, then, in saying that in this matter I do not know where I stand?

62. You are Truth, and in you I see that if I am touched by the high opinion others hold of me, it should be not for my own sake but so that my neighbor may profit thereby. And whether this is the case, I do not know. In this respect I know myself less clearly than I know you. I beg you to reveal myself to me as well, O my God, so that I may confess the wounded condition I diagnose in myself to my brethren, who will pray for me.

Let me try again, and question myself more carefully. If I am anxious that my neighbor shall profit by praising me, why am I less concerned when some other person is unjustly criticized than when I am myself? Why does an affront offered to myself bite more deeply than one flung at another person in my hearing, given that the injustice of it is the same in either case?

Do I really not know the answer? Is there nothing left to say, but that I am deluding myself[170] and not acting truthfully[171] with heart and tongue in your sight? Remove this madness far from me, Lord, lest my own mouth supply me with the sinners's oil to ooze over my head.[172]

38, 63. Needy and poor am I,[173] but I am the better for recognizing it and lamenting it in secret, and seeking your mercy until my shortcomings are made good and my imperfect self brought to perfection in a peace which the gaze of the arrogant will never descry. But words proceed from the mouth, and actions are observed by other people, and this is fraught with peril, because a hankering for praise will garner every little tribute of approval it can beg, to bolster some fancied pre-eminence of its own. This is a real temptation to me, and even when I am accusing myself of it, the very fact that I am accusing myself tempts me to further self-esteem. We can make our very contempt for vainglory a ground for preening ourselves more vainly still, which proves that what we are congratulating ourselves on is certainly not contempt for vainglory; for no one who indulges in it can be despising it.[174]

39, 64. Within our own hearts too, yes, deep within, is another wicked temptation of the same class. Some there are who are complacent about themselves although they are not liked by others, or even actively disliked; and such people may make no attempt to be likeable. But self-satisfied though they are, they are very displeasing to you, not only because they make a virtue out of what is not good, but also because they arrogate your good gifts to themselves, or perhaps acknowledge them as yours but claim them as their due, or again recognize them as the gifts of your grace, but hug the grace to themselves, grudging it to others and refusing to share the joy.

You see the fear in my heart, hemmed in as I am by all these dangers and struggles, and many another like them. It is not that I have ceased to inflict these wounds on myself; rather I am conscious that ever and anew you are healing them.

---

170. See Gal 6:3.
171. See Jn 3:21; 1 Jn 1:6.
172. See Ps 140(141):5.
173. See Ps 108(109):22.
174. In other words, it is possible to be proud even of humility. There is no escape except the mercy and truth of God.

Summary of all his discoveries

40, 65. O Truth,[175] is there any road where you have not walked with me, teaching me what to avoid and what to aim at, whenever I referred to you the paltry insights I had managed to attain, and sought your guidance? I surveyed the external world as best I could with the aid of my senses,[176] and studied the life my body derives from my spirit, and my senses themselves. Then I moved inward to the storehouse of my memory, to those vast, complex places amazingly filled with riches beyond counting; I contemplated them and was adread.[177] No single one of them could I have perceived without you, but I found that no single one of them was you. But what of myself, the discoverer, I who scanned them all and tried to distinguish them and evaluate each in accordance with its proper dignity? Some things I questioned as my senses reported them, others I felt to be inextricably part of myself; I classified and counted the very messengers, and in the ample stores of memory I scrutinized some items, pushed some into the background and dragged others into the light: what, then of me? No, I was not you, either, not even I as I did all this: the faculty, that is, by which I achieved it, not even that faculty in me was you; for you are that abiding Light[178] whom I consulted throughout my search. I questioned you about each thing, asking whether it existed, what it was, how highly it should be regarded; and all the while I listened to you teaching me and laying your commands upon me.

It is still my constant delight to reflect like this; in such meditation I take refuge from the demands of necessary business, insofar as I can free myself. Nowhere amid all these things which I survey under your guidance do I find a safe haven for my soul except in you; only there are the scattered elements of my being collected, so that no part of me may escape from you.

From time to time you lead me into an inward experience quite unlike any other, a sweetness beyond understanding. If ever it is brought to fullness in me my life will not be what it is now, though what it will be I cannot tell. But I am dragged down again by my weight of woe, sucked back into

---

175. See Jn 14:6. Christ, the Truth, the Mediator implicitly present throughout this book, here becomes explicitly needed.
176. Here Augustine begins a recapitulation of the mystical ascent at Ostia (IX,10,24-25) and that described at X,6,8.
177. See Hab 3:2.
178. See Jn 1:9; 8:12; 9:5; 12:46; 1 Jn 1:5.

everyday things and held fast in them;[179] grievously I lament, but just as grievously am I held. How high a price we pay for the burden of habit! I am fitted for life here where I do not want to be, I want to live there but am unfit for it, and on both counts I am miserable.

41, 66. So now under the three headings of temptation I have taken stock of the sickly state to which my sins have reduced me, and I have called upon your right hand for saving help.[180] I have seen your blazing splendor, but with a wounded heart; I was beaten back, and I asked, "Can anyone reach that?" I was flung far out of your sight.[181] You are the Truth,[182] sovereign over all. I did not want to lose you, but in my greed I thought to possess falsehood along with you, just as no one wants to tell lies in such a way that he loses his own sense of what is true. That was why I lost you, for you did not consent to be possessed in consort with a lie.

The Mediator, priest and victim

42, 67. Whom could I find to reconcile me to you? Should I go courting the angels? With what prayer or by what rites could I win them to my cause? Many have there been who tried to make their way back to you and, finding themselves insufficient by their own powers, had recourse to such means as these, only to lapse into a fancy for visions that tickled their curiosity.[183] They were deservedly deluded for they sought you in arrogance, thrusting out their chests in their haughty knowledge instead of beating them in penitence; and so they attracted to themselves the spiritual powers of the air[184] as their true kin, fit accomplices and allies of their pride. These spirits used magical powers to beguile their clients, who were seeking a mediator to purge them of their impurities, but found none; for there was no one there but the devil, disguised as an angel of light.[185] Being without a fleshly body himself, he strongly appealed to the pride of fleshly humans. They were mortal and sinful, whereas you, Lord, to whom they sought, though proudly, to be reconciled, are immortal and

---

179. See XIII,9,10 for "weight," and Plotinus, *Enneads* IV,8,1.
180. See Pss 59:7(60:5); 102(103):3; 107:7(108:6); Mt 4:23.
181. See Ps 30:23(31:22).
182. See Jn 14:6.
183. Apparently Neo-Platonists of a superstitious bent who practiced theurgy; he links the vice of *curiositas* to them.
184. See Eph 2:2.
185. See 2 Cor 11:14.

without sin. What we needed was a mediator to stand between God and men[186] who should be in one respect like God, in another kin to human beings, for if he were manlike in both regards he would be far from God, but if Godlike in both, far from us; and then he would be no mediator. By the same token that spurious mediator, by whose means pride was deservedly duped in keeping with your secret decree, does have one thing in common with human beings, namely sin; and he appears to have something else in common with God because, not being clad in mortal flesh, he is able to flaunt himself as immortal. But in fact since death is the wage sin earns[187] he has this in common with humans, that he lies under sentence of death as surely as they do.

43, 68. In your unfathomable mercy you first gave the humble certain pointers to the true Mediator, and then sent him, that by his example they might learn even a humility like his.[188] This Mediator between God and humankind, the man Christ Jesus,[189] appeared to stand between mortal sinners and the God who is immortal and just: like us he was mortal, but like God he was just. Now the wage due to justice is life and peace; and so through the justice whereby he was one with God he broke the power of death[190] on behalf of malefactors rendered just,[191] using that very death to which he willed to be liable along with them. He was pointed out to holy people under the old dispensation that they might be saved through faith in his future passion,[192] as we are through faith in that passion now accomplished. Only in virtue of his humanity is he the Mediator; in his nature as the Word he does not stand between us and God, for he is God's equal,[193] God with God,[194] and with him one only God.

69. How you loved us, O good Father, who spared not even your only Son, but gave him up for us evildoers![195] How you loved us, for whose sake he who deemed it no robbery to be your equal was made subservient, even to the point of dying on the cross![196] Alone of all he was free among the dead,[197] for he had

---

186. See 1 Tm 2:5.
187. See Rom 6:23.
188. Contrast the deficiencies he observed in the "books of the Platonists," VII,20,26. This paragraph echoes the scriptural texts that struck him then; see VII,9,13.
189. See 1 Tm 2:5.
190. See 2 Tm 1:10.
191. See Rom 4:5.
192. See Rom 4:5; 1 Tm 2:4.
193. See Phil 2:6.
194. See Jn 1:1.
195. See Rom 8:32.
196. See Phil 2:6,8.
197. See Ps 87:6(88:5).

power to lay down his life and power to retrieve it.[198] For our sake he stood to you as both victor and victim, and victor because victim;[199] for us he stood to you as priest and sacrifice, and priest because sacrifice,[200] making us sons and daughters to you instead of servants[201] by being born of you to serve us. With good reason is there solid hope for me in him, because you will heal all my infirmities[202] through him who sits at your right hand and intercedes for us.[203] Were it not so, I would despair. Many and grave are those infirmities, many and grave; but wider-reaching is your healing power. We might have despaired, thinking your Word remote from any conjunction with humankind, had he not become flesh and made his dwelling among us.[204]

70. Filled with terror by my sins and my load of misery I had been turning over in my mind a plan to flee into solitude, but you forbade me, and strengthened me by your words. *To this end Christ died for all*, you reminded me, *that they who are alive may live not for themselves, but for him who died for them.*[205] See, then, Lord: I cast my care upon you[206] that I may live, and I will contemplate the wonders you have revealed.[207] You know how stupid and weak I am:[208] teach me and heal me.[209] Your only Son, in whom are hidden all treasures of wisdom and knowledge,[210] has redeemed me with his blood. Let not the proud disparage me,[211] for I am mindful of my ransom. I eat it, I drink it,[212] I dispense it to others, and as a poor man I long to be filled[213] with it among those who are fed and feasted. And then do those who seek him praise the Lord.[214]

---

198. See Jn 10:18.
199. See Heb 9:28.
200. See Heb 7:27.
201. See Gal 4:7.
202. See Ps 102(103):3.
203. See Rom 8:34.
204. See Jn 1:14.
205. 2 Cor 5:15.
206. See Ps 54:23(55:22).
207. See Ps 118(119):17-18.
208. See Ps 68:6(69:5).
209. See Pss 24(25):5; 6:3(2).
210. See Col 2:3.
211. See Ps 118(119):22.
212. See Jn 6:55,57; 1 Cor 10:31; 11:29.
213. See Lk 16:21.
214. See Ps 21:27(22:26). The allusion is eucharistic.

Book XI

Time and Eternity

1, 1. Eternity belongs to you, O Lord, so surely you can neither be ignorant of what I am telling you, nor view what happens in time as though you were conditioned by time yourself?

Why then am I relating all this to you at such length? Certainly not in order to inform you. I do it to arouse my own loving devotion toward you, and that of my readers, so that together we may declare, *Great is the Lord, and exceedingly worthy of praise.*[1] I have said already,[2] and will say again, that it is out of love for loving you that I do this, even as we pray for things though Truth tells us that *Your Father knows what you need before you ask him.*[3] We confess to you our miseries and the mercies you have shown us in your will to set us free completely, as you have begun to do already; and by so confessing to you we lay bare our loving devotion. Our hope is that we may cease to be miserable in ourselves and may find our beatitude in you; for you have called us to be poor in spirit, to be meek, to mourn, to hunger and thirst for righteousness, to be merciful and pure-hearted, and to be peacemakers.[4]

See, then, how long a tale I have told you, as best I could and as I truly wanted to, because you first willed that I should confess to you, my Lord and God, for you are good and your mercy endures for ever.[5]

Augustine prays for understanding of the scriptures

2, 2. My pen serves me as a tongue,[6] but when will it find eloquence enough to recount all those exhortations and threats, all that encouragement and guidance, by which you led me to this position where I must preach the

---

1. Pss 47:2(48:1); 95(96):4; 144(145):3.
2. That is, at II,1,1.
3. Mt 6:8.
4. See Mt 5:3-9.
5. See Ps 117(118):1-4.
6. See Ps 44:2(45:1).

word and administer the sacrament to your people? Furthermore, even had I skill to relate it all in order, the dripping moments of time are too precious to me.[7] I have long burned with desire to meditate on your law,[8] that there I might confess to you both what I know and what I still find baffling, your dawning light in me and the residual darkness that will linger until my weakness is swallowed up by your strength. I am chary of frittering away on anything else the hours I find free from such needful activities as bodily refreshment, mental concentration, the duties I owe to the people and others I do not owe but render nonetheless.[9]

3. O Lord my God, hear my prayer,[10]
may your mercy hearken to my longing,[11]
a longing on fire not for myself alone
but to serve the brethren I dearly love;
you see my heart and know this is true.
Let me offer in sacrifice to you the service of my heart and tongue,
but grant me first what I can offer you;
for I am needy and poor,[12]
but you are rich unto all who call upon you,[13]
and you care for us though no care troubles you.
Circumcise all that is within me from presumption
and my lips without from falsehood.[14]
Let your scriptures be my chaste delight,
let me not be deceived in them
nor through them deceive others.
Hearken, O Lord, have mercy, my Lord and God,[15]
O Light of the blind, Strength of the weak—who yet are Light to those
who see and Strength to the strong—
hearken to my soul,

---

7. A water-clock, clepsydra, measured time by the dripping away of a known quantity of water.
8. See Ps 1:2.
9. In addition to preaching and performance of the liturgy a bishop had heavy judicial responsibilities.
10. See Ps 60:2(61:1).
11. See Ps 9B:38 (10:17).
12. See Ps 85(86):1.
13. See Rom 10:12.
14. See Ex 6:12.
15. See Jer 18:19; Ps 26(27):7.

hear me as I cry from the depths,[16]
for unless your ears be present in our deepest places
where shall we go[17] and whither cry?
Yours is the day, yours the night,[18]
a sign from you sends minutes speeding by;
spare in their fleeting course a space for us
to ponder the hidden wonders of your law:
shut it not against us as we knock.[19]
Not in vain have you willed so many pages to be written,
pages deep in shadow, obscure in their secrets;
not in vain do harts and hinds seek shelter in those woods,
to hide and venture forth,
roam and browse, lie down and ruminate.
Perfect me too, Lord, and reveal those woods to me.[20]
Lo, your voice is joy to me,
your voice that rings out above a flood of joys.
Give me what I love;
for I love indeed, and this love you have given me.
Forsake not your gifts, disdain not your parched grass.
Let me confess to you all I have found in your books,
Let me hear the voice of praise,[21]
and drink from you,
and contemplate the wonders of your law[22]
from the beginning when you made heaven and earth
to that everlasting reign when we shall be with you in your holy city.[23]

4. Have mercy on me, Lord, and hearken to my longing;[24] for I do not think it arises from this earth, or concerns itself with gold or silver or precious stones, with splendid raiment or honors or positions of power, with the pleasures of the flesh or with things we need for the body and for this our

---

16. See Ps 129(130):1.
17. See Ps 138(139):7-8.
18. See Ps 73(74):16.
19. See Mt 7:7-8; Lk 11:9-10.
20. See Ps 28(29):9; in Old Latin: *Vox Domini perficientis cervos et revelabit silvas.*
21. See Ps 25(26):7.
22. See Ps 118(119):18.
23. That is, from Gn 1:1 to Rev 22:21. He does not attempt here to comment on the whole Bible, but in this book and the two following he moves from creation to the Sabbath rest at the end of it, which prefigures eternity.
24. See Pss 26(27):7; 9B:38(10:17).

life of pilgrimage; for all these things are provided for those who seek your kingdom and your righteousness.[25] Look and see, O my God, whence springs my desire. The unrighteous have told me titillating tales, but they have nothing to do with your law, O Lord;[26] and see, that law is what stirs my longing. See, Father, have regard to me and see and bless my longing, and let it be pleasing in your merciful eyes[27] that I find grace before you,[28] so that the inner meaning of your words may be opened to me as I knock at their door.[29] I beg this grace through our Lord Jesus Christ, your Son, the man at your right hand,[30] the Son of Man whom you have made strong to stand between yourself and us as mediator.[31] Through him you sought us when we were not seeking you,[32] but you sought us that we might begin to seek you. He is the Word through whom you made all things,[33] and me among them, your only Son through whom you called your believing people to be your sons by adoption,[34] and me among them; through him, then, do I make my plea to you, through him who sits at your right hand to intercede for us,[35] for in him are hidden all treasures of wisdom and knowledge.[36] And they are what I seek in your books. Moses wrote of him; Christ told us so himself,[37] and he is the Truth.

In the Beginning God made heaven and earth

3, 5. Let me listen, so that I may understand how you made heaven and earth in the beginning. Moses wrote that statement; he wrote it and went away, and made his passover, his passing from you to you;[38] and so he is not here face to face with me now. If he were, I would take hold of him and ask him and in your name implore him to open these mysteries to me. I would bend my bodily ears to the sounds that broke from his mouth,

25. See Mt 6:33.
26. See Ps 118(119):85.
27. See Ps 18:15(19:14).
28. See Dn 3:40.
29. See Mt 7:7-8; Lk 11:9-10.
30. See Ps 79:18(80:17).
31. See 1 Tm 2:5.
32. See Rom 10:20.
33. See Jn 1:1-3.
34. See Gal 4:5.
35. See Rom 8:34.
36. See Col 2:3.
37. See Jn 5:46.
38. See IV,9,14, where the sinner passes from "God in his tranquillity to God in his anger"; here, by contrast, is the saint's passover.

though if he spoke Hebrew those sounds would knock in vain at the door of my perception, for nothing of what was said would reach my mind, whereas if he spoke Latin I would know what he was saying. But how would I know whether he spoke the truth? If I were to ascertain that too, could it be on his assertion? No; undoubtedly within myself, in that inner habitation of my thought, the truth that is neither Hebrew nor Greek nor Latin nor any vernacular would speak to me without bodily organ of mouth or tongue, and without any clatter of syllables would tell me, "He is speaking the truth"; and then with instant certainty I would say to that man who served you, "What you say is true."

But since I cannot question him, who spoke truthfully because you, O Truth, had filled him, I beg you yourself, O Truth, my God, to pardon my sins,[39] and as you granted that servant of yours the grace to say those things, grant also to me the grace to understand them.

4, 6. Heaven and earth plainly exist, and by the very fact that they undergo change and variation they cry out that they were made.[40] If anything was not made, yet exists, there is no element in it that was not present earlier; for change and variation imply that something is made that was not previously there. Heaven and earth further proclaim that they did not make themselves: "We are, because we have been made; we did not exist before we came to be, as though to bring ourselves into being." And their visible existence is the voice with which they say this. It was you who made them, Lord: you are beautiful, so it must have been you, because they are beautiful; you who are good must have made them, because they are good; you who are, because they are. Yet not in the same way as you, their creator, are they beautiful and good, nor do they exist as you exist; compared with you they have neither beauty nor goodness nor being. We know this, and we thank you for the knowledge, yet compared with your knowledge ours is but ignorance.

God creates in his Word

5, 7. But how did you make heaven and earth? What tool did you employ for so vast an enterprise? You cannot have gone to work like a human

---

39. See I,5,5: divine mercy is needed for both right speaking and right listening.
40. This is the same starting-point that Augustine took in the ascent to God at Ostia (IX,10,25) and that is recorded at X,6,9, but this time he begins from scripture.

craftsman, who forms a material object from some material in accordance with his imaginative decision. Whatever design his mind's eye conjures up within, the mind has power to impose upon the material, but where would he get this power, if you had not made his mind? He merely stamps a form on matter already in existence and in possession of its being, such as clay or stone or wood or gold or any other stuff of the kind. And whence would these derive their existence, unless you had established them in being? You made the craftsman's body; you made the mind which exercises control over his limbs; you made the material he needs to fashion anything; you made the skill that equips him to master his art and visualize within his mind the plan to which he will give outward expression. You made the perceptive senses which can interpret the design in the mind and transfer it to the material to produce the thing he is making, and then report back to the mind on what has been made, so that the craftsman may test it against the truth that rules him within himself, to ensure that it is made properly. All these things praise you, the creator of them all.

But you, how do you make them? How did you make heaven and earth, O God? You certainly did not use either heaven or earth as your workshop when you made heaven and earth, nor did you work in the air or in the waters, because these too belong to heaven and earth; nor can you have made the whole universe anywhere within the whole universe, because there was no place in it where such work could be done before it was made and given its being. Nor did you hold in your hand some material from which to fashion heaven and earth, for where would you have obtained any material you had not made, in order to use it for making something else? Is there anything that exists at all, if not because of you?

Clearly, then, you spoke and things were made. By your word you made them.[41]

6, 8. But how did you speak? Surely not in the same way as you did when a voice came from the cloud, saying, *This is my beloved Son?*[42] That utterance came and went; it had a beginning and an end. Its syllables made themselves heard and then faded away, the second following the first, the third following the second, and so on in due order until the last one followed the others, and silence fell after the last. From this it is self-evident that your voice made itself heard through the movement of a

---

41. See Ps 32(33):9,6.
42. Mt 3:17; see Mt 17:5; Lk 9:35.

created thing,[43] which was the temporal instrument of your eternal will. Then these words of yours, in their temporal expression, would be reported by the outward ear to the mind of any discerning listener whose inner ear was attuned to your eternal Word. The mind would then compare the words sounding in time with your silent Word in eternity, and say, "These are something different, totally different. They are far below me and have no being, since they are fleeting and ephemeral; but the Word of my God is above me and abides for ever."[44] It seems, then, that if you made use of audible, evanescent words to say that heaven and earth should come to be, and that was how you made heaven and earth, there must have been some material thing in existence before you made heaven and earth, so that such a voice might use the creature's temporal movements to make itself audible in time. But no material thing did exist before heaven and earth; or, if there was such a thing, you undoubtedly must have made it without using transitory speech, since you meant to use it as the vehicle of that transitory utterance in which you would say that heaven and earth should come to be. Whatever that thing was from which such an utterance might be produced, it could not have existed at all unless you had made it. So what word did you speak to bring into being that material object, from which those other words were to proceed?

This Word is eternal

7, 9. You are evidently inviting us to understand that the word in question is that Word who is God, God with you who are God;[45] he is uttered eternally, and through him are eternally uttered all things. This does not mean that one thing was said, and then, when that was finished, another thing, so that everything could be mentioned in succession; no, all things are uttered simultaneously in one eternal speaking. Were this not so, time and change would come into it, and there would be neither true eternity nor true immortality. I know this, my God, and I give you thanks for it. I know, and I confess to you, Lord,[46] and everyone who is grateful for assured truth knows it with me, and blesses you. We know this, Lord, we

---

43. That is, probably, the air.
44. See Is 40:8.
45. See Jn 1:1.
46. See Mt 11:25-27; Lk 10:21-22.

know it, because insofar as a thing is no longer what it once was, or is now what it once was not, that thing is dying or rising to new life; but in your Word there is no cessation or succession, for all is truly immortal and eternal. Thus in that Word who is coeternal with yourself you speak all that you speak simultaneously and eternally, and whatever you say shall be comes into being.[47] Your creative act is in no way different from your speaking. Yet things which you create by speaking do not all come to be simultaneously, nor are they eternal.

The eternal Word is the Beginning

8, 10. Why is this, I ask, O Lord my God? I do understand to some degree, but I do not know how to articulate it, except like this: Everything which begins to exist and then ceases to exist does so at the due time for its beginning and cessation decreed in that eternal Reason where nothing begins or comes to an end. This eternal Reason is your Word, who is the Beginning in that he also speaks to us.[48] The gospel records that he claimed this by word of mouth, making his claim audible to people's outward ears that they might believe him and seek him within themselves and find him in the eternal Truth where he, our sole teacher,[49] instructs apt disciples. There it is that I hear your voice, O Lord, the voice of one who speaks to me, because anyone who truly teaches us speaks to us directly, whereas one who is no true teacher does not speak to us, though speak he may. After all, can anyone teach us, other than stable Truth? When some changeable creature advises us, we are but led to that stable Truth, where we truly learn as we stand still and listen to him, and are filled with joy on hearing the Bridegroom's voice,[50] and surrender ourselves once more to him from whom we came. He is the Beginning for us in the sense that if he were not abidingly the same, we should have nowhere to return to after

---

47. This eternity of the creative Word is the essential background to Augustine's long exploration of the mystery of time, which occupies most of the present book. He will show that time is not a primordial medium into which God's acts are inserted, nor a first principle alongside the Word; time is itself the product of the creative Word.
48. See Jn 8:25, a notoriously difficult text in the Greek. The present paragraph plays on the links between *the beginning* of Gn 1:1, Jn 1:1 and Jn 8:25, all being identified with Christ according to an interpretation already found in Ambrose, *Hexameron* I,4,15.
49. See Mt 23:8.
50. See Jn 3:29.

going astray.[51] When we turn back from our errant ways it is by acknowledging the truth that we turn back, and he it is who teaches us to acknowledge it, because he is the Beginning who speaks to us.

9, 11. In this Beginning you made heaven and earth, O God. You made them in your Word, your Son, your Power, your Wisdom,[52] your Truth, wonderfully speaking and in a wondrous way creating. Who can understand this? Who explain it? What is this light that shines through the chinks of my mind and pierces my heart, doing it no injury? I begin to shudder yet catch fire with longing: I shudder inasmuch as I am unlike him, yet I am afire with longing for him because some likeness there is.[53] Wisdom it is, none other than Wisdom, that shines through my darkness, tearing apart the cloud that envelops me; yet I fall away from it and am plunged into obscurity once more, lost in the murk and rubble that are my punishment, for so wasted away is my strength to the point of destitution[54] that I cannot even support the good that I have, until you, O Lord, who are mercifully disposed toward all my sins, heal all my ailments too. And I know you will, for you will rescue my life from decay, crown me in pity and mercy, and overwhelmingly satisfy my desire with good things; and my youth will be renewed like an eagle's.[55] We are already saved, but in hope, and in patience we look forward to the fulfillment of your promises.[56]

Let everyone who has the aptitude listen to your spoken word within; for my part I will begin with confidence from your word in scripture, and cry out, *How magnificent are your works, O Lord! In wisdom you have created all things.*[57] This wisdom is no other than the Beginning, and in that Beginning you have made heaven and earth.

---

51. In IV,16,31 Augustine reflected that because the soul's true home is eternity, we are in no danger of finding it fallen into ruin when we return after an absence.
52. See 1 Cor 1:24.
53. Compare the "region of unlikeness," VII,10,16.
54. See Ps 30:11(31:10).
55. See Ps 102(103):3-5. According to a belief going back at least to Aristotle, the hooked upper section of an aging eagle's beak grew out so far beyond the lower half that the bird became unable to open its mouth. In imminent danger of death from starvation, the eagle hammered its beak against a rock to rid itself of the surplus, and then could eat again. Augustine expounds the idea in his *Exposition of Psalm* 102,9, seeing the rock as a symbol of Christ.
56. See Rom 8:24-25.
57. Ps 103(104):24.

"What was God doing before that?" Meaningless question

10, 12. People who ask us, "What was God doing before he made heaven and earth?" are obviously full of their stale old nature.[58] "If he was at leisure," they say, "and not making anything, why did he not continue so thereafter and for ever, just as he had always done nothing prior to that? If some change took place in God, and some new volition emerged to inaugurate created being, a thing he had never done before, then an act of will was arising in him which had not previously been present, and in that case how would he truly be eternal? God's will is not a created thing; it exists prior to the act of creation, because nothing would be created unless the creator first willed it. Now, God's will belongs to the very substance of God. But if some element appears in God's substance that was previously not there, that substance cannot accurately be called eternal. On the other hand, if God's will that creation should occur is eternal, why is creation not eternal as well?"

11, 13. People who take that line do not yet understand you, O Wisdom of God and Light of our minds. They do not yet understand how things which receive their being through you and in you come into existence; they strive to be wise about eternal realities, but their heart flutters about between the changes of past and future found in created things, and an empty heart it remains.[59] Who is to take hold of it and peg it down, that it may stand still for a little while and capture, if only briefly, the splendor of that eternity which stands for ever, and compare it with the fugitive moments that never stand still, and find it incomparable, and come to see that a long time is not long except in virtue of a great number of passing moments which cannot all run their course at once? They would see that in eternity nothing passes, for the whole is present, whereas time cannot be present all at once. Can they not see that whatever is past has been pushed out of the way by what was future, and all the future follows on the heels of

---

58. Sign of the "old man"; see Rom 6:6; Eph 4:22; Col 3:9. The Manichees certainly asked this question in a polemical spirit; other Gnostic groups apparently also did. Philosophers had long grappled with the mysteries of eternity and time: Plotinus, *Enneads* III,7, explored it at length and influenced Augustine; behind Plotinus stood Plato's *Timaeus* 37D-38D and Aristotle's *Physics* IV,10-14. But Augustine's polemic here against Manichean questions is to be read within the whole context of his meditation on the mystery of the creative Word. To imagine God subject to time, as we are, and eternity as no more than an endless succession of "times," is to make us a little less unlike God (see XI,9,11). Augustine is tackling the difficulty inherent in the Christian affirmation of an absolute beginning.

59. See Ps 5:10(9).

the past, and the whole of both past and future flows forth from him who is always present, and is by him created? Who shall take hold of the human heart, to make it stand still and see how eternity, which stands firm, has neither future nor past, but ordains future and past times? Has my hand the strength for this, or my mouth the persuasiveness to achieve such a thing?

12, 14. However, I will set about replying to the questioner who asks, "What was God doing before he made heaven and earth?" But I will not respond with that joke someone is said to have made: "He was getting hell ready for people who inquisitively peer into deep matters"; for this is to evade the force of the question. It is one thing to see the solution, and something different to make fun of the problem. So I will not give that reply. I would rather have answered, "What I do not know, I do not know," than have cracked a joke that exposed a serious questioner to ridicule and won applause for giving an untrue answer. Instead I will state that you, our God, are the creator of every created thing; and, if we take "heaven and earth" to cover all that is created, I boldly make this assertion: Before God made heaven and earth, he was not doing anything; for if he was doing or making something, what else was he doing but creating? And no creature was made before any creature was made. I wish I could know everything that I desire to know to my own profit with the same certainty with which I know that.

13, 15. If any giddy-minded person wanders off into fantasy about epochs of time before creation, and finds it amazing that you, God almighty, who are the creator of all things, you who are the architect of heaven and earth and hold everything in your hand, should through measureless ages have been at rest before undertaking this huge task, such a person should wake up and realize that his amazement is misplaced. How could measureless ages have passed by if you had not made them, since you are the author and creator of the ages?[60] Or what epochs of time could have existed, that had not been created by you? And how could they have passed by, if they had never existed? If there was a "time" before you made heaven and earth, how can it be said that you were not at work then, you who are the initiator of all times? For of course you would have made that time too; there could not have been any passing times before you created times. If, therefore, there was no time before heaven and earth

---

60. See Heb 1:2.

came to be, how can anyone ask what you were doing then? There was no such thing as "then" when there was no time.

16. Nor can it be said that you are "earlier in time" than all eras of time, for that would mean that there was some kind of time already in existence before you. You have precedence over the past by the loftiness of your ever-present eternity, and you live beyond all the future, because future times are future, but as soon as they have arrived they will be past, whereas you are ever the same, and your years fail not.[61] Your years do not come and go. Our years pass and new ones arrive only so that all may come in turn, but your years stand all at once, because they are stable: there is no pushing out of vanishing years by those that are coming on, because with you none are transient. In our case, our years will be complete only when there are none left. Your years are a single day,[62] and this day of yours is not a daily recurrence, but a simple "Today," because your Today does not give way to tomorrow, nor follow yesterday. Your Today is eternity, and therefore your Son, to whom you said, *Today have I begotten you,*[63] is coeternal with you. You have made all eras of time and you are before all time, and there was never a "time" when time did not exist.

Time, a creature of God—what is it?

14, 17. There was therefore never any time when you had not made anything, because you made time itself. And no phases of time are coeternal with you, for you abide, and if they likewise were to abide, they would not be time. For what is time? Who could find any quick or easy answer to that? Who could even grasp it in his thought clearly enough to put the matter into words? Yet is there anything to which we refer in conversation with more familiarity, any matter of more common experience, than time? And we know perfectly well what we mean when we speak of it, and understand just as well when we hear someone else refer to it. What, then, is time? If no one asks me, I know; if I want to explain it to someone who asks me, I do not know. I can state with confidence, however, that this much I do know: if nothing passed away there would be

---

61. See Ps 101:28(102:27); Heb 1:12.
62. See Ps 89:4(90:3); 2 Pt 3:8.
63. Ps 2:7; Acts 13:33; Heb 1:5; 5:5.

no past time; if there was nothing still on its way there would be no future time; and if nothing existed, there would be no present time.

Now, what about those two times, past and future: in what sense do they have real being, if the past no longer exists and the future does not exist yet? As for present time, if that were always present and never slipped away into the past, it would not be time at all; it would be eternity. If, therefore, the present's only claim to be called "time" is that it is slipping away into the past, how can we assert that this thing *is*, when its only title to being is that it will soon cease to be? In other words, we cannot really say that time exists, except because it tends to non-being.[64]

15, 18. Nonetheless we speak of a long time or a short time, and we do so only of time past or time in the future. For example, we call a hundred years ago a long time in the past, and likewise a hundred years hence a long time in the future; but we call—say—ten days ago a short time past, and ten days hence a short time in the future. But on what grounds can something that does not exist be called long or short? The past no longer exists and the future does not exist yet. We ought not, therefore, to say, "That is a long time," but, when speaking of the past, we should say, "That was long," and of the future, "That will be long."

O my Lord, my Light,[65] will your truth not deride us humans for speaking so? This long time in the past: was it long when it was already past, or earlier than that, when it was still present? If the latter, yes, then it might have been long, because there was something to be long; but if it was already past it no longer existed, and therefore could not have been long, since it was not in existence at all. We ought not, therefore, to say, "That era in the past was a long one," for we shall not find anything that was long, for since that point at which it became past time it has no longer had any being. Rather, we ought to say, "That era of time was long while it was present," because while it was present it was long. It had not yet passed away and so passed out of existence, and so there was something there which could be long. But when it passed away it ceased to be long at that very point when it ceased to be at all.

---

64. This is the heart of the matter for Augustine. He pursues the argument relentlessly throughout the rest of this book, revealing time as something elusive that slips the more swiftly through our fingers the more we try to analyze it or justify our habit of measuring it. The inexorable rush of time toward non-being reveals the fragility of time-bound, time-conditioned creatures, whose only refuge from their native nothingness is the eternity of God.

65. See Mi 7:8; Ps 26(27):1.

19. Now, human mind, let us consider whether present time can be long, as you seem to think it can, since you have been granted the power to be aware of duration and to measure it. Answer my questions, then. Is the present century a long period of time? Before you say yes, reflect whether a hundred years can be present. If the first of them is running its course, that year is present, but ninety-nine others are future and therefore as yet have no being. If the second year is running its course, one year is already past, another is present, and the remainder are still to come. In the same fashion we may represent any one of the intervening years of the century as present, and always the years that preceded it will be past, and those that follow it future. Evidently, then, a hundred years cannot be present.

Well then, consider whether the one current year at least can be present. If we are in the first month of it, the other months are in the future; if we are in the second, the first month is already past and the rest do not yet exist. Even the current year, then, is not present in its totality, and if it is not present in its totality, the year is not present; for a year consists of twelve months, and while any one of them is current that one is present, but the others are either past or future.

But we must go further, and notice that the current month is not in fact present, because only one day of it is: if we are on the first day, the rest are future; if on the last, the others are past; if on any day in the middle, we shall be midway between past and future days.

20. Look where this leaves us. We saw earlier that present time was the only one of the three that might properly be called long, and now this present time has been pared down to the span of a bare day. But let us take the discussion further, because not even a single day is present all at once. It is made up of night hours and day hours, twenty-four in all. From the standpoint of the first hour all the rest are still future; the last hour looks to all those already past; and any one we pick in between has some before it, others to follow. Even a single hour runs its course through fleeing minutes: whatever portion of it has flown is now past, and what remains is future. If we can conceive of a moment in time which cannot be further divided into even the tiniest of minute particles, that alone can be rightly termed the present; yet even this flies by from the future into the past with such haste that it seems to last no time at all. Even if it has some duration, that too is divisible into past and future; hence the present is reduced to vanishing-point.

What kind of time, then, can be referred to as "a long time"? Future time, perhaps? Then we must not say, "That is a long time," because there is as yet nothing to be long; we will have to say, "That will be long." But when will it be so? If at the point of speaking that period is still in the future, it will not be long, because nothing yet exists to be long; if, however, at the moment when we speak it has begun to exist by emerging from the non-existent future, and so has become present, so that there is something in existence to be long, then this present time proclaims itself incapable of being long for the reasons already discussed.

16, 21. All the same, Lord, we are conscious of intervals of time, and we compare them with each other and pronounce some longer, others shorter. We also calculate by how much this period of time is longer or shorter than that other, and we report that the one is twice or three times as long as the other, or that it is the same length. But when we measure periods of time by our awareness of them, what we measure is passing time. Could anyone measure past periods that no longer exist, or future periods that do not yet exist? Only someone who is bold enough to claim that what has no being can be measured. So then, while time is passing it can be felt and measured, but once past it cannot, because it no longer exists.

17, 22. I am asking questions, Father, not making assertions: rule me, O my God, and shepherd me.[66] For who would make so bold as to tell me that there are not really three tenses or times—past, present and future—as we learned as children and as we in our turn have taught our children, but that there is only present, since the other two do not exist? Or is the truth perhaps that they do exist, but that when a future thing becomes present it emerges from some hiding-place, and then retreats into another hiding-place when it moves from the present into the past? Where, otherwise, did soothsayers see future events, if they do not yet exist? What has no being cannot be seen. Nor would people who tell stories about the past be telling true tales if they had no vision of those past events in their minds; and if the events in question were non-existent they could not be seen. The future and the past must exist, then?

---

66. See Pss 22(23):1; 27(28):9.

18, 23. Allow me, Lord, to press the question further: O my hope,[67] do not let me lose the thread. If future and past things do exist, I want to know where they are. If this is not yet within my compass, I do know at any rate that, wherever they are, they are not there as future or past, but as present. For if in that place too future things are future, they are not there yet; and if there too past things are past, they are there no longer. Clearly, then, wherever they are and whatever they are, they can only be present. Nonetheless, when a true account is given of past events, what is brought forth from the memory is not the events themselves, which have passed away, but words formed from images of those events which, as they happened and went on their way, left some kind of traces in the mind through the medium of the senses. This is the case with my childhood, which no longer exists: it belongs to past time which exists no longer, but when I recall it and tell the story I contemplate the image of it which is still in my memory.[68]

Whether something similar occurs in the prediction of future events, in that the seer has a presentiment of images which exist already, I confess, O my God, that I do not know. But this I undoubtedly do know, that we often plan our future actions beforehand, and that the plans in our mind are present to us, though the action we are planning has as yet no being, because it is future. When we set about it, and begin to do what we were planning, then the action will have real being, because then it will be not future but present.

24. However the mysterious presentiment of future events may be explained, only what exists can be seen. But what already exists is not future but present. Therefore when it is claimed that future events are seen, it is not that these things are seen in themselves, because they have as yet no existence, being still future. It may be, however, that their causes, or signs of them, are seen, because these already exist; hence they are not future but present to the people who discern them, and from them future events may take shape in the mind and can be foretold. These ideas in the mind also exist already, and can be inwardly contemplated by people who predict the future.

---

67. See Ps 70(71):5.
68. This tying of speculation about time to the phenomenon of memory is one of Augustine's particularly original contributions.

Let me take an example from a wealth of such occurrences. I watch the dawn, and I give advance notice that the sun is about to rise. What I am looking at is present; what I foretell is future. Not that the sun is future, of course—no, that exists already, but its rising is future; it has not yet happened, yet unless I could imagine the sunrise in my mind, as I do now while I speak of it, I would be unable to forecast it. The dawn, which I am watching in the sky, is not the sunrise, but only precedes it; and similarly the picture I have in my mind is not the sunrise either. But these two realities are present and open to observation, so that the future event can be announced before its time.

We must conclude, then, that future events have no being as yet, and if they have no being yet they do not exist, and if they do not exist it is absolutely impossible for anyone to see them. But they can be predicted on the basis of other things which are already present and hence can be seen.

19, 25. You are the king of your creation; tell me, then: how do you instruct people's minds about the future? You did so teach the prophets. What method can you adopt for teaching what is future, when to you nothing is future at all? Would it be better to say that you teach what is present but has a bearing on the future? Yes, because what does not exist obviously cannot be taught. This method of yours is far above the reach of my mind; it is too much for me[69] and of myself I cannot see it, but I will see it with your help, when you grant me this gift, O gracious light of my secret eyes.[70]

20, 26. What is now clear and unmistakable is that neither things past nor things future have any existence, and that it is inaccurate to say, "There are three tenses or times: past, present and future," though it might properly be said, "There are three tenses or times: the present of past things, the present of present things, and the present of future things." These are three realities in the mind, but nowhere else as far as I can see, for the present of past things is memory, the present of present things is attention, and the present of future things is expectation.[71] If we are allowed to put it that way, I do see three tenses or times, and admit that they

---

69. See Ps 138(139):6.
70. See Eccl 11:7; Ps 37:11(38:10).
71. This triad, which recurs in XII,15,18, is important for Augustine's thought. Some commentators see it as a pattern for *The Confessions* as a whole: Books I-IX = *memoria*, Book X = *contuitus*, Books XI-XIII = *expectatio*. It has links also with the triad *esse … nosse … velle* in XIII,11,12, where the soul's likeness to the Trinity is considered.

are three. Very well, then, let the phrase pass, "There are three tenses or times: past, present and future," as common usage improperly has it: let people go on saying this. I do not mind, nor will I put up any opposition or offer correction, provided we understand what we are saying, and do not assert that either the future or the past exists now. There are few things, in fact, which we state accurately; far more we express loosely, but what we mean is understood.

21, 27. I said just now[72] that we measure periods of time as they pass, so as to declare this interval twice as long as that, or this equal to that, and report anything else about segments of time that our measurements have revealed. It follows, then, that we measure these intervals of time as they are passing by, as I remarked, and if anyone asks me, "How do you know that?" I must be allowed to reply, "I know it because we do in fact measure them; but what does not exist we cannot measure, and past and future do not exist." But how can we measure present time, when it has no extension?[73] We can only hope to measure it as it passes by, because once it has passed by there will be no measuring; it will not exist to be measured.

But when it is measured, where does it come from, by what path does it pass, and whither go? Where from, if not from the future? By what path, if not the present? Whither, if not into the past? It comes, then, from what is not yet real, travels through what occupies no space, and is bound for what is no longer real. But what are we trying to measure, if not time that does have some extension? We speak of "half as long," "double the time," "three times as long," "equal in length," and make similar statements about time only in reference to extended time, or duration. Where then is this duration which will give us a chance to measure passing time? In the future, whence it has come to pass us by? But we do not measure what does not yet exist. In the present, perhaps, through which it passes on its way? But where there is no extension we cannot measure. In the past, then, to which it has gone? But we cannot measure what no longer exists.

22, 28. My mind is on fire to solve this most intricate enigma. O Lord, my God, my good Father, through Christ I beg you not to shut against me the door to these truths, so familiar yet so mysterious. Do not slam the door in the face of my desire, nor forbid me entrance to that place where I may watch these things grow luminous as your mercy sheds its light upon

---

72. That is, in XI,16,21.
73. That is, the ideal present is a point, which has position but no magnitude.

them, Lord. To whom should I put my questions about them? And to whom should I confess my stupidity with greater profit than to you, who do not weary of my intense, burning interest in your scriptures? Give me what I love; for I love indeed, and this love you have given me. Give this to me, Father, for you truly know how to give good gifts to your children,[74] give me this gift, for I have only just begun to understand, and the labor is too much for me[75] until you open the door.[76] Through Christ I implore you, in the name of that holy of holies,[77] let no noisy person stand in my way. I too have believed, and so I too speak.[78] This is my hope, for this I live: to contemplate the delight of the Lord.[79] See how old you have made my days;[80] they are slipping away and I know not how.

We speak of one time and another time, of this period of time or that; we ask, "How long did that man speak?" or "How long did he take to do it?" We say, "What a long time it is since I saw so-and-so," and "This syllable has twice the length of that short one." We say these things and listen to them, we are understood and we understand. They are perfectly plain and fully familiar, yet at the same time deeply mysterious, and we still need to discover their meaning.

Movements of the heavenly bodies are not time itself,
but only markers of it

23, 29. I was once told by a certain learned man that the movements of the sun, moon and stars themselves constitute time. I did not agree with him. Why, in that case, should not the movements of all corporeal things constitute time? Suppose the luminaries of heaven were to halt, but a potter's wheel went on turning, would there not still be time by which we

---

74. See Mt 7:11.
75. See Ps 72(73):16 (Old Latin).
76. See Mt 7:7-8; Lk 11:9-10.
77. *In nomine eius sancti sanctorum*: obscure. In view of the context (desire to enter) and particularly of Ps 72(73):17 (*until I enter the Lord's sanctuary and understand*), which immediately follows the verse just alluded to, it seems that Augustine is thinking of an entrance effected by Christ for all his followers, as described in Heb 9:1-15; 10:11-19. But the plural (*sancta sanctorum*) is more common in references to this. Others therefore take *sancti* in apposition to *eius*, that is, Christ, and translate, "in his name who is the holy of holies" or "the holiest of all holy ones."
78. See Ps 115(116):10.
79. See Ps 26(27):4.
80. See Ps 38:6(39:5) (Old Latin).

could measure those rotations, and say either that all of them took the same time, or (if the speed of the wheel varied) that some were of longer duration, others shorter? And when we said this, would we too not be speaking within time; and in the words we used, would there not be some long syllables and some short; and why could that be said of them, unless because some of them had taken a longer time to pronounce than others?

Through this small thing, O God, grant our human minds insight into the principles common to small things and great. The stars and the other luminaries in the sky are there to mark our times and days and years. Yes, granted; but as I would not assert that the revolution of that little wooden wheel itself constituted a day, so my learned informant on the other hand had no business to say that its gyrations did not occupy a space of time.

30. I want to know the essence and nature of time, whereby we measure the movement of bodies and say, for instance, that one movement lasts twice as long as another. Now I have a question to ask. Taking the word "day" to apply not only to the period of sunlight on earth—day as opposed to night, that is—but to the sun's whole course from the east and back to the east again, in the sense that we say, "So many days elapsed," meaning to include the nights, and not reckoning the nights as extra time over and above the days; taking it, then, that the movement of the sun in its circular course from the east back to the east completes a day, this is my question: Is it the movement itself that constitutes a day? Or the time it takes? Or both? If the movement constitutes a day, then it would still be one day if the sun were to achieve its circuit in an interval of time equivalent to a single hour. If it is the time it takes, there would not be a day if the space between one sunrise and the next were as short as an hour; the sun would have to go round twenty-four times to make up a day. If both were required—a complete circuit of the sun and the customary duration of this—we could not call it a day if the sun traveled through its whole circuit in the space of an hour, nor could we if the sun stopped and as much time elapsed as it usually takes to run its whole course from morning to morning.

My question now is not, therefore, what is it that we call a day, but what is time itself, the time whereby we would be able to measure the sun's revolution and say that it had been completed in only half the usual time, if the circuit had occupied only that space of time represented by twelve hours? We could compare the two periods in terms of time and say that one was twice the length of the other, and this would still be possible even if the sun sometimes took the single period, and sometimes the double, to circle from the east and back to the east again. Let no one tell me, then, that time is simply the motion of the heavenly bodies. After all, at the prayer of a certain man the sun halted so that he could press home the battle to victory.[81] The sun stood still, but time flowed on its way, and that fight had all the time it needed to be carried through to the finish.

I see, therefore, that time is a kind of strain or tension.[82] But do I really see it? Or only seem to see? You will show me, O Light, O Truth.

24, 31. Are you commanding me to agree with someone who says that time is the motion of a body? You do not so command me. No corporeal object moves except within time: this is what I hear; this is what you tell me. But that a corporeal object's movement is itself time I do not hear; this you do not say. When a body moves, I measure in terms of time how long it is in motion, from the moment when it begins until its motion ceases. If I did not notice when it began, and it continues to move without my seeing when it stops, I cannot measure the time, except perhaps the interval between the moment when I began to watch and that when I ceased to observe it. If my observation is prolonged, I can only say that the process went on for a long time; I cannot say exactly how long, because when we add a definite indication of a length of time we do so by reference to some agreed standard. "This is as long as that," we say, or "This is twice as long as that other," or something similar. If, on the other hand, we have been able to note the position of some corporeal object when it moves (or when parts of it move, if, for example, it is being turned on a lathe), and we have observed its starting-point and its point of arrival, then we are able to state how much time has elapsed while the movement of the object was effected from the one place to the other, or how long it has taken to revolve on its axis.

Therefore if the motion of an object is one thing, and the standard by which we measure its duration another, is it not obvious which of the two has the stronger claim to be called time? Moreover, if the motion is irregular, so that the object is sometimes moving and sometimes stationary, we measure not only its motion but also its static periods in terms of time, and

---

81. See Jos 10:12-13.
82. *Distentio:* extension, but with a subjective charge of distraction or anxiety of soul, like being stretched on a rack. See 26,33 below.

say, "Its stationary periods were equivalent in length to its phases of motion," or "It was stationary for two or three times as long as it was in motion," or whatever else our calculation has ascertained or estimated roughly—more or less, as we customarily say. Clearly, then, time is not the movement of any corporeal object.

25, 32. I confess to you, Lord,[83] that even today I am still ignorant of what time is; but I praise you, Lord, for the fact that I know I am making this avowal within time, and for my realization that within time I am talking about time at such length, and that I know this "length" itself is long only because time has been passing all the while. But how can I know that, when I do not know what time is? Or perhaps I simply do not know how to articulate what I know? Woe is me, for I do not even know what I do not know!

Behold me here before you, O my God; see that I do not lie.[84] As I speak, this is the true state of my heart. You, you alone, will light my lamp, O Lord; O my God, you will illumine my darkness.[85]

Perhaps time is tension of our consciousness

26, 33. Am I not making a truthful confession to you when I praise you for my ability to measure time? But this must mean, O my God, that though I can measure it, I do not know what I am measuring! I measure the movement of a body in terms of time, but surely I am by that same calculation measuring time itself? Would it be possible for me to measure a body's motion, to calculate how long it lasts and how long the object takes to travel from here to there, without also measuring the time within which the motion occurs? With what, then, do I measure time itself? Do we measure a longer time by the standard of a shorter, as we use the cubit to measure the span of a cross-beam? That indeed seems to be how we measure the quantity of a long syllable by that of a short syllable, and decide that the former is twice as long. Similarly we measure the length of poems by the length of their lines, and the length of the lines by the length of the feet, and the length of each foot by the length of its syllables, and the length of a long syllable by that of a short syllable. We do not reckon by the

83. See Ps 9:2(1); Mt 11:25; Lk 10:21.
84. See Gal 1:20.
85. See Ps 17:29(18:28).

number of pages—that would be to impose a spatial, not a temporal standard—but by the pronunciation as voices recite them and die away. We declare, "That is a lengthy poem, for it consists of so many lines; the lines are long, since each is composed of so many feet; the feet are long, since each extends over so many syllables; and a syllable is long, when it is twice the quantity of a short one."

But the mensuration of time by these methods yields no result that is absolute, since it may happen that the sound of a shorter line, spoken with a drawl, actually lasts longer than that of a longer one hurried over. The same holds for the whole poem, a foot, and a syllable.

I have therefore come to the conclusion that time is nothing other than tension: but tension of what, I do not know, and I would be very surprised if it is not tension of consciousness itself.[86] What am I measuring, I beg you to tell me, my God, when I say in imprecise terms, "This is longer than that," or even, precisely, "This is twice that"? That I am measuring time, I know; but I am not measuring future time, because it does not yet exist, nor present time, which is a point without extension, nor past time, which exists no more. What, then, am I measuring? Time as it passes by, but not once it has passed? That was what I said earlier.[87]

27, 34. Stick to it, now, my mind, and pay close attention. God is our ally;[88] and he made us, not we ourselves.[89] Mark where truth brightens to the dawn!

Suppose now that a physical voice begins to sound ... and goes on sounding ... and is still sounding ... and now stops. Now there is silence, and that voice is past and is a voice no longer. Before it sounded forth it was a future thing, so it could not be measured because it did not yet exist; neither can it be now, because it exists no more. Perhaps, then, it could be measured while it was sounding forth, because something did then exist that could be measured? But at that time it was not standing still; it was but

---

86. Augustine's typical contribution is to locate the mystery of time within the conscious mind. Plotinus' statement that "the soul contained an unquiet faculty," something restless that by aspiring toward what seemed a fuller life than Eternity brought time into being (see *Enneads* III,7,11), has been adduced as a predecessor, but Plotinus is referring to the All-Soul, the Cosmic Soul.

87. That is, in XI,16,21;21,27.

88. See Ps 61:9(62:8).

89. See Ps 99(100):3. The allusion has special point here. Throughout the preceding argument Augustine has been exposing the self-delusory habits of thought which tempt us to deny our radical tendency to non-being, our ephemerality, by pretending to some kind of permanence. We have in reality no control over the constant "passing away" which is the law of our being. Only God, our creator, is eternal: "he made us."

a fleeting thing that was speeding on its way. Was it therefore any more measurable while sounding than before or after? Only as something transient was it extended over a period of time whereby it might be measured —only as transient, because the present moment has no duration. If it is argued that the sound could, nevertheless, be measured while it lasted, consider this: another voice begins to sound and is still sounding in a continuous, steady tone. Let us measure it, then, while it is sounding, for once it has fallen silent it will be a thing of the past, and nothing measurable will then exist. By all means let us measure it now, and state how long it lasts.

Ah, but it is still sounding, and there is no way of timing it except from its beginning, when the sound orginated, to its end, when it ceases. Obviously we measure any interval of time from some inception to some ending. Hence the sound of a voice which has not yet finished cannot be measured in such a way that anyone can say how long or how short it is, nor can it be declared to be of the same length as something else, or half the length, or twice the length, or anything of the kind. But once finished, it will not exist. So by what criteria will it then be subject to measurement?

All the same we do measure periods of time, not periods which as yet have no being, nor those which have ceased to be, nor those which have no duration, nor those which have no terminus. We measure neither future nor past nor present nor passing time. Yet time we do measure.

35. Take the line, *Deus, creator omnium.*[90] This line consists of eight syllables, short and long alternating. The four short ones—the first, third, fifth and seventh —are thus half the length of the four long ones—the second, fourth, sixth and eighth. Each of these latter lasts twice as long as each of the former; I have only to pronounce the line to report that this is the case, insofar as clear sense-perception can verify it. Relying on this unmistakable evidence of my ear I measure each long syllable by the criterion of a short one, and perceive that it is twice the quantity. But the syllables make themselves heard in succession; and if the first is short and the second long, how am I to hold on to the short one, how am I to apply it to the long one as a measuring-rod in order to discover that the long one has twice the quantity, when the long one does not begin to sound until the short one has ceased? Am I to measure the long one while it is present? Impossible, because I cannot measure something unfinished. But its

90. Ambrose's evening hymn; see IX,12,32 for a translation and indications of Augustine's affection for it.

completion is its passing away, so what now exists for me to measure? Where is the short syllable I was going to use as a standard? What has become of the long one I want to measure? Both have made their sound, and flown away, and passed by, and exist no more; yet I do my calculation and confidently assert that insofar as the testimony of my trained ear can be trusted, the short is half the long, the long twice the short; and obviously I am speaking about a space of time. I can only do this because the syllables have passed away and are completed. Evidently, then, what I am measuring is not the syllables themselves, which no longer exist, but something in my memory, something fixed and permanent there.

36. In you, my mind, I measure time. Do not interrupt me by clamoring that time has objective existence, nor hinder yourself with the hurly-burly of your impressions. In you, I say, do I measure time. What I measure is the impression which passing phenomena leave in you, which abides after they have passed by: that is what I measure as a present reality, not the things that passed by so that the impression could be formed. The impression itself is what I measure when I measure intervals of time. Hence either time is this impression, or what I measure is not time.

What about when we measure silences, and say that this silent pause lasted as long as that sound? Do we not strain our thought to retain the feeling of a sound's duration, as though it were still audible, so as to be able to estimate the intervals of silence in relation to the whole space of time in question? Without any articulate word or even opening our mouths we go over in our minds poems, their lines, a speech, and we assess their developmental patterns and the time they occupied in relation to one another; and our estimate is no different from what it would have been if we had been reciting them aloud.

Suppose a person wishes to utter a fairly long sound, and has determined beforehand in his own mind how long it is to be. He must have first thought through that period of time in silence and committed the impression of it to memory; then he begins to utter the sound, which continues until it reaches the predetermined end. Or rather, it does not "continue," because the sound is evidently both something already heard and something still to be heard, for the part of it already completed is sound that has been, but the part that remains is sound still to be. Thus it is carried through as our present awareness drags what is future into the past. As the future dwindles the past grows, until the future is used up altogether and the whole thing is past.

28, 37. But how can a future which does not yet exist dwindle or be used up, and how can a past which no longer exists grow? Only because there are three realities in the mind which conducts this operation. The mind expects, and attends, and remembers, so that what it expects passes by way of what it attends to into what it remembers. No one, surely, would deny that the future is as yet non-existent? Yet an expectation of future events does exist in the mind. And would anyone deny that the past has ceased to be? Yet the memory of past events still lives on in the mind. And who would deny that the present has no duration, since it passes in an instant? Yet our attention does endure, and through our attention what is still to be makes its way into the state where it is no more. It is not, therefore, future time which is long, for it does not exist; a long future is simply an expectation of the future which represents it as long. Nor is the past a long period of time, because it does not exist at all; a long past is simply a memory of the past which represents it as long.

38. Suppose I have to recite a poem I know by heart. Before I begin, my expectation is directed to the whole poem, but once I have begun, whatever I have plucked away from the domain of expectation and tossed behind me to the past becomes the business of my memory, and the vital energy of what I am doing is in tension between the two of them: it strains toward my memory because of the part I have already recited, and to my expectation on account of the part I still have to speak. But my attention is present all the while, for the future is being channeled through it to become the past. As the poem goes on and on, expectation is curtailed and memory prolonged, until expectation is entirely used up, when the whole completed action has passed into memory.

What is true of the poem as a whole is true equally of its individual stanzas and syllables. The same is true of the whole long performance, in which this poem may be a single item. The same thing happens in the entirety of a person's life, of which all his actions are parts; and the same in the entire sweep of human history, the parts of which are individual human lives.

Our time and God's eternity

29, 39. Because your mercy is better than many a life[91] I confess that my life is no more than anxious distraction; but in my Lord, the Son of Man, your right hand upholds me.[92] He stands as mediator between you, the one God, and us, the many,[93] who are pulled many ways by multifarious distractions. In him your right hand holds me fast, so that I may grasp that for which I have been grasped myself, and may be gathered in from dispersion in my stale days to pursue the One, forgetting the past and stretching undistracted not to future things doomed to pass away, but to my eternal goal. With no distracted mind but with focused attention I press on to the prize of our heavenly calling,[94] to that place where I yearn to hear songs of praise[95] and contemplate your delight,[96] which neither comes, nor slips away.

Now as my years waste away amid groaning[97] you are my solace, Lord, because you are my Father, and you are eternal. But I have leapt down into the flux of time where all is confusion to me. In the most intimate depths of my soul my thoughts are torn to fragments by tempestuous changes until that time when I flow into you, purged and rendered molten by the fire of your love.

30, 40. I will stand still,[98] then, and find firm footing in you, in your Truth who is shaping me to himself, and no longer will I tolerate the questions of people who, sickly under sin's punishment, crave more than they can take in. "What was God doing before he made heaven and earth?" they ask. "Why did it enter his head to make something, when he had never made anything before?" Grant them, Lord, the grace to think clearly what they are saying, and to realize that the word "never" has no meaning where time does not exist. If God is said never to have done something, that simply means that he did not do it at any time.[99] Let such people see, then, that there cannot be any time apart from creation, and stop talking

---

91. See Ps 62:4(63:3).
92. See Pss 17:36(18:35); 62:9(63:8). So time, the sign of our ephemerality which we are prone to deny, becomes the place where grace finds us in the incarnate Word.
93. See 1 Tm 2:5.
94. See Phil 3:12-14.
95. See Ps 25(26):7.
96. See Ps 26(27):4.
97. See Ps 30:11(31:10).
98. See Phil 4:1; 1 Thes 3:8.
99. That is, "before" and "after" are words expressing relationships between events within the totality of events. They have no application to anything that stands outside the totality of events altogether.

nonsense.[100] Let them even stretch their minds to what lies ahead[101] and understand that you exist before all ages of time, because you are the eternal creator of all times, and that no time is coeternal with you, nor any creature whatsoever, even if any was created outside time.[102]

31, 41. How deep is that mystery hidden in the secret recesses of your being, O Lord, my God! And how far from it have the consequences of my sins hurled me! Heal my eyes, that I may rejoice with you in your light.

It could be said with certainty that if there is anywhere a person whose mind is so richly endowed, whose knowledge and foresight are so vast, that he knows all past and all future things in the same way that I know a song that is very familiar to me, such a mind is wonderful, so amazing as to fill us with awe, since nothing that has happened and nothing still to come throughout the ages is hidden from it, even as nothing in the song I am singing is hidden from me, whatever portions of it have passed away since its opening, and whatever parts remain before its end. But far be it from us to suppose that you, the creator of the universe, creator of souls and bodies, know all things future and past in this fashion! Perish the thought! Far, far more wonderful is your mode of knowing, and far more mysterious. When a person is singing words well known to him, or listening to a familiar song, his senses are strained between anticipating sounds still to come and remembering those sung already; but with you it is quite otherwise. Nothing can happen to you in your unchangeable eternity, you who are truly the eternal creator of all minds. As you knew heaven and earth in the beginning, without the slightest modification in your knowledge, so too you made heaven and earth in the beginning without any distension in your activity.

Let anyone who understands this praise you, and anyone who does not understand it praise you no less. Oh, how high and glorious you are, who make the humble-hearted your home![103] You help the downtrodden to their feet,[104] and they do not fall, for their high dignity is yourself.

---

100. See Ps 143(144):8.
101. See Phil 3:13.
102. Augustine is thinking of the possibility that the angels may have been, a question he discusses in his *Unfinished Literal Commentary on Genesis* III,7 and *The City of God* XII,16.
103. See Ps 137(138):6; Dn 3:87; Is 57:15.
104. See Pss 144(145):14; 145(146):8.

Book XII

Heaven and Earth

1, 1. The words of your holy scripture have knocked at the door of my heart, O Lord, and in this poverty-stricken life of mine my heart is busy about many things concerning them.[1] The penury of human understanding is apt to lead to excessive wordiness, for to seek requires more talking than to find, to ask takes longer than to obtain, and the hand that knocks puts in more effort than the hand that receives. But we cling to your promise: who shall rob it of its force? If God is for us, who is against us?[2] *Ask, and you will obtain; seek, and you will find; knock, and the door will be opened to you. For everyone who asks, obtains, and the seeker will find, and to the one who knocks the door will be opened:*[3] these are your promises; and who need fear to be deceived by the promises of Truth himself?

Heaven's heaven is the spiritual creation

2, 2. My lowly tongue lauds your sublime majesty,[4] for you have made heaven and earth: this heaven which I see, and the earth on which I tread, and this frame of clay I carry—you made them all.[5] But where, Lord, is that *heaven's heaven* of which we hear in the psalm: *Heaven's heaven is for the Lord; but he has assigned the earth to humankind?*[6] Where is that heaven we cannot see, in comparison with which all we can see is but earth? This whole material world has been endowed with beauty of form even in its furthest parts, the lowest of which is our earth (though not uniformly

---

1. See Lk 10:40-42, Martha and Mary, who in a tradition followed by Augustine (Sermon 104,3,4) represent respectively the active and the contemplative lives, or the life of this world and the life in heaven. The contrast is continued in the following lines.
2. See Rom 8:31.
3. Mt 7:7-8; Lk 11:9-10; see Jn 16:24.
4. See Rom 14:11.
5. See I,6,7; IX,11,28.
6. Ps 113(115):16, relying on the LXX; the sense of the Hebrew is slightly different.

throughout, for the material world is not the same or wholly present everywhere); yet compared with *heaven's heaven* the heaven that overarches our earth is itself no better than earth. And not without good reason are those two vast realities—our earth and our sky—to be regarded as mere lowly earth beside that unimaginable heaven which is for the Lord, not for humankind.

Formless matter, the abyss

3, 3. This earth was, moreover, neither visible nor organized; it was an abyss of inconceivable depth over which no light dawned, because it had no form.[7] This is why you commanded your writer to record that *darkness loured over the abyss,*[8] for what does that mean, except complete absence of light? If light had existed, where would it have been, if not overhead, lifted on high and shedding its radiance from there over everything? So if there was as yet no light, what else can the presence of darkness signify but the mere absence of light?[9] Over it all, then, there was darkness, simply because over it all there was no light, just as there is silence where there is no sound. What does it mean to say that silence reigns, if not that sound is absent? Have you not yourself taught this soul which confesses to you, Lord, have you not taught me[10] that before you imparted form and distinction to that formless matter there was nothing—no color, no shape, no body, no spirit? Yet not nothing at all, no, not that either, for there was some kind of formlessness with no differentiation.[11]

4, 4. What could this be called? How could the meaning of that statement be conveyed to slower minds, except by some familiar expression? Nowhere in the world can anything be found more akin to total formless-

---

7. No *species*. The word is nearly equivalent to *forma*, the principle of differentiation and individuation which makes a thing what it is. Augustine has just evoked unformed matter, "invisible" because there is nothing to see where there is not distinction. The endowing of formless matter with form or *species* is thought of as particularly the action of the creative Word. But though in this paragraph Augustine evokes formless matter as existing, waiting for the Word, he is careful to note elsewhere (that is, in *The Literal Meaning of Genesis* I,15, 29) that this is a logical, not a temporal, priority: matter and form created simultaneously, as when a person speaks he utters both sound and intelligible words in the same act. See 29, 40 below.
8. Gn 1:2.
9. That is, darkness is a mere negation, not a hostile kingdom set over against the kingdom of light, as the Manichees held.
10. See Ps 70(71):17.
11. See Wis 11:18.

ness than "earth" or "the deep." Lying so far below us, they are less distinctive than other, radiant, lofty objects and all resplendent things. I am therefore justified, I think, in assuming that when the earth is said to be *invisible and unorganized*, this is a convenient way of making clear to people what formless matter is, the matter which you had created undifferentiated in order to make from it the world in all its form and distinction.

5, 5. When our thought looks for something to grasp in this, or for something the senses can apprehend, it says to itself, "There is no intelligible reality here, such as life or justice, because 'matter' belongs to bodily things; but there is no reality perceptible to the senses either, because in something *invisible and unorganized* there is nothing that can be seen or perceived." If human speculation runs on these lines, it would be well advised to aim at knowledge by way of unknowing, or be content with an ignorance that is yet a kind of knowledge.

6, 6. But for my own part, Lord, if I am to confess to you with tongue and pen all that you have taught me about this primal matter, in earlier days I heard it mentioned but failed to understand what it was, when people who were equally devoid of understanding told me about it, and I pictured it to myself under innumerable forms of all kinds, which is to say that I was not thinking of it as it truly was at all. My mind passed in review disgusting, hideous forms, distortions of the natural order, certainly, but forms nonetheless. I dubbed "formless" not something that really lacked all form, but what had a kind of form from which, if it were to appear, my gaze would turn away as from something weird and grotesque, and liable to upset weak human sensibility very badly. But what I thus imagined was not formless in the sense that it lacked all form, but formless only by comparison with other things of fairer form; and clear thinking was beginning to convince me that I must eliminate the last vestiges of form entirely if I wished to gain a notion of what true formlessness would be. And this I could not do. I would have found it easier to deem anything that entirely lacked form non-existent, than to conceive of something midway between form and nothingness, neither formed existence nor nothingness, formless and all but non-existent.

Hence my intellect gave up asking questions of my imagination, filled as this was with pictures of formed corporeal things which it could shuffle and vary at will; and I turned my attention to the bodily things themselves, and more carefully examined their mutability. They cease to be what they formerly were, and begin to be what they were not, and I came to suspect that this transition from one form to another involves passing through formlessness, rather than through absolute non-being; but I was anxious to know, and not merely suspect.

So, as I was saying, if my voice and my pen are to confess to you everything that you have disentangled for me concerning this problem, how many of my readers will have enough stamina to take it in? Still, that is no reason for my heart to withhold honor from you, or to stop singing your praises for all that it understands but cannot record here. The mutability of mutable things itself gives them their potential to receive all those forms into which mutable things can be changed. And what is this mutability? A soul? A body? The form of a soul or of a body? No; I would call it "a nothing-something" or "an is-that-is-not," if such expressions were allowed. And yet it must have had some kind of being, to be capable of receiving those visible and organized forms.

7, 7. And whence would it have any kind of being, if not from you, from whom derive all things[12] which to any degree have being? They are far from you, not by any spatial distance, but in the measure that they are unlike you; for it is you, Lord, you who vary not from one time to another, who are never inconsistent in your action from one time to another, but are Being-Itself, ever unchanging, ever the selfsame.[13] *Holy, Holy, Holy, Lord God almighty,*[14] you it is who have created something out of nothing, and created it in that Beginning who is from your very self, in your Wisdom, born of your own substance. Not from your own substance did you make heaven and earth: if you had, they would have been equal to your only-begotten Son and hence to yourself, and it would in no way have been right for them to be equal to you, these things which were not from your substance. Apart from yourself nothing existed from which you might make them, O God, undivided Trinity and threefold Unity, and therefore you made heaven and earth out of nothing—heaven and earth, a great thing and a small thing, because you are omnipotent and your goodness led you to make all good things, a mighty heaven and a tiny earth. You were; but nothing else was, from which you might make heaven and earth, two realities: one near to yourself, the other bordering on nothingness; one, to which you alone would be superior, the other, than which nothing would be lower.

---

12. See Rom 11:36; 1 Cor 8:6.
13. *Idipsum*, see IX,4,11 and the note there.
14. Is 6:3; Rv 4:8.

8, 8. But *heaven's heaven* was for you, Lord.[15] As for the earth, which you have given to us mortals to gaze upon and touch, it was not like the earth we see and touch today. It was *invisible and unorganized,* an abyss over which no light dawned; or, rather, it was a darkness overwhelming the abyss, which means it outdarkened the darkness of the deepest ocean. The abyss we know, the deep ocean of waters now visible, admits even in its most unfathomable depths some semblance of light which is perceptible to the fish and slithering creatures[16] that live down on the ocean floor; but the primal abyss was almost nothingness, for it was still totally without form, although it did exist, since it had the capacity to receive form. For you, Lord, made the world from formless matter, and that formless matter that was almost nothing at all you made from nothing at all, intending to create from it all the great things which fill us humans with wonder.

Truly marvelous is this material heaven which you established as a vault separating water from water when on the second day, after creating light, you said, *Let there be a vault,*[17] and so it came to be. You called the vault "sky," for it was to be the heaven or sky overarching our earth and sea. (These you were to make when on the third day you gave visible form to the formless matter you had made before there were any days.) You had indeed made a heaven before any day existed, but that was *heaven's heaven* far above this sky of ours; we know this because it was *in the beginning* that you *created heaven and earth.*[18] The *earth* here referred to, which you had already made, was the formless matter, invisible, unorganized and deeper than the deepest darkness; and from this invisible, unorganized earth, from this thing that was almost nothing, you were to make all these things of which our changeable world consists in its inconsistency. Its very mutability, so evident to us, makes possible our awareness and demarcation of passing times, because this is what the rolling seasons are—the changes that occur in creatures as various forms proliferate and develop. But the aforementioned invisible earth is the matter underlying all forms.

•

15. See Ps 113(115):16.
16. See Gn 1:20-22.
17. Gn 1:6.
18. Gn 1:1.

There was no time there

9, 9. This is the reason why the Spirit who instructed your servant, Moses, says nothing about time and is silent on the subject of days when he records that you made heaven and earth in the beginning. It is clear that this *heaven's heaven* which you made in the beginning is some kind of intellectual creation.[19] Participating in your eternity, though in no sense coeternal with you, O Trinity, this intellectual creation largely transcends its mutability through the intense bliss it enjoys in contemplation of you, and by holding fast to you[20] with a constancy from which it has never fallen since its first creation, it is independent of the spinning changes of time.

Not even primal formlessness, however, the invisible and unorganized earth, is mentioned in the counting of the days. Where there is no form, neither is there order, and nothing comes or passes away; and where this does not happen there are certainly no days, nor any variation between successive periods of time.[21]

10, 10. O Truth, illumination of my heart,
let not my own darkness speak to me!
I slid away to material things, sank into shadow,
yet even there, even from there, I loved you.
Away I wandered, yet I remembered you.
I heard your voice behind me,[22] calling me back,
yet scarcely heard it for the tumult of the unquiet.
See now, I come back to you,
fevered and panting for your fountain.[23]
Let no one bar my way,
let me drink it and draw life from it.
Let me not be my own life:
evil was the life I lived of myself;
I was death to myself; but in you I begin to live again.

---

19. He is thinking of angels, though his language resembles that used by Neo-Platonists of the "inferior gods."
20. See Ps 72(73):28, a favorite verse with Augustine.
21. As he showed in Book X, time only begins with the creation of mutable things. He there showed that eternity stands above all temporal succession; here he sees primal formless matter to be below it.
22. See Ez 3:12; Is 30:21.
23. See X,27,38; IX,10,23.

Speak to me yourself, converse with me.

I have believed your scriptures,

but those words are full of hidden meaning.

11, 11. Loud and clear have you spoken to me already in my inward ear, O Lord, telling me that you are eternal, and to you alone immortality belongs,[24] because no alteration of form, no motion, changes you. Nor does your will vary with changing times, for a will that can be sometimes one thing, sometimes another, is not immortal. In your sight[25] this is clear to me, but I beg you that it may grow clearer still, and in that disclosure I will prudently stand firm beneath your wings.

Again, Lord, loud and clear have you spoken to me in my inward ear, to tell me that you have made all natures and substances which are not what you are and yet have being; that alone is not from you which has no being. You have told me also that if our will moves away from you, who are, toward anything which less truly is, that movement is transgression and sin, but no one's sin either harms you or disturbs the order of your reign at any point, first or last. In your sight this is clear to me, but I beg you that it may grow clearer still, and in that disclosure I will prudently stand firm beneath your wings.

12. Loud and clear have you spoken to me once more in my inward ear, to tell me that no creature is coeternal with you, not even a created being whose entire pleasure is in you alone. Drinking deeply from you in unswerving fidelity, such a creature shows no trace of mutability at any point, for it is bound fast by the whole strength of its love to you, who are always present to it; and having nothing to expect in the future, nor any memories to relegate to the past, it is neither affected by change nor a prey to distended consciousness. How blessed is such a creature, if any such there be! Its beatitude is to hold fast to your beatitude, its blessedness to have you as its everlasting guest and enlightener. Nothing can I find that I would more readily call *heaven's heaven, which belongs to the Lord* than this your household, which contemplates your entrancing beauty, never tiring, never turning aside to any other joy. This pure mind builds up your family of holy, spiritual beings, united in perfect concord on the founda-

---

24. See 1 Tm 6:16.
25. See Ps 18:15(19:14).

tion of peace; it is the mind of all the citizens of your holy city in that heaven above the heaven we see.[26]

13. If a soul has been on a long journey,[27] how can it know whether it yet thirsts for you, whether yet its tears have become its daily bread as every day it hears the taunt, *Where is your God?*[28] How can it know whether yet it has but one plea to make to you, that it may dwell in your house all the days of its life?[29] And what is its life, but yourself? And what are your days but your eternity; what else are they but your years that fail not, because you are ever the same?[30] Your household has never journeyed to any far country, and though it is not coeternal with you, yet by holding fast to you unceasingly and without wavering it suffers none of the vicissitudes of time; from this let any soul capable of grasping it learn how far above all temporal change are you, the eternal. In your sight this is clear to me, but I beg you that it may grow clearer still, and in that disclosure I will prudently stand firm beneath your wings.

14. It is quite evident now that in the alterations to which creatures of the last and lowest degree are subject there is some kind of formlessness. Who, except someone who wanders amid the foolish notions of his own mind and is whirled about by his fantasies, who, I ask, except such a person, will tell me that when all form is diminished and reduced to nothing, and all that remains is the formlessness through which a being passed as it was changed from one form into another, any temporal succession can still be found? Such a thing is entirely impossible, because there is no time where there is no variation or movement, and no variation where no form exists.

Summary of foregoing remarks on spiritual and material creation

12, 15. In the light of these considerations, O my God, I observe insofar as you enable me and urge me to knock, and open to my knocking,[31] that you made two kinds of creatures which are unaffected by the passage of time, although neither is coeternal with you. One was so formed that

26. See Eph 2:19; 4:3.
27. See Lk 15:13; the prodigal son reappears.
28. Ps 41:3,4,11(42:2,3,10).
29. See Ps 26(27):4.
30. See Ps 101:28(102:27).
31. See Mt 7:7-8; Lk 11:9-10.

without any slackening in its contemplation, without any intervening period of change, and without suffering any mutation in itself in spite of its mutability, it finds its total fulfillment in your eternal immutability. The other was created so formless that it lacked all capacity to be changed from one form to another, whether of motion or of rest, and so become subject to time.

But you did not leave it to its formlessness, because these two things I have mentioned, heaven and earth, were what you made before all days, in the beginning. *The earth was invisible and unorganized, and darkness loured over the abyss.*[32] These words suggest formlessness, so that the truth may gradually lay hold on the minds of those who are unable to think of an absolute privation of all form without pushing the idea to nothingness. From this formlessness were to be made another heaven and the visible, organized earth, and the beauty of fully formed water, and whatever else would thereafter constitute our world. In the making of this world a succession of days is mentioned, because the nature of these things is such that temporal succession is needed in their case to bring about ordered modifications of motion or form.

13, 16. This, then, is the view I take at present, O my God, when I hear your scripture declare, *In the beginning God made heaven and earth; but the earth was invisible and unorganized, and darkness loured over the abyss,* without mentioning that you made them on any particular day in a series. I take this view provisionally for two reasons: first, on account of *heaven's heaven,* that intellectual heaven where it is the prerogative of intelligence to know all at once, not partially, nor in riddles, nor as reflected in a mirror, but totally, in open manifestation, face to face;[33] not needing to know one thing, then another, but knowing all at once, as I have said, without any succession of time; and secondly on account of the invisible and unorganized earth, where also there was no succession of time, for succession implies that one thing is followed by another, and where there is no form there cannot be any question of one thing, then another.

My present view, then, is that it was on account of these two realities—the one formed from the very first and the other formless through and through, the one a heaven, but a heaven above our heavens, the other an earth, but an earth invisible and unorganized—on account of these two

---

32. Gn 1:2.
33. See 1 Cor 13:12.

it was that your scripture states, without mentioning days, *In the beginning God made heaven and earth;* for it immediately adds a line to show what "earth" it means. And by recording that on the second day a vault was established and called "heaven" or "sky,"[34] it indicates of what heaven it had been speaking before it began to count the days.

Some people disagree with me about the spiritual and material creation

14, 17. How amazing is the profundity of your words! We are confronted with a superficial meaning that offers easy access to the unlettered; yet how amazing their profundity, O my God, how amazingly deep they are! To look into that depth makes me shudder, but it is the shudder of awe, the trembling of love. I regard with intense hatred all who attack the scriptures;[35] if only you would slay them with your double-edged sword,[36] that they might be enemies no longer! How dearly would I love them to be slain in that respect, that they might live to you!

There are others, however, who, so far from carping at the Book of Genesis, speak highly of it. "The Spirit of God, who caused those verses to be written by his servant, Moses," these people declare, "did not intend to convey that meaning. No, he did not intend us to understand them in the way you have explained, but differently, according to our interpretation." You must be the judge, you, the God of us all, as I reply to them as follows.[37]

15, 18. You will surely not claim that everything Truth told me so loudly in my inward ear concerning the eternity of the creator was false? Can it be untrue that his substance varies not one whit throughout time, and that his will is not separate from his substance? From that I infer that he does not first will something, then something else; whatever he wills, he wills once only and all together and eternally, not in repetitive fashion, nor this today and that tomorrow, nor willing later what he did not will previously, nor

---

34. See Gn 1:7-8.
35. See Ps 138(139):21-22.
36. See Ps 149:6; Heb 4:12.
37. From this point Augustine argues with Catholic interpreters whose understanding differs from his own.

going back later on what he wanted earlier. A will like that is subject to change, and anything changeable is not eternal; but our God is eternal.[38]

Another thing that he imparts to my inward ear is that our expectation of future events turns into direct attention to them when they come to pass, and this attention becomes memory when they have passed away. Now it is obvious that any awareness which varies like this is mutable, and nothing mutable is eternal, whereas our God is eternal.

These are the truths I gather, and by combining them I discover that my God, the eternal God, did not bring creation into being by some new act of will, nor is his knowledge subject to any impermanence.

19. Well, my opponents, what have you to say to that? Are these statements incorrect? "No," they say. What does that mean? You surely are not going to accuse me of error when I claim that every formed nature, and all matter capable of receiving form, is from him alone who is supremely good, and supremely exists? "We do not dispute that either," they reply. What is your objection, then? Would you deny that there is a sublime order of creation which by pure love clings so closely to the true God, the truly eternal God, that, even though not coeternal with him, it never loosens its grip or slips away from him into any temporal succession or the vicissitudes of time, but rests in utterly real contemplation of him alone? You, O God, show yourself to anyone who loves you according to your bidding, and are wholly sufficient to him,[39] so that such a one turns not aside from you or to himself. This order of creation is God's house,[40] neither terrestrial nor some massive celestial building, but a spiritual structure which shares your eternity, and is unstained for ever. You have established it to last for ever, and your ordinance will not pass away.[41] Yet it is not coeternal with you, for it did have a beginning: it was created.

20. Before its creation we find no mention of time, for wisdom is known to be the eldest of all created things.[42] The wisdom here referred to is obviously not the Wisdom who is fully coeternal with you, his Father, who are our God, and equal to you;[43] no, not that Wisdom through whom all things

38. See Ps 47(48):15.
39. See Jn 14:8-9, 21.
40. See Ps 26(27):4.
41. See Ps 148:6.
42. See Sir 1:1-5.
43. See Phil 2:6.

were created,[44] not that Beginning in whom you made heaven and earth. The wisdom of which I speak is a created wisdom, the intellectual order of being which by contemplating the Light becomes light itself. Wisdom it is called, but it is a created wisdom, and as there is a vast difference between Light as source and that which is lit up by another,[45] the difference is just as great between Wisdom that creates and the wisdom that has been created. A comparable gulf exists between the justice that justifies us and the justice created in us by that act of justification, which is why even we are said to be "your justice" in the words of a certain servant of yours: *so that in him we might become the justice of God.*[46] Well then, the first of all creatures was wisdom understood in this way, created wisdom, which is the rational, intelligent mind of your chaste city. That city on high is our mother, and she is free[47] and eternal in heaven[48]—and what heaven can that be, if not the *heaven's heaven* which praises you, *heaven's heaven* which belongs to the Lord?[49] We find no mention of time prior to this wisdom, since what was created before all else necessarily precedes time, which is also a creature; but it is preceded by the eternity of the creator himself. From him came its origin: not a temporal beginning, for time did not yet exist, but the dawn of its creation.

21. It therefore derives its being from you, our God, in such a way that it is entirely different from you; it is not Being-Itself.[50] Not only before it came to be, but even in its life, we find no time, because it has the capacity to look upon your face always[51] and never turns its gaze away. Accordingly no change or variation affects it; but all the same it contains within it a potential for change which would cause it to darken and grow cold, did it not cling to you with immense love, shining with your light like noonday never dimmed and burning with your fire.

O lightsome house, so fair of form, I have fallen in love with your beauty, loved you as the place where dwells the glory of my Lord,[52] who fashioned you and claims you as his own. My pilgrim-soul sighs for you,

---

46. See Col 1:16.
47. Similar language in Plotinus, *Enneads* IV,3,17;V,3,8.
48. 2 Cor 5:21.
49. See Gal 4:26.
48. See 2 Cor 5:1.
49. See Pss 148:4; 113(115):16.
50. See IX,4,11; 10,24; XII,7,7.
51. See Mt 18:10.
52. See Ps 25(26):8.

and I pray him who made you to claim me also as his own within you, for he made me too. Like a lost sheep I have gone astray,[53] but on the shoulders of my shepherd, your builder, I hope to be carried back to you.[54]

22. Now, my opponents, you whom I was addressing, those of you at least who believe that Moses was God's trusty servant and that his books are the utterance of the Holy Spirit, what have you to say? Does such a house of God exist, not indeed coeternal with God, yet in its own way eternal in heaven,[55] in which you will look in vain for temporal succession, because nothing of the kind is to be found there? For any creature which finds its good in always holding fast to God[56] transcends all distension of being and all the fleeting passage of time. "Yes, it does exist," they say.

Which point, then, do you allege to be false out of those which my heart cried out to my God as it listened to his praises resounding within it? Do you dispute my statement that there was unformed matter, and that where no form existed there was no order? But where there was no order, neither could there be any succession of periods of time. Yet this thing that was almost nothing derived from him insofar as it was not quite nothing, because whatever is, whatever in any fashion exists, is from him. "We do not dispute this either," they say.

Augustine's response to those who disagree

16, 23. In your presence, O my God, I want to discuss some matters with those who acknowledge as true what your Truth never ceases to tell me within my own mind. As for the people who will not concede this, they may bark as much as they please until they deafen themselves; I will merely attempt to persuade them to be quiet, and so open a way by which your word may reach them. If they refuse and rebuff me, I beg you, my God, not to answer me with silence.[57] Speak to me yourself within my heart in truth, for you alone speak so. Then I will get rid of those people

---

53. See Ps 118(119):176.
54. See Lk 15:4-5.
55. See 2 Cor 5:1.
56. See Ps 72(73):28.
57. See Ps 27(28):1.

who blow into the dust only to stir up earth and get it into their eyes;[58] then let me retire to my private room[59] and sing my songs of love to you, giving vent to my inarticulate groans[60] as I walk my pilgrim way, remembering Jerusalem and lifting up my heart[61] toward her. To her would I stretch out, to Jerusalem my homeland, Jerusalem my mother,[62] and to you who are her ruler, her illuminator, Father, guardian and husband, her chaste, intense delight, her unshakable joy: to you who are the fullness of good things beyond all telling, and all good things at once, because you are the one supreme and true Good. Let me not waver from my course before you have gathered all that I am, my whole disintegrated and deformed self, into that dearly loved mother's peace, where are lodged the first-fruits of my spirit,[63] and whence I draw my present certainty, so that you may reshape me to new form, new firmness, for eternity, O my God, my mercy.[64]

To those, however, do I address myself in the following lines, who do not decry all these true statements as errors, but respect your holy scripture, written through the agency of holy Moses, and attribute to it, as we do, the loftiest normative authority, but who contradict us nonetheless on certain points. Do you, our God, stand as arbiter between my confessions and their contradictions.

17, 24. "Although your assertions are true," they say, "it was not those two realities that Moses had in mind when in response to the revealing Spirit he said, *In the beginning God made heaven and earth.* By the name *heaven* he did not mean to indicate the spiritual or intellectual creation which unceasingly contemplates the face of God,[65] nor did he indicate formless matter by the name *earth.*"

What, then?

"What we say is what the author meant," they reply. "We can explain what he enunciated in those words."

And what is that?

---

58. Apparently a metaphor derived from the circus, but possibly also an ironic allusion to God's creative act of breathing into dust at Gn 2:7, destructively parodied by the opponents Augustine is attacking.

59. See Mt 6:6.

60. See Rom 8:26.

61. This familiar phrase, "Lift up your hearts," was in use in the liturgy from at least the mid-third century; see Cyprian, *On the Lord's Prayer* 31. Augustine occasionally used it as a shorthand (and deliberately discreet) way of referring to the whole eucharistic liturgy.

62. See Gal 4:26.

63. See IX,10,24.

64. See Ps 58:18(59:17).

65. See Mt 18:10.

"By *heaven and earth* he intended to signify this whole visible world in brief and comprehensive terms first of all," they say, "so that afterward, by means of a series of days, he could enumerate one by one all those things which it pleased the Holy Spirit to have mentioned separately in this way. The race to whom he was speaking was crude and of carnal disposition; they were the kind of people to whom he judged it impossible to convey an idea of any works of God other than visible ones."

With regard to the invisible and unorganized earth and the dark abyss, from which in the next verse the whole array of visible things familiar to all of us are shown to be created and assigned to their places, these objectors agree that it is not unreasonable to understand this as formless matter.

25. What now of another opinion, which holds that the terms *heaven* and *earth* are used by anticipation to mean this same formless, confused matter? It can be called by these names because from it were created and perfected our visible world, with all its assortment of beings so plainly evident, this world which in customary speech is often called "heaven and earth."

Another view again is that both invisible and visible nature are quite appropriately styled *heaven and earth*, and that under these two names is comprised the entire universe which God made in his Wisdom, that is, in the Beginning. According to this opinion the terms *heaven* and *earth* are used by anticipation to indicate the still formless matter which is common to all things, both invisible and visible; this usage is justified because all these creatures were made not from God's own substance but out of nothing; they are not Being-Itself like God[66] and a certain mutability is inherent in all of them, whether they abide, as does the eternal house of God, or suffer change, as do the human soul and body. From this primal matter, still formless but undoubtedly capable of receiving form, heaven and earth were to be made, that is, both invisible and visible creation in their formed state. Under this double name, however, are included both the *invisible and unorganized earth* and the *darkness louring over the abyss*, but with this distinction: the invisible and unorganized earth is understood to be corporeal matter before it received the distinguishing qualities of form, while the darkness lowering over the deep stands for spiritual matter before its impetuous flux was restrained and it was illumined by wisdom. So runs the theory: what are we to make of it?

---

66. See IX,4,11;10,24; XII,7,7.

26. Anyone so minded might advance yet another opinion, namely that when we read *In the beginning God made heaven and earth*, the words do not refer to invisible and visible natures already perfect and formed, but to the still unformed seeds of things, the matter capable of being formed and created, because in it were potentially present, though mingled confusedly, and not yet distinguished by qualities and forms, all those things which are now distributed in their various ranks, the spiritual and the corporeal creation which we now call, respectively, heaven and earth.

The author's intention must be sought, in charity

18, 27. Having listened to all these divergent opinions and weighed them, I do not wish to bandy words, for that serves no purpose except to ruin those who listen.[67] The law is an excellent thing for building us up provided we use it lawfully, because its object is to promote the charity which springs from a pure heart, a good conscience and unfeigned faith,[68] and I know what were the twin precepts on which our Master made the whole law and the prophets depend.[69] If I confess this with burning love, O my God, O secret light of my eyes,[70] what does it matter to me that various interpretations of those words are proffered, as long as they are true? I repeat, what does it matter to me if what I think the author thought is different from what someone else thinks he thought? All of us, his readers, are doing our utmost to search out and understand the writer's intention, and since we believe him to be truthful, we do not presume to interpret him as making any statement that we either know or suppose to be false. Provided, therefore, that each person tries to ascertain in the holy scriptures the meaning the author intended, what harm is there if a reader holds an opinion which you, the light of all truthful minds, show to be true, even though it is not what was intended by the author, who himself meant something true, but not exactly that?[71]

---

67. See 2 Tm 2:14.
68. See 1 Tm 1:4-5, 8.
69. See Mt 22:40.
70. See Ps 37:11(38:10).
71. Augustine's recognition that meanings other than those intended by the writer can legitimately be discovered in the sacred text is grounded in his conviction that the God of truth who inspired the writer and guarantees the text abides also in the minds of believing readers, and that though

19, 28. True it is, Lord, that you made heaven and earth. And it is true that your Wisdom, in whom you made all things,[72] is the Beginning. It is also true that this visible world consists of the great regions we call heaven and earth, and that these names, "heaven" and "earth," can be used as a brief, compendious phrase to connote all the natural things made and created within them. Again, it is true that every changeable thing suggests to us the notion of a certain formlessness, whereby that creature can receive form, or can be changed and transformed into something else. It is true that any being which holds fast to immutable form with such constancy that, though changeable in itself, it does not change, is not subject to variations of time. It is also true that formlessness, which is close to nothingness, cannot experience any passage of time either. It is true that a substance from which something else is made can by a certain convention of speech be given proleptically the name of the thing which is to issue from it: hence the formless matter from which heaven and earth were made could have been called "heaven and earth." It is true that, out of all formed creatures, nothing is nearer to formlessness than earth and the deep. It is true that you, from whom all things come,[73] made not only what is created and formed, but also matter with the potential to be created and formed. It is true that anything which is formed from what is unformed is formless first, and then formed.[74]

20, 29. All these valid points of view are available to people who entertain no doubts about their truth because you have granted them the grace to discern these matters with the inner eye, and they believe unwaveringly that your servant Moses spoke in a truthful spirit.[75] On the basis of these agreed truths, then, one person picks out one meaning to explain the words, *In the beginning God made heaven and earth*, and says, "This means that in his Word, coeternal with himself, God made both intelligible and sensible creation, or spiritual and corporeal." Another chooses differently: "*In the beginning God made heaven and earth* means that in his Word, coeternal with himself, God made the whole vast bulk of this corporeal world, together with all the array of natures known to us which it

God makes use of human words, they are never adequate fully to express his mystery; there is always a "plus" of meaning.

72. See Ps 103(104):24.
73. See Rom 11:36; 1 Cor 8:6.
74. That is, according to logical, not temporal, priority; see XII,29,40 and the note at XII,3,3.
75. Or "in the Spirit of Truth"; see Jn 14:17.

contains." Another adopts a different interpretation again: "*In the beginning God created heaven and earth* means that in his Word, coeternal with himself, he made the formless matter underlying his spiritual and material creation." Another view is taken by the one who says, "*In the beginning God made heaven and earth* means that in his Word, coeternal with himself, God made the formless matter of his corporeal creation; contained within it in a still confused state were the heaven and earth which in this vast world we now perceive as distinct and formed." Yet another takes the view that "*In the beginning God made heaven and earth* simply means that at the very inception of his making and working God made that formless matter which contained heaven and earth in a confused state, and from it they now stand forth plain to see, together with all that is in them."

21, 30. The situation is the same with regard to our understanding of the words that follow. Confronted by all the true interpretations I have listed, each of us chooses differently to explain the next verse, *The earth was invisible and unorganized, and darkness loured over the abyss.* One says, "It means that God's corporeal creation was still only the formless matter whence corporeal things would come; it was still devoid of order and lacked light." Another makes a different choice: "*The earth was invisible and unorganized, and darkness loured over the abyss* means that this totality which is called heaven and earth was still formless, dark matter, but from it the corporeal heaven and the corporeal earth would emerge, together with all the beings within them which our corporeal senses recognize." Another prefers the explanation: "*The earth was invisible and unorganized, and darkness loured over the abyss* means that this totality, here called heaven and earth, was still unformed, dark matter, but from it were to be made the intelligible heaven (elsewhere called *heaven's heaven*[76]) and the earth, that is, the whole of corporeal nature, including our material sky; thus the entire creation, both invisible and visible, would be made from it." Another selects the interpretation which says, "*The earth was invisible and unorganized, and darkness loured over the abyss* suggests that scripture did not assign the names 'heaven' and 'earth' to that unformed matter, but the formlessness, it says, was there, and it called this formlessness an invisible, unorganized earth and a dark abyss. From this formless matter it had already told us that God made

---

76. See Ps 113(115):16.

heaven and earth, that is, his spiritual and corporeal creation." Another holds that *"The earth was invisible and unorganized, and darkness loured over the abyss* means that the formlessness was already a kind of matter, from which, as scripture has told us in the preceding verse, God made heaven and earth, that is, the entire corporeal mass of the world, divided into two great regions, an upper and a lower, together with all the familiar, everyday creatures within them."

22, 31. It may be that someone will attempt to undermine the last two positions mentioned by arguing as follows: "If you will not allow that this formless matter should seem to be given the name 'heaven' and 'earth,' you will have to admit that there must have been something which God had not made, something from which he was going to make heaven and earth; for scripture does not relate that God made this prime matter, unless we take it to be covered by the phrase 'heaven' and 'earth,' or 'earth' alone, when we are told, *In the beginning God made heaven and earth.* Although when the following verse states that *the earth was invisible and unorganized*, the writer may have chosen so to designate formless matter, we have no right to understand 'earth' in this verse any differently from the earth which God is said to have made in the preceding verse: *he made heaven and earth.*"

When the proponents of the two views we put last on our list (or of one or the other of them) hear this objection, they will reply, "We certainly do not deny that this primal matter was made by God. From God come all things that are exceedingly good,[77] and just as we declare what is created and formed to be better, so too we acknowledge that what has the potential to be created and formed is less good, but good all the same. Now scripture does not record that God made this formless matter, but neither does it record that he made many other things—the cherubim and seraphim,[78] for instance, and the other ranks which the apostle specifically mentions: *thrones, sovereignties, authorities and powers;*[79] and it is self-evident that God made all these. Moreover, if the words, *he made heaven and earth,* are taken to be a complete statement, what are we to say of the waters over which the Spirit of God hovered? For if they are to be understood as included when 'earth' is named, how can the same word, 'earth,' mean

---

77. See Gn 1:31.
78. See Gn 3:24; Is 37:16; 6:2.
79. Col 1:16.

formless matter, when the waters we see are so fairly formed? Or, if we do accept that 'earth' means formless matter, why does scripture say that out of this same formlessness a vault was fashioned and called 'sky,' without saying that the waters were made? They are not still formless and invisible, these waters that we watch flowing and formed so fair. Or, if it is alleged that they received their form only when God said, *Let the water below the vault be gathered into one place,*[80] so that this gathering itself would be their endowment with form, what is to be said of the waters above the vault?[81] They could not have been worthy of so honorable a station if they were still unformed, yet scripture says nothing of any word spoken to give form to them. We must conclude, then, that if Genesis is silent about God's making something, still a healthy faith and clear intellect are in no doubt that God did make it. No sane teaching will presume to claim that because we hear those waters mentioned in Genesis, but find no mention of their being made, we should on those grounds suppose them coeternal with God. Why then should we not by the same token understand, under Truth's tutelage, that formless matter too—the formless matter which this verse of scripture calls an *invisible and unorganized earth* and a *dark abyss*—was made by God out of nothing and is therefore not coeternal with him? And should we not understand it thus even though the account has omitted to say when formless matter was made?"

23, 32. I have listened to these arguments and examined them insofar as my weakness permits—the weakness I confess to you, my God, though you know it—and I observe that two kinds of disagreement may arise when something is announced by truthful informants through signs.[82] One is when the dispute is about the facts themselves, the other when it concerns the intention of the person who announces them. It is one thing to seek the truth about the making of the created universe, and another to inquire what Moses, that most excellent servant in your household of faith,[83] wished his reader or hearer to understand from his words. With regard to the former, I will have no truck with any who think they know things which are in fact untrue. With regard to the latter, neither will I have anything to do with those who think that Moses could have said what is

80. Gn 1:9.
81. See Gn 1:7.
82. That is, words, which are a kind of signs, as he remarks in *The Teacher* II,4.
83. See Heb 3:5.

untrue. But as for those who feed on your truth in the wide pastures of charity,[84] let me be united with them in you, and in you find my delight in company with them. Let us approach the words of your book together, and there seek your will as expressed through the will of your servant, by whose pen you have dispensed your words to us.

24, 33. A great variety of interpretations, many of them legitimate, confronts our exploring minds as we search among these words to discover your will. Is there any one of us who is so sure of having found it that he can declare with as much confidence that Moses meant this or that in his narrative, as that so-and-so is true, whether Moses meant that or something different? For see, my God: I am your servant;[85] I have dedicated this writing to you as my sacrificial confession, and I pray that by your mercy I may fulfill my vows to you;[86] see now with how much confidence I assert that you made all things, invisible and visible, in your immutable Word. But am I prepared to state so confidently that Moses intended nothing else but this when he wrote, *In the beginning God made heaven and earth*? In your truth I see that this is certain, but I do not see with equal certainty into his mind, so as to be sure that he was thinking this when he wrote the words. It is possible that when he wrote, *In the beginning*, he meant simply "at the very outset of the creative process." Again, he could have wished us to understand "heaven and earth" in this context not as any already formed and perfect nature, whether spiritual or corporeal, but as both kinds in an inchoate and still unformed condition. I see indeed that, whichever of these was being stated, it could have been stated truly; but I do not see which of them was in his mind when he wrote the words. I have no doubt, however, that whether his mental gaze was directed to one of these meanings, or to some other which I have not recorded, a man of such stature will have seen what was true and expressed it fittingly.

25, 34. Let no one henceforth try to pick a quarrel with me[87] by telling me, "Moses did not mean what you say; he meant what I say." If instead the objector had asked, "How do you know that Moses intended the meaning that you get out of his words?" I would be obliged to meet the

---

84. See Eph 3:18-19.
85. See Ps 115(116):16.
86. See Ps 115(116):18.
87. See Gal 6:17.

challenge calmly, and I would perhaps reply on the lines I have already indicated, or somewhat more fully if he proved stubborn. But when he says, "He did not mean what you say, but what I say," yet does not deny that what each of us says is true, then, O life of the poor, O my God, in whose tender embrace there is no contradiction, then rain down gentleness into my heart, that I may patiently put up with such people, who say this to me not because they are godlike and have seen what they assert in the heart of your servant, but because they are proud, and without having grasped Moses' idea they are infatuated with their own, not because it is true but because it is theirs. Were this not the case they would look with equal favor on a valid opinion held by someone else, just as I am favorably disposed to what they say when they talk good sense, not because the exegesis is theirs but because it is true. Indeed, once it is true, it is no longer their property. If they love it because it is true, then it belongs to me as well as to them, because it is a common bounty for all lovers of truth.

But when they contend that Moses did not mean what I say, but what they say, I reject their claim and have no time for it, because even if what they say is correct, so reckless an assertion is a mark of presumption, not of knowledge; it is the fruit of no vision but of conceit.

This is why we must tremble before your judgments, O Lord, for your Truth is not mine, nor his, nor hers, but belongs to all of us whom you call to share it in communion with him, at the same time giving us the terrible warning not to arrogate truth to ourselves as private property, lest we find ourselves deprived of it.[88] For anyone who appropriates what you provide for all to enjoy, and claims as his own what belongs to all, is cast out from this commonwealth, cast out to what is truly his own, which is to say from the truth to a lie; for anyone who lies is speaking from what is his own.[89]

35. Pay heed, O God, most excellent judge, you who are very Truth, pay heed to what I am going to say to this man who contradicts me; pay heed, for I say it in your presence and in that of my brethren, who make lawful use of the law for the promotion of charity;[90] pay heed, and mark what I shall say to him, if this finds favor with you. The brotherly, irenic reply I will offer him is this: "If we both see that what you say is true, and we both

88. See 1 Tm 6:5.
89. See Jn 8:44, though Augustine's argument strictly requires the invented sense: "When he speaks from what is his own, he is lying."
90. See 1 Tm 1:8.5.

see that what I say is true, where do we see it? I certainly do not see it in you, nor do you in me; we both see it in the immutable truth itself which towers above our minds.[91] Since, then, we do not argue about that light of the Lord our God, why should we argue about the thought in the mind of our neighbor? We cannot see that, for it is not available to us in the way that unchangeable truth offers itself to us to be seen; even if Moses himself appeared to us and said, 'This is what was in my mind,' we still should not see his thought; we would only believe him. Let us not *go beyond what is written, inflated with pride and playing one off against another.*[92] Rather let us love the Lord our God with our whole heart, our whole soul and our whole mind, and our neighbor as ourselves.[93] Unless we believe that Moses meant whatever he did mean in his books with an eye to those twin commandments of charity, we shall make the Lord out to be a liar,[94] by attributing to our fellow-servant a purpose which is at odds with the Lord's teaching. Since, then, so rich a variety of highly plausible interpretations can be culled from those words, consider how foolish it is rashly to assert that Moses intended one particular meaning rather than any of the others. If we engage in hurtful strife as we attempt to expound his words, we offend against the very charity for the sake of which he said all those things."

"If I had been Moses"

26, 36. All the same, O my God, you who lift up my lowliness, who are rest amid my labor, who hear my confessions and forgive my sins,[95] you command me to love my neighbor as myself, and in view of that precept I cannot believe that Moses, your devotedly faithful servant, received a meaner gift than I would have hoped and desired should be given to me, had I been born at the time he was and put by you in precisely the same place, so that my heart and tongue might dispense those writings which would benefit all nations so long afterward, and would by their eminent authority, acknowledged throughout the world, subjugate all erroneous,

---

91. See X, 26, 37.
92. 1 Cor 4:6.
93. See Mt 22:37-39; Mk 12:30-31; Lk 10:27.
94. See 1 Jn 1:10; 5:10.
95. See Mt 6:15; Mk 11:25.

proud doctrines. I would have wanted, had I been Moses at that time —well, we all come from the same lump of clay after all,[96] and is any human being anything, except because you are mindful of him?—as[97] I say, if I had been in his place then, and the task of writing the Book of Genesis had been laid upon me, I would have wished that such a gift of eloquence should be given me, and such skill in weaving words, that readers unable to understand how God creates would not reject what I said as too difficult for them, while those who could already understand it, whatever might be the true idea they had arrived at by their own reasoning, should not find that their idea had been overlooked in your servant's few words. Finally I would hope to have written in such a way that if anyone else had in the light of truth seen some other valid meaning, that too should not be excluded, but present itself as a possible way of understanding in what I had said.

How fruitful are these verses of Genesis!

27, 37. A spring wells up in quite a small space, yet by means of its branching streams it is a source of richer fertility, and waters wider tracts of countryside, than can any one of the derivative streams alone, far though this may flow from its parent fount. So too the steward you entrusted[98] with the telling of your story confined his message within a small compass, yet this narrative, destined to supply a theme for many messengers of the word, is a spring whence rivers of limpid truth gush forth. Everyone draws for himself whatever truth he can from it about these questions, each a different point, and then hauls his discovery through the meandering channels of his own discourse, which are somewhat longer.

On reading or hearing the scriptural words some people think of God in the guise of a man, or as some huge being possessed of immense power, who arrived at a sudden new decision to make heaven and earth outside himself, as though located at a distance from him, and made them like two vast solid structures, above and below, within which everything would be contained. And when they hear, *God said, Let there be ...* whatever it is,

---

96. See Rom 9:21.
97. See Ps 8:5(4).
98. See Ti 1:7.

and this thing *came to be*, they think his words began and ended, echoing through a space of time and then fading away, and that as soon as they were finished the object God had ordered to exist sprang into existence. And many similar notions fill their minds, derived from life in the flesh, to which they are accustomed. Such people are still children with their carnal outlook,[99] but while their weakness is cradled in scripture's humble mode of discourse as though in their mother's arms, their faith is being built up for salvation, since they hold it as certain and firmly believe that God made all those natural things which their senses observe all round them in amazing variety. If any one of these people should disdain this mode of expression as not grand enough, and in his feeble pride lean out of the nest where he was reared—alas, he will fall, poor wretch! Have pity on him, Lord God, lest passers-by trample on the unfledged squab; send your angel to put him back in the nest, that he may survive until he is ready to fly.[100]

28, 38. There are others for whom these words are no longer a nest. For them they are shady thickets in which they espy hidden fruit; they fly to and fro joyfully, chattering as they search it out, and plucking it. When they read or hear these words they perceive that all past and future eons of time are transcended by your steadfast permanence, O eternal God, but that nonetheless there is no creature subject to time which you have not made. Your will is identical with yourself, and you made all things by no change of will whatever, without the emergence of any volition which had not previously been present. You made them all, not from your own substance, in that image of yourself that gives form to all things, but out of nothing, as formless matter quite unlike yourself, which was yet destined to be formed through your image by returning to you, the One,[101] in proportion to the capacity of each, as imparted to it according to its kind. Thus they would become exceedingly good,[102] whether they remain closely grouped about you or, arrayed in ever-widening circles

---

99. See 1 Cor 3:1-3; 2:14.
100. For the "nest" of the Church, see IV,16,31. In Sermon 51,5,6, Augustine congratulates his hearers: "How safely and securely you learn, you who are still baby chicks in the nest of the faith, and are fed on spiritual food! I was not so lucky. Thinking myself ready to fly, I left the nest, only to fall instead of flying. But the merciful Lord picked me up to save me from being trampled to death by passers-by, and restored me to the nest."
101. This language recalls the Neo-Platonists' idea of "return to the One," correlative to their doctrine of emanation; see Plotinus, *Enneads* III,8,10.
102. See Gn 1:31.

through time and space, they bring about changes or themselves beautifully evolve. All these things do such people perceive, and they rejoice
over them in the light of your truth, to the limited degree possible here
below.

39. Another interpreter concentrates on the words, *In the beginning
God made ...* and prefers to think of Wisdom as the Beginning, because
Wisdom also speaks to us.[103] Another again concentrates on the same
words, but understands "beginning" to mean the first stage in the creation
of things, and so takes *In the beginning God made ...* to mean simply, "He
first made...."

Among those who understand *In the beginning ...* to be a statement that
you made heaven and earth in Wisdom, one will hold that when the text
says "heaven and earth" it is the formless matter with the potential to be
created into heaven and earth that is so designated; another will take the
words to mean natures already formed and distinct; another will read there
that one nature, the spiritual, was already formed, and called "heaven," but
that by the name "earth" we should understand the other, unformed nature
of corporeal matter.

As for those who take the names "heaven and earth" to signify the still
unformed matter from which heaven and earth were to be formed, even
they do not agree. One understands the formless matter to be that from
which both intelligible and sensible creatures would come; another thinks
that it means that from which would emerge only this vast corporeal mass
perceptible to our senses, enfolding in its huge bosom all these natures so
evident and accessible to us.

Nor is there unanimity among those who believe that in this text it is
creatures already deployed and assigned to their places that are referred to
as "heaven and earth," for one takes it to mean both invisible and visible
creation, but another the visible creation only, in which we look up at a
luminous sky from a dark earth, and all the beings within them.

29, 40. Anyone, however, who takes *In the beginning God made ...* to
mean nothing more than "He first made ... " has no coherent way of understanding "heaven and earth" except as the primal matter from which
heaven and earth were to be formed, which is to say the primal matter of
the whole universe, of all creation both intelligible and corporeal; for if
this person argues that "heaven and earth" means the universe already

---

103. See Jn 8:25, and Augustine's development of this at XI,8,10.

formed, we have the right to ask him, "If God made that first, what did he make next?" Our disputant will not find anything else subsequent to the whole universe, and so he will be disconcerted by the question, "How can that be 'first,' if nothing else came after it?"

If, though, he means that God made first a formless, and then a formed universe, there is nothing contradictory in his position, provided he is able to distinguish between what precedes in virtue of eternity, what precedes in time, what has precedence in the order of choice, and what has a purely logical priority.

In virtue of eternity: in the way that God precedes all things.

In time: as the flower appears before the fruit.

In the order of choice: the fruit takes precedence over the flower.

By logical priority: the sound precedes the song.

Among these four kinds of priority which I have enumerated the first and the last are very difficult to understand, but the two middle ones are quite easy.

Rare indeed, and exceedingly arduous for us, Lord, is contemplation of your eternal being which, though immutable in itself, makes mutable creatures, and is in this sense prior to them.

Then again, whose mind is so acute as to discern without great labor how the sound must be prior to the song, because song is formed sound? While it is possible for something to exist in an unformed state, what does not exist cannot be formed. In this sense, matter is prior to what is made out of it. This does not mean that matter enjoys any power to make that thing—rather it is made itself—nor that it has any priority in time, for we do not first utter unformed sounds, tunelessly, and then later shape them to the form of a song. Nor do we work on them as we might make a chest out of wood, or some vessel out of silver; these materials are, of course, anterior even in time to the forms of objects made from them. But this is not the case with a song. When someone is singing we hear sound and song both at once; it is not as though formless noise were heard first and then given the form of the song. If some kind of sound is audible in advance, it dies away, and then there will be nothing of it left which you could take up again and compose into a song by employing your musical skill. The song, therefore, happens in its sound, and this sound is the matter of the song. This very sound is what is formed so as to become song. And therefore, as I was saying, the matter, sound, has priority over the form that is sung, but not a priority in the sense of having power to create, for the sound is not the composer of what is to be sung; it is merely made available to the mind of the singer by the bodily organ he uses when he sings. Neither has the sound any temporal priority, for it is uttered simultaneously with the song. Nor has it any precedence in the order of choice, for no one would think sound more excellent than song, since the song is not mere sound, but sound endowed with beautiful form. But the sound does have logical priority, because it is not the song that is given form to make it into sound, but the sound which is formed to turn it into song.

This example may help anyone who can follow the argument to understand that primal matter was made first and called "heaven and earth" because from it heaven and earth were made. We must understand, though, that "first" does not mean earlier in time, because it is the forms of things that give rise to time, whereas matter was formless; but once time exists, we can observe within time both matter and form. Yet nothing can be told with regard to formless matter without our seeming to attribute to it a temporal priority, although in terms of value it is of the lowest rank, things endowed with form being unquestionably better than what is unformed; and certainly it is preceded by the eternity of its creator. And rightly, so that the matter from which something was to be made should itself be made from nothing.

Conclusion: the one Truth, many human approaches

30, 41. Amid this profusion of true opinions let Truth itself engender concord; may our God have mercy upon us[104] and grant us to make lawful use of the law for the purpose envisaged by his commandment, pure charity.[105] In that perspective, if anyone asks me which of them is what Moses, your servant, intended, these writings are no true confession of mine unless I confess to you, "I do not know." Yet I do know that these opinions are valid (I do not speak here of the carnal-minded, of whom I have said as much as I thought necessary;[106] the words of your book, teaching lofty truths in humble guise and many things in small compass,

---

104. See Ps 66:2(67:1).
105. See 1 Tm 1:8.5. In this opening sentence Augustine again echoes Terence, *Andria* 68 (see X,23,34 and the note there), but this time inverts the meaning of that text in an invocation to the Trinity: "our God ... Truth ... Charity."
106. That is, at XII,27,37.

do not frighten them, those promising children). But let all of us who, as I acknowledge, discern rightly and speak truly on these texts, love one another and likewise love you,[107] our God, the fount of truth, if truth is really what we thirst for, and not illusions. Let us also honor this same servant of yours whom you filled with your Spirit and entrusted with the promulgation of your scripture, by believing that when he wrote these things he had in mind what you revealed to him to be the best of all meanings in the light of truth, and with respect to the profit it would yield.

31, 42. Accordingly when anyone claims, "He meant what I say," and another retorts, "No, rather what I find there," I think that I will be answering in a more religious spirit if I say, "Why not both, if both are true? And if there is a third possibility, and a fourth, and if someone else sees an entirely different meaning in these words, why should we not think that he was aware of all of them, since it was through him that the one God carefully tempered his sacred writings to meet the minds of many people, who would see different things in them, and all true?"[108]

Of this I am certain, and I am not afraid to declare it from my heart, that if I had to write something to which the highest authority would be attributed, I would rather write it in such a way that my words would reinforce for each reader whatever truth he was able to grasp about these matters, than express a single idea so unambiguously as to exclude others, provided these did not offend me by their falsehood. It would therefore be over-hasty to conclude that Moses did not enjoy the same favor from you, O my God, and I am unwilling to think so. I am convinced that when he wrote those words what he meant and what he thought was all the truth we have been able to discover there, and whatever truth we have not been able to find, or have not found yet, but which is nonetheless there to be found.

32, 43. Finally, Lord, what if human vision is incomplete? Does that mean that anything you intended to reveal by these words to later generations of readers—you who are God, not flesh and blood—was[109] hidden from your good Spirit, who will, I pray, lead me into the right land?[110] Is this not the case even if the man through whom you spoke to us had

---

107. See Dt 6:5; Mt 22:37-39; Mk 12:30-31; Lk 10:27; 1 Jn 4:7.
108. Augustine can recognize that pluralism is not only inevitable but even desirable, because he is certain that all interpretations which subject themselves to truth are bound to meet in the one Truth eventually. See his invocation to God, "the light of all truthful minds," in XII,18,27.
109. See Mt 16:17; 1 Cor 15:20.
110. See Ps 142(143):10.

perhaps only one of the true meanings in mind? If he did, by all means let that one which he intended be taken as paramount. But as for us, Lord, we beg you to point out to us either that sense which he intended or any other true meaning which you choose, so that whether you take occasion of these words to make plain to us the same thing that you showed him, or something different, you still may feed us[111] and no error dupe us.

Mark how much we have written about so few words, O Lord my God, how remarkably much! If we continue in this style, where shall we find sufficient energy or time to cover all your books? Grant me, then, to make my confession to you more briefly as I comment on them, and to select one meaning only, one that is inspired by you as true, certain and good, even if many suggest themselves in those places where indeed many may. For this is the assurance on which I make my confession: that if I manage to expound the sense intended by the writer who served you, that will be correct and the best course I could take, and that I must endeavor to do; but if I do not succeed in that, I may at least say what your Truth wills to reveal to me through the words of Moses, since it was your Truth who communicated to him also whatever he willed.

---

111. See IX,10,24.

Book XIII

The Days of Creation,
Prophecy of the Church

1, 1. Upon you I call, O God, my mercy,[1] who made me and did not forget me when I forgot you. Into my soul I call you, for you prepare it to be your dwelling by the desire you inspire in it. Do not forsake me now when I call upon you, who before ever I called on you forestalled me[2] by your persistent, urgent entreaties, multiplying and varying your appeals that I might hear you from afar, and turn back, and begin to call upon you who were calling me.[3] You have blotted out all the evils in me that deserved your punishment, Lord, not requiting me for the work of my hands, by which I defected from you to my own unmaking, and you have anticipated all my good actions, rewarding the work of your own hands that made me;[4] for before ever I was, you were; I did not even exist to receive your gift of being; yet lo! now I do exist, thanks to your goodness. Over all that I am, both what you have made me and that from which you made me, your goodness has absolute precedence. You had no need of me. Am I so valuable as to be a help to you, my Lord and my God? Did you will me to serve you so that you might be spared fatigue in your work, or because your power might be diminished if my homage were wanting to it? Nor did you will me to pay cult to you as I would cultivate the earth, as though you feared to stay uncultivated for want of cult from me! No, you command me to serve you and worship you that it may be well with me of your bounty, who have granted me first to exist, that I may enjoy well-being.

---

1. See Ps 58:18(59:17).
2. See Ps 58:11(59:10).
3. The opening of this last book echoes that of Book I: Augustine's invocation of God is preceded by and dependent on God's prevenient grace.
4. See Pss 17:21(18:20); 118(119):73.

Why did God create?

2, 2. Solely by your abundant goodness has your creation come to be and stood firm, for you did not want so good a thing to be missing. It could be of no profit to you, nor equal to yourself as though proceeding from your own substance,[5] yet there was the possibility of its existing as your creation. What advance claim did heaven and earth have upon you, when you made them in the Beginning? Let your spiritual and corporeal creation speak up and tell us what rights they had. In your Wisdom you made them,[6] so that on your Wisdom might depend even those inchoate, formless beings, whether of the spiritual or the corporeal order, beings plunging into excess or straying into far-off regions of unlikeness to yourself.[7] Even in its unformed state the spiritual was of higher dignity than any formed corporeal thing, and a corporeal being, even unformed, had more dignity than if it had had no existence at all. Thus these formless things would have depended on your Word even had they not by that same Word been summoned back to your unity and received form, and become, every one of them, exceedingly good[8] because they are from you, the one supreme Good. What prior entitlement had they to exist even as formless things, when they could not exist at all except by your creation?

3. As for corporeal matter, did that have some pre-emptive claim upon you to exist at least in an invisible and unorganized state? No: how could it, when it could not even be, except because you made it? Since it did not exist, it could have acquired no right to existence that could be urged in your presence. And what of the inchoate spiritual creation: did it earn the right at least to exist as dark and wavering like the deep ocean, but utterly unlike yourself? Only through the same Word that gave it being could it be converted to him who made it and become light at his illumination, not indeed as his equal, but by being shaped and conformed to him who, being in the form of God, is equal to you.[9] For just as, in the case of a corporeal creature, to be is not the same thing as to be beautiful (otherwise it would be impossible for it to be ugly), so too for a created spirit to live is not the same thing as to live in accord with wisdom, for otherwise it would be

---

5. See Phil 2:6.
6. See Ps 103(104):2.
7. See Lk 15:13 and VII,10,16 above.
8. See Gn 1:31.
9. See Rom 8:29; Phil 2:6.

infallibly wise. But such a creature's good is to hold fast to you always,[10] lest by turning away it lose the light it acquired by its conversion, and slip back into the old life, dark and abysmal.[11] We ourselves, who in respect of our souls are also your spiritual creatures, were once turned away from you who are our Light; in that earlier life we were darkness,[12] and even now we labor in our residual gloom, until in your only Son we become your righteousness;[13] for that righteousness is like God's high and holy mountains, while your judgments, which were all the being we then had, are like the deep.[14]

Not for any deserving on the creature's side

3, 4. Among your first acts of creation you said, *Let there be light, and light was made.*[15] It seems to me reasonable to refer this to your spiritual creation, which was already alive in some fashion and capable of receiving your illumination. But just as it had in no way deserved well of you or earned the right to be alive like that, neither had it any claim on you to be illumined. Its unformed state would not have been pleasing to you, had it not also become light; but this could not happen merely in virtue of its existence, for it needed to contemplate the Light which would shed radiance upon it, and hold fast to that. It would thus be indebted to your free grace both for its initial life and for its life in the beatitude which it won by changing for the better in being converted to you, who can change neither for better nor for worse. You alone are, because you alone exist in utter simplicity, for with you to live is the same thing as to live in blessedness, since you yourself are beatitude.

4, 5. What, then, would have been lacking to that Good which is your very self, even if these things had never come to be at all, or had remained in their unformed state? It was no need on your part that drove you to make them. Out of your sheer goodness you controlled them and converted them

---

10. See Ps 72(73):28.
11. Throughout these chapters Augustine is drawing a parallel between the *formation* of the creature from formless matter and the *conversion* of the spiritual creature to God, both seen as the work of the second person of the Trinity, the Word.
12. See Eph 5:8.
13. See 2 Cor 5:21.
14. See Ps 35:7(36:6). In his *Exposition of Psalm* 35,9, Augustine explains that the rising sun illuminates the mountains first, then the valleys; the mountains represent the apostles.
15. Gn 1:3.

to their form; it was not as though your own happiness stood in need of completion by them. Their imperfection is displeasing to you who are perfect in the sense that you will them to be perfected and so become pleasing to you, not in the sense that you are yourself imperfect and look to reach your own perfection by helping them to theirs. Your good Spirit[16] hung poised above the waters,[17] but the waters did not support him, as though he needed them to rest upon. When your Spirit is said to rest upon people,[18] it means that he causes them to rest in himself. Rather did your unassailable, immutable will, sufficient in itself unto itself, brood over the life you had made, over the creature for which life is not the same as beatitude, for it is alive even in its own dark turbulence; but it has the prospect of being converted to him who made it, that so it may live more and more fully on the fount of life, and in his light see light,[19] and so be perfected, illumined, and beatified.[20]

God's Spirit, Third Person of the Trinity

5, 6. Ah, now I have found what I was looking for! In symbolic form a Trinity now dawns clear for me, the Trinity which is yourself, my God. You, Father, made heaven and earth in that Beginning who originates our wisdom, that is to say in the Wisdom who is your Son, coequal and coeternal with yourself. And already we have spoken at length of heaven's heaven,[21] and of the invisible and unorganized earth, and spoken too of the abyss, dark with the unstable flux of spiritual formlessness and destined so to remain until it should be converted to him from whom it drew such life as it had. But once illuminated by him it was transformed into a life so beautiful that it became the heaven overarching that other heavenly vault to be established later between upper and lower waters.[22] I understood already that the name "God" signified the Father who made these things, and the name "Beginning" the Son in whom he made them; and believing as I did that my God is a Trinity, I sought for a Trinity among his holy utter-

---

16. See Ps 142(143):10.
17. See Gn 1:2.
18. See Nm 11:25; Is 11:2; 1 Pt 4:14.
19. See Ps 35:10(36:9).
20. This is already a trinitarian pattern, which becomes explicit in the following chapter.
21. See Ps 113(115):16.
22. See Gn 1:6.

ances. And there was your Spirit poised above the waters! Here, then, is the Trinity who is my God: Father, Son and Holy Spirit, creator of the whole created universe.

6, 7. But then why was it?—O truth-speaking Light, I bring my heart to you lest it beguile me with empty thoughts: dispel its darkness and tell me, I beg you, through Charity, our mother, I beg you, tell me, why was it that only after naming heaven, and the invisible and unorganized earth, and the darkness over the deep, did your scripture mention your Spirit, last of all? Was it because he had to be introduced in such a way that he could be described as poised overhead? This could not be said of him unless something else was mentioned first, over which your Spirit could hover. He could not be poised above Father or Son, nor could he be rightly said to hang poised at all, if there were nothing over which he could hover. Some object therefore had to be mentioned first, and only then could he be referred to, since it was not fitting for him to be presented in any way other than as hovering like this. But why could he not be introduced otherwise?

7, 8. Anyone with enough mental agility should here follow your apostle, who tells us that *the love of God has been poured out into our hearts through the Holy Spirit who has been given us.*[23] But then, minded to instruct us on spiritual matters,[24] the apostle points out a way of loftiest excellence, the way of charity;[25] and he kneels before you[26] on our behalf, entreating you to grant us some understanding of the charity of Christ, which is exalted above all knowledge.[27] This is why the Spirit, who is supereminent Love, was said to be poised above the waters at the beginning.

To whom should I speak, and how express myself, about the passion that drags us headlong into the deep, and the charity that uplifts us through your Spirit, who hovered over the waters? To whom should I say this, and in what terms? These are not literally places, into which we plunge and from which we emerge: what could seem more place-like than they, yet what is in reality more different? They are movements of the heart, they are two loves. One is the uncleanness of our own spirit, which like a flood-tide sweeps us down, in love with restless cares; the other is the holi-

---

23. Rom 5:5.
24. See 1 Cor 12:1.
25. See 1 Cor 12:31.
26. See Eph 3:14.
27. See Eph 3:19.

ness of your Spirit, which bears us upward in a love for peace beyond all care, that our hearts may be lifted up to you,[28] to where your Spirit is poised above the waters, so that once our soul has crossed over those waters on which there is no reliance we may reach all-surpassing rest.[29]

8, 9. An angel was swept away; the human soul was swept away; and they had shown that all spiritual creatures would have been engulfed in darkness, had you not said at that first moment, *Let there be light,*[30] and brought light into being; and had not every obedient intelligence in your heavenly city clung fast to you and found its rest in your Spirit, who unchangingly broods over everything subject to change. Otherwise the very heaven above our heaven would have been a dark abyss in itself, whereas now it is light in the Lord.[31] When spirits slide away from you they are stripped of their vesture of light and exposed in their native darkness, and then their unhappy restlessness amply proves to us how noble is each rational creature you have made, for nothing less than yourself can suffice to give it any measure of blessed rest, nor indeed can it be its own satisfaction. For it is you, Lord, who will light up our darkness.[32] From you derives our garment of light, and in you our darkness will be bright as noon.[33]

Give me yourself, O my God, give yourself back to me. Lo, I love you, but if my love is too mean, let me love more passionately. I cannot gauge my love, nor know how far it fails, how much more love I need for my life to set its course straight into your arms, never swerving until hidden in the covert of your face.[34] This alone I know, that without you all to me is misery, woe outside myself and woe within, and all wealth but penury, if it is not my God.

9, 10. It cannot be denied, surely, that the Father too was borne aloft over the waters, and the Son? If the expression means poised in a place, after the manner of a body, then the Holy Spirit was not poised there either; but if it means that the eminence of unchangeable Godhead is far above all that is changeable, then certainly the one God, Father, Son and Holy Spirit, was poised above the waters. Why, then, was this stated of your Spirit only?

---

28. See Col 3:1-2 and the note at XII,16,23.
29. See Ps 123(124):5. In his *Exposition of Psalm* 123,9, Augustine explains that these "unsubstantial waters" represent sin.
30. Gn 1:3.
31. See Eph 5:8.
32. See Ps 17:29(18:28).
33. See Is 58:10.
34. See Col 3:3; Ps 30:21(31:20).

Why of him alone, as though he were in a place, when it is no place; and why only of him who alone is said to be your Gift?[35]

Because, I think, in your Gift we find rest, and there we enjoy you.[36] Our true place is where we find rest. We are borne toward it by love, and it is your good Spirit[37] who lifts up our sunken nature from the gates of death.[38] In goodness of will is our peace.[39] A body gravitates to its proper place by its own weight. This weight does not necessarily drag it downward, but pulls it to the place proper to it: thus fire tends upward, a stone downward. Drawn by their weight, things seek their rightful places. If oil is poured into water, it will rise to the surface, but if water is poured onto oil it will sink below the oil: drawn by their weight, things seek their rightful places. They are not at rest as long as they are disordered, but once brought to order they find their rest. Now, my weight is my love, and wherever I am carried, it is this weight that carries me.[40] Your Gift sets us afire and we are borne upward; we catch his flame and up we go. In our hearts we climb those upward paths,[41] singing the songs of ascent.[42] By your fire, your beneficent fire, are we enflamed, because we are making our way up to *the peace of Jerusalem*. For *I rejoiced when I was told, We are going to the Lord's house*.[43] There shall a good will find us a place, that we may have no other desire but to abide there for ever.[44]

10, 11. How blessed is that creature which knew no different lot! Indeed, it might itself have been something very different, had not your Gift, the

---

35. See Acts 2:38.
36. *Te fruimur*. Augustine's classic distinction between *uti* ("to make use of") and *frui* ("to enjoy") is illustrated by his definition of the latter: "to enjoy is to cling by love to something for its own sake" (*Teaching Christianity* I,4,4).
37. See Ps 142(143):10.
38. See Ps 9:14-15(13).
39. See Lk 2:14.
40. Plato had envisaged the human soul as midway between God and the material world. Augustine, finding little difficulty in reconciling Platonic ethics with his Christianity, developed a doctrine of natural "love" in all creatures, bearing them by inexorable "weight" to their proper destinies. But human beings are a special case, both because of the variety of conflicting "loves" within the soul resulting from Adam's fall, and because of our capacity to choose between our "loves" and decide which to satisfy. Hence the need for an ordering of love within us if we are to reach that blessedness where all desires and impulses are brought to rest. The third person of the Trinity, already associated in scripture with fire (see Acts 2:34) and with love (see Rom 5:5), is linked with the notion of "weight" by Wis 11:21. Compare, in *The Confessions*, IV,15,27; VII,7,11;17,23; and the famous X,27,38.
41. See Ps 83:6(84:5).
42. This title was given to Pss 119-133(120-134).
43. Ps 121(122):6,1.
44. See Ps 60:8(61:7).

Spirit who broods over all that is mutable, raised it up without the least delay, from the moment it was made, and summoned it with the words, *Let there be light*. And light it became. In our case there are distinct periods of time, for we were darkness once, and then we became light.[45] Not so for that creature: what it would have been, had it not been illumined, was announced, and announced in such a way that it might seem to have once been all darkness and chaotic flux; but this was to show why it was made capable of becoming something different, enlightened by conversion to the Light that never fails.[46]

Let anyone grasp this who can, or else let him seek understanding from you. Why should he pester me, as though I had the power to illumine anyone coming into this world?[47]

11, 12. Can anyone comprehend the almighty Trinity? Everyone talks about it—but is it really the Trinity of which they talk? Rare indeed is the person who understands the subject of his discourse, when he speaks of that. People argue and wrangle over it, yet no one sees that vision unless he is at peace.

I wish they would turn their attention to the triad they have within themselves. It is, to be sure, a triad far distant from the Trinity, but I propose it as a topic on which they may exercise their minds, by way of experiment and in order to make clear to themselves how great the difference is. The triad I mean is being, knowledge and will.[48] I am, and I know, and I will. Knowingly and willingly I exist; I know that I am and that I will; I will to be and to know. Let anyone with the wit to see it observe how in these three there is one inseparable life: there is one life, one mind and one essence. How inseparable they are in their distinctness! Yet distinction there is. Everyone has himself readily available for inspection; let each, then, scrutinize himself, and see what he can find, and tell me.

But when he has verified this unity between his powers, he must not suppose that what he has discovered is that which exists immutably above our creaturely minds, that which unchangeably is and unchangeably knows and unchangeably wills. Do these three coexistent acts constitute

---

45. See Eph 5:8.
46. See Sir 24:6.
47. See Jn 1:9.
48. This chapter states explicitly what has been hinted several times earlier: that in the activities of the human mind can be discerned an image of the triune God. The doctrine develops through Augustine's writings, to reach its final form in *The Trinity* IX-XV; compare *The City of God* XI.

the Trinity? Or are all three found in each Person, so that each is this triple reality? Or are both these propositions true, the simplicity and the complexity being reconciled in some way beyond our comprehension, since the Persons are defined by their mutual relationships yet infinite in themselves? Thus the Godhead exists and is known to itself and is its own all-sufficient joy without variation for ever, Being-Itself in the manifold greatness of its unity. Who can find any way to express this truth? Who dare make any assertion about it?

Allegorical interpretation of Gn 1. Day One: Light

12, 13. But let my faith go further, and say to the Lord my God, "Holy, holy, holy,[49] Lord my God, in your name, Father, Son and Spirit, were we baptized, and in your name, Father, Son and Holy Spirit, we administer baptism,"[50] for among us too has God in his Christ created a heaven and an earth: the spiritual and the carnal members of his Church.[51] Before our earth was formed by his teaching it was invisible and unorganized,[52] and we were shrouded in the darkness of ignorance, because you castigated humankind for its sin[53] and your judgments are deep as a chasmic abyss.[54] But your mercy did not forsake us in our misery, for your Spirit hovered over the water; and you said, *Let there be light; repent, for the kingdom of heaven is near, repent, and let there be light.*[55] And because our souls were deeply disquieted within themselves we remembered you, O Lord, from our muddy Jordan; we called you to mind in that mountain which, though lofty as yourself, was brought low for us.[56] Disgusted with our darkness,

---

49. See Is 6:3; Rv 4:8.
50. See 1 Cor 1:15; Mt 28:19.
51. See 1 Cor 3:1. The following chapters interpret the creation narrative of Gn 1 as an allegory of the action of the Spirit in the Christian Church. Augustine begins with baptism.
52. See Gn 1:2.
53. See Ps 38:12(39:11).
54. See Ps 35:7(36:6).
55. Gn 1:3; Mt 3:2; 4:17. The juxtaposition of these texts is not arbitrary: *Let there be light* are the first words spoken by God in Gn 1, and *Repent* is the first word both of John in his baptizing mission (Mt 3:2) and of Jesus (Mt 4:17). Creation and re-creation are correlative.
56. See Ps 41:6-7(42:5-6). This psalm, which echoes through the following paragraphs, is interpreted by Augustine in his *Exposition of Psalms* 41,1 as a song of catechumens hastening to baptism. It was apparently sung by the candidates in procession to the baptistery in Africa in Augustine's time. The mountain *equal to God* (Phil 2:6) is Christ, brought low in the Incarnation.

we were converted to you, and light dawned. See now, we who once were darkness are now light in the Lord.[57]

13, 14. But as yet we know this only by faith, not by anything we see,[58] for we have been saved indeed, but in hope, and hope that is seen is hope no longer.[59] Deep still calls unto deep, but now in the roar of your waterfalls.[60] Paul himself, even Paul, who says, *Not as spiritual persons could I speak to you, but only as carnal,*[61] even he does not consider himself to have laid hold on his salvation already, but, forgetting what lies behind him, he stretches out to what lies ahead,[62] groaning and oppressed[63] because his soul is athirst for the living God, like a parched deer running to springs of water and panting, "When shall I reach it?"[64] He longs to have his heavenly habitation put on over his earthly vesture;[65] and he calls to those deeper in the abyss than himself, *Conform yourselves no longer to the standards of this world, but allow yourselves to be reformed by the renewal of your minds,* and *Do not be childish in your outlook; be babes in your innocence of evil, but mature in mind;* and again, *You stupid Galatians! Who has bewitched you?*[66] But he calls to them no longer in his own voice. In your voice he calls to them, for you sent your Spirit from heaven[67] through Christ who ascended on high[68] and threw open your floodgates that your gifts might cascade upon us and your rushing river bring joy to your city.[69]

For him does Paul, the Bridegroom's friend,[70] sigh with longing, for to him has Paul dedicated the first-fruits of his spirit,[71] but still he groans

---

57. See Eph 5:8.
58. See 2 Cor 5:7.
59. See Rom 8:24.
60. See Ps 41:8(42:7); Augustine understands the psalmist's words, *Deep calls to deep*, of human preachers, themselves sinful, appealing to human hearers (see *Exposition of Psalm* 41,13); but the appeal is now charged with new power.
61. 1 Cor 3:1.
62. See Phil 3:13.
63. See 2 Cor 5:4.
64. See Ps 41:2-3(42:1-2). Augustine recounts in section 3 of his exposition of this psalm that deer kill snakes, and after doing so suffer intense thirst. Another convenient allegory.
65. See 2 Cor 5:2.
66. Rom 12:2; 1 Cor 14:20; Gal 3:1.
67. See Wis 9:17.
68. See Ps 67:19(68:18).
69. See Ps 45:5(46:4).
70. See Jn 3:29.
71. That is, through the life of faith; see IX,10,24; XII,16,23.

within himself as he awaits the adoption that will set his whole self free.[72] For Christ he yearns, for he is a member of the bride, but on Christ's behalf he is jealous, for he is the Bridegroom's friend. Not for his own rights is he jealous, but for Christ's; not in his own voice but in the thunder of your waterfalls he calls out to that deeper abyss, alert with jealous fear lest, as once the serpent seduced Eve by his wiles, she too may lose the purity of her singleminded devotion to our Bridegroom, your only Son.[73]

What, then, is this fair light? A light by which we shall see him as he is,[74] a light to put an end to the tears that have become bread to me, daily, nightly, as I hear the unceasing taunt, "Where is your God?"[75]

14, 15. And I too ask, "Where are you, my God?" But this is where you are. I find a little respite[76] in you when I pour out my soul in rising above myself with a shout of joy and praise, the clamor of a pilgrim keeping festival.[77] Yet still my soul is sad, because it slips back and becomes an abyss once more, or rather, it feels itself to be still in the depths.

But my faith takes it to task, that faith which you have kindled, lamp-like, on my nocturnal path: "Why so sorrowful, my soul, why do you disquiet me? Trust in the Lord; his word is a lamp for your feet.[78] Keep your hope high and persevere until night, nurturer of the wicked, shall pass away, until the Lord's anger shall pass.[79] We too were once children of his wrath;[80] once darkness,[81] we carry that residual gloom in bodies marked for death because of sin,[82] but hope on until day dawns and shadows disperse.[83] Hope in the Lord. In the morning I shall stand in his presence and contemplate him,[84] and I will praise him for ever."

In the morning I will stand and see my God, who sheds the light of salvation on my face,[85] who will breathe life even into our mortal bodies

---

72. See Rom 8:23.
73. See 2 Cor 11:3.
74. See 1 Jn 3:2.
75. See Ps 41:4(42:3).
76. See Jb 32:20.
77. See Ps 41:5(42:4).
78. See Pss 41:6.12(42:5.11); 118(119):105.
79. See Is 26:20.
80. See Eph 2:3.
81. See Eph 5:8.
82. See Rom 8:10.
83. See Sg 2:17.
84. See Ps 5:5(3).
85. See Ps 42(43):5.

through the Spirit who dwells in us[86] and has been mercifully hovering over the dark chaos of our inner being. By this we have received, even on our pilgrim way, the pledge[87] that we are children of the light already. Saved only in hope we may be,[88] but we are at home in the light and in the day. No longer are we children of the night or of darkness,[89] as once we were. But you alone distinguish between us and the night-born in this present uncertainty where human knowledge falters, for you test our hearts, and call light "day" and darkness "night."[90] Who but you can tell them apart? Yet what do we possess that we have not received from you, since from the one same lump you have formed us for honorable service, and others for common use?

Day Two: The vault of scripture

15, 16. Moreover you alone, our God, have made for us a vault overhead in giving us your divine scripture.[91] The sky will one day be rolled up like a book,[92] but for the present it is stretched out above us like the skin of a tent,[93] for your divine scripture has attained an even nobler authority now that the mortal writers through whom you provided it for us have died. And you know, Lord, you know[94] how you clothed human beings in skins when they became mortal in consequence of their sin.[95] That is why you are said to have stretched out the vault that is your book, stretched out like the skin of a tent those words of yours so free from discord,[96] which you have canopied over us through the ministry of mortal men. The firm authority inherent in your revelation, which they have passed on to us, is by their very death spread more widely over all the world below, for in

---

86. See Rom 8:11.
87. See 2 Cor 1:22; 5:5.
88. See Rom 8:24.
89. See 1 Thes 5:5.
90. See Gn 1:4-5; Ps 16(17):3.
91. See Gn 1:7. The vault or sky, allegorically understood as the scriptures, is referred to by Ps 103(104) as a tent (hence skin, since in the ancient world tents were ordinarily made of skins). Since Gn 3:21 links skins with mortality, Augustine concludes that the mortality and death of the scriptural writers effectively stretched out, that is, made more widely available, their writings.
92. That is, a papyrus scroll; see Is 34:4.
93. See Ps 103(104):2.
94. See Tb 3:16; 8:9; Jn 21:15-17.
95. See Gn 3:21 and VII,18,24.
96. That is, Old and New Testaments agree.

their lifetime it had not been raised so high or extended so far. At that time you had not yet stretched out the sky like a tent, nor had you caused their death to become resoundingly famous far and wide.

17. Let us contemplate the heavens, the work of your fingers, O Lord;[97] clear away that cloud you have spread beneath them, hiding them from our eyes. There is the witness you have borne to yourself, and to little ones it imparts wisdom.[98] Out of the mouths of infants and sucklings evoke perfect praise, O my God.[99] We know no other books with the like power to lay pride low[100] and so surely to silence the obstinate contender who tries to thwart your reconciling work by defending his sins. Nowhere else, Lord, indeed nowhere else do I know such chaste words,[101] words with such efficacy to persuade me to confession, to gentle my neck beneath your kindly yoke[102] and invite me to worship you without thought of reward. Grant me understanding of your words, good Father, give me this gift, stationed as I am below them, because it is for us earth-dwellers that you have fashioned that strong vault overhead.

18. Above this vault are other waters,[103] and these, I believe, are immortal, immune to earthly decay. Let them praise your name,[104] let them praise you, your angelic peoples above the heavens, who have no need to look up at the vault and learn by reading your word in it; for they behold your face unceasingly[105] and there read without the aid of time-bound syllables the decree of your eternal will. They read it, they make it their choice, they love it; they read it always, and what they read never passes away, for in their act of choosing and loving they read the unchangeable constancy of your purpose. Their book is never closed, their scroll never rolled up,[106] for you are their book and are so eternally, because you have assigned them their place above the vault you strongly framed over the weakness of your lower peoples. Into that vault we look up, there to recog-

---

97. See Ps 8:4(3). The Holy Spirit is understood to be signified by the *finger of God* (Lk 11:20); since the sacred writers were inspired by the Spirit they are called God's "fingers." Augustine is praying for understanding of the scriptures.

98. See Ps 18:8(19:7).

99. See Ps 8:3(2).

100. See Ez 30:6.

101. See Ps 11:7(12:6) and VII,21,27.

102. See Mt 11:29-30.

103. See Gn 1:7.

104. See Ps 148:4-5.

105. See Mt 18:10.

106. See Is 34:4.

nize the mercy which manifests you in time, you who have created time; *for your mercy is heaven-high, O Lord, and your faithfulness reaches to the clouds.*[107] Clouds are wafted away, but heaven abides. Preachers of your word are wafted away out of this life into another, but your scripture remains stretched above your people everywhere until the end of the world. Then will even sky and earth be swept away,[108] but your utterances will stand unmoved, because though the tent is folded and the grass where it was pitched withers with all its verdure, your Word abides for ever.[109] Not as he is, but tantalizingly, as though veiled by cloud and mirrored in his heaven,[110] does this Word appear to us now, for though we are the beloved of your Son, it has not yet appeared what we shall be.[111] He peeps through the trellis of our flesh, and coaxes us, and enkindles our love until we run after him, allured by his fragrance.[112] *But when he appears, we shall be like him, because we shall see him as he is.*[113] Our seeing then, Lord, will be the vision of you as you are, but this is not granted to us yet.

16, 19. As you exist in all fullness, so too do you alone possess the fullness of knowledge: you unchangeably exist, unchangeably know and unchangeably will. Your essence knows and wills unchangeably; your knowledge is and wills unchangeably; your will is and knows unchangeably. It therefore does not seem fitting to you that the unchangeable Light should be known by the changeable being it illumines in the same way as it knows itself. This is why my soul is like an arid land before you,[114] for as it cannot illumine itself from its own resources, neither can it slake its thirst from itself. So truly is the fount of life with you, that only in your light will we see light.[115]

---

107. Ps 35:6(36:5).
108. See Mt 24:35.
109. See Is 40:6-8. In the preceding sentences the thought moves through stages of increasing permanence in the revelation of God: preachers, scripture, God's utterances, the Word.
110. See 1 Cor 13:12.
111. See 1 Jn 3:2.
112. See Sg 2:9; 1:3.
113. 1 Jn 3:2.
114. See Ps 142(143):6.
115. See Ps 35:10(36:9).

Day Three: Bitter sea, dry land, fruitfulness

17, 20. Who else gathered people brewing bitterness into a single mass?[116] All of them are bent on the same quest for earthly, temporal happiness; this is the object of all they do, though the waves of care that toss them to and fro are endlessly varied. Who called them together if not you, Lord, who commanded that the waters be gathered into a single mass and dry land emerge,[117] athirst for you? To you even the sea belongs, for you made it and your hands formed the dry earth.[118] It is not the bitter brine of those conflicting wills that earns the name "sea," but their gathering; for you control even the unruly urges of our souls, and set limits to their onrush, boundaries where their surging waves must break.[119] Thus your sway over all things imposes order, and you create "sea."

21. But you have other souls in view as well, souls athirst for you,[120] whose very different aim marks them out clearly from the surrounding sea. Their thirst you quench from the sweet waters of your secret fountain, that the earth too may yield its increase.[121] And yield it does: at the command of its Lord and God the soil of our souls grows fertile in works of mercy according to its kind.[122] We fructify in love of our neighbors[123] by assisting them in their bodily needs, for, having seed of similar kind within ourselves, we learn compassion from our own weakness. So we are impelled to succor the needy in the way we would wish to be relieved ourselves, were we in the same distress. This means not only the easy provision that could be likened to seed-bearing grass; we may also be called upon to supply the stout, oak-like protection of a fruit-bearing tree, which in its benign strength can lift an injured person clear of the grasp of a powerful oppressor, and furnish protective shade by the unshakable firmness of just judgment.

---

116. Variously in his commentaries on the psalms and on Job Augustine thinks of this world as a sea, for example, *Exposition of Psalm* 64, 9: "This world is figuratively called a sea because it is rendered bitter by its saltiness and turbulent by storms. In it live people who by their perverted and depraved lusts behave like fishes devouring each other." In the present text it represents the pagan, unbelieving world from which God forms his Church.
117. See Gn 1:9.
118. See Ps 94(95):5.
119. See Jb 38:10-11.
120. See Ps 62:2(63:1).
121. See Ps 84:13(85:12).
122. See Gn 1:12.
123. See Mt 22:39; Mk 12:31.

Day Four: Lamps of wisdom and knowledge

18, 22. And so I pray you, Lord: as you cause joy and strength to spring and grow, even so let the truth spring up: let it sprout from the earth, and let righteousness look down from heaven,[124] and let luminaries be set in the firmament.[125] Let us break our bread for the hungry and bring the homeless poor under our roof, let us clothe the naked and not spurn our own kin.[126] When these fruits are burgeoning on earth, take heed and see that it is good. Then may swift dawn break for us, so that rising from this lowly crop of active works to the delights of contemplation, we may lay hold on the Word of Life above,[127] and appear like luminaries for the world, firmly set in the vault that is your scripture. There you school us to mark the distinction between realities of the mind and sensible things, as between day and night, or between souls devoted to the life of the mind and others preoccupied with sensible matters. No longer then is it you alone who in the secret recesses of your own judgment separate light from darkness, as before that vault was made; for now that your grace is manifested throughout the world your spiritual children too, set in the vault and plainly visible, may shine upon the earth, separate day from night, and mark distinct periods of time.[128] This is because old things have passed away now and all is made new;[129] our salvation is nearer now than when we first believed; night is far gone and day is breaking.[130] You crown the year with your blessing,[131] sending laborers into your harvest[132] where others have toiled over the sowing.[133] Different workers you send to sow new crops, which will be reaped at the end.[134]

Accordingly you grant our requests when we pray to you, and bless the passing years of a just person, but your years do not pass,[135] and in your

124. See Ps 84:12(85:11). In his *Exposition of Psalm* 84,13-14, Augustine interprets truth springing from the earth as the birth of Christ from Mary, and also as the truthful word of confession evoked from humankind.
125. See Gn 1:14.
126. See Is 58:7-8.
127. See Phil 2:15-16; 1 Jn 1:1.
128. See Gn 1:14-18.
129. See 2 Cor 5:17.
130. See Rom 13:11-12.
131. See Ps 64:12(65:11).
132. See Mt 9:38.
133. See Jn 4:38.
134. See Mt 13:39; those reapers will be angels.
135. See Ps 101:28(102:27).

unchanging eternity you are preparing a barn for the harvest of our fleeting years.

You lavish your heavenly blessings on the earth at due times, as determined by your eternal counsel; [23.] for to one person is granted the gift of speaking with wisdom, like the greater light you made, for the benefit of those who find their joy in the brilliant transparency of truth as in the light of early morning; to another is given through the grace of the same Spirit an ability to put the knowledge he has into words, and this is like the lesser light;[136] to another is granted gifts of healing, to another miraculous powers, to another prophecy, to another discernment between spirits, and to yet another various tongues. All these are like stars. All of them are the work of one and the same Spirit, who allots appropriate gifts to different people as he wills, and causes stars to shine out clearly for the benefit of all.[137]

As for knowledge expressed in apt words, comprising all those sacred signs[138] which wane and wax like the moon,[139] and the other gifts which in their diversity I likened to stars, all these differ so greatly from the glorious wisdom in which the aforesaid day rejoices that they are but rulers of the night. Nonetheless they are necessary for those people to whom your very prudent servant could speak only as carnal, not as spiritual persons,[140] whereas among the mature he speaks wisdom.[141] A sensual person is like a small child in Christ, in need of milk until he is robust enough to eat solid food and his eyes have the strength to stand exposure to the sun. Meanwhile, however, he does not live in a night devoid of all illumination, but must be content with the light of moon and stars.

These things you teach us[142] with consummate wisdom in your book, which is the vault you provide for us, O our God, so that they may all become plain to us through contemplation of your wonders. Still, though, we must discern them through signs, and transient phases, and passing days and years.

---

136. The distinction between wisdom and knowledge corresponds to that between contemplation and action suggested earlier in this chapter.

137. See 1 Cor 12:7-11.

138. See 1 Cor 13:2.

139. Augustine is perhaps thinking of sacred signs under the old dispensation, which have waned under the new.

140. See 1 Cor 3:1.

141. See 1 Cor 2:6.

142. Here and in XIII,18,22 the verb is *disputo*, reflecting the use of disputation in teaching.

19, 24. "But first you must wash, get yourselves clean, purge the wickedness from your souls and take it out of my sight, that dry land may appear. Learn to do good, champion the orphan and defend the rights of the widow, that your earth may yield nourishing crops and fruit-bearing trees, and then come back and let us discuss matters," says the Lord,[143] "so that there may be lights in the vault of heaven to shed their radiance on earth."

Remember the rich man in the gospel who was seeking guidance from a good teacher as to what he ought to do to win eternal life. Let that good teacher (whom he believed to be a man and no more, whereas Christ is good because he is God)—let that good teacher tell him that if he wishes to attain to life, he must keep the commandments, steer clear of bitter malice and wickedness, refrain from killing, adultery and theft, and never tell lies against anyone. Then dry land will have a chance to appear and bear the fruits of honor toward his mother and father and love for his neighbor. *I have done all this*, the young man says.[144] Then where do these rampant thorns come from, if your land is fruitful? Go and root out the wild clumps of avarice, sell your possessions, get yourself rich fruit by giving to the poor, for you will have treasure in heaven. If you want to be perfect, follow the Lord in the company of those to whom he speaks wisdom,[145] he who knows which gifts to assign to the day and which to the night, so that you may know too, and there may be lights in the vault of heaven to shine for you as well. This will not happen unless your heart is there; and that in turn will not happen unless your treasure is deposited there,[146] as you have heard from your good teacher.

But the barren earth was saddened,[147] and thorns choked the word.[148]

25. As for you, race of the elect,[149] weaklings in the world's esteem,[150] who have left all to follow the Lord, march after him and rout the strong,[151] march after him, you beautiful feet.[152] Shine in the firmament that the

143. See Is 1:16-18; this is God's answer in the "disputation."
144. See Mt 19:16-22; Mk 10:17-22; Lk 18:18-23.
145. See 1 Cor 2:6.
146. See Mt 6:21.
147. See Lk 18:23.
148. See Mt 13:7.22.
149. See 1 Pt 2:9.
150. See 1 Cor 1:27.
151. See 1 Cor 1:7.
152. See Is 52:7; Rom 10:15, the feet of those who preach the good news.

heavens may proclaim his glory.[153] Separate the light of the mature, who yet are not angels, from the darkness of the little ones, who yet are not to be despaired of; shine over the whole earth, and let the day, radiant with its sun, tell out the word of wisdom to the day, and the night, steeped in moonlight, proclaim the word of knowledge[154] to the night.[155] Let moon and stars lend brightness to the night, but let not the night overwhelm them with its darkness, for they do illumine it, in its measure.

As though God were once more commanding, *Let there be lights in the vault of heaven,*[156] there came a sudden noise from on high as though a violent wind were sweeping through, and tongues like fire appeared, separating and coming to rest on each one of them.[157] So they became luminaries in the vault of heaven, endowed with the word of life.[158] Run everywhere, you holy fires, you fires so beautiful, for you are the light of the world, and your place is not under a meal-tub.[159] He to whom you have given yourselves is exalted, and now he has exalted you. Run, then, and make him known to all nations.[160]

Day Five: Sea creatures represent signs and sacraments

20, 26. Let the sea conceive and bring forth your works, and let the waters produce living things that crawl;[161] for you have become God's spokesmen, separating worth from dross.[162] Through you he was able to say, *Let the waters bring forth living things that crawl* (not "living souls," which the dry land alone was to produce, but crawling things), *and birds to fly above the earth;*[163] for these aquatic creatures represent your holy signs, O God. Amid the waves of this world's temptations they swarmed, thanks to the efforts of your saints, to the end that the Gentiles might be stamped

---

153. See Ps 18:2(19:1).
154. See 1 Cor 12:8.
155. See Ps 18:3(19:2).
156. Gn 1:14.
157. See Acts 2:2-3.
158. See Phil 2:15-16; 1 Jn 1:1.
159. See Mt 5:14-15.
160. See Mt 28:19.
161. See Gn 1:20-22.
162. See Jer 15:19. The thought seems to be that the evangelists, whom Augustine is still addressing, by producing signs and wonders effect a discrimination between those who accept the gospel and those who refuse it.
163. Gn 1:20.

with your name in baptism. Among them were also some prodigious and wonderful feats,[164] suggested by the massive whales. The birds represent the voices of your messengers, who flew above the earth and close to the sky which is your book, for this book was the authority set over them, and wherever they might travel they always stayed beneath it. Never a word, never an utterance of theirs, but the rumor of it was heard as their sound echoed throughout the world and their words to the ends of the earth,[165] because you, Lord, caused them to multiply by your blessing.

27. Am I to be charged with lying or with causing confusion, by failing to draw a distinction between the luminous comprehension of these mysteries in the vault of heaven, and the corporeal works achieved far below in the waves of the sea? It is true that the characteristics of certain things are fixed and finalized, and not subject to development over successive generations, and among these are the splendors of wisdom and knowledge; but these same realities work themselves out in the sphere of bodily things in a great variety of forms which constantly increase and multiply through your blessing, O God. You have made kindly provision for the learning processes of us mortals, so prone to weariness, by arranging that our minds should attain to understanding as one single truth is figuratively expressed and enunciated in many different ways through the variations to which corporeal things are subject. The waters it was that produced these things, but in response to your creative Word. It was the needs of peoples estranged from your eternal truth that produced them, but only at the preaching of your gospel, for though it was the waters themselves that threw up these prodigies, in the sense that the bitter weariness of those waters occasioned them, they emerged only at your bidding.

28. All these things of your making are lovely, and lo, you who made them are more lovely still, unutterably more. If Adam had not fallen away from you, that briny sea would not have gushed from him, the deeply curious and stormily swollen and unstable flux that is the human race. And then there would have been no need for the deeds performed and the words spoken by your stewards[166] amid the pounding waves, words and deeds material and sensible, yet fraught with sacramental power.

This is what the creeping things and birds suggest to me at present, for even though people have been baptized and initiated, and have submitted

---

164. See Acts 2:11.
165. See Ps 18:4(19:3).
166. See 1 Cor 4:1.

to these material sacraments, they would proceed no further, did their souls not rise to a new level of spiritual life, and move on from elementary doctrine toward maturity.[167]

Day Six: Animals, the living soul

21, 29. What now emerges, then, are neither living things that crawl, nor anything from the depths of the sea: at your command the land, which stands clear from the bitter sea, throws up a *living creature*.[168] This creature no longer stands in need of baptism as the pagans do, and as it did itself while sunk beneath the waters, for since you ordained baptism as the means of entry into the kingdom of heaven no one can get in by any other way.[169] Nor does this creature demand prodigious miracles to prompt it to faith; it is not like people who refuse to believe unless they see signs and wonders,[170] for already it is believing earth, clearly demarcated from the waves of the sea and their bitter unbelief; and tongues serve as a sign to unbelievers, not to the faithful.[171]

Neither does this dry land, which you have established upon the waters,[172] need those flying creatures which the waters produced at your command. Send your word to the land through your messengers: we recount their works, yet it is you who work in them,[173] enabling their work to give rise to a living soul. The land indeed produces it, in the sense that it is the land's need that occasions your preachers' efforts there, just as it was the sea's need that occasioned their summoning from it living things that crawl and birds to fly beneath the vault of heaven. The land needs these no longer, though at that table which you have prepared in the presence of believers[174] it eats a fish raised up from the deep, raised up for the very purpose of watering the parched land.[175]

---

167. See Heb 6:1-3.
168. Gn 1:24.
169. See Jn 3:5.
170. See Jn 4:48.
171. See 1 Cor 14:22.
172. See Ps 135(136):6.
173. See Phil 2:13.
174. See Ps 22(23):5.
175. The initial letters of five Greek words (Jesus Christ, Son of God, Savior) spell ΙΧΘΥΣ, fish. A fish was therefore used from early times as a symbol of Christ, and particularly of his resurrection from the deep waters of death. The reference here is eucharistic.

Although birds are the sea's progeny, they flock over the land,[176] for though human unbelief was the reason why the evangelists' voices were originally needed, believers are daily encouraged and blessed by them too. Nonetheless it is from the land that the living soul takes its rise, because only believers profit by so restraining themselves from attachment to this world[177] that each soul, once dead through trying to live in death-dealing depravity,[178] may live instead for you,[179] who to a pure heart are life-giving delight.

30. No longer must your ministers work with the methods they used amid the waters of unbelief, announcing their message and conveying their meaning through miracles and signs and symbolic expressions. The attention of ignorant people is attracted by such things and gives birth to a wondering fear of the unknown that lies behind these signs; for since Adam's children have forgotten you, and now hide from your presence[180] and become the abyss, no other access to faith is open to them. But now it is on land that stands clear from the eddying deep that your ministers must work, and there make themselves an example to the faithful[181] by living alongside them and arousing them to imitation.

Thus it comes about that believers do not merely listen, but listen with a view to acting on what they hear, when they are bidden, *Seek God, and your soul will live,*[182] and so the earth will bring forth a living creature; and again, *Shape yourselves no longer to the standards of this world,*[183] but restrain yourselves from it. The soul that dies by craving lives by avoiding what it craved. Restrain yourselves from the monstrous savagery of pride, from the luxurious inertia of self-indulgence, and from sham pretension to knowledge,[184] so that wild beasts may become gentle, domestic animals responsive, and snakes harmless.[185] These animals symbolize the impulses of the soul; but arrogant self-importance and wallowing in lust and poisonous curiosity are the impulses of a soul that is dead, though not dead in such a

---

176. See Gn 1:22.
177. See Jas 1:27.
178. See 1 Tm 5:6.
179. See 2 Cor 5:15.
180. See Gn 3:8.
181. See 1 Thes 1:7.
182. Ps 68:33(69:32).
183. Rom 12:2.
184. See 1 Tm 6:20.
185. The three classes of animals created on the same day as human beings are taken to represent the three temptations of Jn 2:16, which parody the Trinity: Father, Spirit, Son.

way as to be motionless. It dies by forsaking the fountain of life,[186] and thus is welcomed by this passing world and shaped to it.

31. But the fountain of eternal life is your Word, O God, which passes not,[187] and so it is by your word that we are dissuaded from drifting away. *Shape yourselves no longer to the standards of this world,* we are warned. Through this fount of life the land can produce a living being; that is to say, by your word, delivered through your evangelists, it is enabled to bring forth a soul that restrains itself from excesses by imitating those who imitate your Christ.[188] To act so is to act *according to its kind,*[189] for friendship prompts us to emulation,[190] as Paul suggests when he urges, *Adapt yourselves to me, as I have adapted myself to you.*[191]

The wild beasts in this living soul will thus become good and gentle in their conduct, as you have commanded us to be: *Be gentle in all you do, and you will be loved by everyone.*[192] The domestic animals will be good too, discovering that when they have eaten they do not suffer from excess, and when they have not eaten they feel none the worse.[193] The snakes will be good, not dangerous and liable to hurt people but astute and wary,[194] given to exploring the nature of this world of time to whatever degree is necessary that through created things eternity may be glimpsed and understood.[195] These animals are the servants of reason and are truly alive when they are held back from fatally dissipating themselves, and tamed to goodness.

Humanity in God's image and likeness

22, 32. Our attachment to this world brought us to death's door by evil living; but see, O Lord, our God and creator, once the soul has controlled its hankering for worldly things, and has begun to revive by living a good life, and that word which you spoke through your apostle has become a

---

186. See Jer 2:13.
187. See Jn 1:1; 4:14; 6:69; Mt 24:35.
188. See 1 Cor 4:16; 11:1.
189. Gn 1:21.
190. See Eccl 4:4 (Old Latin).
191. Gal 4:12.
192. Sir 3:19(17).
193. See 1 Cor 8:8.
194. See Gn 3:1; Mt 10:16-17.
195. See Rom 1:20.

reality in it: *Shape yourselves no longer to the standards of this world,* something else follows, for you immediately added, *but allow yourselves to be reformed by the renewal of your minds.* You do not say, "reformed according to your kind," as though imitating some neighbor who had gone ahead, or taking some better person as the norm for your lives. No, for you, O God, did not say, "Let there be man, according to his kind," but *Let us make man according to our image and likeness,*[196] for you meant us to discern your will for ourselves. Such was your steward's aim[197] in urging, *Allow yourselves to be reformed by the renewal of your minds, that you may be able to discern what is God's will, what is good and pleasing to him and perfect,*[198] for while he had begotten children through the gospel[199] he did not want them to remain for ever babies whom he must feed on milk and care for like a nurse.[200] This is why you do not say, "Let there be man," but, *Let us make ... ;* nor do you say, "according to his kind," but, *according to our image and likeness.*

A person thus made new considers your truth and understands it. He does not need some other human being to explain it to him so that he may imitate his own kind; you explain it to him, so that he can discern for himself what is your will, what is good and pleasing to you and perfect. And since he now has the capacity to understand, you teach him to contemplate the Trinity in Unity, the Unity that is Trinity. This is why after the plural expression, *Let us make man,* the singular is implied by the next verse, *So God made man in his own image,*[201] and after the plural *according to our image and likeness* the singular is suggested by *in the image of God he created him.* In this way man is renewed in the knowledge of God in accordance with the image of his creator.[202] He becomes a Spirit-filled person, fit to judge of any matters that call for judgment, though he himself is not subject to the judgment of his fellows.

23, 33. "Judging everything" means that human beings have dominion over the fish of the sea and the birds in the sky and all domestic animals

---

196. Gn 1:26.
197. See 1 Cor 4:1.
198. Rom 12:2.
199. See 1 Cor 4:15.
200. See 1 Cor 3:1-2; 1 Thes 2:7.
201. Gn 1:27.
202. See Col 3:10.

and wild beasts, and the whole earth, and all reptiles that crawl there.[203] They exercise it through their intelligent minds, which give them insight into whatever concerns the Spirit of God. Were this not the case, human beings, for all their high dignity, would not understand; they would be on a level with senseless beasts and become like them.[204]

This is why in your Church, O God, persons gifted with the Spirit judge of spiritual things in virtue of the grace you have given her,[205] for we are of your craftsmanship, created for good works.[206] Judgment is exercised not only by the holders of spiritual authority but by those also who are subject to them in the Spirit, for it is in this sense that you have created humanity male and female in the sphere of your spiritual grace: in respect of bodily sexuality male and female here have no significance, any more than do differences between Jew and Greek, slave and free.[207] Spirit-filled persons, then, whether they rule or obey, judge in the light of the Spirit,[208] but not in respect of the splendors of wisdom ablaze in the vault of heaven,[209] for it would be presumptuous to pass judgment on an authority so sublime. Nor do they judge your book itself, because to that we submit our intellects, even if something in it is less than luminous, holding it certain that what is impenetrable to our gaze is nonetheless spoken rightly and with truth; for even a person who is already in the Spirit, already made new in the knowledge of God in accordance with the image of our creator,[210] must be a doer of the law,[211] not a judge of it.

Nor, again, can such a person judge of the distinction between spiritual and carnal people. These are known in your sight, our God, but are not yet clearly distinguished in ours by the criterion of any deeds, which might enable us to tell them by their fruits.[212] You, Lord, know them already, and have drawn your distinction and issued your call, before ever you made the firmament.

---

203. See Gn 1:26.
204. See Ps 48:13(49:12).
205. See 1 Cor 3:10.
206. See Eph 2:10.
207. See Gal 3:28.
208. See 1 Cor 2:15.
209. See Gn 1:15.17.
210. See Col 3:9-10.
211. See Jas 4:11.
212. See Mt 7:20.

Nor, finally, does such a person, however spiritual, judge of the mudbound races of this world, for what business of his are outsiders,[213] when he cannot know which of them will forsake the sea for your sweet grace, and which will remain in that unendingly bitter godlessness?

34. This is why human beings whom you have created in your image did not receive dominion over the luminaries set in the heavenly vault, nor over the hidden heaven itself, nor over the day and the night which you called into being before you established the vault, nor over the amassed waters known as sea. But they were entrusted with dominion over the fish of the sea and the birds in the sky and all domestic cattle, and over the whole land and all the reptiles that crawl upon it. They judge and approve what they find done rightly, but condemn anything they find amiss; and this they do through the celebration of those rites whereby people whom your mercy has sought out in the vast ocean are initiated;[214] or at the solemn rite which makes present the fish raised up from the deep and devoutly eaten by the faithful;[215] or by preaching, which through exegesis, discussion and argument attempts to make plain the meaning of your words, while subjecting itself always to the authority of your book as though winging its way beneath the sky; and through blessing and invoking you, so that as these sounds break from our mouths and make themselves heard, the populace may answer, "Amen."[216] That all these explanations have to be delivered through the spoken word is due to the needs of that abyss which is this world and the blindness of the flesh, for when people cannot see the truth under consideration, it must be dinned into their ears. Although the birds flock over the land, they originate from the waters, and we can see why.

A person endowed with the Spirit also exercises judgment by approving what he finds proper and rebuking anything he finds amiss in the activities and conduct of the faithful. He commends their almsgiving as he would fruitful soil; and he judges favorably the affections tamed to gentleness that characterize a living soul, its chastity, fasting,[217] and devout reflection on the experiences of the senses. In short, he can be said to exercise judgment in areas where he also has authority to correct what is wrong.

---

213. See 1 Cor 5:12.
214. That is, baptism.
215. That is, eucharist.
216. A liturgical context, clearly. This paragraph gives insight into a bishop's occupations.
217. See 2 Cor 6:5-6.

Increase and multiply

24, 35. But now to something puzzling: what sort of mystery have we here?[218] You bless human beings, O Lord, commanding them to increase and multiply and fill the earth.[219] Are you giving us some kind of hint here? Do you not mean us to understand something? You did not confer the same blessing on the light, which you named "day," or on the vault of the sky, or on its luminaries, or on stars, earth or sea: why not? I would have said that you, our God, who created us according to your image, willed to lavish this blessing on humankind exclusively; yes, that is what I would have said, were it not that you gave it equally to the fish and the sea monsters, bidding them swarm and fill the waters of the sea, and commanding the birds also to flock over the land.[220] Or again I might have said that this blessing was restricted to those classes of creatures which give birth and propagate themselves, if I had found it also applied to shrubs and bushes and land animals. But the fact is that the command, *Increase and multiply*,[221] is not addressed to vegetation or trees, or to beasts or reptiles, although all these keep up their numbers and conserve their species by giving birth, as do fish and birds and humans.

36. What am I to say, then, O my Light, O Truth? That this is without significance, and idly so expressed? That is unthinkable, most careful Father: far be it from a servant of your word to say such a thing. If I do not understand what you mean to convey by this saying, let better men make better use of it—people more intelligent than I, in the measure of the wisdom you have granted to each of them.[222] But may my confession too be pleasing in your sight when I confess that I do not believe, Lord, that you spoke in these terms to no purpose. I will not pass over in silence the meaning that comes to my mind when this passage is read, for it is true in itself, and I do not see what is to stop me from responding sensitively to figurative expressions in your books.

Now I know that something may be signified in a variety of ways through material means, yet understood in only one way by the mind, or, conversely, understood in multiple ways by the mind, although signified in only one way materially. An example is love of God and our neighbor: it

---

218. See Sir 39:26.
219. See Gn 1:28.
220. See Gn 1:22.
221. Gn 1:22.28.
222. See Rom 12:3; 1 Cor 3:5.

is simple in itself, but in what a variety of mysterious ways, in what tongues without number, and in any one tongue through what innumerable modes of speech is it given tangible expression! This corresponds to the way in which the offspring of the waters increases and multiplies.

Then consider another example, you who read this: observe that scripture offers us a single truth, couched in simple words, when it tells us, *In the beginning God made heaven and earth.* But is it not interpreted in manifold ways? Leaving aside fallacious and mistaken theories, are there not divergent schools of true opinion? This corresponds to the increase and multiplication of human progeny.

37. So then, if we consider the nature of creatures as they are in themselves, not allegorically but literally, the command, *Increase and multiply*, is appropriate to all those which are propagated from seed. If, however, we take it for granted that the statement is figurative—and I am inclined to think that this was what scripture intended, for it cannot have confined this blessing to the offspring of sea creatures and humans without good reason—then we do indeed find things multiplying everywhere: among both spiritual and corporeal creatures, represented by heaven and earth; among souls both righteous and unjust, described as light and darkness; among the sacred writers through whom the law was mediated, described as the vault fixed firm between upper waters and lower; in the throng of peoples brewing bitterness, who are called "sea"; in the zeal of devout souls, represented by dry land; in the works of mercy appropriate to this present life,[223] described as self-seeding plants and fruit-bearing trees; in spiritual gifts bestowed for the good of all,[224] symbolized by the celestial luminaries; in impulses trained to temperance, described as the "living soul."

In all these instances we discover multiplication, increase and growth, but we do not find anything able to increase and multiply in the way that one truth may be articulated in various modes, or one articulation understood in many different senses; this we find only amid signs displayed by corporeal things and concepts of the mind. Deep-seated carnality and its needs suggest that we take the offspring of the waters to represent signs displayed materially; but the fecundity of our human reason leads us to interpret the breeding of humans as a symbol of truths processed by the intelligence. And we believe that this, Lord, is why your command, *Increase and multiply*, was issued to each of these two; for I assume that by

---

223. See 1 Tm 4:8.
224. See 1 Cor 12:7.

this blessing you granted us the faculty and the power both to articulate in various forms something we have grasped in a single way in our minds, and to interpret in many different senses something we have read, which, though obscure, is couched in simple terms.

Thus the waters of the sea are filled, for it takes a variety of signs to stir them; and so too do human generations populate the land whose aridity bespeaks its thirst for knowledge, the land where reason holds sway.[225]

God assigns them their food

25, 38. I also want to say what the following verses of your scripture bring to mind, Lord my God. I will say it without scruple, because I shall be speaking the truth that is in me by your inspiration, since you have willed me to say what these words mean to me. I do not believe I could speak truthfully under inspiration from anyone other than you, since you are the Truth, whereas all human beings are liars.[226] Thus anyone who tells lies is speaking from what is his own,[227] and in order to speak the truth, I must speak from what is yours.

Well now, you gave us *for food every seeding plant that grows on earth, and every tree that bears fruit yielding seed.*[228] These you gave not to us alone but also to all birds in the sky and land animals and serpents, but you did not give them to the fish or the huge whales. This accords with what we were saying earlier: that these fruits of the earth symbolize and represent in allegorical terms the works of mercy produced by fertile soil to meet the needs of this present life. The charitable Onesiphorus was soil of this type, and you showed mercy to his household because he often relieved Paul's hardships and was not ashamed to consort with a prisoner.[229] Other brethren did the same and bore similar fruit by supplying from Macedonia what Paul needed.[230] But how disappointed he was over certain other trees which failed to bear him the fruit they owed: *The first time I offered my defense*, he says, *no one stood by me. One and all, they left me in the lurch:*

---

225. That is, the sea means carnal-mindedness, only moved to response as signs multiply; human progeny stands for mental concepts.
226. See Jn 14:6; Ps 115(116):11.
227. See Jn 8:44.
228. Gn 1:29-30.
229. See 2 Tm 1:16.
230. See 2 Cor 11:9.

may it not be held against them.[231] For we owe food to those who dispense intelligent teaching to others from their own penetration into divine mysteries, and on this score it is due to them as human beings. We owe it to them also as "living creatures," in that they offer themselves as an example to be followed in every kind of self-restraint. Finally we owe it to them as to birds, in that flocks of blessings fly from them over the land; indeed, *their sound echoed throughout the world.*[232]

26, 39. Only those who find this food delicious are nourished by it; people whose god is their belly[233] do not enjoy it. As for those who supply the food, it is not what they give that is the fruit, but the intention with which they give. I can plainly see the source of that man's joy who served God, and not his own belly;[234] I see it, and with all my heart I rejoice with him. True, he had received the gifts which the Philippians had sent him through Epaphroditus,[235] but all the same I can see the real source of his joy. What brings him joy feeds him. He is speaking the truth when he tells them, *I am splendidly joyful in the Lord to see you putting forth new shoots of care for me. You used to show your care, but then you wearied.*[236] Long-drawn-out weariness had left them too withered and shriveled to bear fruit in good works, so now Paul rejoices on their account, in that fresh green shoots are appearing, rather than on his own, in having his poverty relieved. He therefore continues, *I am not suggesting that I lack anything. Whatever circumstances I am in, I have learned to be content with them; I know how to endure privation, but I also know how to have enough and to spare. I have been thoroughly initiated into the art of withstanding plenty and hunger, abundance and penury. I am capable of anything in him who strengthens me.*[237]

40. Whence, then, springs your joy, great Paul?[238] What brings you joy, and what nourishes you, a man made new in the knowledge of God,

---

231. 2 Tm 4:16.
232. Ps 18:5(19:4).
233. See Phil 3:19.
234. Paul; see Rom 16:18.
235. See Phil 4:18.
236. Phil 4:10. The original Greek has *you had no opportunity*, but the Latin version used by Augustine translated this as *taedium habuistis*, which meaning controls his thought in the following lines.
237. Phil 4:11-13.
238. *Paule magne*, a play of words, since *paulus* means "small."

modeled on the image of your creator,[239] a creature truly alive in your heroic continence, a winged tongue uttering mysteries?[240] All these types of living beings are entitled to eat the food in question, as we know. What is your food, then? Joy! Let me hear your next words: *All the same, you did well to share with me in my trouble.*[241]

This is what he rejoices over, and on this he feeds, that they have acted well, not that his own distress has been alleviated. *When I was hard beset you led me into spacious freedom,*[242] he says to you, because he has learned to withstand both abundance and penury in you, who strengthen him.

For you know yourselves, Philippians, he continues, *that in the early days of my mission, when I set out from Macedonia, no church entered into partnership with me in the business of disbursements and receipts except yourselves alone, for you sent contributions even to Thessalonica, once and then a second time, to defray my expenses.*[243] Now he rejoices in their resumption of these good works and delights over the new growth they are showing, as though over a once-fertile field brought back into good heart.

41. Are we to understand from his words, *You sent to defray my expenses,* that their settling of his money affairs was his motive for such joy? No, not that. How do we know it was not? Because he himself goes on to say, *Not that I seek your gift: all I seek is the fruit accruing to you.*[244] From you, my God, I have learned to distinguish between gift and fruit. The gift is the actual thing given by the person who supplies these necessary goods: it may be cash, food, drink, clothing, shelter, assistance of some kind. But the fruit is the good, upright will of the giver. Our good Master does not simply say, *Anyone who welcomes a prophet;* he specifies: *inasmuch as he is a prophet.* And he says not simply, *Anyone who welcomes a just person,* but adds, *inasmuch as he is a just person.* Only so will the one receive a prophet's reward and the other the reward of a just person. Again, he says not only, *Anyone who gives a cup of cold water to one of my little ones,* but adds, *simply because he is a disciple,* and then goes on to promise, *I tell you, he will not miss his reward.*[245] The gift consists in welcoming the prophet, welcoming the just person, and

---

239. See Col 3:9-10.
240. See 1 Cor 14:2.
241. Phil 4:14.
242. Ps 4:2(1).
243. Phil 4:15-16.
244. Phil 4:17.
245. Mt 10:41-42.

handing a cup of cold water to a disciple; but the fruit consists in doing it precisely because the other is a prophet, or a just person, or a disciple. Elijah was fed by a widow who knew that she was feeding a man of God and did it for that reason, and so she sustained him with fruit; but the food brought him by the raven was no more than a gift:[246] not the spirit of Elijah but only the outer man was fed, the outer man who could have died for lack of such food.

27, 42. I would say, therefore, what I believe to be true in your sight, Lord, with regard to uninstructed and unbelieving persons, the kind who need preliminary rites and spectacular miracles if they are to be initiated into faith and won over, the people who, as we have said, are typified by fishes and whales. When such people welcome your servants, offering them bodily refreshment or any kind of timely assistance in their daily lives, but do so without knowing why it should be done or what is implied, they do not truly feed their guests, nor are the guests fed by them, because no holy or upright will prompts the hosts' actions, nor do your servants yet find in the gifts received any fruit over which to rejoice. So true is it that our spirit feeds on what gives it joy. This is why the fishes and whales are not permitted to eat the foods which spring up only from soil already marked out and emergent from the bitter waves of the sea.

God saw that it was exceedingly good (against the Manichees)

28, 43. And you looked upon all the things you have made, O God, and lo, they are exceedingly good;[247] we too look upon them, and even in our eyes they are exceedingly good. In every successive act of creation you had commanded some class of creature to be, and it came into being, and you saw that each was good. Seven times, according to my count, does scripture relate that you looked on what you have made and found it good; but this eighth time you looked on all your works together, and lo, not merely are they good, but taken as a whole they are exceedingly good. Severally good, they are exceedingly good all together. Every beautiful body conveys the same message, for a body consisting of beautiful limbs is far more beautiful than its component parts individually, because

---

246. See 1 Kgs 17:6-16.
247. See Gn 1:31.

though each one has its own loveliness, it is only through their exquisite coordination that the whole organism attains its perfection.

29, 44. I now applied my mind to discover whether you really did look upon your works seven or eight times when you found them pleasing, and I discovered in your act of seeing no element of temporality which would explain to me how you could have looked so many times at what you had made. I therefore appealed to you: "Surely, Lord, this scripture of yours is true, since you are its author and you are truthful—indeed, Truth itself?[248] Why, then, do you tell me that there is no element of time in your seeing, whereas your scripture tells me that day after day you saw that your work was good? I was even able to count these occasions, and find out how many times you looked at your creatures."[249]

You reply to me, because you are my God, and you speak loudly in your servant's inner ear, bursting through my deafness,[250] you cry out to me, "Listen, human creature: what my scripture says, I myself say, but whereas scripture says it in terms of time, my Word is untouched by time, because he subsists with me eternally, equal to myself. What you see through my Spirit, I see, just as what you say through my Spirit, I say.[251] You see these things in terms of time, but I do not see in time, nor when you say these things in temporal fashion do I speak in a way conditioned by time."

30, 45. I heard your answer, O Lord my God, and from this truth I sucked out a drop of sweetness. I understood why some people do not find your creatures pleasing; they hold that you were driven by necessity when you built such things as the heavens and the constellations, and that these had already been created somewhere else and by some other power. You, they say, merely assembled them, fitted and welded them together when you were laboriously constructing the ramparts of the world after vanquishing your enemies, to barricade them in and ensure that they would never again

---

248. See Jn 3:33; 14:6.
249. Brief recapitulation of his considerations in Book XI (temporal creation as related to the eternal creator) and Book XII (veracity of scripture).
250. See X,27,38.
251. This may include Augustine's authoritative teaching as bishop, as well as statements made by the human scriptural authors. God's answer to Augustine powerfully draws together Word and scripture, Spirit and Church, eternity and time, divine unity and human fragmentation.

rebel against you.[252] Other things, such as all the animals and the minutest life-forms and everything that clings to the soil by its roots, they do not believe you made or even put together at all; a hostile intelligence, some other nature not created by you and working against you, spawned and shaped them in the lower regions of the world.[253] People who allege this are mad, because they do not contemplate your works through your Spirit, nor recognize you in them.

31, 46. It is different for people who see creation through your Spirit, for you are seeing it through their eyes. Thus when such people see that these things are good, you are seeing that they are good; whatever created things please them for your sake, it is you who are arousing their delight in these things; and anything that gives us joy through your Spirit gives you joy in us. Yet scripture asks, *Who knows the reality of anyone, except that person's own inward spirit? So too no one knows the reality of God except God's own Spirit. But we,* says scripture, *we have not received the spirit of this world, but the Spirit which is of God, that we may know what gifts have been bestowed on us by God.*[254]

Plainly I am bound to say that no one knows the reality of God except the Spirit of God. How, then, can we too know the gifts that God has given us? This is the answer that comes to me: if we know something through his Spirit, it is still true to say that *no one knows* it *except God's own Spirit;* for just as it could rightly be said to people who spoke in the Spirit of God, *It is not you who are speaking,*[255] so too is it rightly said to those who know anything in the Spirit of God, "It is not you who are knowing this." With equal justice could it be said to people who contemplate creation in the Spirit of God, "It is not you who are seeing this." If, then, seeing something in God's Spirit, they perceive it to be good, it is evidently not they, but God, who sees that it is good.

One point of view, therefore, is that of someone who thinks a good thing evil; of such people mention has been made already. Another approach is to see that it is good, as many do who find your good creation pleasant, but fail to find you within it, and look for their enjoyment in

---

252. The Manichees are envisaged here and in the following sentences: the captive powers of darkness had been built into the fabric of the universe, according to their system.
253. The captive powers were supposed to have dropped their aborted fetuses, which fell to earth, developed and propagated themselves, giving rise to animals.
254. 1 Cor 2:11-12.
255. Mt 10:20.

creation itself rather than in you. Different from both is the attitude of one who sees it as good in such a way that their God views its goodness through the person's human eyes. This means that God is loved in what he has made. But he could not be loved were it not through the Spirit he has given us, *because the love of God has been poured out into our hearts through the Holy Spirit bestowed upon us.*[256] Through him we see that everything is good which in any degree has being, because it derives from him who has being in no degree at all, but is simply *He Is.*[257]

Summary of literal exegesis; man and woman

32, 47. Thanks be to you, O Lord. We contemplate heaven and earth, whether this be understood as the upper and lower regions of your material creation, or your spiritual as distinct from your embodied creatures. We see also the adornment of these parts, of which either the whole bulk of the physical world, or the entire created universe, consists, for we see light created and separated from darkness. We behold the vault of heaven, which means either the barrier between the spiritual waters on high and the lower waters which constitute the primordial matter of the world, or else the airy space of sky through which birds freely wander, since this too goes by the name "heaven." Across it they wing their way between the waters which sail overhead in cloudy vapor, bedewing the earth even on fine nights, and the heavy waters that surge on earth. We contemplate the beauty of waters gathered together in the wide expanses of the sea,[258] and the dry land, still bare as it rises from the sea, or endowed with visible, organized form to bring forth plants and trees. We see the lamps shining on high, the sun flooding the day and the moon and stars bringing solace to the night, and all of them serving to indicate periods of time and mark its passage. On every side we see the watery world teeming with fish and whales, and with birds too, because their flight is upborne on air made denser by evaporation from the waters. We regard the fair face of the earth adorned with land animals; and we see humankind, made in your image and likeness, set over all these irrational living creatures in virtue of this

---

256. Rom 5:5. This text, already quoted in XIII,7,8, is a fitting climax to this book devoted to the Spirit, who was seen hovering over the waters in its early chapters.
257. Ex 3:14.
258. Literally "the fields of the sea," a probable allusion to Virgil, *Aeneid* X,214: "wide fields of waters."

same image and likeness to you, which resides in its reason and intelligence. And just as within the human soul one faculty deliberates and takes decisions, while another must be submissive and obedient, so too was woman made physically subordinate to man. Though equal to him by nature in her rational mind and intelligence, with respect to bodily sexuality she was subjected to the male, even as the impulse to action must be submissive in order to conceive from the rational mind the sagacity to act aright.

All these things we see. Severally they are good, and together they are exceedingly good.

Summary of allegorical exegesis

33, 48. Your creation sings praise to you[259] so that we may love you, and we love you so that praise may be offered to you by your creation. Created things have their beginning and their end in time, their rising and setting, their growth and decline, their beauty of form and their formlessness; and thus they have their morning and evening, though sometimes this is hidden, sometimes plainly seen. Inevitably so, because they were made by you out of nothing: not made from you, nor from any matter not of your making, nor from anything pre-existent, but from concreated matter: that is, matter which you created formless at the same instant that you gave it form, without any interval. Although the primal matter of heaven and earth is something other than the form of heaven and earth, you made their matter from nothingness, and their formed condition from unformed matter, and both simultaneously, so that form followed on the heels of matter without the least interruption or lapse of time.

34, 49. We also scrutinized the text to discover what figurative meaning you intended to suggest in willing these things to happen, or at any rate to be written, in this particular order. And in your Word, your only Son, we saw them severally as good and collectively as exceedingly good; for what we saw was heaven and earth, the Head and the body of the Church[260] which you predestined before time began, when there was neither morning nor evening.

---

259. See Ps 144(145):10; Dn 3:57.
260. See Col 1:18.

But when you began to give effect in time to your predetermined plan, when you purposed to bring your hidden decrees[261] to light and give form to our unformed state (formless it was because with our sins weighing us down we had been dragged away from you into the darkness of the deep, but your good Spirit[262] was hovering overhead to help us in our time of need), then you justified the godless,[263] marked them out from the wicked, and established the vault of your authoritative scripture between the upper creatures who were docile to you, and the lower who were subject to them.

Then you gathered the great horde of unbelievers into a cohesive mass, which would throw into relief the zealous efforts of the faithful who were to bear fruit for you in works of mercy, even to the point of distributing their worldly goods to the poor[264] and so winning wealth in heaven.

After this you kindled special lamps in the vault; these are your saints, entrusted with the word of life,[265] whose sublime authority was attested by their spiritual gifts.[266] Through them you drew forth sacraments from corporeal matter, palpable miracles and doctrine in harmony with your overarching scripture, all designed to instill faith into unbelieving Gentiles, though apt to shed their benediction upon the faithful as well.

Then you gave form to the believing soul, the soul truly alive because by robust self-control it had reduced its impulses to good order. Its mind was now subject to you alone, and needed no human norm to imitate, for you made it new after your own image and in your likeness, and subordinated its rational activity to the sovereignty of intellect, as woman is to man.

Finally you willed that all your ministers, whose work is necessary in this present life to bring your faithful to maturity, should be provided for in the temporal sphere by these same faithful, whose services will bear fruit for the life to come.

All these things we see to be exceedingly good, because you see them in us, you who have given us the Spirit to enable us to see them, and in them to love you.

---

261. See Ps 50:8(51:6).
262. See Ps 142(143):10.
263. See Rom 4:5.
264. See 1 Cor 13:3.
265. See Phil 2:15-16; Jn 6:69.
266. See 1 Cor 12:7.

Conclusion: rest on the seventh day

35, 50. Give us peace, Lord God, for you have given us all else;[267] give us the peace that is repose, the peace of the Sabbath, and the peace that knows no evening.[268] This whole order of exceedingly good things, intensely beautiful as it is, will pass away when it has served its purpose: these things too will have their morning and their evening.[269]

36, 51. But the seventh day has no evening and sinks toward no sunset, for you sanctified it that it might abide for ever. After completing your exceedingly good works you rested on the seventh day, though you achieved them in repose; and you willed your book to tell us this as a promise that when our works are finished (works exceedingly good inasmuch as they are your gift to us) we too may rest in you, in the Sabbath of eternal life.

37, 52. And then you will rest in us, as now you work in us, and your rest will be rest through us as now those works of yours are wrought through us. But you yourself, Lord, are ever working, ever resting. You neither see for a time nor change for a time nor enjoy repose for a time, yet you create our temporal seeing and time itself and our repose after time.[270]

38, 53. We, therefore, see these things you have made, because they exist, but for you it is different: they exist because you see them. Moreover when we see that they exist, we see it outside ourselves, but when we see that they are good, we see it by inner vision, whereas you see them as created in no other place than where you saw them as non-existent things you willed to create.

Once our heart had conceived by your Spirit we made a fresh start and began to act well, though at an earlier stage we had been impelled to wrongdoing and abandoned you; but you, O God undivided and good, have never ceased to act well. Some of our works are indeed good, thanks to your Gift,[271] but they will not last for ever, and when they are done we hope that we shall rest in your immense holiness.[272] But you, the supreme

---

267. See Is 26:12; Nm 6:26.
268. See 2 Thes 3:16.
269. See Gn 1:5-31.
270. See I,4,4: some of the antitheses there are echoed in the present chapter.
271. That is perhaps "your Spirit," the Gift of God; compare XIII,9,10.
272. This is the rest and peace toward which the whole of *The Confessions* has tended from I,1,1; compare I,5,5, through all the restlessness of the long search. At the end of *The City of God* XXII,30, Augustine will similarly evoke the Sabbath rest: "Then will God seem to take his

Good, need no other good and are eternally at rest, because you yourself are your rest.

What human can empower another human to understand these things? What angel can grant understanding to another angel? What angel to a human? Let us rather ask of you, seek in you, knock at your door. Only so will we receive, only so find, and only so will the door be opened to us. Amen.[273]

---

rest on the seventh day, for he will cause the seventh day, that is, ourselves, to rest in God himself.... There we shall be still and see, see and love, love and praise."

273. See Mt 7:7-8, quoted especially at the beginning of his search through Gn 1, at XII,1,1.

Index of Scripture

(prepared by Michael Dolan)

Index

(prepared by Joseph Sprung)

*Citations are to book [Roman number], chapter,
and paragraph (in parentheses).*

A Bibliographic Guide to Augustine
and
the Confessions

(prepared by William Harmless, S.J.)

Augustine's Life And Theology: Introductions

The best place to begin one's study of Augustine is with Peter Brown's landmark biography, *Augustine of Hippo: A Biography*, rev. ed. (Berkeley: University of California Press, 2000). Originally published in 1968, this beautifully written work does much to bring Augustine and his complex world alive to contemporary readers. It is studded with fine insights into Augustine's personality and struggles. The revised edition has two lengthy chapters that incorporate perspectives from newly discovered works (the Dolbeau sermons and the Divjak letters). Also excellent is Serge Lancel's *Saint Augustine*, trans. Antonia Nevill (London: SCM Press, 2002). Lancel draws on a wide range of archeological discoveries from Roman North Africa to illuminate Augustine's world. He also gives more attention than Brown does to the intricacies of Augustine's theology and offers helpful summaries of Augustine's major theological works. Other useful surveys and introductions to Augustine's life and theology include:

Bonner, Gerald. "Augustinus (uita)." In *Augustinus-Lexikon*, 1:519-550. Ed. Cornelius Mayer. Basel: Schwabe, 1986.

Chadwick, Henry. *Augustine: A Very Short Introduction*. New York: Oxford University Press, 2001.

_____. *Augustine of Hippo: A Life*. New York: Oxford University Press, 2009.

Harrison, Carol. *Augustine: Christian Truth and Fractured Humanity*. Christian Theology in Context. New York: Oxford University Press, 2000.

Madec, Goulven. *Introduction aux 'Revisions' et à la lecture des oeuvres de saint Augustin*. Collection des Études Augustiniennes, Série Antiquité 150. Paris: Institut d'Études Augustiniennes, 1996.

Vessey, Mark, ed. *A Companion to Augustine*, Blackwell Companions to the Ancient World. Oxford: Wiley-Blackwell, forthcoming, 2012.

Reading Augustine: A Guide to Texts and Translations

The entire corpus of Augustine's writings is gradually being translated into English in the series of which this translation of *Confessions* is part: *The Works of Saint Augustine: A Translation for the 21st Century*, eds. John E. Rotelle and Boniface Ramsey (Hyde Park, NY: New City Press, 1990-   ). Because Augustine was such a prolific writer, knowing what of his work to read or how best to read him in context can prove daunting not only to newcomers but even to scholars. A recent anthology that allows one to survey the richness and wide breadth of Augustine's writings is that of William Harmless, ed. and trans., *Augustine in His Own Words* (Washington, DC: Catholic University of America Press, 2010). This compilation devotes a chapter to each of Augustine's major works (*Confessions, The Trinity,* and *City of God*) and to each of his major controversies (against the Manicheans, against the Donatists, and against the Pelagians); it also has chapters on Augustine's work as a philosopher, bishop, preacher, and interpreter of the Bible. There are two other major recent anthologies. One is Daniel H. Doyle's collection, *Saint Augustine: Essential Sermons,* trans. Edmund Hill (Hyde Park, NY: New City Press, 2007). This selects key sermons from the nearly 1000 sermons of Augustine's that have been preserved. A second is Roland Teske's *Saint Augustine: Selected Writings on Grace and Pelagianism* (Hyde Park, NY: New City Press, 2011). This guides readers through the vast literature associated with Augustine's final and enormously influential controversy with the Pelagians. Other translations of Augustine's works can be found in other multi-volume series: Fathers of the Church (Catholic University of America Press), Ancient Christian Writers (Newman Press, Paulist Press), and the Library of Christian Classics (Westminster). One widely used, but quite dated, translation is the 8-volume collection in the Nicene and Post-Nicene Fathers (1886-1888; reprint: Peabody, MA: Hendrickson, 1995); these are also available online at various Internet websites.

Augustine was a brilliant Latin stylist and should be read in the original if possible. For those who can read Latin, the bulk of Augustine's works can be found in J.P. Migne, Patrologia Latina, vols. 32-47. Migne reproduced the excellent 17th-century edition of the Benedictines of St. Maur. The Italian publishers of Augustine's works, the Nuova Biblioteca Agostiniana (NBA), have posted this classic Maurist edition on the Internet: http://www.augustinus.it/latino/index.htm. This older edition of Augustine's works is slowly being replaced by modern critical editions in the Corpus Scriptorum Ecclesiasticorum Latinorum (CSEL) and the Corpus Christianorum, Series Latina (CCL).

Reference Works

One excellent research tool is *Augustine Through the Ages: An Encyclopedia,* ed. Allan D. Fitzgerald (Grand Rapids, MI: Eerdmans, 1999). This 900-page work surveys every aspect of Augustine's life, writings, theology, and influence. Articles are written by the leading English-speaking Augustinian scholars. Also excellent, but incomplete, is the *Augustinus-Lexikon,* ed. Cornelius Mayer (Basel: Schwabe, 1986-), 3 volumes to date; individual articles are written in German, English or French.

Confessions: Studies

The major biographies of Augustine do a fine job of guiding readers through the story recorded in *Confessions,* providing the historical and cultural background and adding critical perspectives to Augustine's own self-presentation. See Brown, *Augustine of Hippo* (pp. 7-124 and 151-175); and Lancel, *Saint Augustine* (pp. 3-120). Also helpful is the classic study by John J. O'Meara,

The Young Augustine: An Introduction to the Confessions of St. Augustine, 2ⁿᵈed. (1956; reprint: New York: Alba House, 2001). For an introduction to the literary character of the text, see Gillian Clark, *Saint Augustine: The Confessions*, Landmarks of World Literature (Cambridge: Cambridge University Press, 1993). For a book-by-book commentary, see Kim Paffenroth and Robert Peter Kennedy, eds. *A Reader's Companion to Augustine's Confessions* (Louisville: Westminster John Knox, 2003). More advanced students should consult J.J. O'Donnell, *Augustine: Confessions*, 3 volumes (New York: Oxford University Press, 1991); volume 1 has the Latin text, while volumes 2 and 3 offer a detailed paragraph-by-paragraph commentary. O'Donnell presumes readers have a strong command of Latin. Also valuable is the introduction and commentary by Aimé Solignac in the French edition of *Confessions*, Bibliothèque Augustinienne, vols. 13-14, rev. ed. (Paris: Desclée de Bouwer, 1992). There is a vast scholarly literature on *Confessions*. What follows is a small selection of scholarly studies for more advanced students:

Archambult, Paul J. "Augustine, Memory, and the Development of Autobiography." *Augustinian Studies* 13 (1982): 23-30.

_____. "Augustine, Time, and Autobiography as Language." *Augustinian Studies* 15 (1984): 7-13.

BeDuhn, Jason D. *Augustine's Manichaean Dilemma*. Vol. 1: *Conversion and Apostasy, 373-388 C.E.* Divinations: Rereading Late Ancient Religion. Philadelphia: University of Pennsylvania Press, 2009. BeDuhn, a specialist in Manicheanism, examines how Augustine's former co-religionists would have read his "apostasy" from Manicheanism.

_____. "Augustine Accused: Megalius, Manichaeism, and the Inception of the *Confessions*." *Journal of Early Christian Studies* 17 (2009): 85-124.

Bochet, Isabelle. *"Le Firmament de l'Écriture": L'herméneutique augustinienne*. Collection des Études Augustiniennes: Série Antiquité 172. Paris: Institut d'Études Augustiniennes, 2004. A massive and insightful study of the way Augustine draws on the Psalms and on the letters of Paul in his *Confessions*.

Bonner, Gerald. "Augustine's Conversion: Historical Fact or Literary Device." *Augustinus* 37 (1993): 103-119.

Bowery, Anne-Marie. "You Are What You Read: Reading the Books of Augustine's *Confessions*." *Augustinian Studies* 39 (2008): 101-112.

Brachtendorf, Johannes. *Augustins 'Confessiones'*. Darmstadt: Wissenschaftliche Buchgesellschaft, 2005.

Bright, Pamela. "En-Spirited Waters: Baptism in the *Confessions* of Augustine." In *The Early Church in its Context: Essays in Honor of E. Ferguson*, 48-58. Eds. A.J. Malherbe, F.W. Norris, J.W. Thompson. Leiden: Brill, 1998.

Burns, J. Patout. "Ambrose Preaching to Augustine: The Shaping of Faith." In *Augustine: Second Founder of the Faith*, 373-386. Eds. Joseph C. Schnaubelt and Frederick van Fleteren. New York: Peter Lang, 1990.

_____. "Augustine's Distinctive Use of the Psalms in the Confessions." *Augustinian Studies* 24 (1993): 133-146.

Burton, Philip. *Language in the* Confessions *of Augustine.* New York: Oxford University Press, 2007.

Cavadini, John C. "Time and Ascent in *Confessions* XI." In *Augustine: Presbyter Factus Sum,* 171-185. Eds. Joseph T. Lienhard et al. Collectanea Augustiniana. New York: Peter Lang, 1993.

_____. "Eucharistic Exegesis in Augustine's *Confessions.*" *Augustinian Studies* 41 (2011): 87-108.

Chadwick, Henry. "History and Symbolism in the Garden at Milan." In *From Augustine to Eriugena: Essays on Neoplatonism and Christianity in Honor of John O'Meara,* 42-55. Eds. F.X. Martin and J.A. Richmond. Washington, DC: The Catholic University of America Press, 1991.

Chin, Catherine M. "Christians and the Roman Classroom: Memory, Grammar, and Rhetoric in *Confessions* X." *Augustinian Studies* 33 (2002): 161-182.

Courcelle, Pierre. *Recherches sur les Confessions de saint Augustin.* 2ⁿᵈ ed. Paris: E. de Boccard, 1968. One of the most important studies of *Confessions* in the 20ᵗʰ century. While dated, it remains a pivotal book.

_____. *Les Confessions de saint Augustin dans la tradition littéraire: Antécédents et postérité.* Collection des Études Augustiniennes, Série Antiquité 15. Paris: Études Augustiniennes, 1963.

Coyle, J. Kevin. "Saint Augustine's Manichaean Legacy." St. Augustine Lecture 2002. *Augustinian Studies* 34 (2003): 1-22. Valuable perspectives on the way Manicheanism shaped Augustine's outlook.

Ferrari, Leo C. "The Pear-Theft in Augustine's *Confessions.*" *Revue des Études Augustiniennes* 16 (1970): 233-242.

_____. "The Theme of the Prodigal Son in Augustine's *Confessions.*" *Recherches Augustiniennes* 12 (1977): 105-118.

_____. "Paul at the Conversion of Augustine (Conf VIII, 12, 29-30)." *Augustinian Studies* 11 (1980): 5-20.

Finn, Thomas M. "Ritual and Conversion: The Case of Augustine." In *Nova et Vetera: Patristic Studies in Honor of Thomas Patrick Halton,* 148-161. Ed. John F. Petruccione. Washington, DC: Catholic University of America Press, 1998.

Fitzgerald, Allan D. "Ambrose and Augustine: *confessio* as *initium iustitiae.*" *Augustinianum* 40 (2000): 173-185.

Fredriksen, Paula. "Paul and Augustine: Conversion Narratives, Orthodox Traditions, and the Retrospective Self." *Journal of Theological Studies* n.s. 37 (1986): 3-34.

Fredouille, J.-C. "Les *Confessions* d'Augustin. Autobiographie au présent." *L'invention du l'autobiographie: D'Hésiode à saint Augustin, Actes du 2e colloque de l'Équipe de recherche sur l'hellénisme post-classique (Paris, 14-16 juin 1990),* 167-178. Eds. M.-F. Baslez, Ph. Hoffman, and L. Pernot. Paris: Presses de l'École Normale Supérieure, 1993.

Harrison, Carol. "Augustine of Hippo's Cassiciacum *Confessions*: Toward a Reassessment of the 390s." *Augustinian Studies* 31 (2000): 219-224 .

Kenney, John Peter. *The Mysticism of Saint Augustine: Re-Reading the Confessions.* New York: Routledge, 2005. In *Confessions,* Books 7 and 9,

Augustine describes several powerful spiritual experiences. This landmark study demonstrates how dramatically Augustine's accounts differ from those of his philosophical dialogue partners, Plotinus and the Neoplatonists.

Kotzé, Annemaré. *Augustine's Confessions: Communicative Purpose and Audience.* Supplements to Vigiliae Christianae 71. Leiden / Boston: Brill, 2004.

Lepelley, Claude. "Un aspect de la conversion d'Augustin: La rupture avec ses ambitions sociales et politiques." *Bulletin de Littérature Ecclésiastique* 88 (1987): 229-246.

Madec, Goulven. "Conuersio." In *Augustinus-Lexikon*, 1:1282-1294. Ed. Cornelius Mayer. Basel: Schwabe, 1986.

_____. "Les *Confessions* comme prière biblique." In *Lectures Augustiniennes*, 111-119. Collection des Études Augustiniennes, Série Antiquité 168. Paris: Institut d'Études Augustiniennes, 2001.

_____. "Le néoplatonisme dans la conversion d'Augustin: État d'une question centenaire (depuis Harnack et Boissier, 1888)." In *Petites Études Augustiniennes*, 51-69. Collection des Études Augustiniennes, Série Antiquité 142. Paris: Institut d'Études Augustiniennes, 1994.

Martin, Thomas F. "Paul the Patient: *Christus Medicus* and the *'Stimulus Carnis'*: A Consideration of Augustine's Medicinal Christology." *Augustinian Studies* 32 (2001): 219-256.

Mathews, Charles T. "The Liberation of Questioning in Augustine's *Confessions.*" *Journal of American Academy of Religion* 70 (2002): 539-560.

McMahon, Robert. *Augustine's Prayerful Ascent: An Essay on the Literary Form of the Confessions.* Athens, GA: Georgia University Press, 1989.

Meconi, David Vincent. "The Incarnation and the Role of Participation in St. Augustine's *Confessions.*" *Augustinian Studies* 29 (1998) 61-75.

O'Connell, Robert J. *St. Augustine's Confessions: The Odyssey of Soul.* Cambridge, MA: Harvard University Press, 1969. A controversial study, but full of important insights.

_____. "Isaiah's Mothering God in St. Augustine's *Confessions.*" *Thought* 58 (1983): 188-206.

_____. "Faith, Reason, and Ascent to Vision in St. Augustine." *Augustinian Studies* 21 (1990): 83-126.

_____. *Images of Conversion in Saint Augustine's Confessions.* New York: Fordham University Press, 1995.

O'Meara, John J. "*Arripui, aperui, et legi*' (*Confessions* VIII, 12, 29)." In *Studies in Augustine and Eriugena*, 24-30. Ed. Thomas Halton. Washington, DC: Catholic University of America Press, 1992.

_____. "Augustine's *Confessions*: Elements of Fiction." In *Augustine: From Rhetor to Theologian*, 77-96. Ed. Joanne McWilliam. Waterloo: Wilfrid Laurier University Press, 1992.

Pollman, Karla, and Mark Vessey, eds. *Augustine and the Disciplines: From Cassiciacum to Confessions.* New York: Oxford University Press, 2005.

Quinn, John M. *A Companion to the* Confessions *of St. Augustine.* New York: Peter Lang, 2002.

Reta, José Oroz. "Prière et recherche de Dieu dans les *Confessions* de saint Augustine." *Augustinian Studies* 7 (1976): 99-118.

Ramirez, J.R.E. "Augustine's Proof for God's Existence from the Experience of Beauty: Confessions X,6." *Augustinian Studies* 19 (1988): 121-130.

Shaw, B.D. "The Family in Late Antiquity: The Experience of Augustine." *Past and Present* 115 (1987): 3-51.

Starnes, Colin. *Augustine's Conversion: A Guide to the Argument of Confessions I-IX*. Waterloo, Ottawa: Wilfrid Laurier University Press, 1990.

Steinhauser, Kenneth B. "The Literary Unity of the *Confessions*." In *Augustine: From Rhetor to Theologian*, 15-30. Ed. Joanne McWilliam. Waterloo, Ontario: Wilfrid Laurier University Press, 1992.

Stock, Brian. *Augustine's Inner Dialogue: The Philosophical Soliloquy in Late Antiquity*. Cambridge: Cambridge University Press, 2011.

Teske, Roland J. "'Homo Spiritualis' in the *Confessions* in St. Augustine." In *Augustine: From Rhetor to Theologian*, 67-76. Ed. Joanne McWilliam. Waterloo, Ontario: Wilfrid Laurier University Press, 1992.

Torchia, N. Joseph. "St. Augustine's Triadic Interpretation of Iniquity in the *Confessions*." In *Augustine: Second Founder of the Faith*, 159-174. Eds. Joseph C. Schnaubelt, Frederick Van Fleteren. Collectanea Augustiniana. New York: Peter Lang, 1990.

Verheijen, Luc. "The *Confessions*: Two Grids of Composition and Reading." In *Augustine: Second Founder of the Faith*, 177-201. Ed. Joseph C. Schnaubelt and Frederick van Fleteren. Collectanea Augustiana. New York: Peter Lang, 1990.

Wetzel, James. "The Force of Memory: Reflections on the Interrupted Self." *Augustinian Studies* 38 (2007): 147-159.

Williams, Rowan, "Augustine's Christology: Its Spirituality and Rhetoric." In *In the Shadow of the Incarnation: Essays in Honor of Brian Daley*, 176-189. Ed. Peter Martens. Notre Dame: University of Notre Dame Press, 2008.

Wright, David F. "Monnica's Baptism, Augustine's Deferred Baptism, and Patricius," *Augustinian Studies* 29 (1998): 1-17 .

Young, Frances. "The *Confessions* of St. Augustine: What is the Genre of this Work?" 1998 St. Augustine Lecture. *Augustinian Studies* 30 (1999): 1-16.

Le Confessioni *di Agostino (402-2002): Bilancio e prospettive: XXXI Incontro di studiosi dell'antichità cristiana, Roma, 2-4 maggio 2002*. Rome: Institutum Patristicum Augustinianum, 2003.

Confessions and Augustine's Broader Theology

The following are a collection of important book-length studies of Augustine. All of these touch upon various themes and ideas relevant to the study of *Confessions*, though in most cases, *Confessions* itself is not their singular focus. I have added occasional comments that note the relevance of the work to the study of *Confessions*:

Arnold, Duane W.H. Arnold and Pamela Bright, ed., *De Doctrina Christiana: a Classic of Western Culture*, Christianity and Judaism in Antiquity, vol. 9 (Notre Dame: University of Notre Dame Press, 1995). Augustine composed *Teaching Christianity* (*De doctrina Christiana*) around the same time as *Confessions*. This important collection of essays highlights how Augustine thought about biblical interpretation during the very period that he was writing *Confessions*.

Ayres, Lewis. *Augustine and the Trinity*. New York: Oxford University Press, 2010. In Book 13 of *Confessions*, Augustine meditates on the Trinity. This landmark study puts those reflections in the context of Augustine's broader trinitarian theology.

Bouton-Touboulic, Anne Isabelle. *L'ordre caché: La notion d'ordre chez saint Augustin*. Collection des Études Augustiniennes, Série Antiquité 174. Paris: Institut d'Études Augustiniennes, 2004.

Brown, Peter. *Religion and Society in the Age of St. Augustine*. 1972; reprint: Eugene, OR: Wipf & Stock, 2007. A classic collection of essays on Augustine's North Africa.

Burnaby, John. *Amor Dei: A Study of the Religion of St. Augustine*. 1938: reprint: Eugene, OR: Wipf & Stock, 2007. A classic study on central themes in Augustine's theology.

Conybeare, Catherine. *The Irrational Augustine*. Oxford Early Christian Studies. New York: Oxford University Press, 2006. A key study of the Cassiciacum dialogues, which Augustine alludes to in Book 9 of *Confessions*.

Dodaro, Robert, and George Lawless, eds. *Augustine and His Critics: Essays in Honor of Gerald Bonner*. New York: Routledge, 2000. A superb collection of essays on many facets of Augustine's thought and career.

Evans, G. R. *Augustine on Evil*. Cambridge: Cambridge University Press, 1982. Augustine says that he was drawn to the Manicheans because of his search to uncover the origins of evil. This traces Augustine's many-sided response to the question.

Fiedrowicz, Michael. *Psalmus vox tottus Christi: Studien zu Augustins Enarrationes in Psalmos*. Freiburg: Herder, 1997. Throughout *Confessions*, Augustine again and again quotes the Psalms. This is a major study of the role of the Psalms in Augustine's life and preaching.

Fredriksen, Paula. *Augustine and the Jews: A Christian Defense of Jews and Judaism*. New York: Doubleday, 2008. Augustine records in Books 5 and 6 of *Confessions* the pivotal intellectual breakthrough he experienced as a result of Ambrose's defense of the Old Testament. In this work, Fredriksen explores how Augustine defended Judaism and the Old Testament against Manichean attacks.

Fux, P.-Y., J.-M. Roessli, and Otto Wermelinger, eds. *Augustinus Afer: Saint Augustin, africanité et universalité. Actes du colloque international, Alger-Annaba, 1-7 avril 2001*. Fribourg: Éditions universitaires, 2003. An important collection of essays exploring Augustine's African roots and pastoral context.

Geest, Paul van. *The Incomprehensibility of God: Augustine as a Negative Theologian*. Leuven: Peeters, 2011. An exploration of Augustine's theological views on the ineffability of God, a theme that runs through *Confessions*.

Harmless, William. *Augustine and the Catechumenate*. Collegeville, MN: The Liturgical Press [A Pueblo Book], 1995. This study includes an analysis of the baptismal rituals that Augustine experienced during his conversion in Milan and the catechesis he received as a catechumen and neophyte under Ambrose's supervision.

Harrison, Carol. *Rethinking Augustine's Early Theology: An Argument for Continuity*. New York: Oxford University Press, 2006. Peter Brown stresses that *Confessions* marked a sharp break in Augustine's thinking on grace; Harrison argues that one needs to see instead certain deeper continuities.

Harrison, Simon. *Augustine's Way into the Will: The Theological and Philosophical Significance of De libero arbitrio*. Oxford Early Christian Studies. New York: Oxford University Press, 2006. Much of the drama of *Confessions* focuses on the struggle of the conversion of Augustine's will. This examines Augustine's earlier thinking about the will.

Hermanowicz, Erika. *Possidius of Calama: A Study of the North African Episcopate in the Age of Augustine*. Oxford Early Christian Studies. New York: Oxford University Press, 2008. Possidius was Augustine's biographer and literary executor.

Hombert, Pierre-Marie. *Gloria Gratiae: Se glorifier en Dieu, principe et fin de la théologie augustinienne de la grâce*. Collection des Études Augustiniennes, Serie Antiquité 148. Paris: Institut d'Études Augustiniennes, 1996.

Hombert, Pierre-Marie. *Nouvelles recherches de chronologie augustiniennes*. Collection des Études Augustiniennes, Série antiquité 163. Paris: Institut d'études augustiniennes, 2000. Hombert argues for a new dating of a number of Augustine's works, including *Confessions*.

Hunter, David G. *Marriage, Celibacy, and Heresy in Ancient Christianity: The Jovinianist Controversy*. Oxford Early Christian Studies. New York: Oxford University Press, 2007. In *Confessions*, Augustine makes the pivotal choice for celibacy. This work helps put some of that struggle into its historical and theological context.

Kolbet, Paul R. *Augustine and the Cure of Souls: Revising a Classical Ideal*. Notre Dame, IN: University of Notre Dame Press, 2010.

Lienhard, Joseph T.; Earl C. Muller; Roland J. Teske, eds. *Augustine: Presbyter Factus Sum*. Collectanea Augustiniana. New York: Peter Lang, 1993. A valuable collection of essays.

Madec, Goulven. *Saint Augustin et la philosophie: Notes critiques*. Collections des Études Augustiniennes, Série Antiquité 149. Paris: Institut d'Études Augustiniennes, 1996.

Madec, Goulven, *Le Christ de saint Augustin: La patrie et la voie*. Paris: Desclée, 2001. At various points in *Confessions*, Augustine discuss shifts in his understanding of Christ. This work puts those shifts into the broader context of his thinking on the mystery of Christ.

Mandouze, André. *Saint Augustin: L'aventure de la raison et de la grâce*. Paris: Études augustiniennes, 1968.

Marrou, Henri-Iréné. *Saint Augustin et la fin de la culture antique*. Paris: Bibliothéque des Écoles Françaises d'Athénes et de Rome, 1938. Augustine was a gifted and highly trained orator. This is one of the classic Augustinian studies of the 20th century, and puts the rhetorical dimension of Augustine into its late antique cultural context.

Merdinger, Jane E. *Rome and the African Church in the Time of Augustine*. New Haven: Yale University Press, 1997.

Perler, Othmar. *Les voyages de saint Augustin.* Collection des Études Augustiniennes, Série Antiquité 36. Paris: Études Augustiniennes, 1969.

Pollmann, Karla. *Doctrina Christiana: Untersuchungen zu den Anfängen der christlichen Hermeneutik unter besonderer Berücksichtigung von Augustinus, De doctrina christiana.* Freiburg: Universitätverlag, 1996.

Ramsey, Boniface. *Ambrose.* The Early Church Fathers. New York: Routledge, 1997. A valuable introduction to the life and works of Augustine's mentor.

Rist, John M. *Augustine: Ancient Thought Baptized.* Cambridge: Cambridge University Press, 1994. An important overview of the philosophical dimensions of Augustine's thought.

Rombs, Ronnie. *St. Augustine and the Fall of the Soul: Beyond O'Connell and His Critics.* Washington, DC: Catholic University of America Press, 2006.

Schnaubelt, Joseph C., and Frederick Van Fleteren, eds. *Augustine: Second Founder of the Faith.* Collectanea Augustiniana. New York: Peter Lang, 1990. A valuable collection of essays.

Six-Means, Horace E. *Augustine and Catholic Christianization: The Catholicization of Roman Africa, 391-408.* New York: Peter Lang, 2011.

Stock, Brian. *Augustine the Reader: Meditation, Self-Knowledge, and the Ethics of Interpretation.* Cambridge, MA: Harvard University Press, 1996.

Stump, Eleonore and Norman Kretzmann, eds. *The Cambridge Companion to Augustine.* New York: Cambridge University Press, 2001. Essays focused on the philosophic elements of Augustine's thought.

Teske, Roland J. *To Know God and the Soul: Essays on the Thought of St. Augustine.* Washington, DC: Catholic University of America Press, 2008.

Wetzel, James. *Augustine and the Limits of Virtue.* New York: Cambridge University Press, 1992. In *Confessions,* Augustine recounts his struggle to live virtuously and concludes that he could not do so without the grace of God. This study explores Augustine's thinking on the quest for virtuous living and the role of grace.

William, Daniel H. *Ambrose of Milan and the End of the Arian-Nicene Conflicts.* Oxford Early Christian Studies. New York: Oxford University Press, 1995. In Book 9 of *Confessions,* Augustine recounts a showdown between Ambrose and the imperial court which tried to seize one of the churches of Milan for the Arians. Augustine would embrace Nicene Christianity. This important study examines a clash that helped shaped Augustine's understanding of orthodoxy.

THE COMPLETE WORKS OF ST. AUGUSTINE
A Translation for the 21st Century

Sermons 184-229 (III/6)
  cloth, 978-1-56548-050-6

Sermons 230-272 (III/7)
  cloth, 978-1-56548-059-9

Sermons 273-305A (III/8)
  cloth, 978-1-56548-060-5

Sermons 306-340A (III/9)
  cloth, 978-1-56548-068-1

Sermons 341-400 (III/10)
  cloth, 978-1-56548-028-5

Sermons Newly Discovered Since 1990
  (III/11)
  cloth, 978-1-56548-103-9

Homilies on the Gospel of John 1-40
  (III/12)
  cloth, 978-1-56548-319-4
  paper, 978-1-56548-318-7

Homilies on the Gospel of John (41-124)
  (III/13) forthcoming

Homilies on the First Letter of John (III/14)
  cloth, 978-1-56548-288-3
  paper, 978-1-56548-289-0

Expositions of the Psalms 1-32 (III/15)
  cloth, 978-1-56548-126-8
  paper, 978-1-56548-140-4

Expositions of the Psalms 33-50 (III/16)
  cloth, 978-1-56548-147-3
  paper, 978-1-56548-146-6

Expositions of the Psalms 51-72 (III/17)
  cloth, 978-1-56548-156-5
  paper, 978-1-56548-155-8

Expositions of the Psalms 73-98 (III/18)
  cloth, 978-1-56548-167-1
  paper, 978-1-56548-166-4

Expositions of the Psalms 99-120 (III/19)
  cloth, 978-1-56548-197-8
  paper, 978-1-56548-196-1

Expositions of the Psalms 121-150 (III/20)
  cloth, 978-1-56548-211-1
  paper, 978-1-56548-210-4

Essential Texts Created for Classroom Use

Augustine Catechism: Enchiridion on Faith Hope and Love
  paper, 978-1-56548-298-2

Essential Expositions of the Psalms
  paper, 978-1-56548-510-5

Essential Sermons
  paper, 978-1-56548-276-0

Instructing Beginners in Faith
  paper, 978-1-56548-239-5

Monastic Rules
  paper, 978-1-56548-130-5

Prayers from The Confessions
  paper, 978-1-56548-188-6

Selected Writings on Grace and Pelagianism
  paper, 978-1-56548-372-9

Soliloquies: Augustine's Inner Dialogue
  paper, 978-1-56548-142-8

Trilogy on Faith and Happiness
  paper, 978-1-56548-359-0

E-books Available

Essential Sermons, Homilies on the First Letter of John, Revisions, The Confessions, Trilogy on Faith and Happiness, The Trinity, The Augustine Catechism: The Enchiridion on Faith, Hope and Love.

Custom Syllabus

Universities that wish to create a resource that matches their specific needs using selections from any of the above titles should contact New City Press.

New City Press — The Works of Saint Augustine Catalog

For a complete interactive catalog of *The Works of Saint Augustine, A Translation for the 21st Century* go to New City Press website at: www.newcitypress.com

Electronic Editions

InteLex Corporation's Past Masters series encompasses the largest collection of full-text electronic editions in philosophy in the world. The Past Masters series, which includes *The Works of Saint Augustine, A Translation for the 21st Century*, published by New City Press, supports scholarly research around the world and is now being utilized at numerous research libraries and academic institutions. The Works of Saint Augustine (Fourth release), full-text electronic edition, is available for subscription from InteLex. The Fourth release includes all 41 of the published volumes as of May 2016. For more information, visit: http://www.nlx.com/home.

About the Augustinian Heritage Institute

In 1990, the Augustinian Heritage Institute was founded by John E. Rotelle, OSA to oversee the English translation of *The Works of Saint Augustine, A Translation for the 21st Century*. This project was started in conjunction with New City Press. At that time, English was the only major Western language into which the Works of Saint Augustine in their entirety had not yet been attempted. Existing translations were often archaic or faulty and the scholarship was outdated. These new translations offer detailed introductions, extensive critical notes, both a general index and scriptural index for each work as well as the best translations in the world.

The Works of Saint Augustine, A Translation for the 21st Century in its complete form will be published in 49 volumes. To date, 41 volumes have been published.

About New City Press of the Focolare

New City Press is one of more than 20 publishing houses sponsored by the Focolare, a movement founded by Chiara Lubich to help bring about the realization of Jesus' prayer: "That all may be one" (John 17:21). In view of that goal, New City Press publishes books and resources that enrich the lives of people and help all to strive toward the unity of the entire human family. We are a member of the Association of Catholic Publishers.

Free Index to *The Works of Saint Augustine*

Download a PDF file that provides the ability to search all of the available indexes from each volume published by New City Press.

Visit http://www.newcitypress.com/index-to-the-works-of-saint-augustine-a-translation-for-the-21st-century.html for more details.